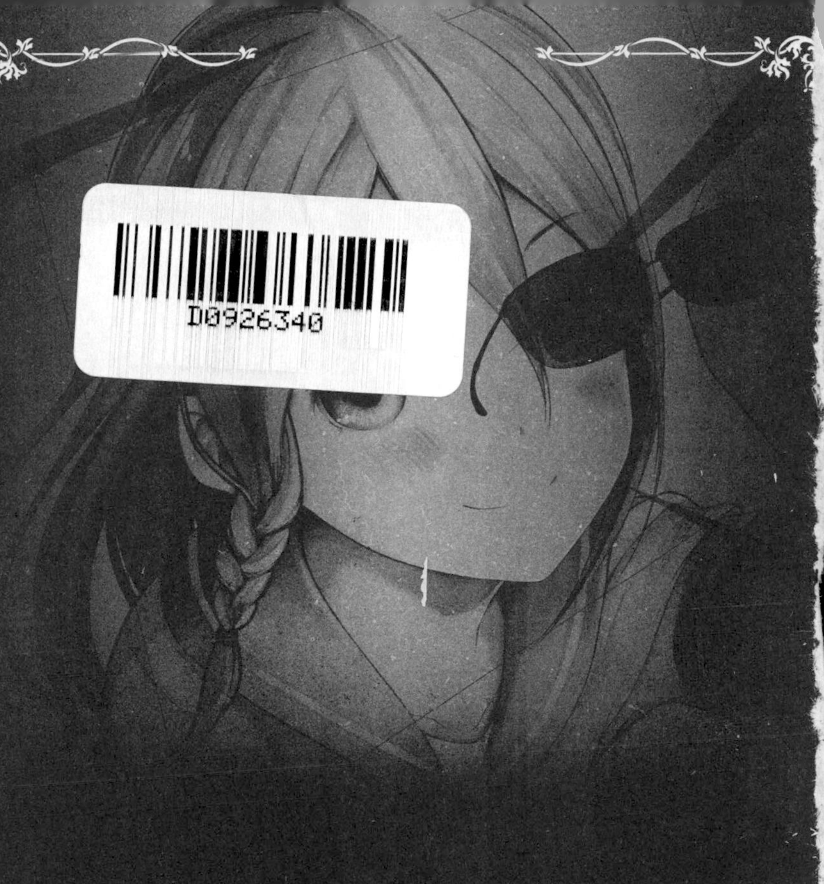

KAGUYA-SAMA
LOVE IS WAR

11

AKA AKASAKA

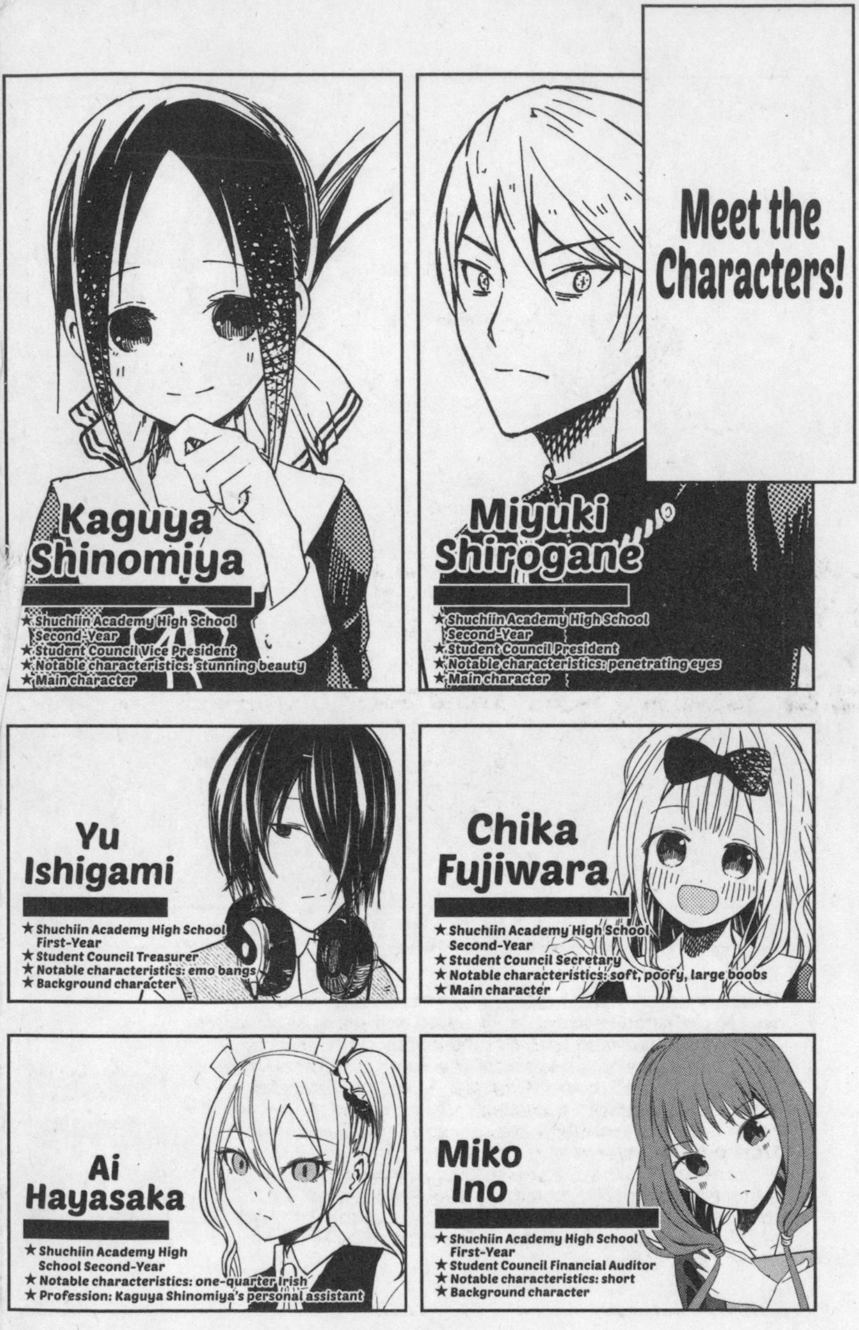

Meet the Characters!
Miyuki Shirogane
★Shuchiin Academy High School Second-Year
★Student Council President
★Notable characteristics: penetrating eyes
★Main character
Kaguya Shinomiya
★Shuchiin Academy High School Second-Year
★Student Council Vice President
★Notable characteristics: stunning beauty
★Main character
Chika Fujiwara
★Shuchiin Academy High School Second-Year
★Student Council Secretary
★Notable characteristics: soft, poofy, large boobs
★Main character
Yu Ishigami
★Shuchiin Academy High School First-Year
★Student Council Treasurer
★Notable characteristics: emo bangs
★Background character
Miko Ino
★Shuchiin Academy High School First-Year
★Student Council Financial Auditor
★Notable characteristics: short
★Background character
Ai Hayasaka
★Shuchiin Academy High School Second-Year
★Notable characteristics: one-quarter Irish
★Profession: Kaguya Shinomiya's personal assistant

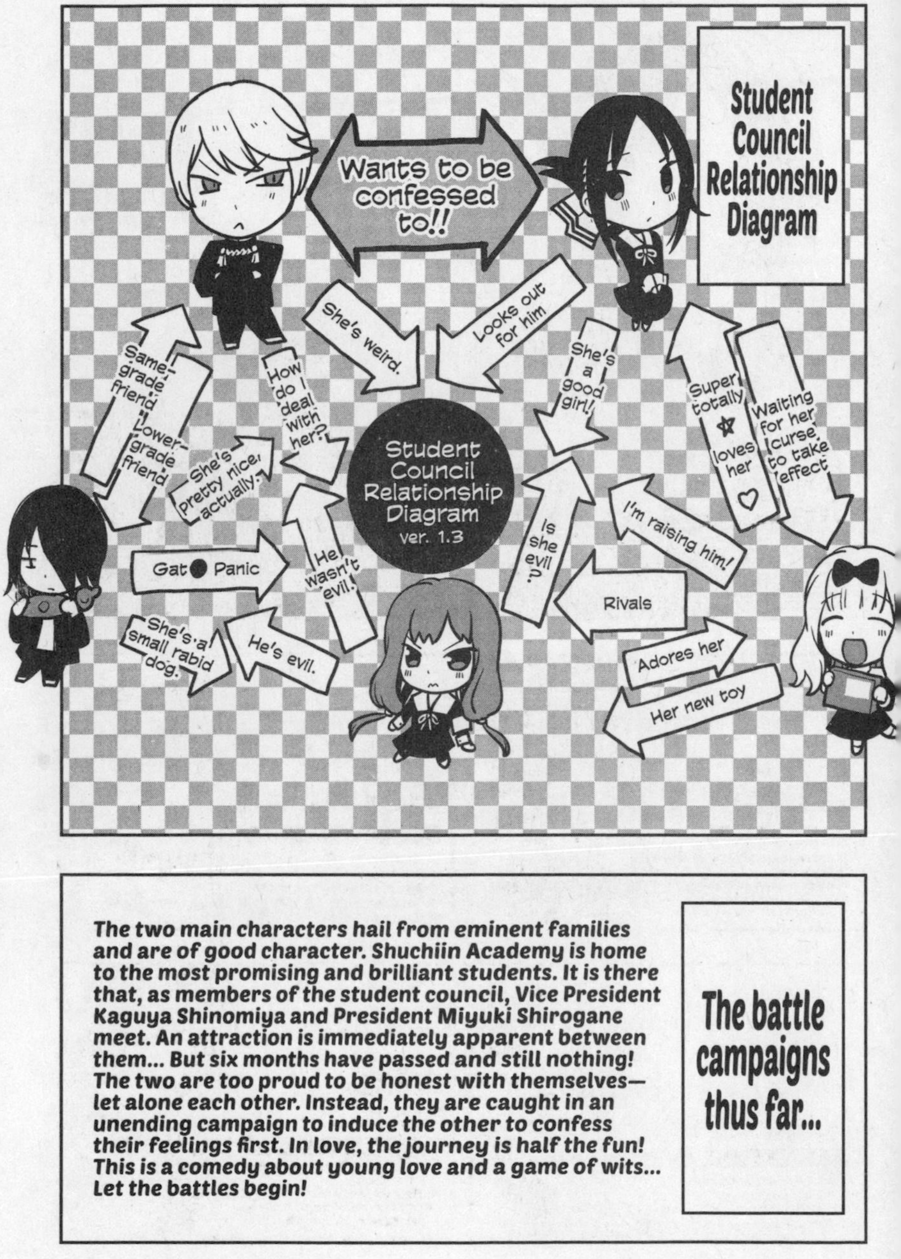
Student Council Relationship Diagram
Wants to be confessed to!!
Looks out for him
She's weird.
Student Council Relationship Diagram ver. 1.3
She's a good girl!
Super totally ☆ loves her ♡
Waiting for her curse to take effect
How do I deal with her?
Same-grade friend
Lower-grade friend
She's pretty nice, actually.
Gat● Panic
He wasn't evil.
Is she evil?
I'm raising him!
Rivals
Adores her
Her new toy
She's a small rabid dog.
He's evil.

The battle campaigns thus far...

The two main characters hail from eminent families and are of good character. Shuchiin Academy is home to the most promising and brilliant students. It is there that, as members of the student council, Vice President Kaguya Shinomiya and President Miyuki Shirogane meet. An attraction is immediately apparent between them... But six months have passed and still nothing! The two are too proud to be honest with themselves—let alone each other. Instead, they are caught in an unending campaign to induce the other to confess their feelings first. In love, the journey is half the fun! This is a comedy about young love and a game of wits... Let the battles begin!

KAGUYA-SAMA LOVE IS WAR

BATTLE CAMPAIGNS 11

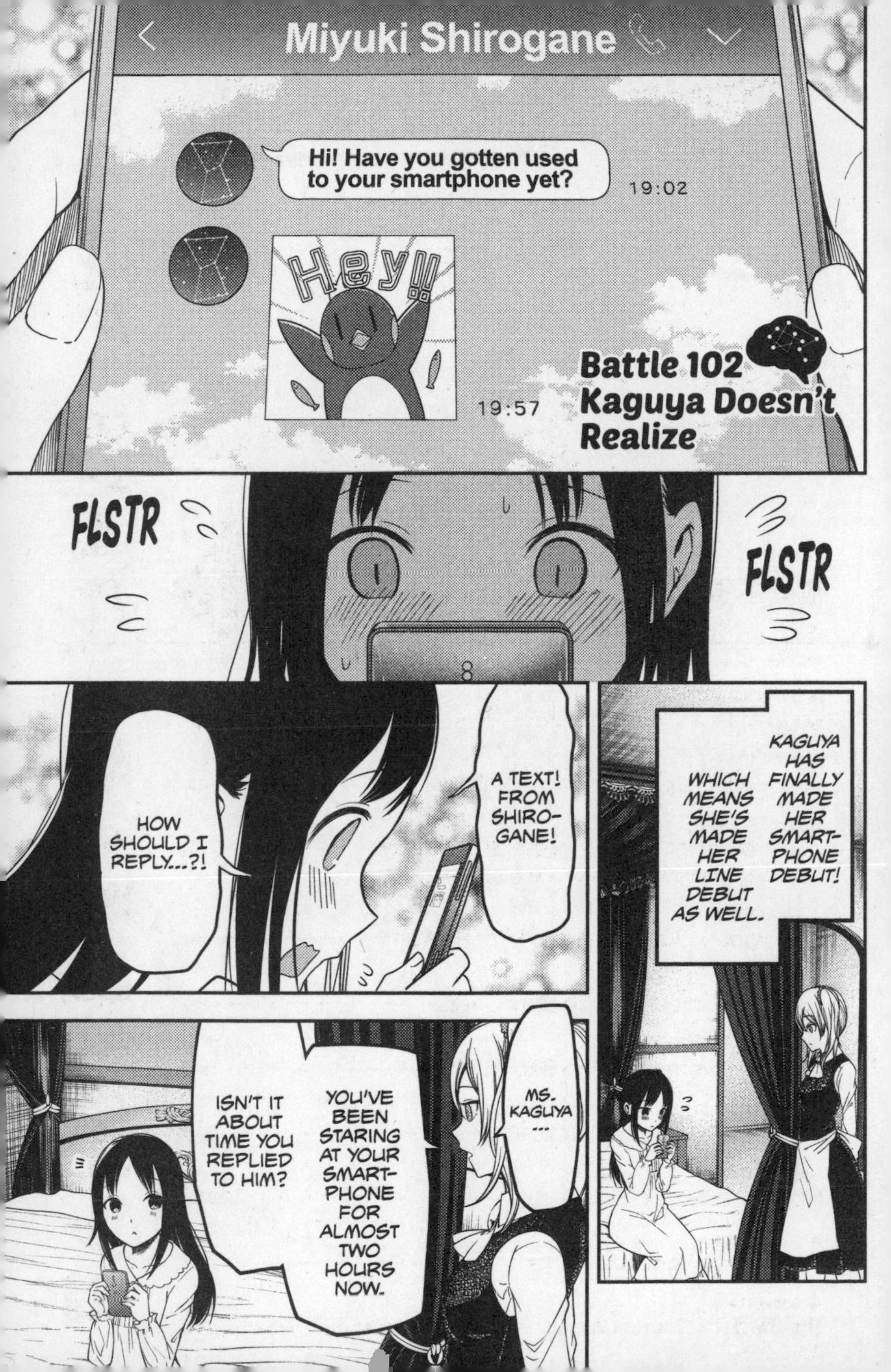
Miyuki Shirogane
Hi! Have you gotten used to your smartphone yet?
19:02
Hey!!
19:57
Battle 102 Kaguya Doesn't Realize
FLSTR
FLSTR
KAGUYA HAS FINALLY MADE HER SMARTPHONE DEBUT!
WHICH MEANS SHE'S MADE HER LINE DEBUT AS WELL.
A TEXT! FROM SHIROGANE!
HOW SHOULD I REPLY...?!
MS. KAGUYA...
YOU'VE BEEN STARING AT YOUR SMARTPHONE FOR ALMOST TWO HOURS NOW.
ISN'T IT ABOUT TIME YOU REPLIED TO HIM?

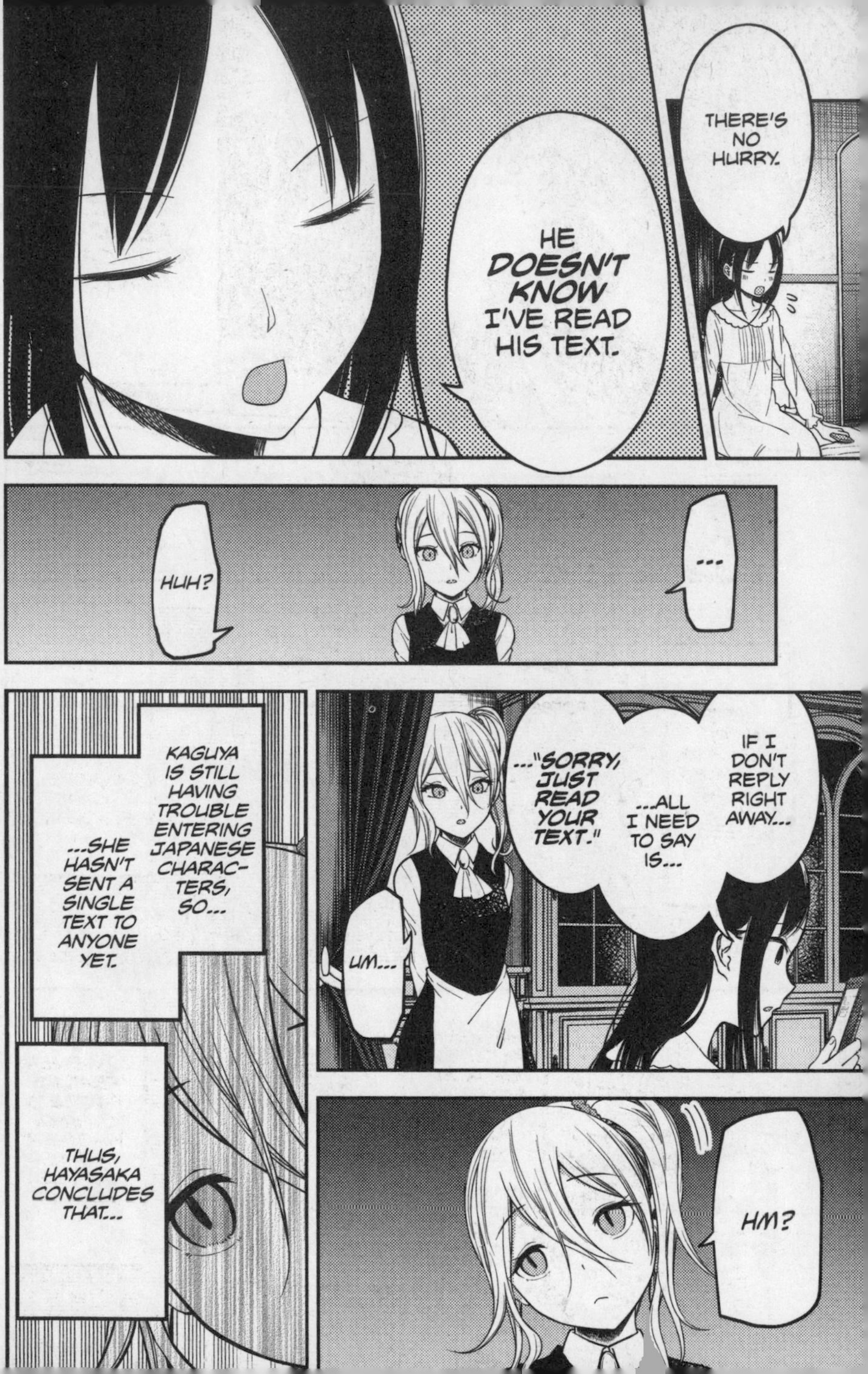
THERE'S NO HURRY.
HE *DOESN'T KNOW* I'VE READ HIS TEXT.
...
HUH?
IF I DON'T REPLY RIGHT AWAY...
...ALL I NEED TO SAY IS...
..."*SORRY, JUST READ YOUR TEXT.*"
UM...
HM?
KAGUYA IS STILL HAVING TROUBLE ENTERING JAPANESE CHARACTERS, SO...
...SHE HASN'T SENT A SINGLE TEXT TO ANYONE YET.
THUS, HAYASAKA CONCLUDES THAT...

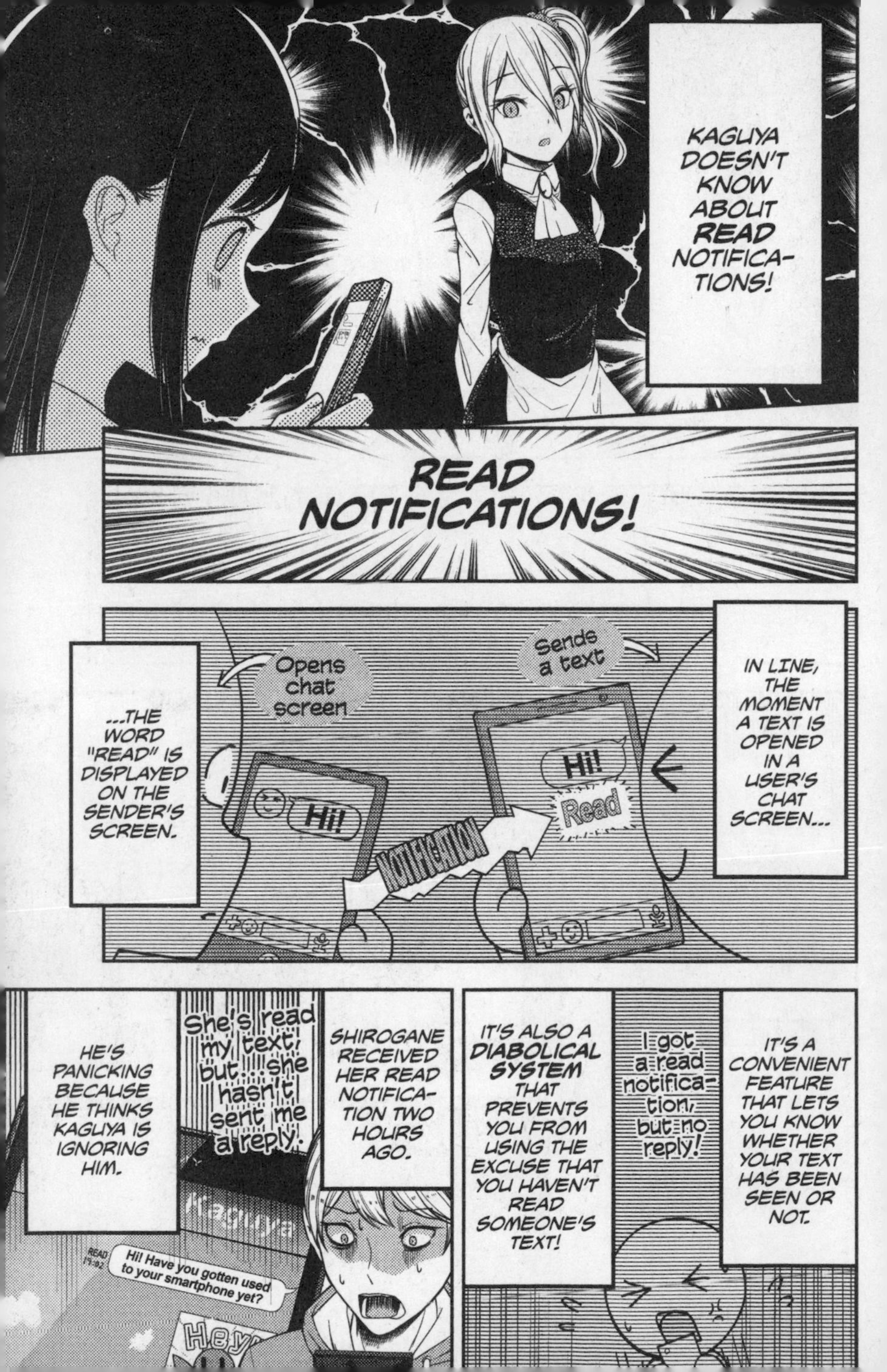
KAGUYA DOESN'T KNOW ABOUT READ NOTIFICATIONS!
READ NOTIFICATIONS!
IN LINE, THE MOMENT A TEXT IS OPENED IN A USER'S CHAT SCREEN...
Sends a text
Hi!
Read
Opens chat screen
NOTIFICATION
Hi!
...THE WORD "READ" IS DISPLAYED ON THE SENDER'S SCREEN.
IT'S A CONVENIENT FEATURE THAT LETS YOU KNOW WHETHER YOUR TEXT HAS BEEN SEEN OR NOT.
I got a read notification, but no reply!
IT'S ALSO A DIABOLICAL SYSTEM THAT PREVENTS YOU FROM USING THE EXCUSE THAT YOU HAVEN'T READ SOMEONE'S TEXT!
SHIROGANE RECEIVED HER READ NOTIFICATION TWO HOURS AGO.
She's read my text, but... she hasn't sent me a reply.
HE'S PANICKING BECAUSE HE THINKS KAGUYA IS IGNORING HIM.
Kaguya
READ
Hi! Have you gotten used to your smartphone yet?

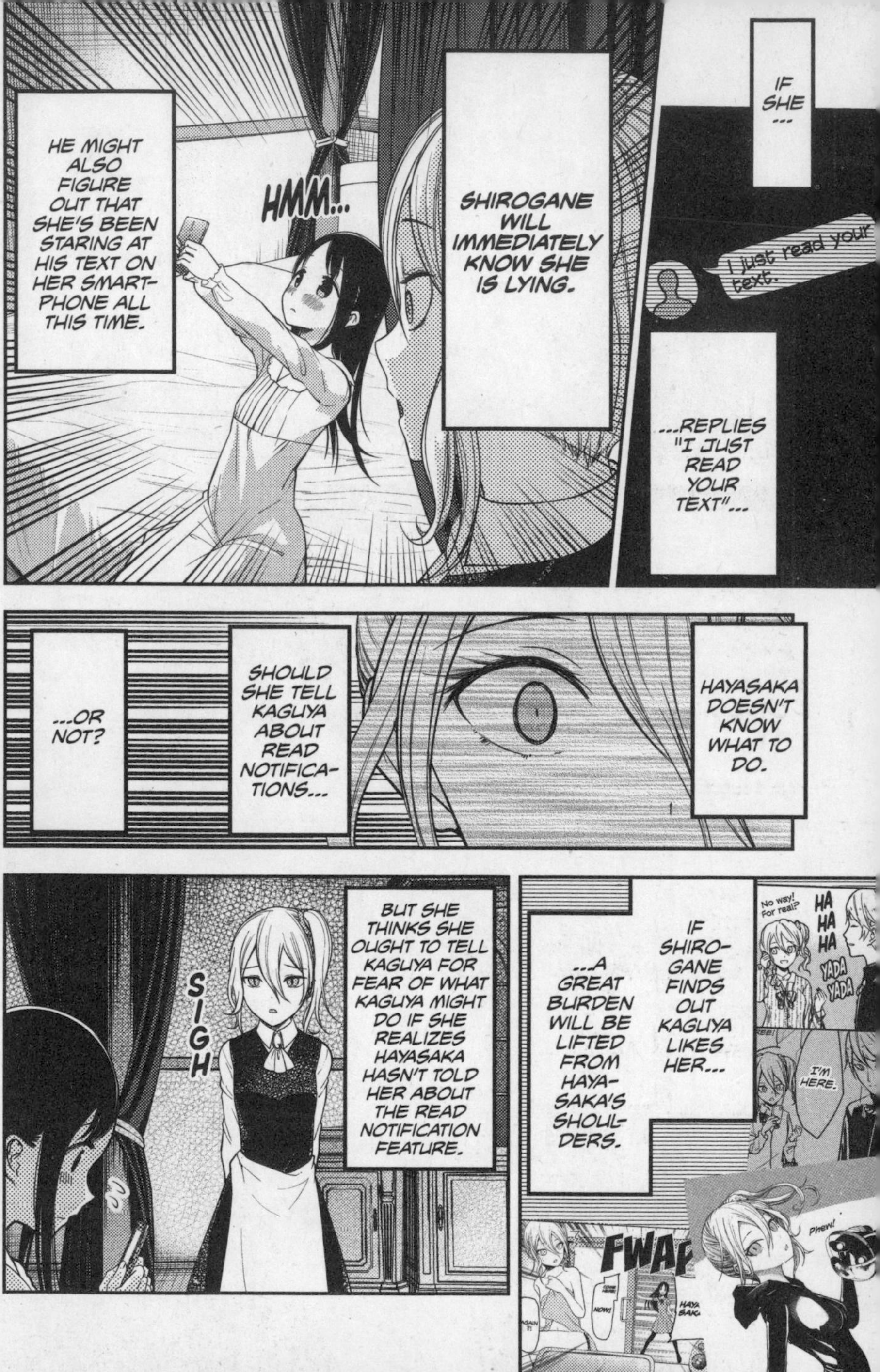
IF SHE ...
I just read your text.
...REPLIES "I JUST READ YOUR TEXT"...
SHIROGANE WILL IMMEDIATELY KNOW SHE IS LYING.
HE MIGHT ALSO FIGURE OUT THAT SHE'S BEEN STARING AT HIS TEXT ON HER SMART-PHONE ALL THIS TIME.
HMM...
HAYASAKA DOESN'T KNOW WHAT TO DO.
SHOULD SHE TELL KAGUYA ABOUT READ NOTIFICA-TIONS...
...OR NOT?
IF SHIRO-GANE FINDS OUT KAGUYA LIKES HER...
...A GREAT BURDEN WILL BE LIFTED FROM HAYA-SAKA'S SHOUL-DERS.
No way! For real!?
HA HA HA
YADA YADA
I'M HERE.
Phew!
FWAP
NOW!
BUT SHE THINKS SHE OUGHT TO TELL KAGUYA FOR FEAR OF WHAT KAGUYA MIGHT DO IF SHE REALIZES HAYASAKA HASN'T TOLD HER ABOUT THE READ NOTIFICATION FEATURE.
SIGH

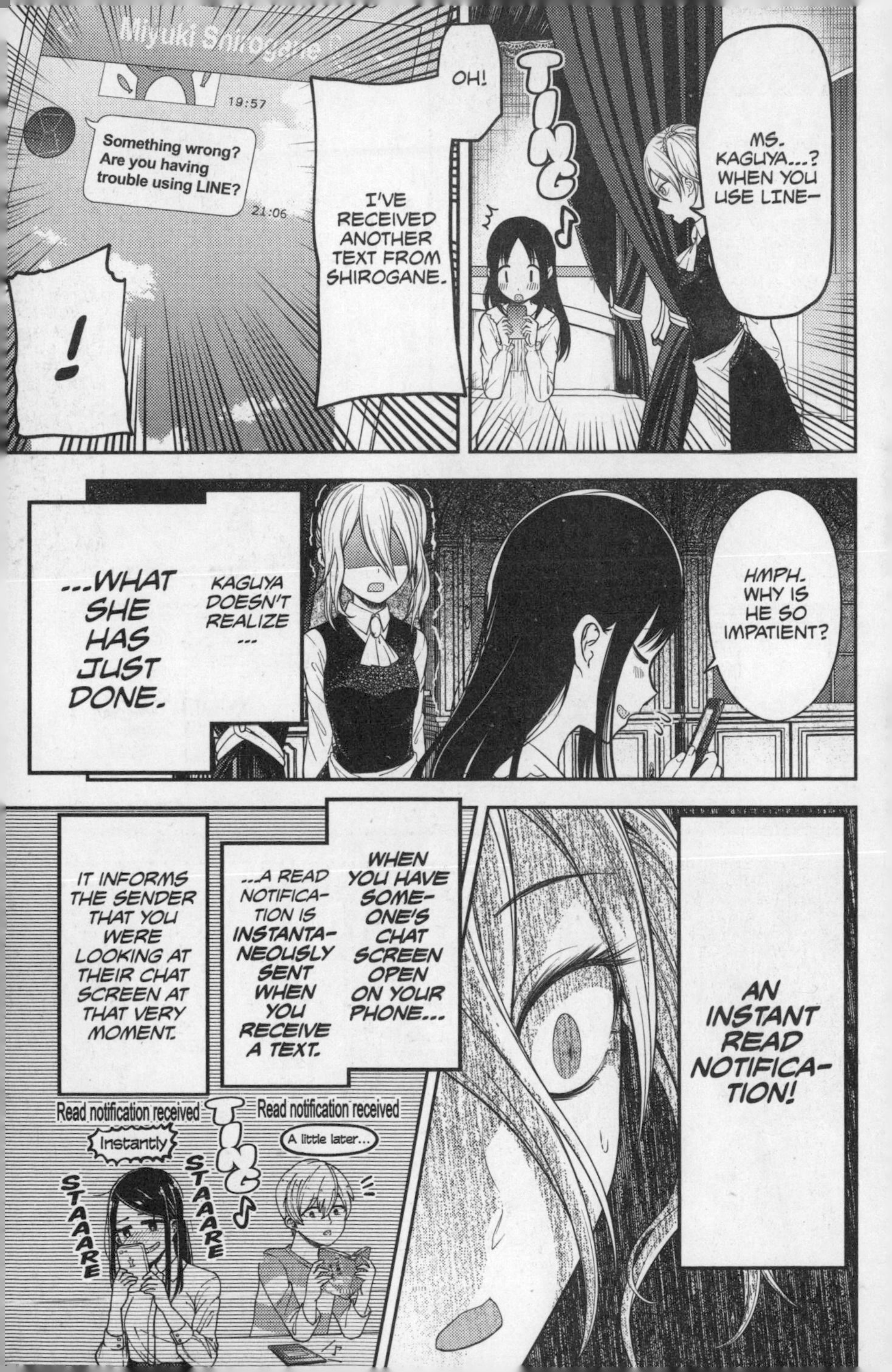
MS. KAGUYA...? WHEN YOU USE LINE—
TING ♪
OH!
I'VE RECEIVED ANOTHER TEXT FROM SHIROGANE.
Miyuki Shirogane
19:57
Something wrong? Are you having trouble using LINE?
21:06
!
HMPH. WHY IS HE SO IMPATIENT?
KAGUYA DOESN'T REALIZE...
...WHAT SHE HAS JUST DONE.
AN INSTANT READ NOTIFICATION!
WHEN YOU HAVE SOMEONE'S CHAT SCREEN OPEN ON YOUR PHONE...
...A READ NOTIFICATION IS INSTANTANEOUSLY SENT WHEN YOU RECEIVE A TEXT.
IT INFORMS THE SENDER THAT YOU WERE LOOKING AT THEIR CHAT SCREEN AT THAT VERY MOMENT.
Read notification received
A little later...
TING ♪
Read notification received
Instantly
STAAARE
STAAARE

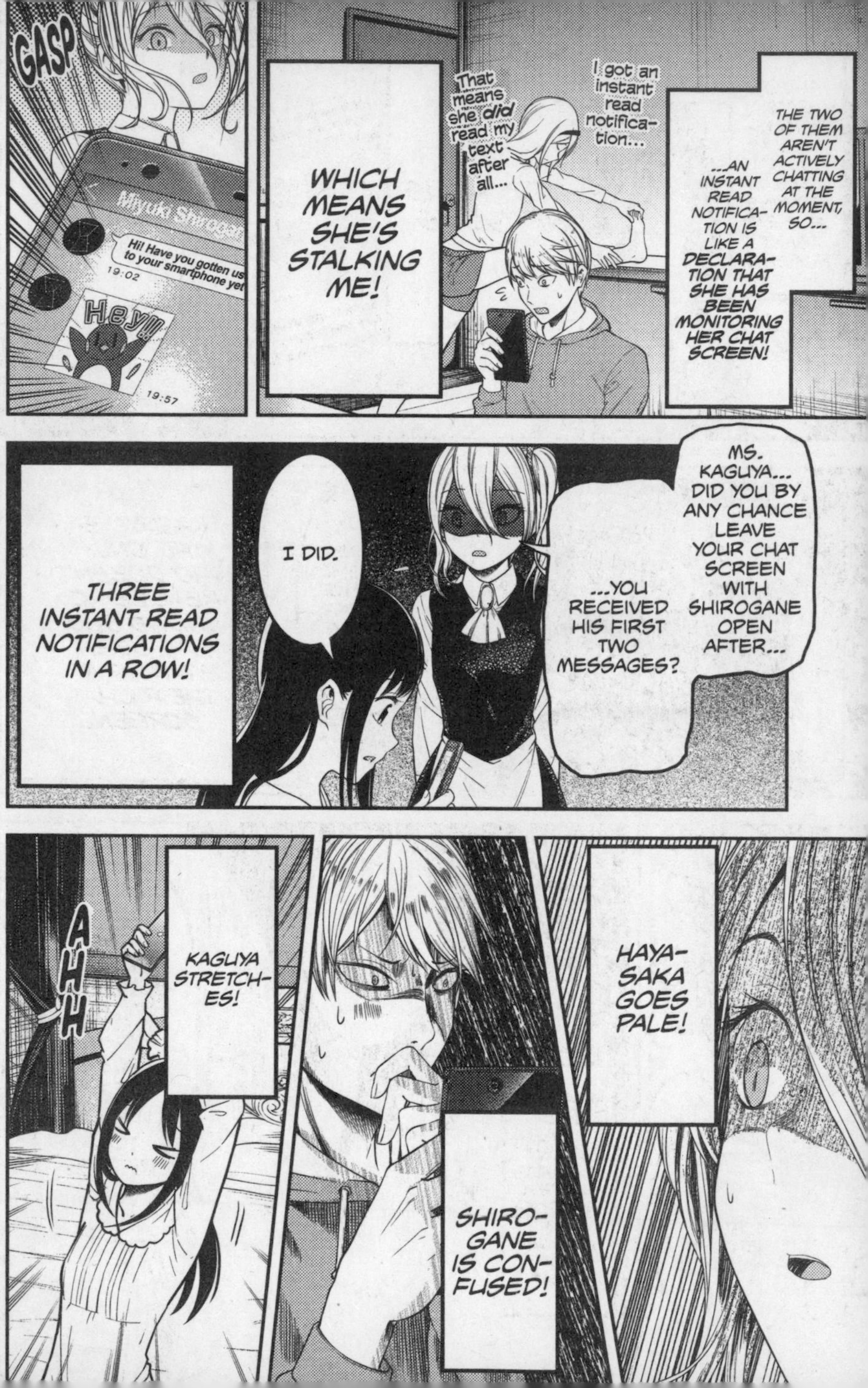

THE TWO OF THEM AREN'T ACTIVELY CHATTING AT THE MOMENT, SO...
...AN INSTANT READ NOTIFICATION IS LIKE A DECLARATION THAT SHE HAS BEEN MONITORING HER CHAT SCREEN!
I got an instant read notification...
That means she *did* read my text after all...
WHICH MEANS SHE'S STALKING ME!
GASP
Miyuki Shiroga
Hi! Have you gotten us
to your smartphone yet
19:02
Hey!!
19:57
MS. KAGUYA... DID YOU BY ANY CHANCE LEAVE YOUR CHAT SCREEN WITH SHIROGANE OPEN AFTER...
...YOU RECEIVED HIS FIRST TWO MESSAGES?
I DID.
THREE INSTANT READ NOTIFICATIONS IN A ROW!
HAYA-SAKA GOES PALE!
SHIRO-GANE IS CON-FUSED!
KAGUYA STRETCH-ES!
AHHH

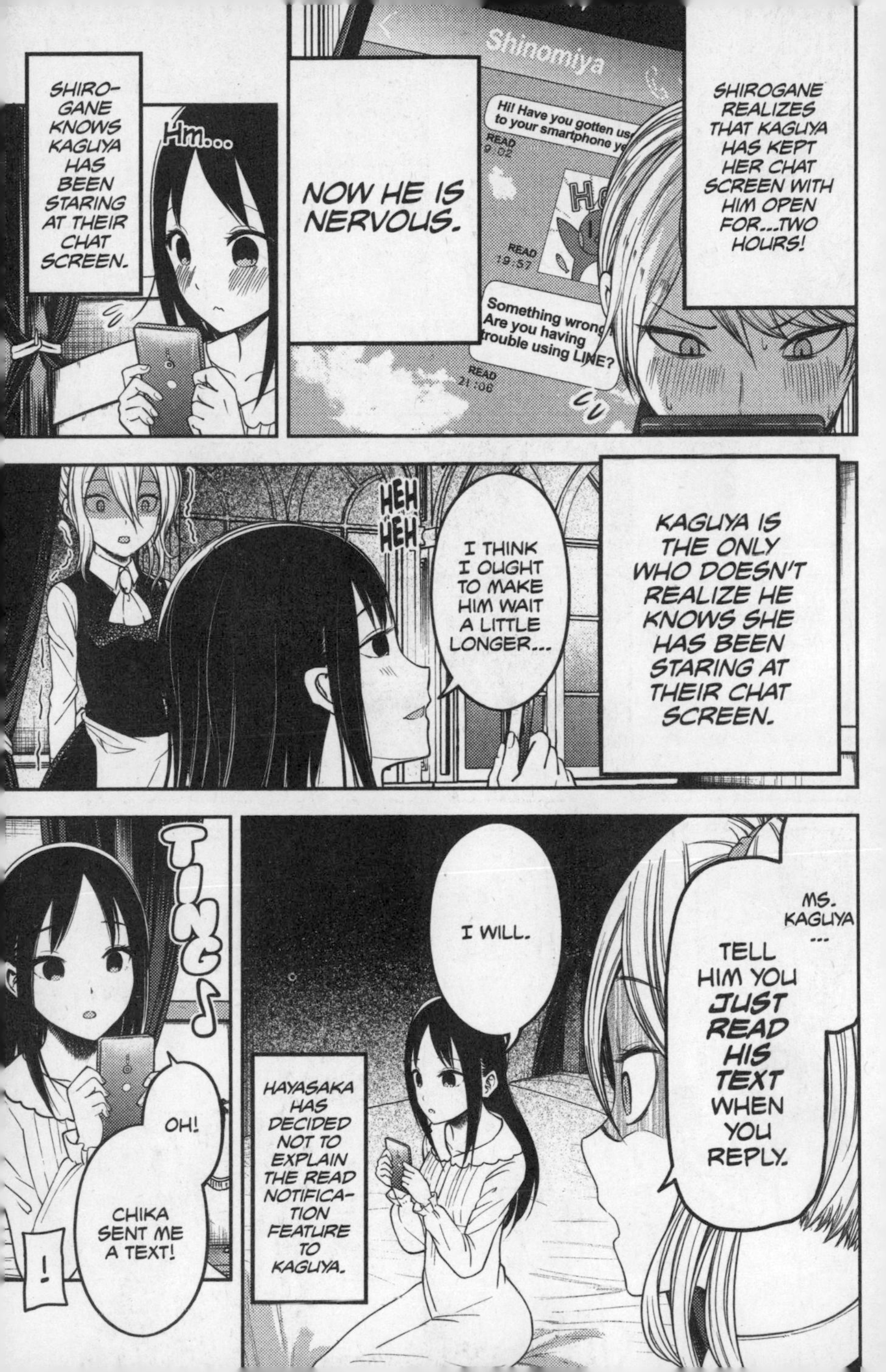
SHIROGANE REALIZES THAT KAGUYA HAS KEPT HER CHAT SCREEN WITH HIM OPEN FOR...TWO HOURS!
Shinomiya
Hi! Have you gotten us to your smartphone ye
READ 9:02
READ 19:57
Something wrong Are you having trouble using LINE?
READ 21:06
NOW HE IS NERVOUS.
SHIROGANE KNOWS KAGUYA HAS BEEN STARING AT THEIR CHAT SCREEN.
Hm...
KAGUYA IS THE ONLY WHO DOESN'T REALIZE HE KNOWS SHE HAS BEEN STARING AT THEIR CHAT SCREEN.
I THINK I OUGHT TO MAKE HIM WAIT A LITTLE LONGER...
HEH HEH
MS. KAGUYA ...
TELL HIM YOU JUST READ HIS TEXT WHEN YOU REPLY.
I WILL.
HAYASAKA HAS DECIDED NOT TO EXPLAIN THE READ NOTIFICATION FEATURE TO KAGUYA.
TING ♪
OH!
CHIKA SENT ME A TEXT!
!

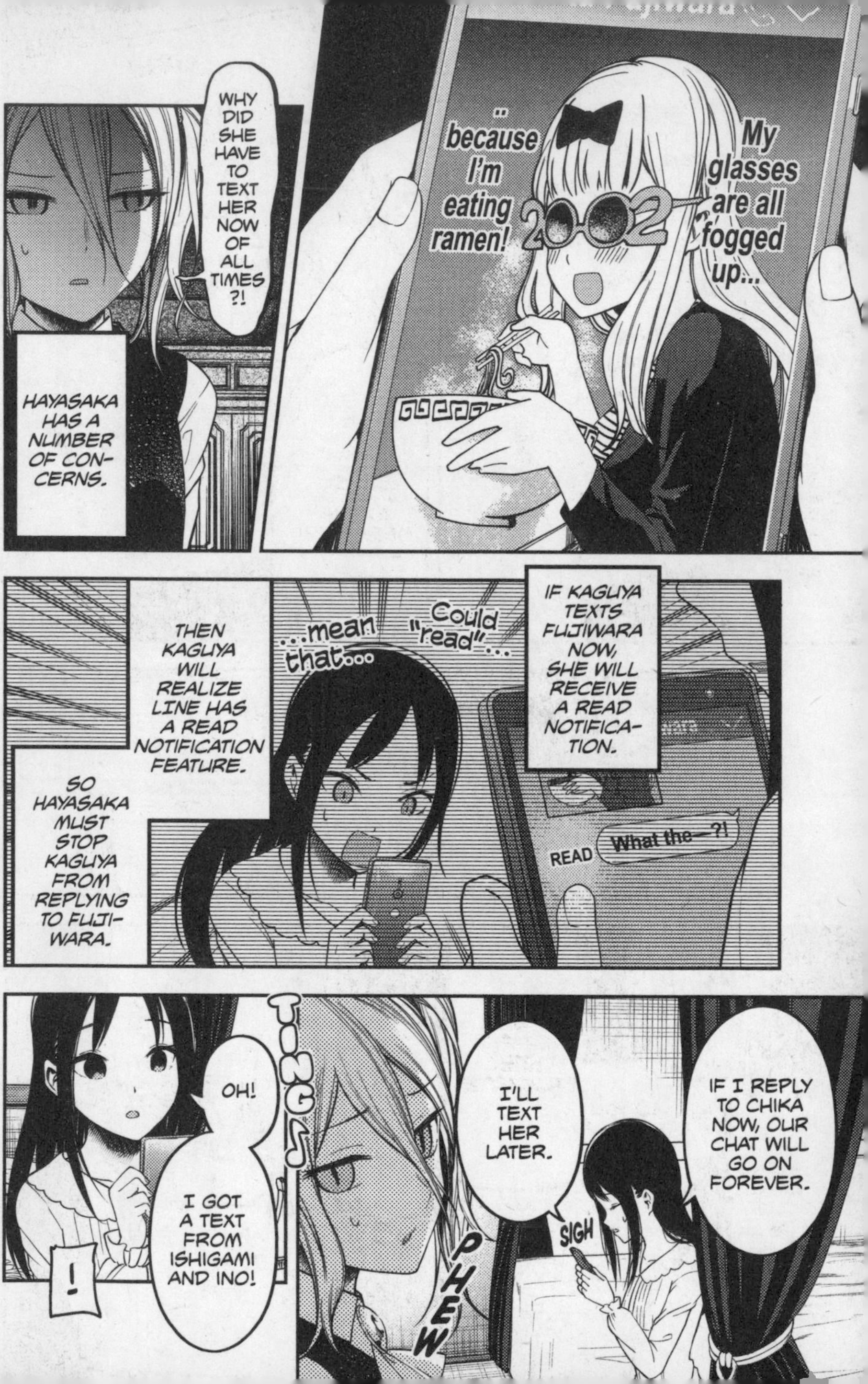
My glasses are all fogged up...
..because I'm eating ramen!
WHY DID SHE HAVE TO TEXT HER NOW OF ALL TIMES?!
HAYASAKA HAS A NUMBER OF CONCERNS.
IF KAGUYA TEXTS FUJIWARA NOW, SHE WILL RECEIVE A READ NOTIFICATION.
READ
What the—?!
Could "read"...
...mean that...
THEN KAGUYA WILL REALIZE LINE HAS A READ NOTIFICATION FEATURE.
SO HAYASAKA MUST STOP KAGUYA FROM REPLYING TO FUJIWARA.
IF I REPLY TO CHIKA NOW, OUR CHAT WILL GO ON FOREVER.
I'LL TEXT HER LATER.
SIGH
PHEW
TING
OH!
I GOT A TEXT FROM ISHIGAMI AND INO!
!

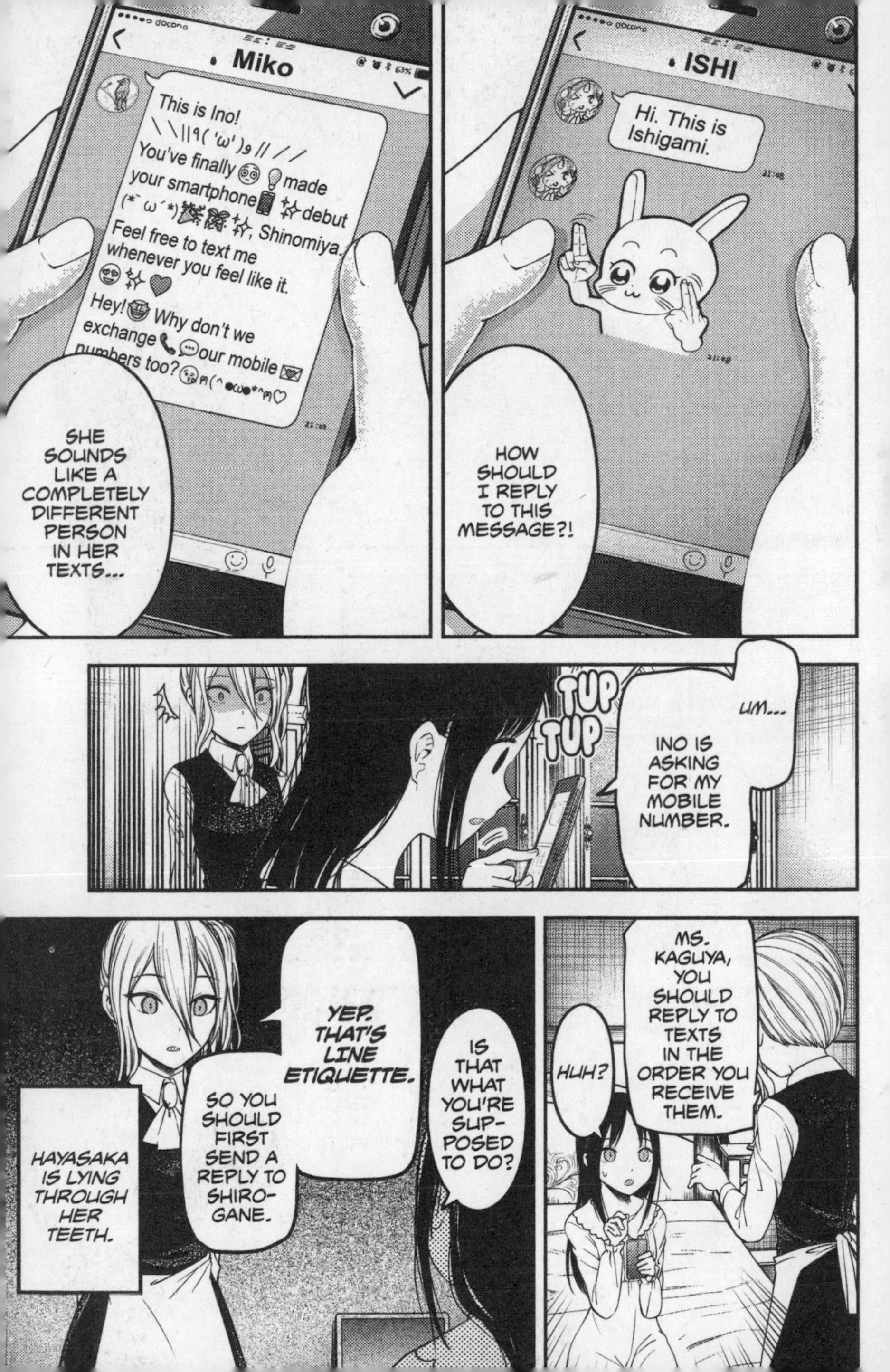
ISHI
Hi. This is Ishigami.
HOW SHOULD I REPLY TO THIS MESSAGE?!
Miko
This is Ino!
\\||٩('ω')و //／／
You've finally made your smartphone debut (*´ω`*), Shinomiya.
Feel free to text me whenever you feel like it.
Hey! Why don't we exchange our mobile numbers too?
SHE SOUNDS LIKE A COMPLETELY DIFFERENT PERSON IN HER TEXTS...
TUP TUP
UM...
INO IS ASKING FOR MY MOBILE NUMBER.
MS. KAGUYA, YOU SHOULD REPLY TO TEXTS IN THE ORDER YOU RECEIVE THEM.
HUH?
IS THAT WHAT YOU'RE SUP-POSED TO DO?
YEP. THAT'S LINE ETIQUETTE.
SO YOU SHOULD FIRST SEND A REPLY TO SHIRO-GANE.
HAYASAKA IS LYING THROUGH HER TEETH.

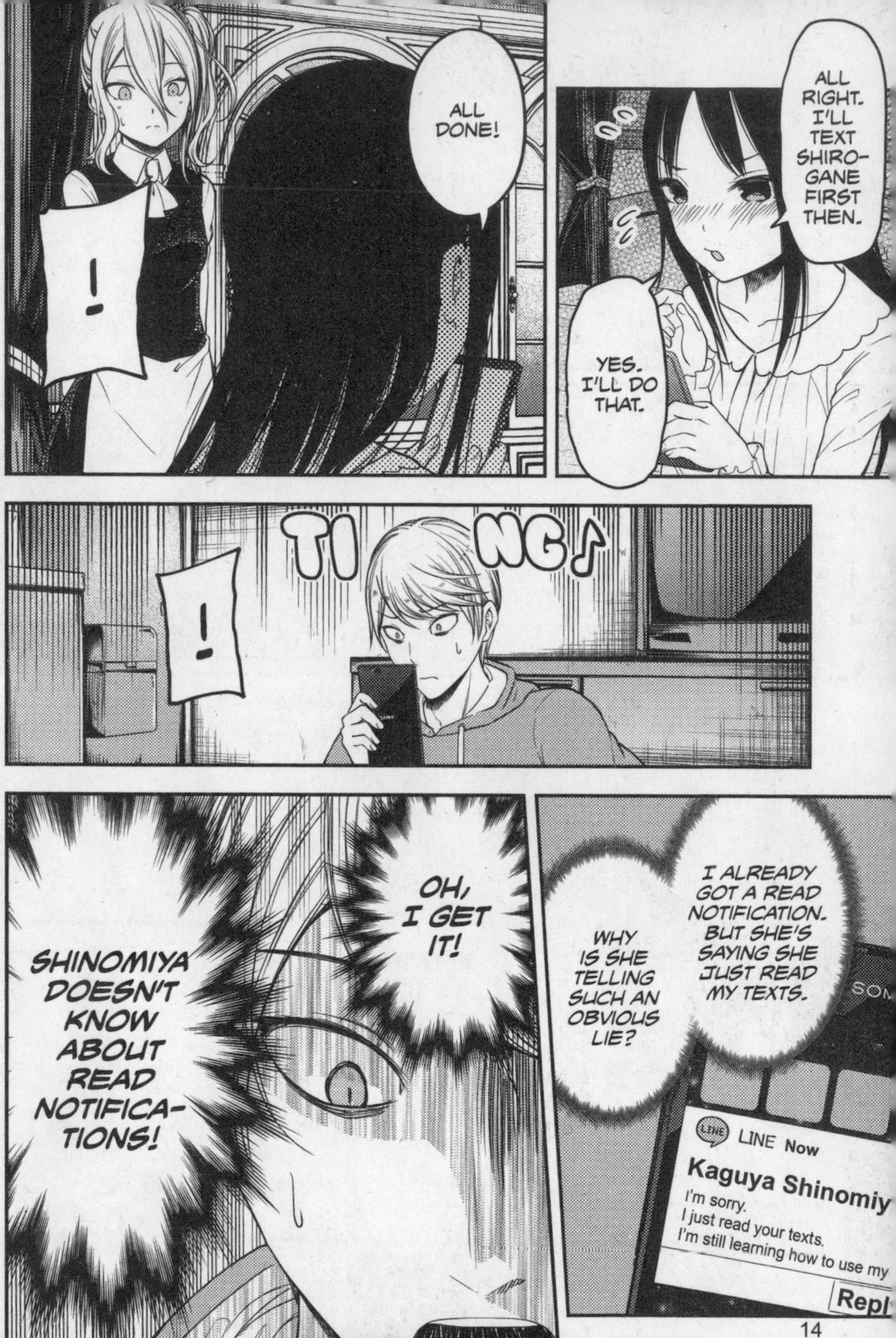
ALL RIGHT. I'LL TEXT SHIROGANE FIRST THEN.
YES. I'LL DO THAT.
ALL DONE!
!
TING♪
!
I ALREADY GOT A READ NOTIFICATION. BUT SHE'S SAYING SHE JUST READ MY TEXTS.
WHY IS SHE TELLING SUCH AN OBVIOUS LIE?
SOM
LINE LINE Now
Kaguya Shinomiy
I'm sorry.
I just read your texts.
I'm still learning how to use my
Repl
OH, I GET IT!
SHINOMIYA DOESN'T KNOW ABOUT READ NOTIFICATIONS!

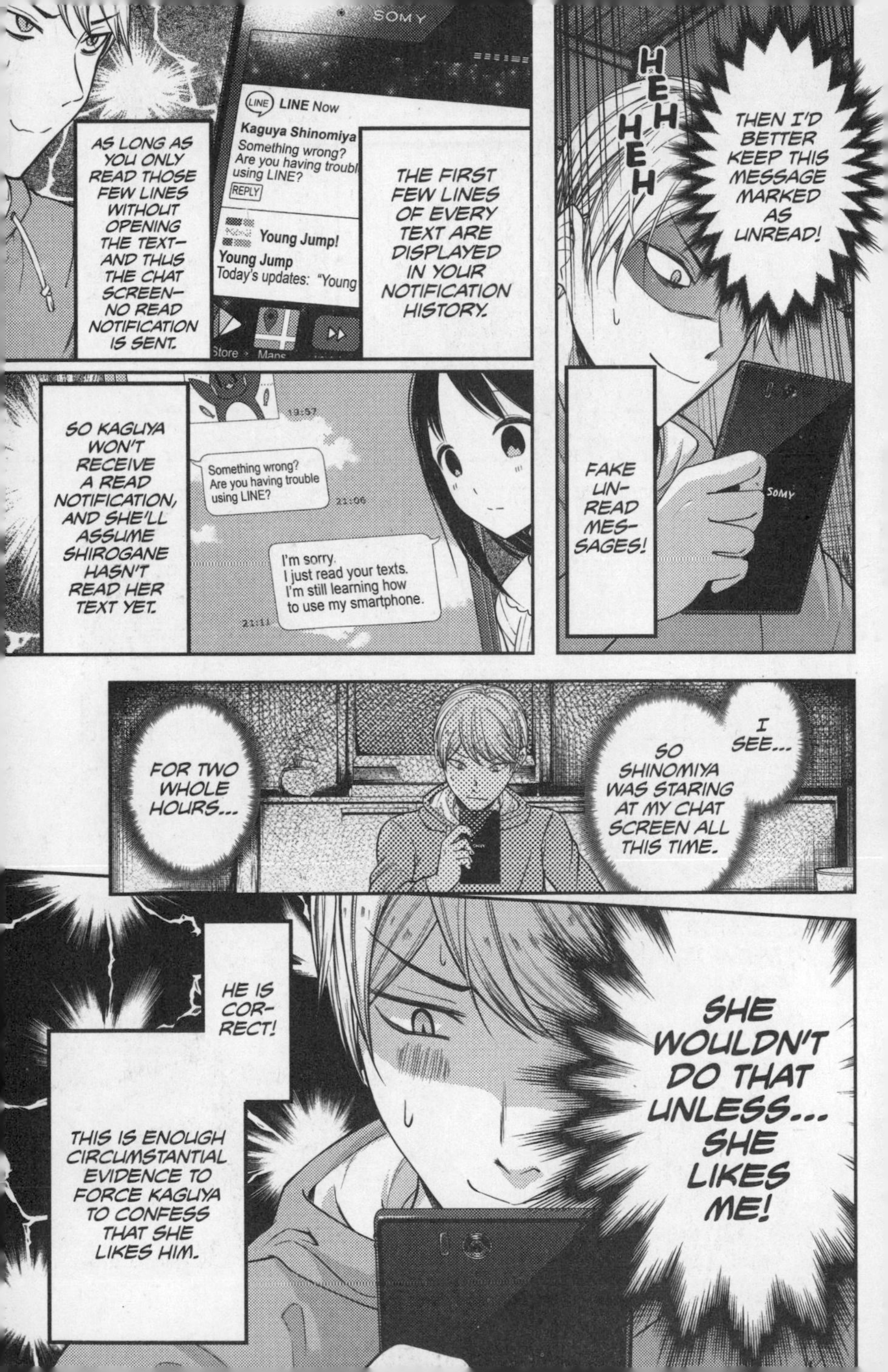
HEHEHEH
THEN I'D BETTER KEEP THIS MESSAGE MARKED AS UNREAD!
FAKE UN-READ MES-SAGES!
SOMY
SOMY
LINE Now
Kaguya Shinomiya
Something wrong? Are you having troubl using LINE?
REPLY
Young Jump!
Young Jump
Today's updates: "Young
Store Maps
THE FIRST FEW LINES OF EVERY TEXT ARE DISPLAYED IN YOUR NOTIFICATION HISTORY.
AS LONG AS YOU ONLY READ THOSE FEW LINES WITHOUT OPENING THE TEXT—AND THUS THE CHAT SCREEN—NO READ NOTIFICATION IS SENT.
19:57
Something wrong? Are you having trouble using LINE?
21:06
I'm sorry. I just read your texts. I'm still learning how to use my smartphone.
21:11
SO KAGUYA WON'T RECEIVE A READ NOTIFICATION, AND SHE'LL ASSUME SHIROGANE HASN'T READ HER TEXT YET.
I SEE...
SO SHINOMIYA WAS STARING AT MY CHAT SCREEN ALL THIS TIME.
FOR TWO WHOLE HOURS...
SHE WOULDN'T DO THAT UNLESS... SHE LIKES ME!
HE IS COR-RECT!
THIS IS ENOUGH CIRCUMSTANTIAL EVIDENCE TO FORCE KAGUYA TO CONFESS THAT SHE LIKES HIM.

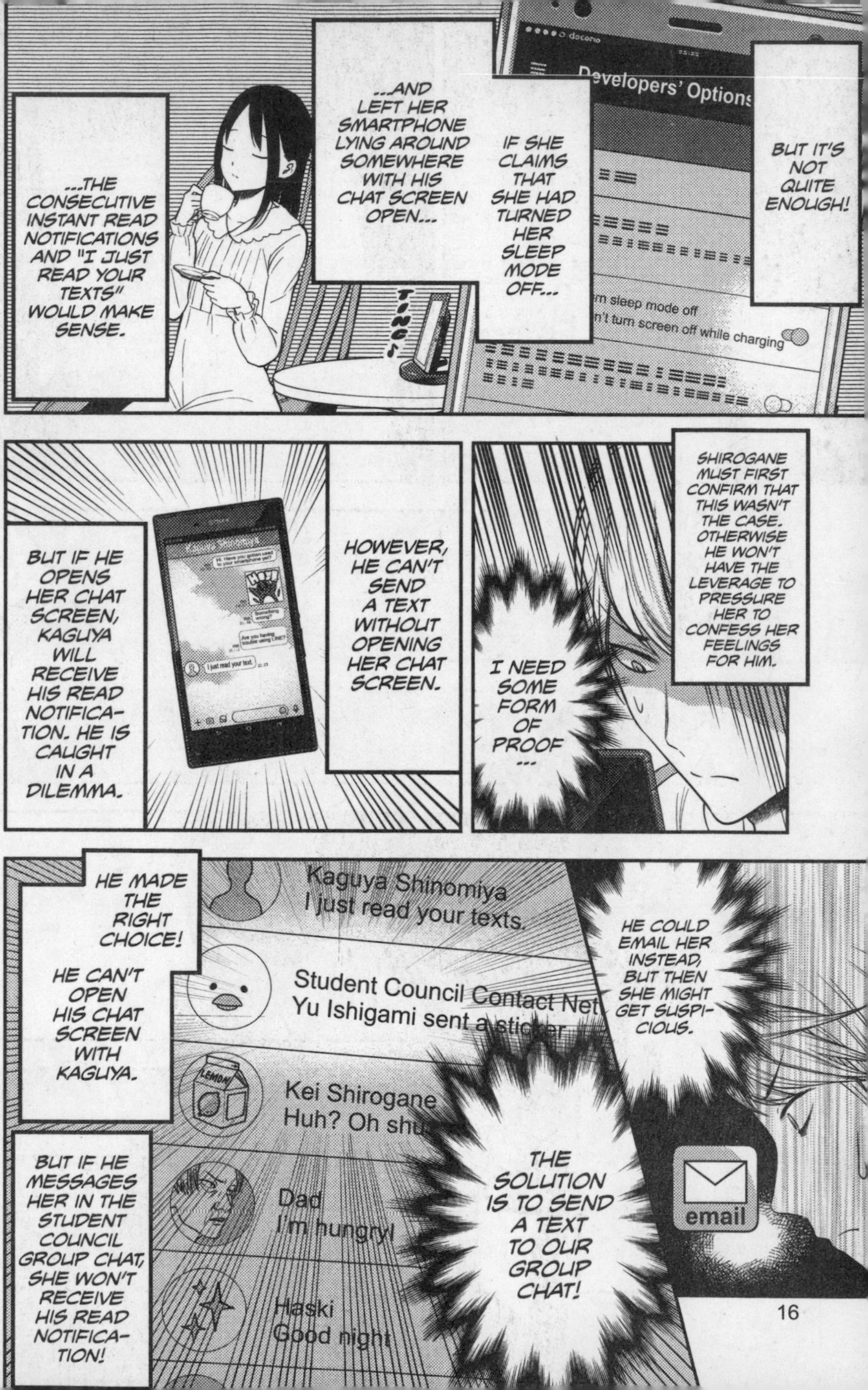
Developers' Options
IF SHE CLAIMS THAT SHE HAD TURNED HER SLEEP MODE OFF...
...AND LEFT HER SMARTPHONE LYING AROUND SOMEWHERE WITH HIS CHAT SCREEN OPEN...
TING♪
...THE CONSECUTIVE INSTANT READ NOTIFICATIONS AND "I JUST READ YOUR TEXTS" WOULD MAKE SENSE.
BUT IT'S NOT QUITE ENOUGH!
SHIROGANE MUST FIRST CONFIRM THAT THIS WASN'T THE CASE. OTHERWISE HE WON'T HAVE THE LEVERAGE TO PRESSURE HER TO CONFESS HER FEELINGS FOR HIM.
I NEED SOME FORM OF PROOF...
HOWEVER, HE CAN'T SEND A TEXT WITHOUT OPENING HER CHAT SCREEN.
Kaguya Shinomiya
I just read your text.
BUT IF HE OPENS HER CHAT SCREEN, KAGUYA WILL RECEIVE HIS READ NOTIFICATION. HE IS CAUGHT IN A DILEMMA.
HE COULD EMAIL HER INSTEAD, BUT THEN SHE MIGHT GET SUSPICIOUS.
email
THE SOLUTION IS TO SEND A TEXT TO OUR GROUP CHAT!
Kaguya Shinomiya
I just read your texts.
Student Council Contact Net
Yu Ishigami sent a sticker
LEMON
Kei Shirogane
Huh? Oh shu
Dad
I'm hungry!
Haski
Good night
HE MADE THE RIGHT CHOICE!
HE CAN'T OPEN HIS CHAT SCREEN WITH KAGUYA.
BUT IF HE MESSAGES HER IN THE STUDENT COUNCIL GROUP CHAT, SHE WON'T RECEIVE HIS READ NOTIFICATION!

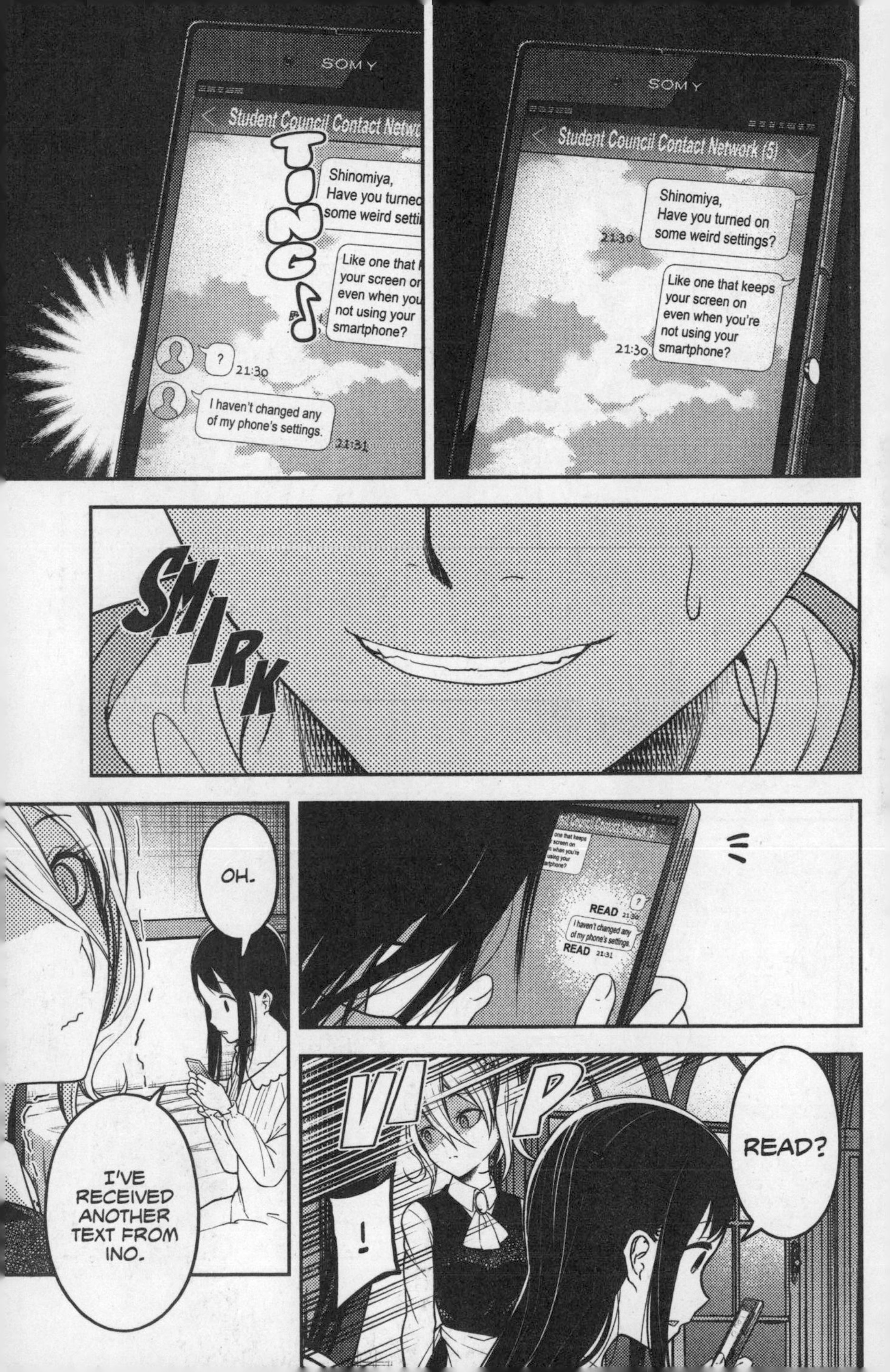
SOMY
Student Council Contact Network (5)
Shinomiya, Have you turned on some weird settings?
21:30
Like one that keeps your screen on even when you're not using your smartphone?
21:30
TING
SOMY
?
21:30
I haven't changed any of my phone's settings.
21:31
SMIRK
READ
?
21:30
I haven't changed any of my phone's settings.
READ
21:31
READ?
VIP
!
OH.
I'VE RECEIVED ANOTHER TEXT FROM INO.

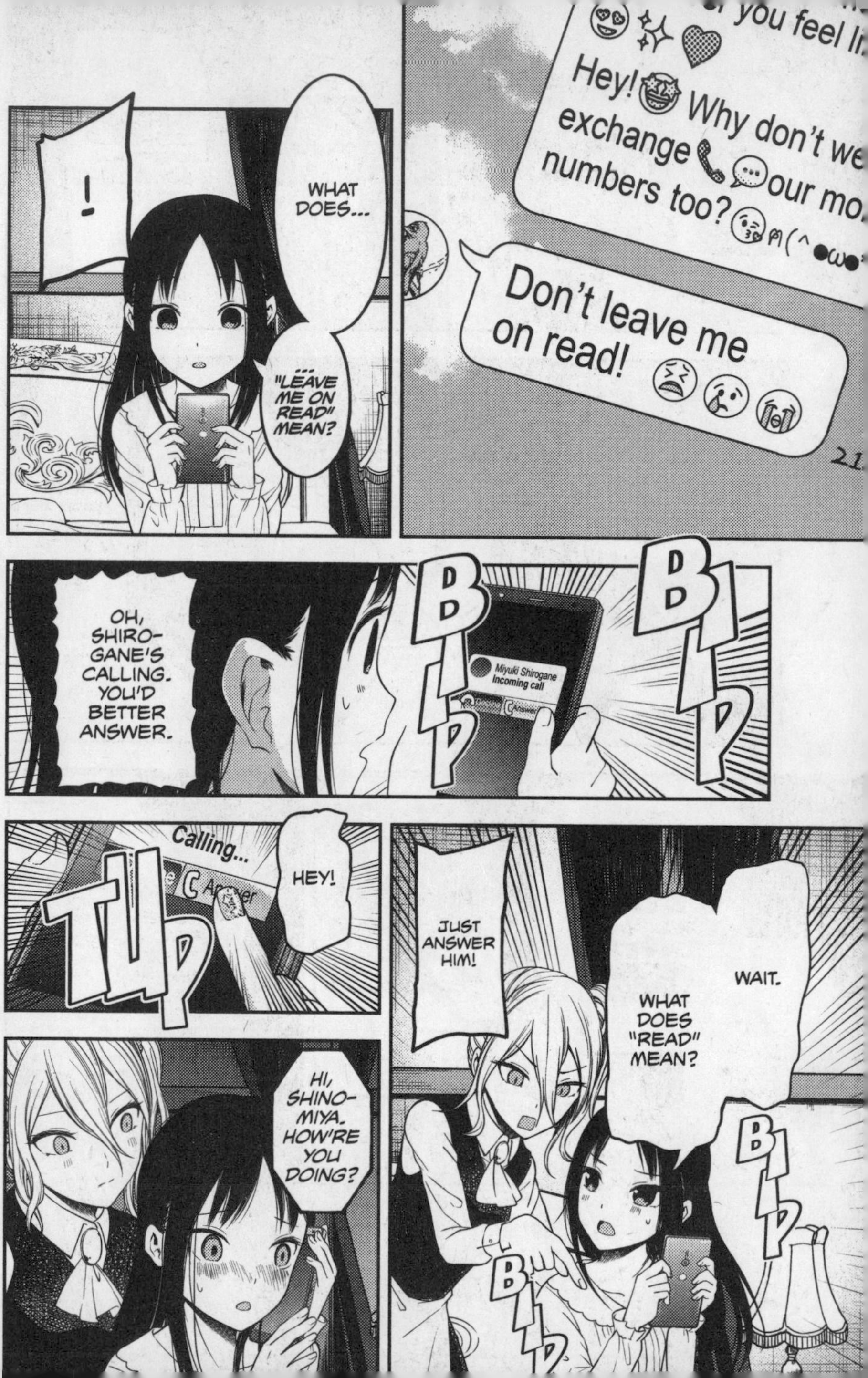

you feel li
Hey! Why don't we exchange our mo numbers too?
Don't leave me on read!
WHAT DOES...
..."LEAVE ME ON READ" MEAN?
!
BIP
BIP
Miyuki Shirogane
Incoming call
Answer
OH, SHIROGANE'S CALLING. YOU'D BETTER ANSWER.
WAIT.
WHAT DOES "READ" MEAN?
JUST ANSWER HIM!
BIP
BIP
HEY!
Calling...
Answer
TUP
HI, SHINOMIYA. HOW'RE YOU DOING?

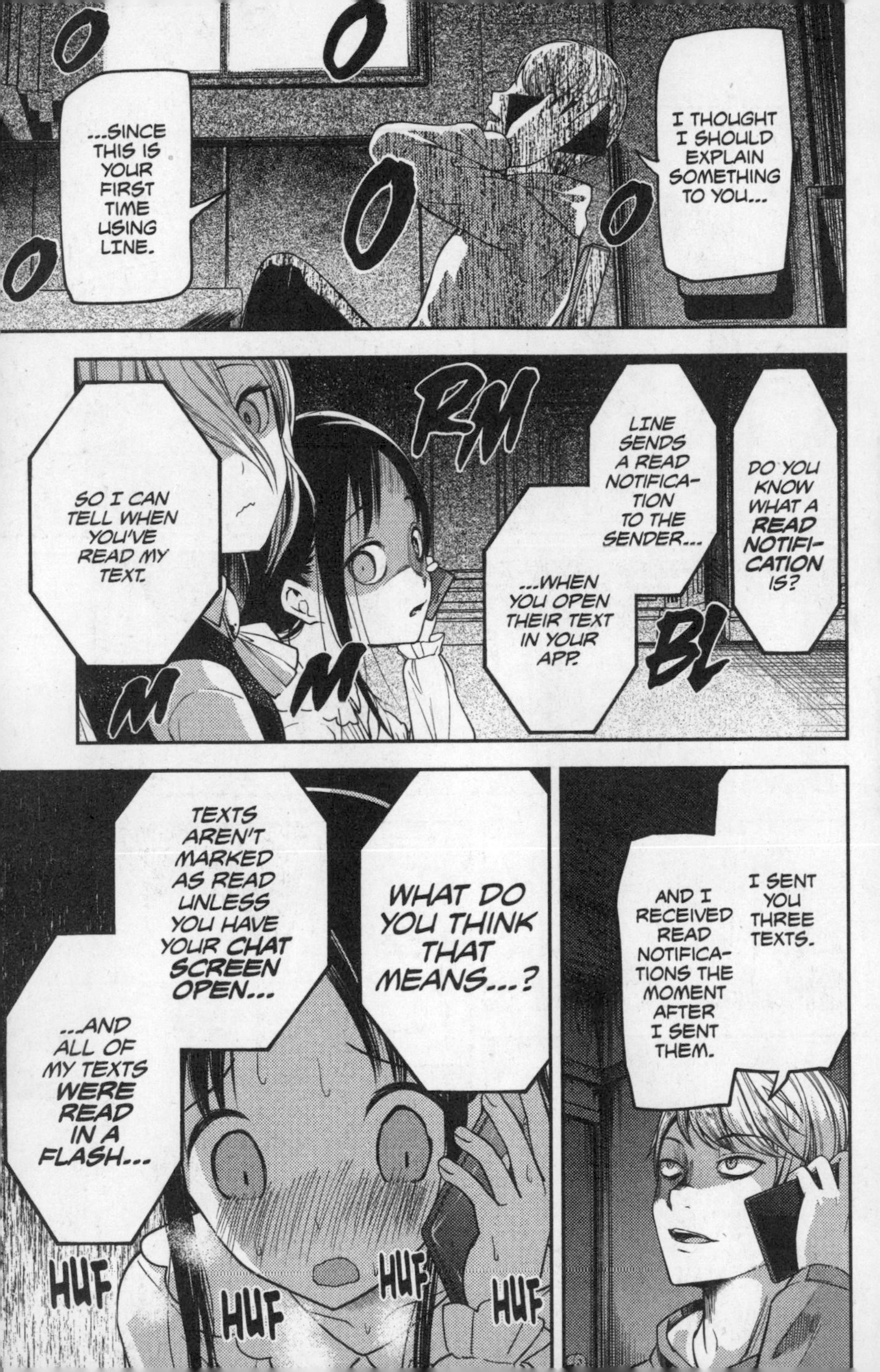
I THOUGHT I SHOULD EXPLAIN SOMETHING TO YOU...
...SINCE THIS IS YOUR FIRST TIME USING LINE.
DO YOU KNOW WHAT A READ NOTIFICATION IS?
LINE SENDS A READ NOTIFICATION TO THE SENDER...
...WHEN YOU OPEN THEIR TEXT IN YOUR APP.
RM
BL
SO I CAN TELL WHEN YOU'VE READ MY TEXT.
M
M
I SENT YOU THREE TEXTS.
AND I RECEIVED READ NOTIFICATIONS THE MOMENT AFTER I SENT THEM.
WHAT DO YOU THINK THAT MEANS...?
TEXTS AREN'T MARKED AS READ UNLESS YOU HAVE YOUR CHAT SCREEN OPEN...
...AND ALL OF MY TEXTS WERE READ IN A FLASH...
HUF
HUF
HUF
HUF

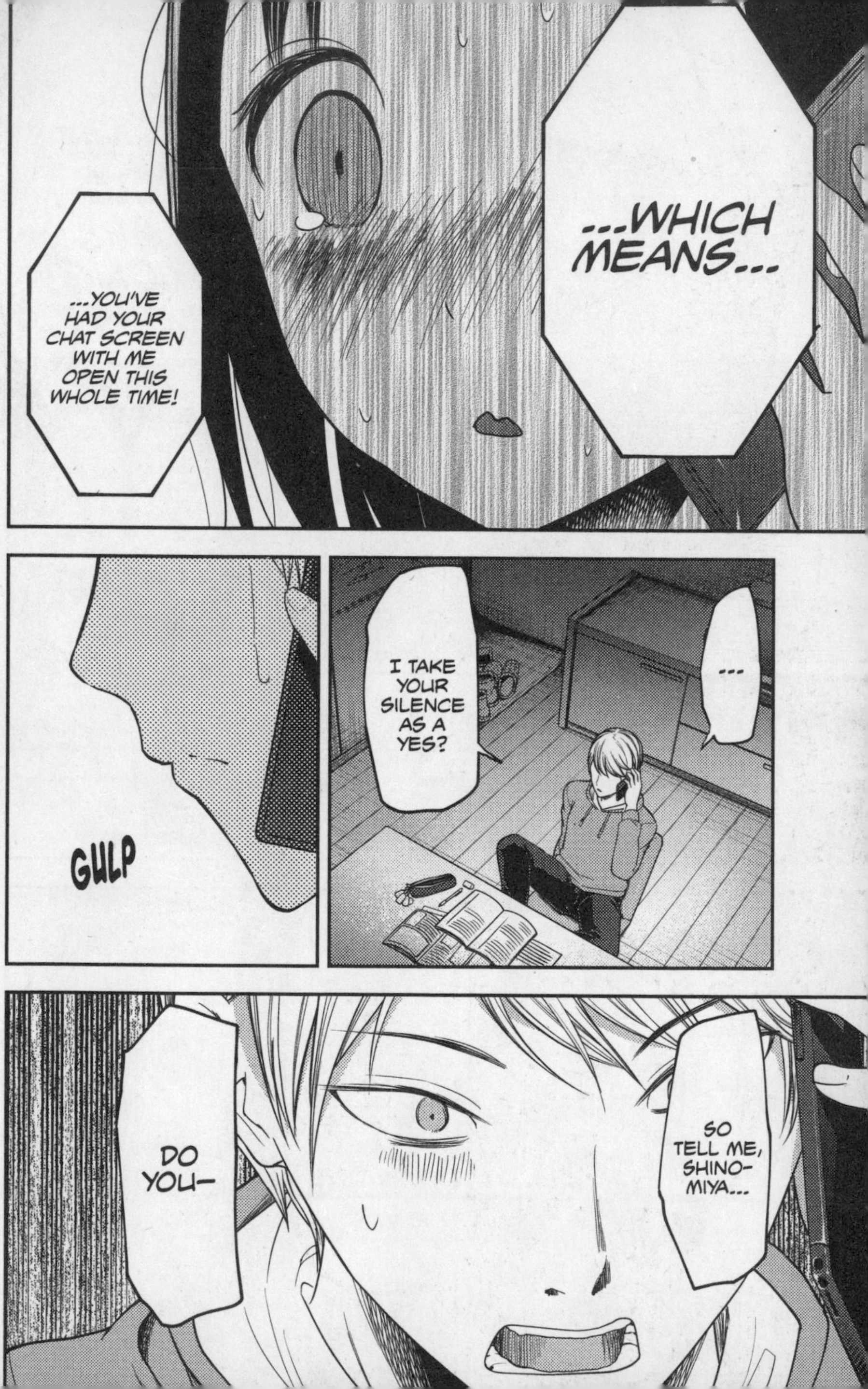
...WHICH MEANS...
...YOU'VE HAD YOUR CHAT SCREEN WITH ME OPEN THIS WHOLE TIME!
...
I TAKE YOUR SILENCE AS A YES?
GULP
SO TELL ME, SHINOMIYA...
DO YOU–

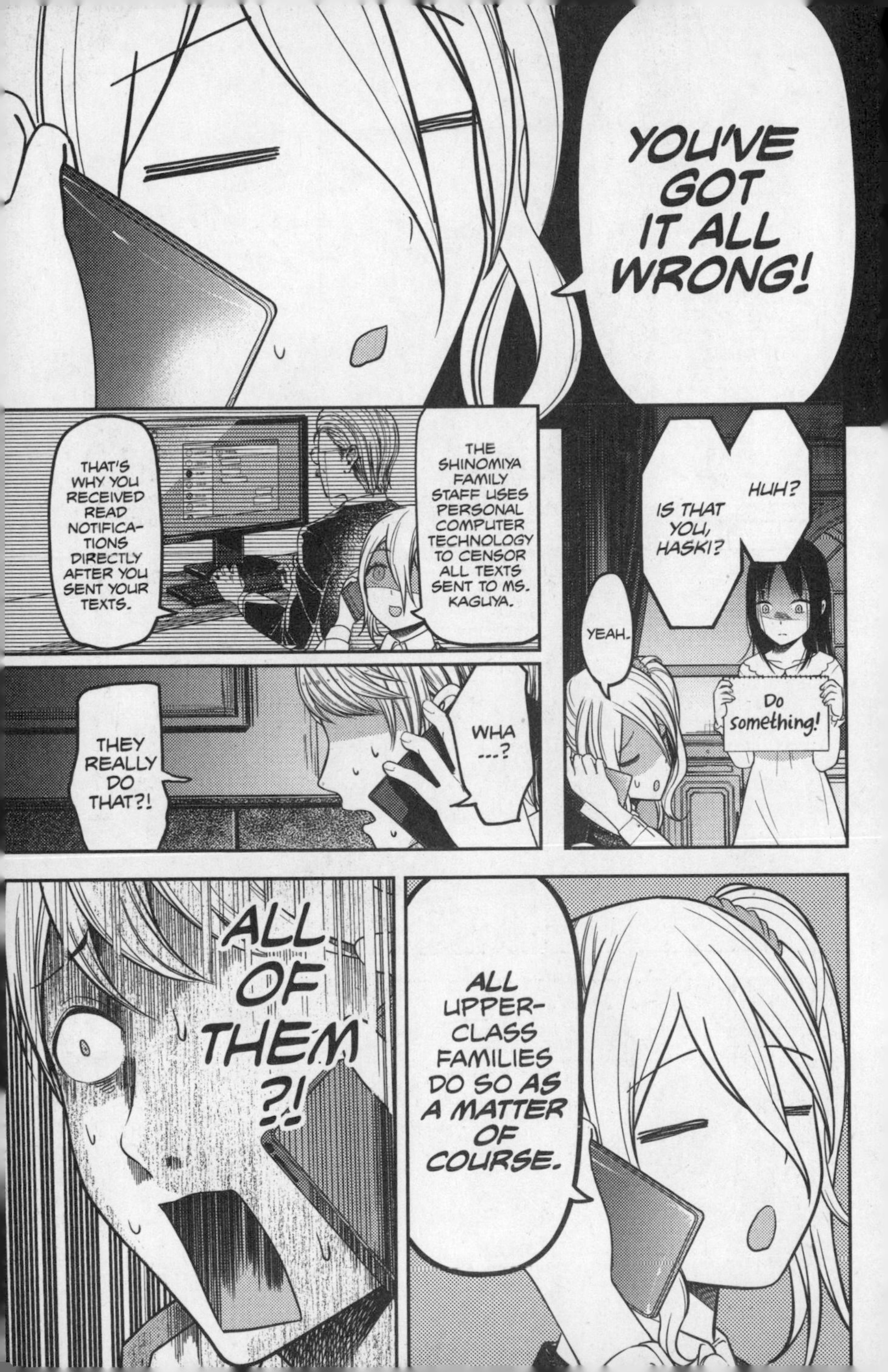
YOU'VE GOT IT ALL WRONG!
HUH?
IS THAT YOU, HASKI?
YEAH.
Do something!
THE SHINOMIYA FAMILY STAFF USES PERSONAL COMPUTER TECHNOLOGY TO CENSOR ALL TEXTS SENT TO MS. KAGUYA.
THAT'S WHY YOU RECEIVED READ NOTIFICATIONS DIRECTLY AFTER YOU SENT YOUR TEXTS.
WHA---?
THEY REALLY DO THAT?!
ALL UPPER-CLASS FAMILIES DO SO AS A MATTER OF COURSE.
ALL OF THEM?!

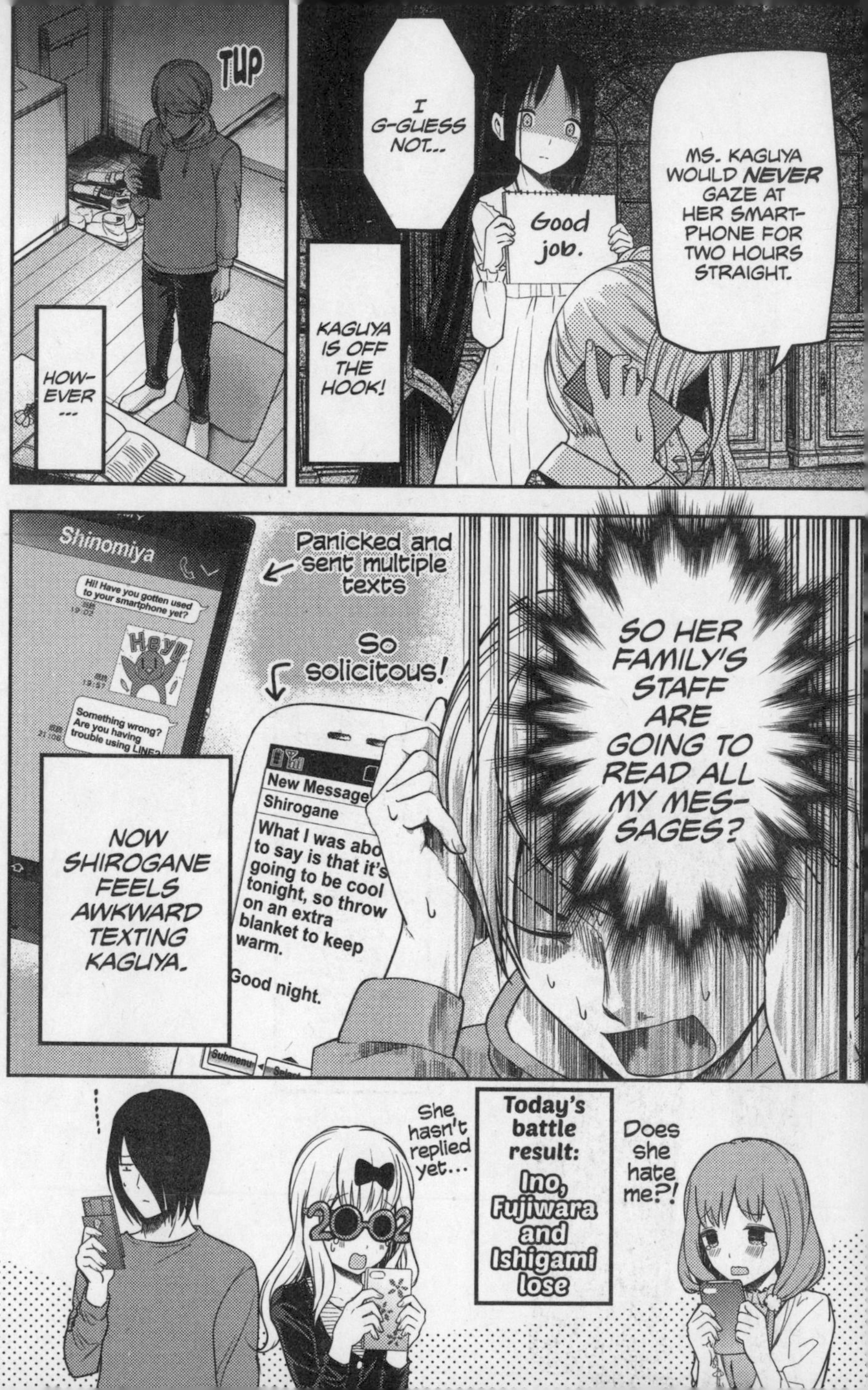
MS. KAGUYA WOULD NEVER GAZE AT HER SMART-PHONE FOR TWO HOURS STRAIGHT.
I G-GUESS NOT...
Good job.
KAGUYA IS OFF THE HOOK!
TUP
HOW-EVER---
SO HER FAMILY'S STAFF ARE GOING TO READ ALL MY MES-SAGES?
So solicitous!
Panicked and sent multiple texts
Shinomiya
Hi! Have you gotten used to your smartphone yet?
Hey!!
Something wrong? Are you having trouble using
New Message
Shirogane
What I was abo to say is that it's going to be cool tonight, so throw on an extra blanket to keep warm.
Good night.
NOW SHIROGANE FEELS AWKWARD TEXTING KAGUYA.
Does she hate me?!
Today's battle result: Ino, Fujiwara and Ishigami lose
She hasn't replied yet...
......

HE EXPLAINED AT GREAT LENGTH THAT DISCORD IS AS GOOD AS LINE. AND THIS WAS THE LOOK ON HIS FACE WHEN KAGUYA DIDN'T UNDER- STAND AND LOOKED PUZZLED.

KAGUYA-SAMA
LOVE IS WAR

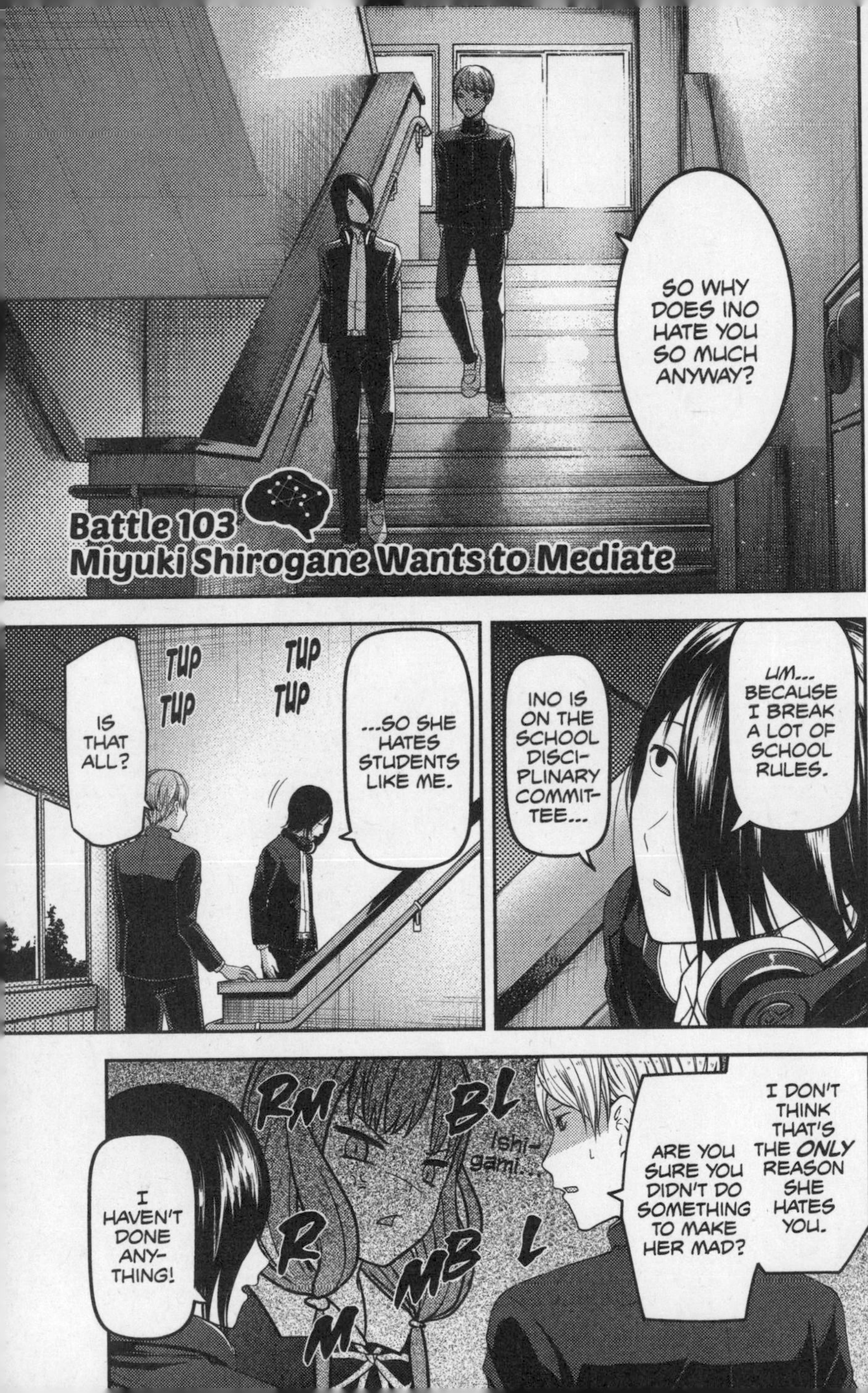
SO WHY DOES INO HATE YOU SO MUCH ANYWAY?
Battle 103 Miyuki Shirogane Wants to Mediate
UM... BECAUSE I BREAK A LOT OF SCHOOL RULES.
INO IS ON THE SCHOOL DISCI-PLINARY COMMIT-TEE...
TUP TUP
...SO SHE HATES STUDENTS LIKE ME.
TUP TUP
IS THAT ALL?
I DON'T THINK THAT'S THE ONLY REASON SHE HATES YOU.
ARE YOU SURE YOU DIDN'T DO SOMETHING TO MAKE HER MAD?
Ishi-gami...
RMBL
RMMBL
I HAVEN'T DONE ANY-THING!

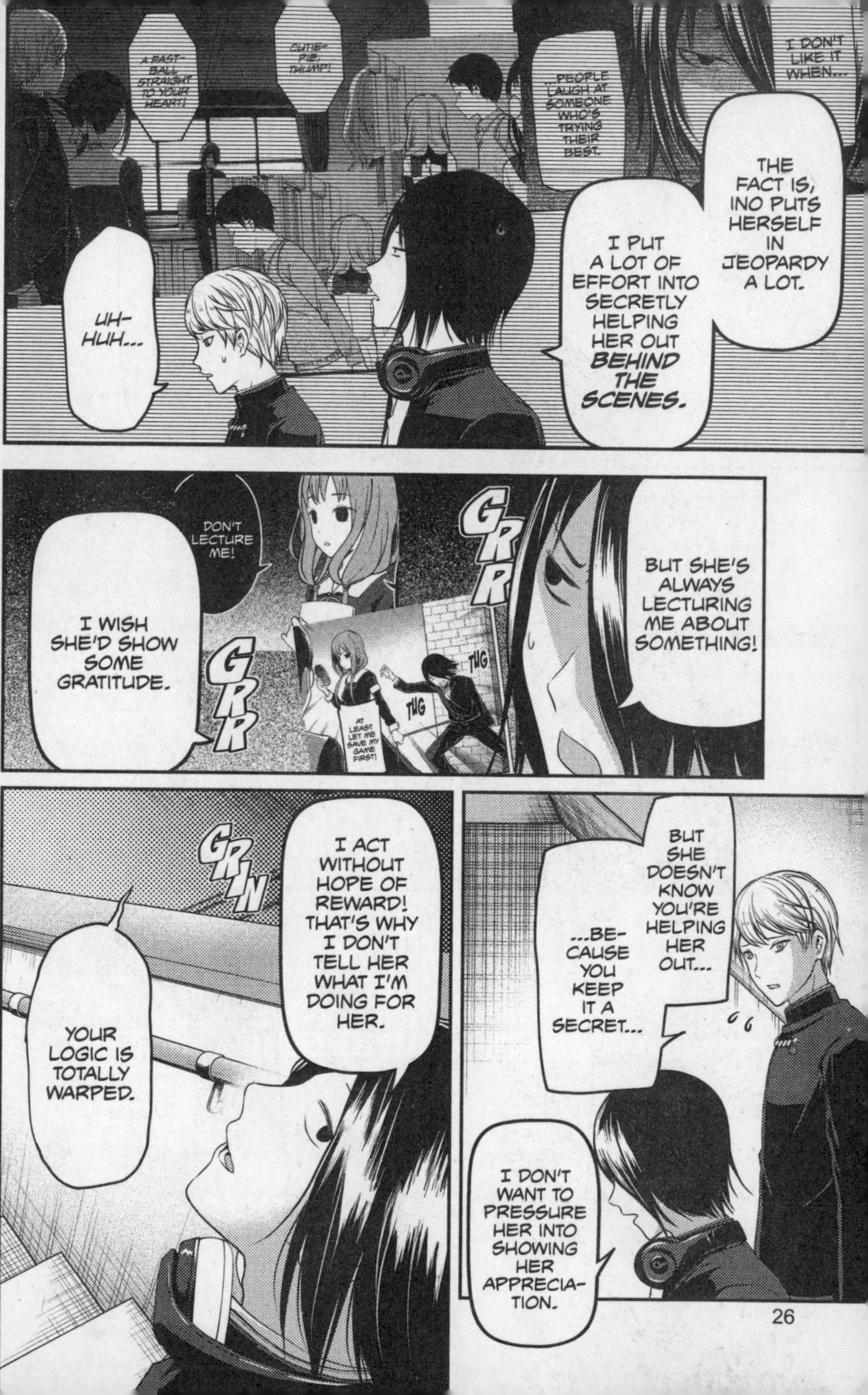
I DON'T LIKE IT WHEN...
...PEOPLE LAUGH AT SOMEONE WHO'S TRYING THEIR BEST.
CUTIE-PIE, THUMP!
A FASTBALL STRAIGHT TO YOUR HEART!
THE FACT IS, INO PUTS HERSELF IN JEOPARDY A LOT.
I PUT A LOT OF EFFORT INTO SECRETLY HELPING HER OUT ***BEHIND THE SCENES.***
UH-HUH...
BUT SHE'S ALWAYS LECTURING ME ABOUT SOMETHING!
GRR
THUG
THUG
DON'T LECTURE ME!
AT LEAST LET ME SAVE MY GAME FIRST!
GRR
I WISH SHE'D SHOW SOME GRATITUDE.
BUT SHE DOESN'T KNOW YOU'RE HELPING HER OUT...
...BECAUSE YOU KEEP IT A SECRET...
I DON'T WANT TO PRESSURE HER INTO SHOWING HER APPRECIATION.
I ACT WITHOUT HOPE OF REWARD! THAT'S WHY I DON'T TELL HER WHAT I'M DOING FOR HER.
GRIN
YOUR LOGIC IS TOTALLY WARPED.

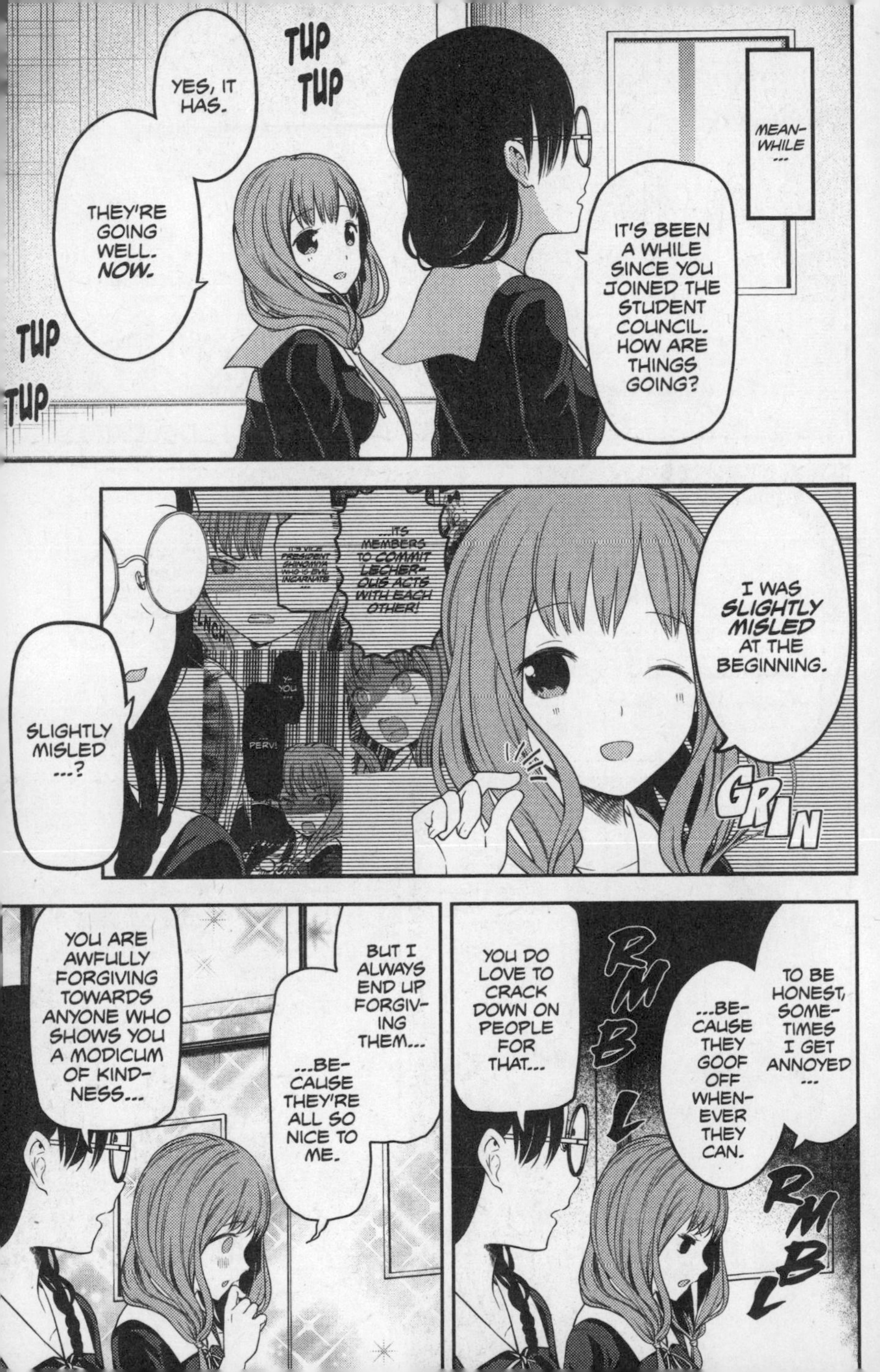
MEAN-WHILE...
IT'S BEEN A WHILE SINCE YOU JOINED THE STUDENT COUNCIL. HOW ARE THINGS GOING?
TUP TUP
YES, IT HAS.
THEY'RE GOING WELL. *NOW.*
TUP TUP
I WAS ***SLIGHTLY MISLED*** AT THE BEGINNING.
GRIN
...ITS MEMBERS TO ***COMMIT LECHEROUS ACTS WITH EACH OTHER!***
IT'S VICE PRESIDENT SHINOMIYA WHO IS EVIL INCARNATE...
Y-YOU...
...PERV!
SLIGHTLY MISLED...?
TO BE HONEST, SOMETIMES I GET ANNOYED...
...BECAUSE THEY GOOF OFF WHENEVER THEY CAN.
RMBL
RMBL
YOU DO LOVE TO CRACK DOWN ON PEOPLE FOR THAT...
BUT I ALWAYS END UP FORGIVING THEM...
...BECAUSE THEY'RE ALL SO NICE TO ME.
YOU ARE AWFULLY FORGIVING TOWARDS ANYONE WHO SHOWS YOU A MODICUM OF KINDNESS...

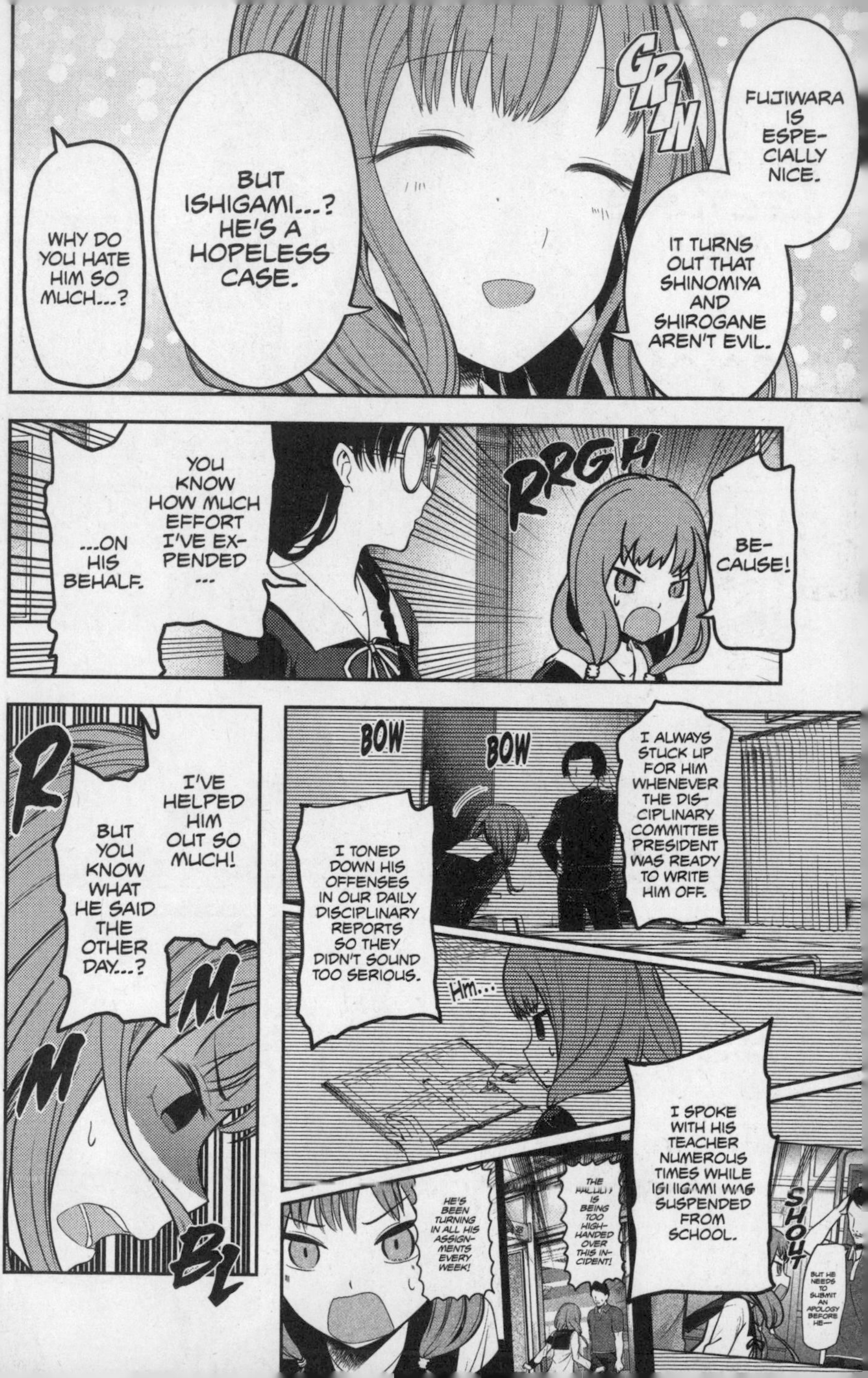
FUJIWARA IS ESPECIALLY NICE.
IT TURNS OUT THAT SHINOMIYA AND SHIROGANE AREN'T EVIL.
GRIN
BUT ISHIGAMI...? HE'S A HOPELESS CASE.
WHY DO YOU HATE HIM SO MUCH...?
BE-CAUSE!
RRGH
YOU KNOW HOW MUCH EFFORT I'VE EXPENDED...
...ON HIS BEHALF.
I ALWAYS STUCK UP FOR HIM WHENEVER THE DISCIPLINARY COMMITTEE PRESIDENT WAS READY TO WRITE HIM OFF.
BOW
BOW
I TONED DOWN HIS OFFENSES IN OUR DAILY DISCIPLINARY REPORTS SO THEY DIDN'T SOUND TOO SERIOUS.
Hm...
I SPOKE WITH HIS TEACHER NUMEROUS TIMES WHILE ISHIGAMI WAS SUSPENDED FROM SCHOOL.
SHOUT
BUT HE NEEDS TO SUBMIT AN APOLOGY BEFORE HE—
THE
IS BEING TOO HIGH-HANDED OVER THIS INCIDENT!
HE'S BEEN TURNING IN ALL HIS ASSIGNMENTS EVERY WEEK!
I'VE HELPED HIM OUT SO MUCH!
BUT YOU KNOW WHAT HE SAID THE OTHER DAY...?
RMMBL

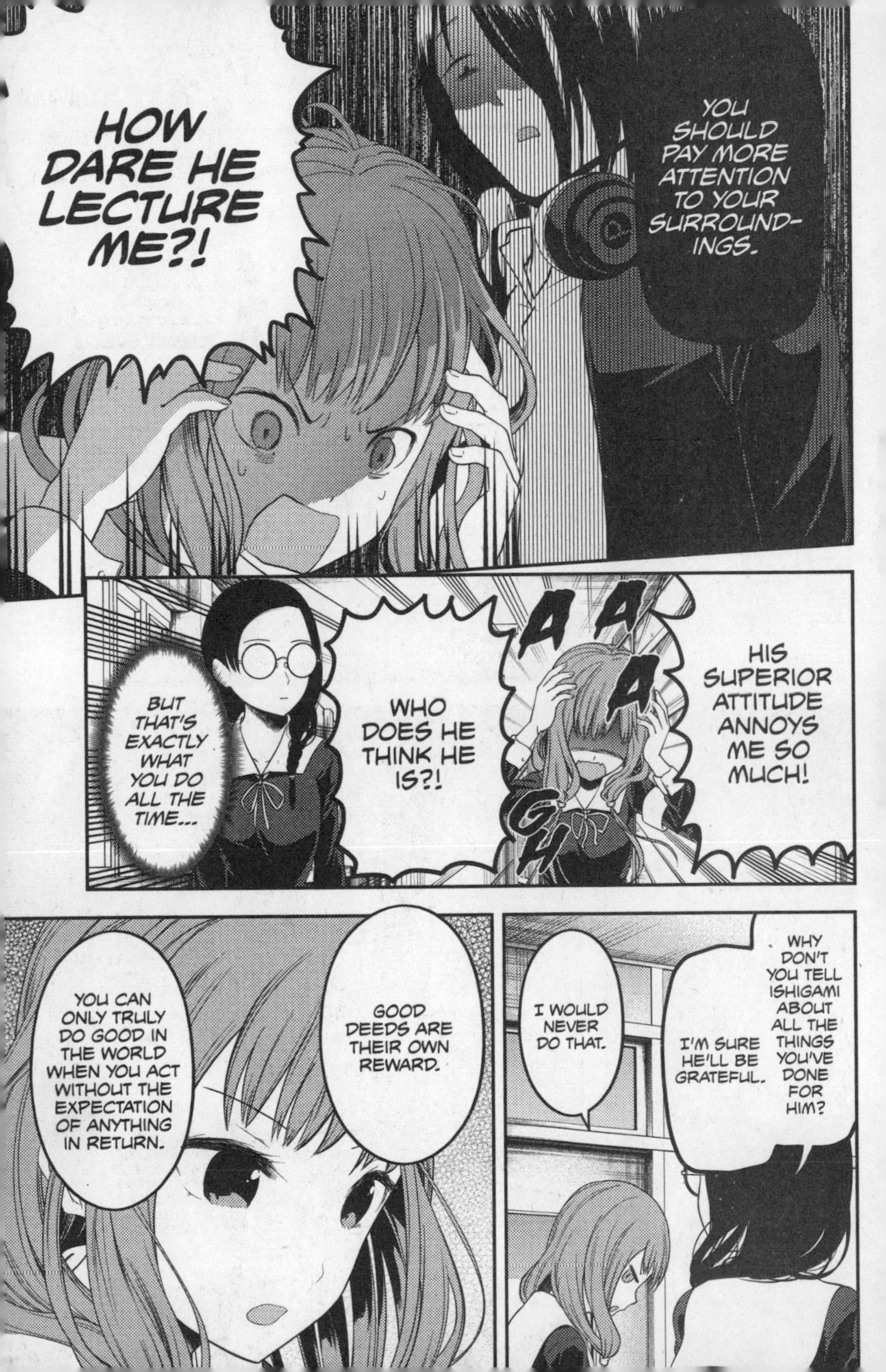
YOU SHOULD PAY MORE ATTENTION TO YOUR SURROUNDINGS.
HOW DARE HE LECTURE ME?!
HIS SUPERIOR ATTITUDE ANNOYS ME SO MUCH!
AAA
GH
WHO DOES HE THINK HE IS?!
BUT THAT'S EXACTLY WHAT YOU DO ALL THE TIME...
WHY DON'T YOU TELL ISHIGAMI ABOUT ALL THE THINGS YOU'VE DONE FOR HIM?
I'M SURE HE'LL BE GRATEFUL.
I WOULD NEVER DO THAT.
GOOD DEEDS ARE THEIR OWN REWARD.
YOU CAN ONLY TRULY DO GOOD IN THE WORLD WHEN YOU ACT WITHOUT THE EXPECTATION OF ANYTHING IN RETURN.

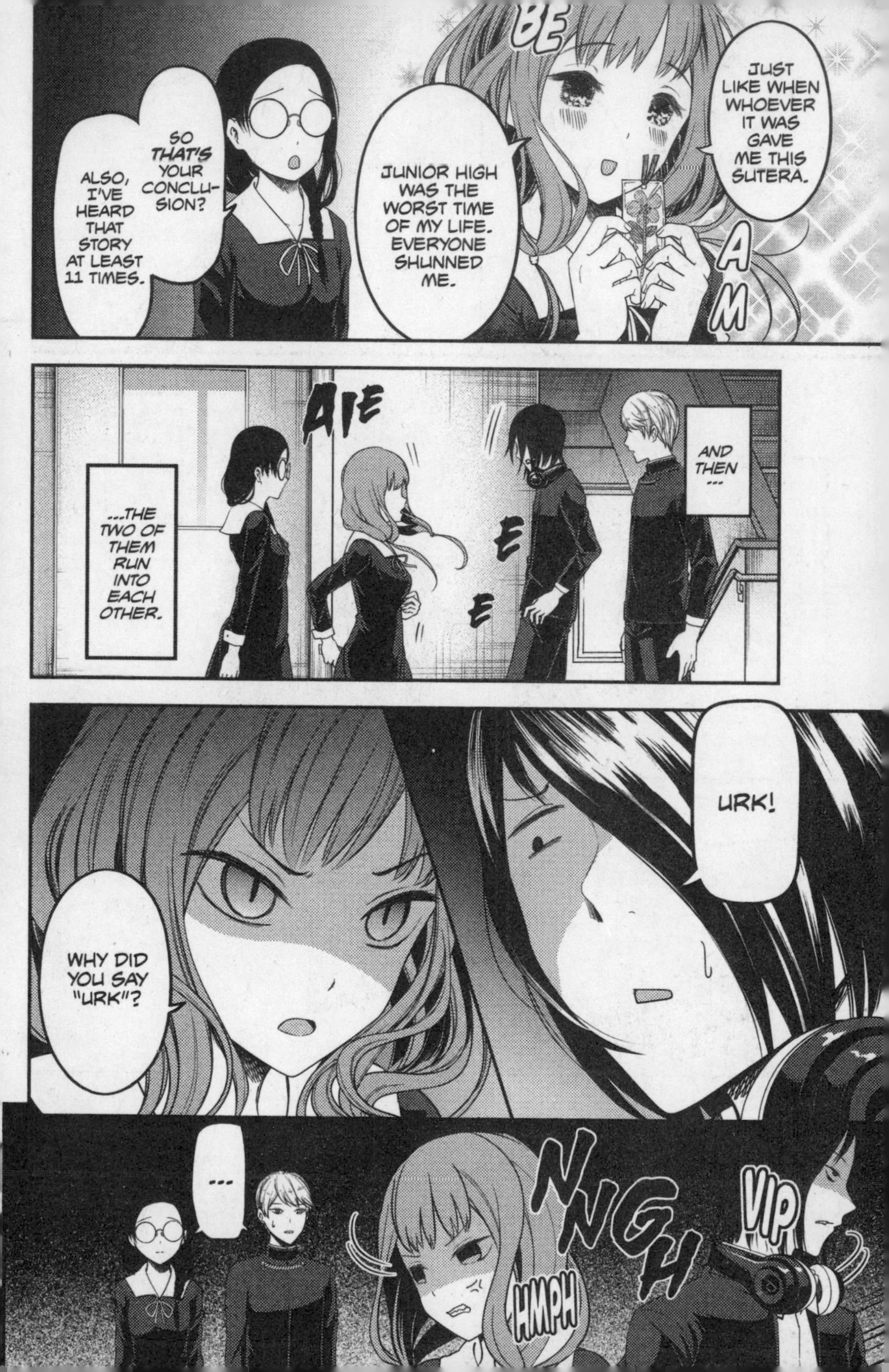
BE
JUST LIKE WHEN WHOEVER IT WAS GAVE ME THIS SUTERA.
AM
JUNIOR HIGH WAS THE WORST TIME OF MY LIFE. EVERYONE SHUNNED ME.
SO THAT'S YOUR CONCLUSION?
ALSO, I'VE HEARD THAT STORY AT LEAST 11 TIMES.
AND THEN ...
EEE
AIE
...THE TWO OF THEM RUN INTO EACH OTHER.
URK!
WHY DID YOU SAY "URK"?
VIP
NNGH
HMPH
...

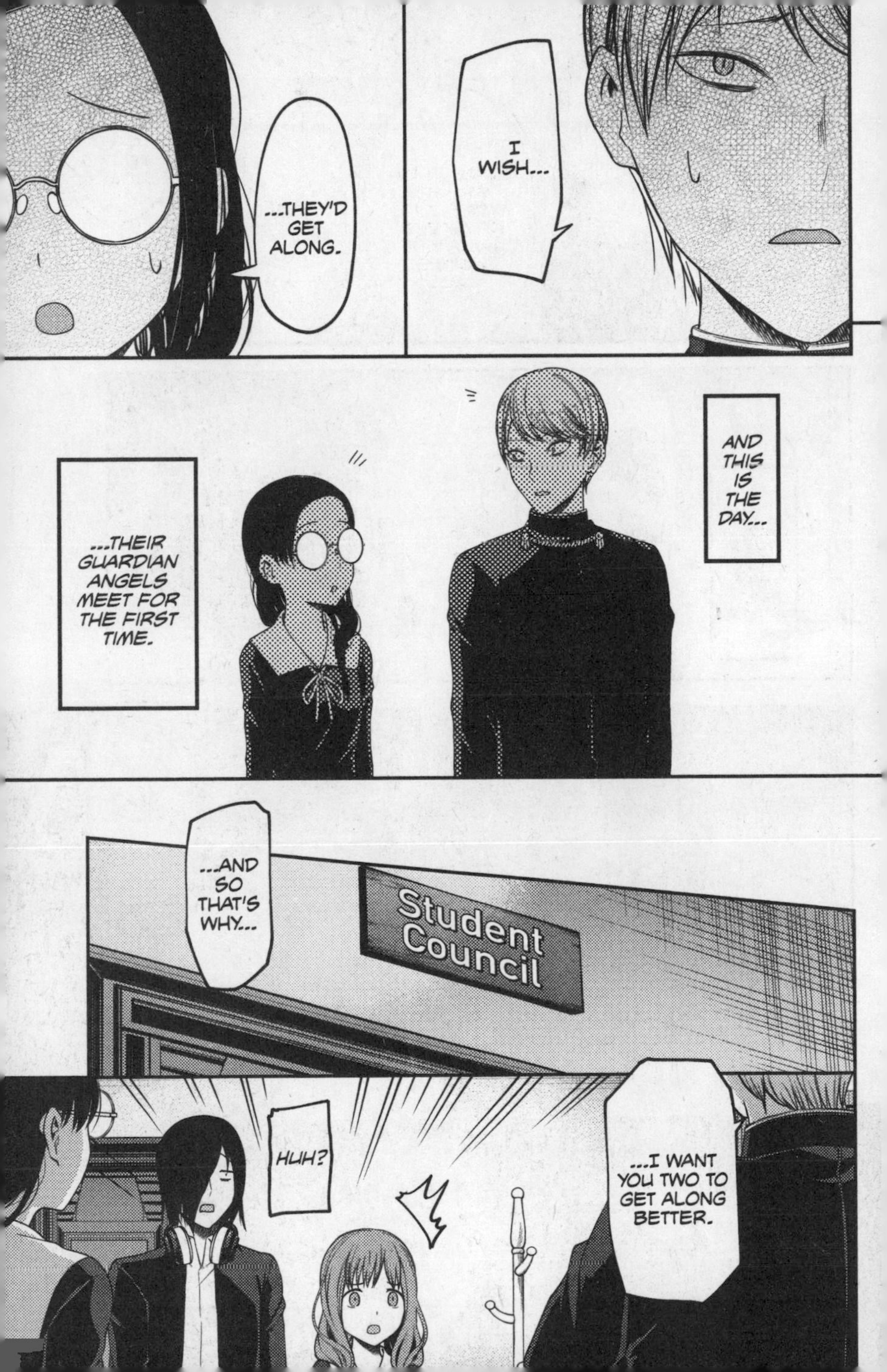
I WISH...
...THEY'D GET ALONG.
AND THIS IS THE DAY...
...THEIR GUARDIAN ANGELS MEET FOR THE FIRST TIME.
...AND SO THAT'S WHY...
Student Council
...I WANT YOU TWO TO GET ALONG BETTER.
HUH?

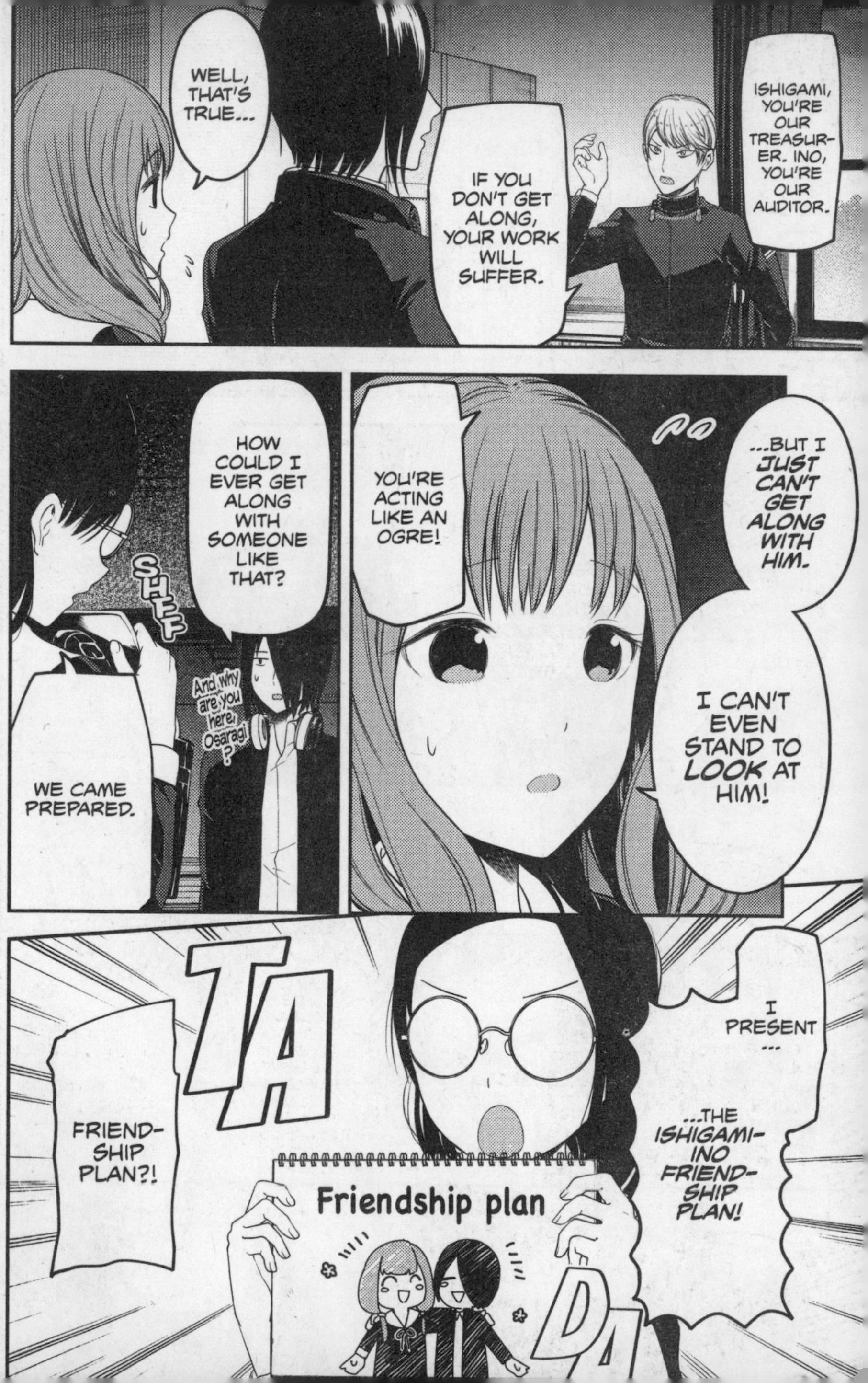
ISHIGAMI, YOU'RE OUR TREASURER. INO, YOU'RE OUR AUDITOR.
IF YOU DON'T GET ALONG, YOUR WORK WILL SUFFER.
WELL, THAT'S TRUE...
...BUT I JUST CAN'T GET ALONG WITH HIM.
I CAN'T EVEN STAND TO LOOK AT HIM!
YOU'RE ACTING LIKE AN OGRE!
HOW COULD I EVER GET ALONG WITH SOMEONE LIKE THAT?
SHFF
And why are you here, Osaragi?
WE CAME PREPARED.
I PRESENT...
...THE ISHIGAMI-INO FRIENDSHIP PLAN!
TA
DA
Friendship plan
FRIENDSHIP PLAN?!

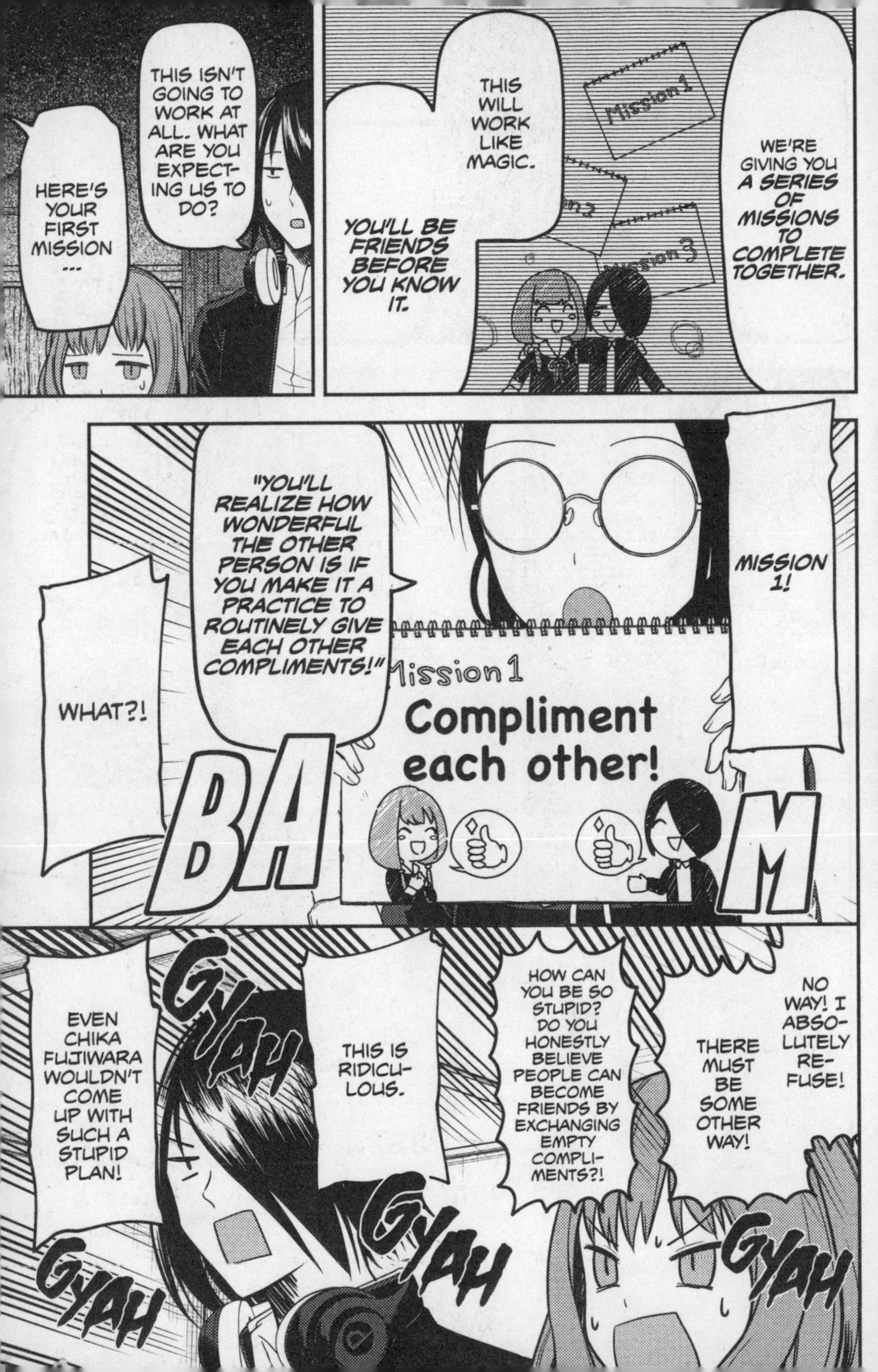
WE'RE GIVING YOU A SERIES OF MISSIONS TO COMPLETE TOGETHER.
Mission 1
Mission 3
THIS WILL WORK LIKE MAGIC.
YOU'LL BE FRIENDS BEFORE YOU KNOW IT.
THIS ISN'T GOING TO WORK AT ALL. WHAT ARE YOU EXPECTING US TO DO?
HERE'S YOUR FIRST MISSION ...
MISSION 1!
Mission 1
Compliment each other!
"YOU'LL REALIZE HOW WONDERFUL THE OTHER PERSON IS IF YOU MAKE IT A PRACTICE TO ROUTINELY GIVE EACH OTHER COMPLIMENTS!"
BAM
WHAT?!
NO WAY! I ABSOLUTELY REFUSE!
THERE MUST BE SOME OTHER WAY!
HOW CAN YOU BE SO STUPID? DO YOU HONESTLY BELIEVE PEOPLE CAN BECOME FRIENDS BY EXCHANGING EMPTY COMPLIMENTS?!
GYAH
THIS IS RIDICULOUS.
EVEN CHIKA FUJIWARA WOULDN'T COME UP WITH SUCH A STUPID PLAN!
GYAH
GYAH
GYAH

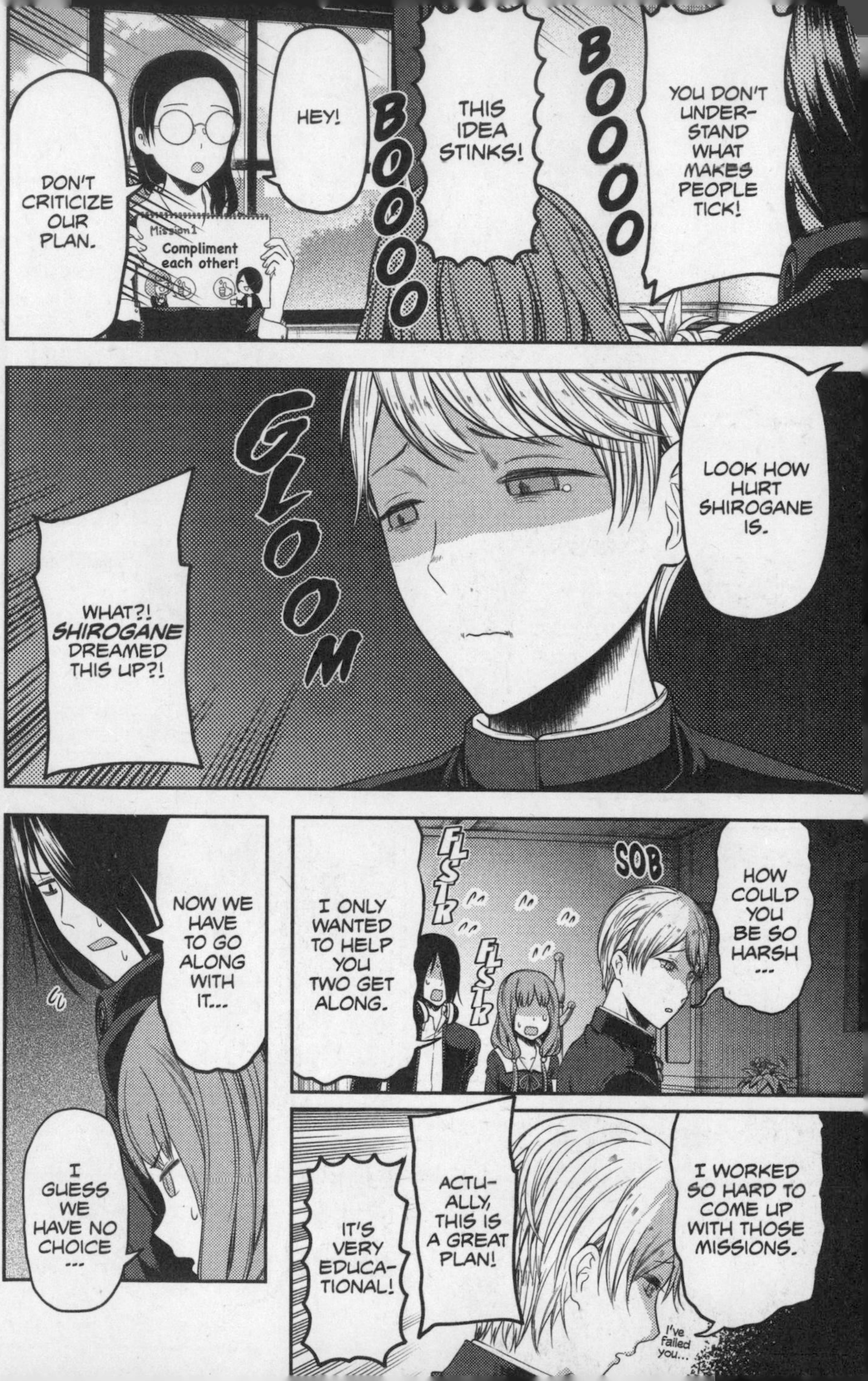
YOU DON'T UNDERSTAND WHAT MAKES PEOPLE TICK!
BOOOOO
THIS IDEA STINKS!
BOOOOO
HEY!
DON'T CRITICIZE OUR PLAN.
Mission1
Compliment each other!
LOOK HOW HURT SHIROGANE IS.
GLOOM
WHAT?! SHIROGANE DREAMED THIS UP?!
HOW COULD YOU BE SO HARSH...
SOB
FLSTR
FLSTR
I ONLY WANTED TO HELP YOU TWO GET ALONG.
I WORKED SO HARD TO COME UP WITH THOSE MISSIONS.
I've failed you...
ACTUALLY, THIS IS A GREAT PLAN!
IT'S VERY EDUCATIONAL!
NOW WE HAVE TO GO ALONG WITH IT...
I GUESS WE HAVE NO CHOICE...

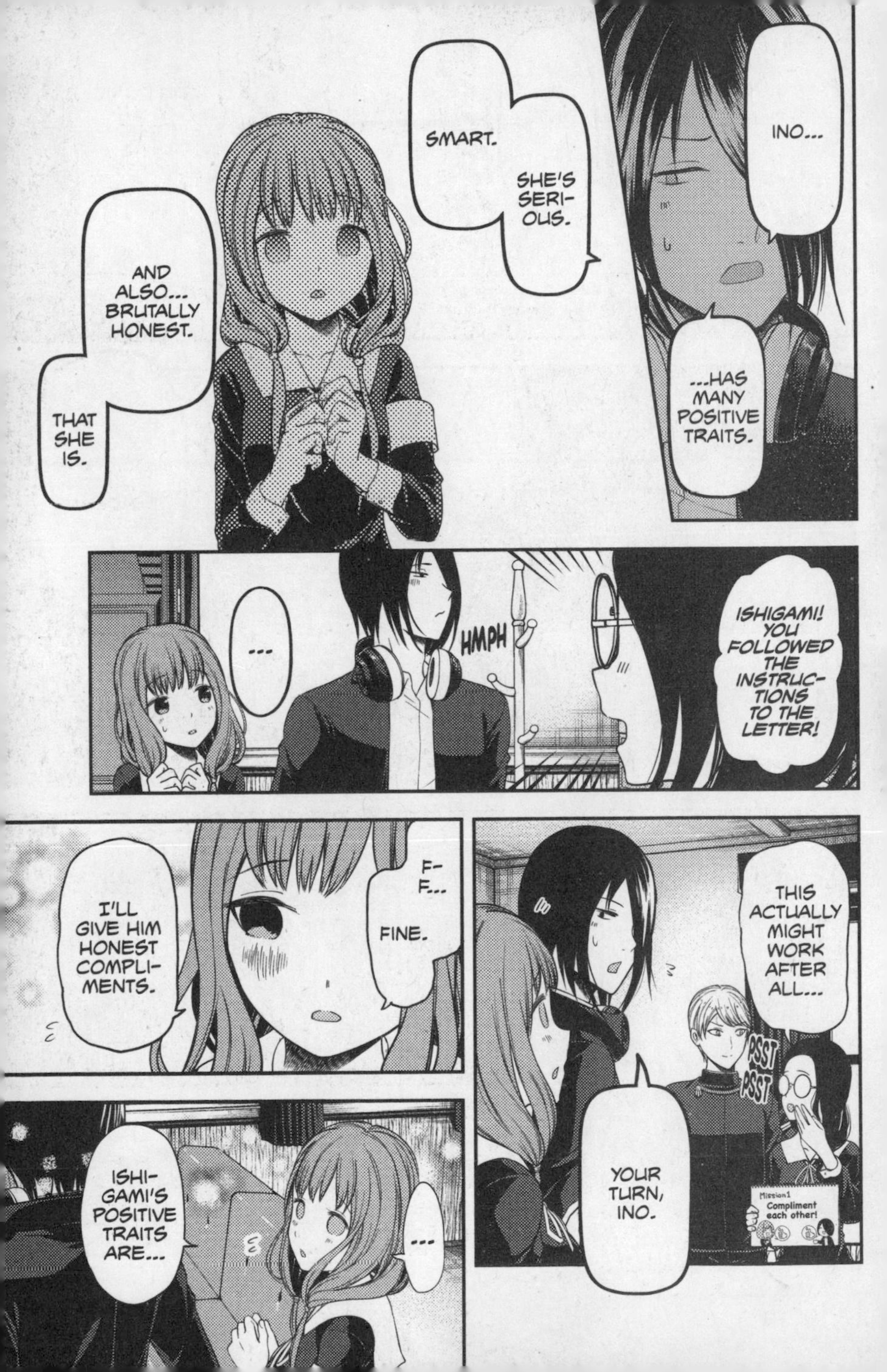
INO...
...HAS MANY POSITIVE TRAITS.
SMART.
SHE'S SERI-OUS.
AND ALSO... BRUTALLY HONEST.
THAT SHE IS.
ISHIGAMI! YOU FOLLOWED THE INSTRUC-TIONS TO THE LETTER!
HMPH
...
THIS ACTUALLY MIGHT WORK AFTER ALL...
PSST PSST
YOUR TURN, INO.
Mission1
Compliment each other!
F-F...
FINE.
I'LL GIVE HIM HONEST COMPLI-MENTS.
...
ISHI-GAMI'S POSITIVE TRAITS ARE...

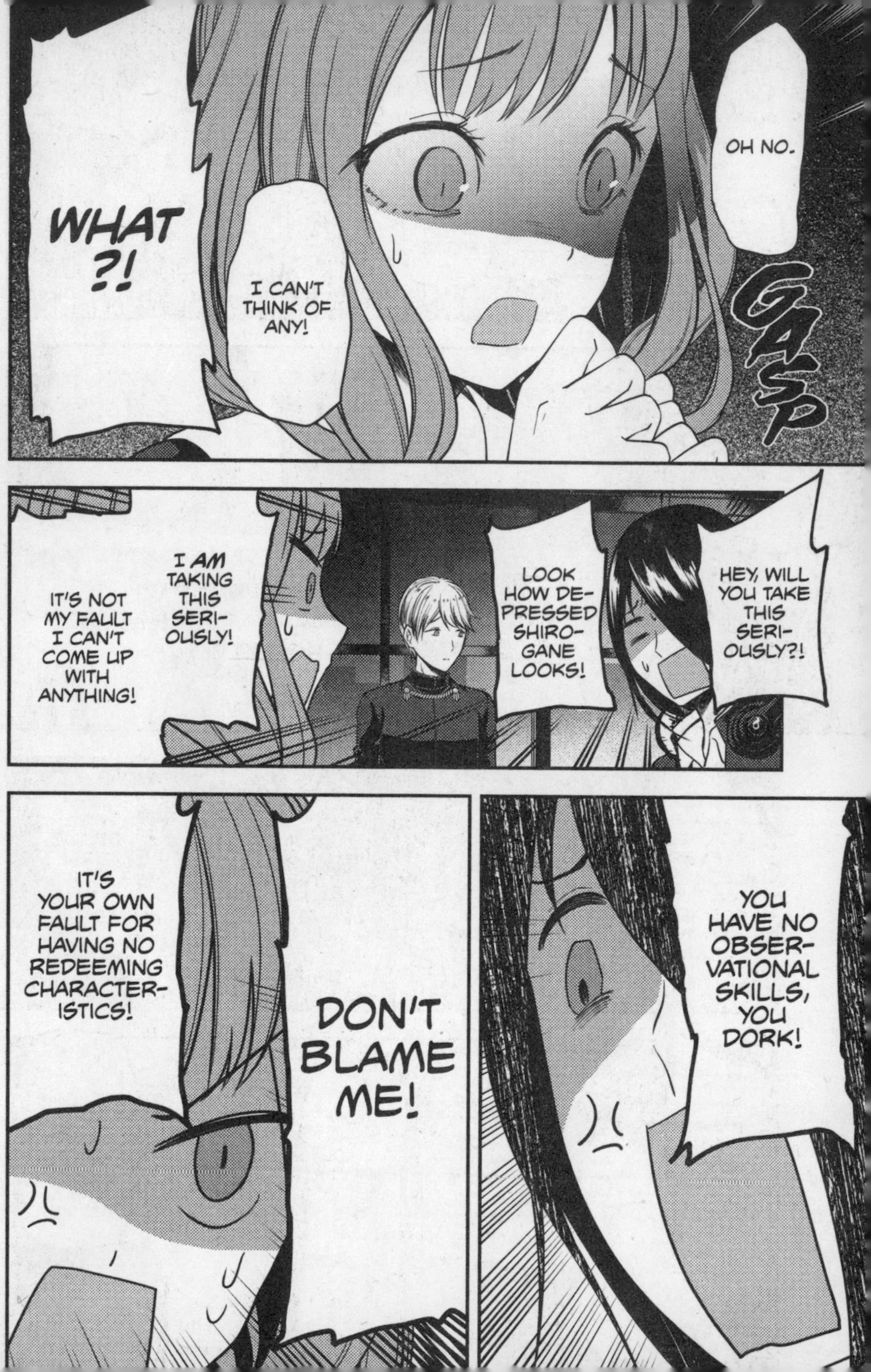
OH NO.
GASP
I CAN'T THINK OF ANY!
WHAT ?!
HEY, WILL YOU TAKE THIS SERIOUSLY?!
LOOK HOW DEPRESSED SHIROGANE LOOKS!
I *AM* TAKING THIS SERIOUSLY!
IT'S NOT MY FAULT I CAN'T COME UP WITH ANYTHING!
YOU HAVE NO OBSERVATIONAL SKILLS, YOU DORK!
IT'S YOUR OWN FAULT FOR HAVING NO REDEEMING CHARACTERISTICS!
DON'T BLAME ME!

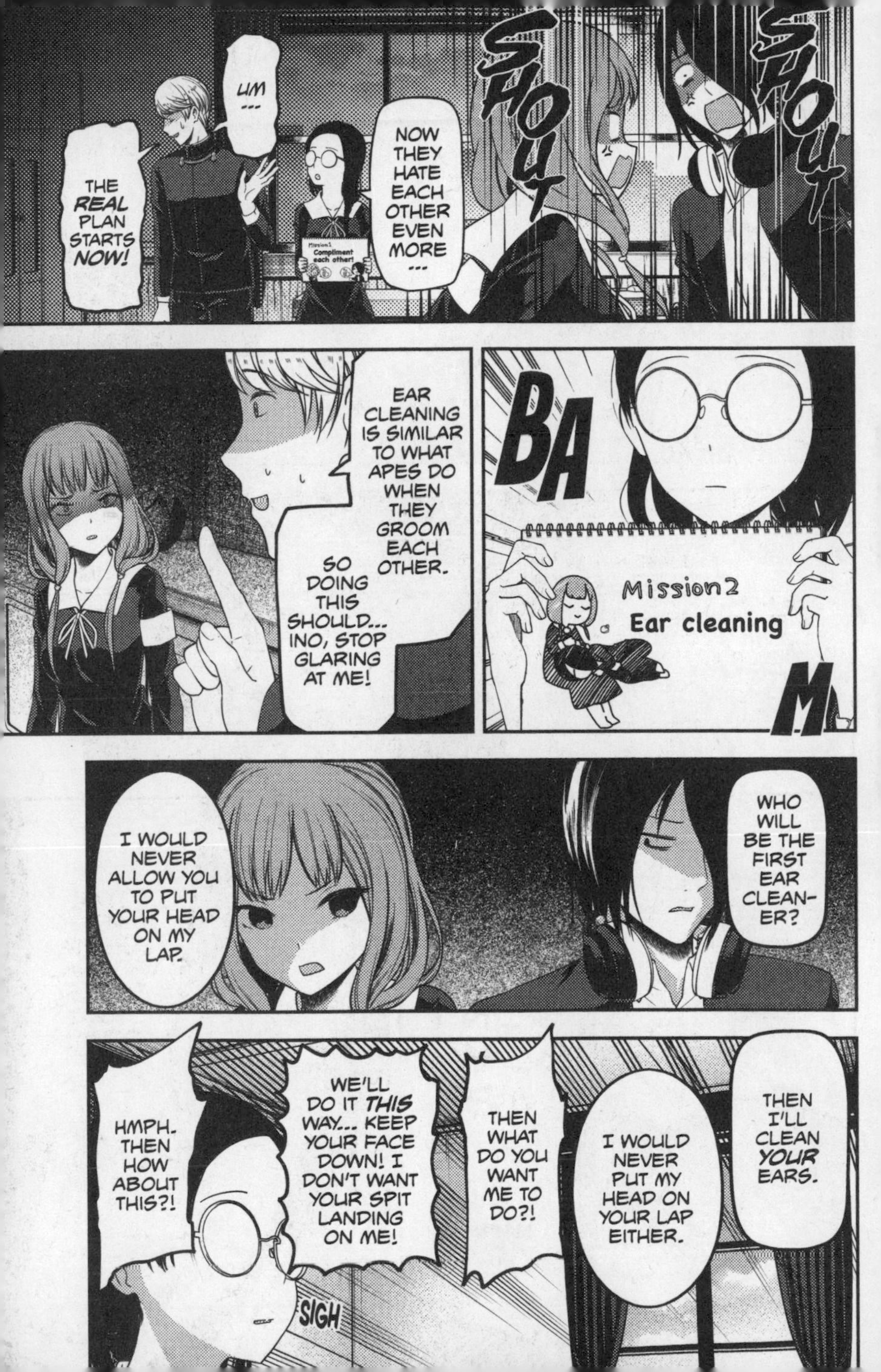
SHOUT
SHOUT
NOW THEY HATE EACH OTHER EVEN MORE...
Mission1 Compliment each other!
UM...
THE REAL PLAN STARTS NOW!
BA
M
Mission2 Ear cleaning
EAR CLEANING IS SIMILAR TO WHAT APES DO WHEN THEY GROOM EACH OTHER.
SO DOING THIS SHOULD... INO, STOP GLARING AT ME!
WHO WILL BE THE FIRST EAR CLEANER?
I WOULD NEVER ALLOW YOU TO PUT YOUR HEAD ON MY LAP.
THEN I'LL CLEAN YOUR EARS.
I WOULD NEVER PUT MY HEAD ON YOUR LAP EITHER.
THEN WHAT DO YOU WANT ME TO DO?!
WE'LL DO IT THIS WAY... KEEP YOUR FACE DOWN! I DON'T WANT YOUR SPIT LANDING ON ME!
HMPH. THEN HOW ABOUT THIS?!
SIGH

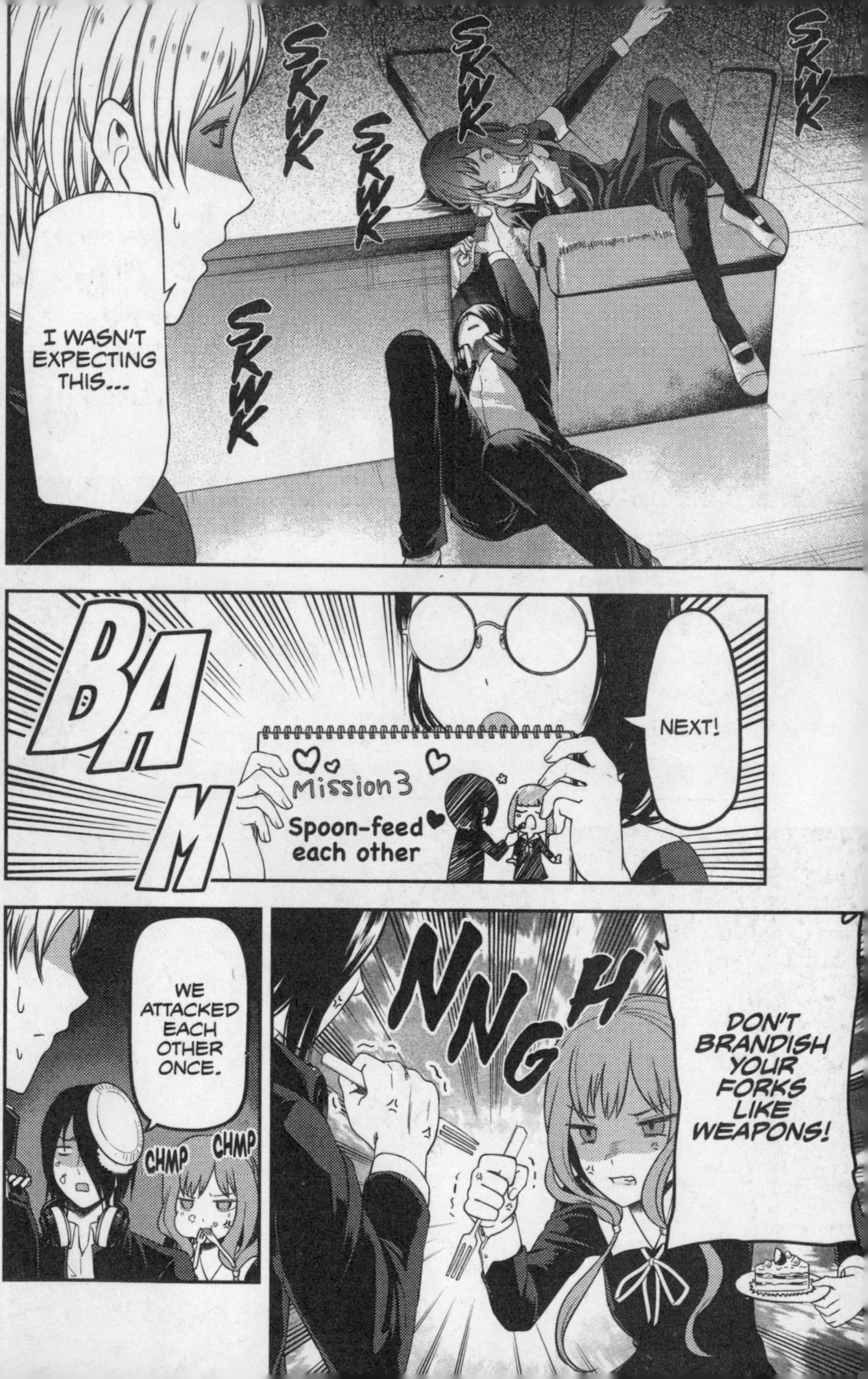
SKWK
SKWK
SKWK
SKWK
SKWK
I WASN'T EXPECTING THIS...
NEXT!
Mission 3
Spoon-feed each other
BAM
NNGH
DON'T BRANDISH YOUR FORKS LIKE WEAPONS!
WE ATTACKED EACH OTHER ONCE.
CHMP
CHMP

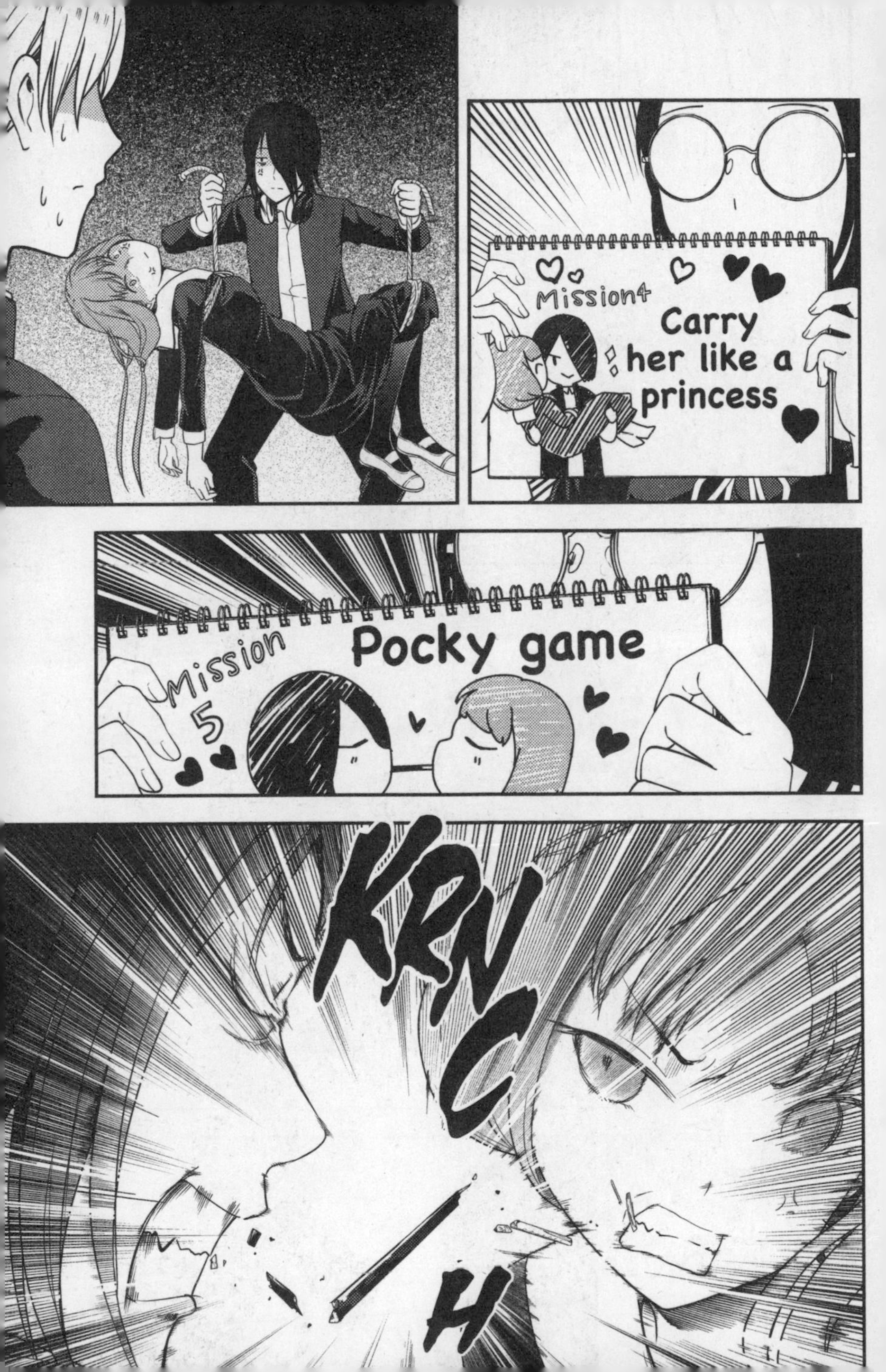
Mission4
Carry her like a princess
Mission 5
Pocky game
KRNCH

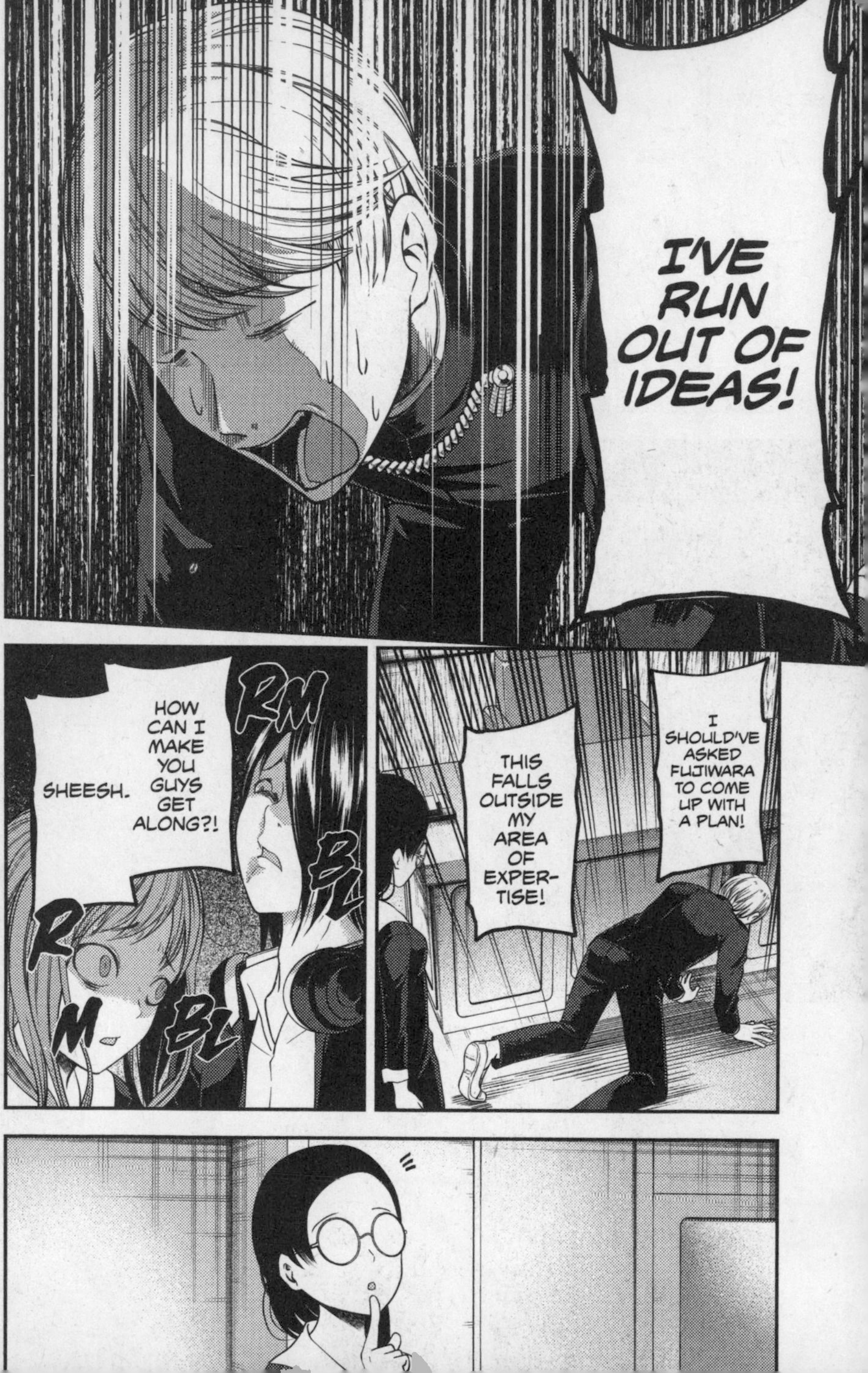
I'VE RUN OUT OF IDEAS!
I SHOULD'VE ASKED FUJIWARA TO COME UP WITH A PLAN!
THIS FALLS OUTSIDE MY AREA OF EXPERTISE!
HOW CAN I MAKE YOU GUYS GET ALONG?!
SHEESH.
RMBL
RMBL
RMBL

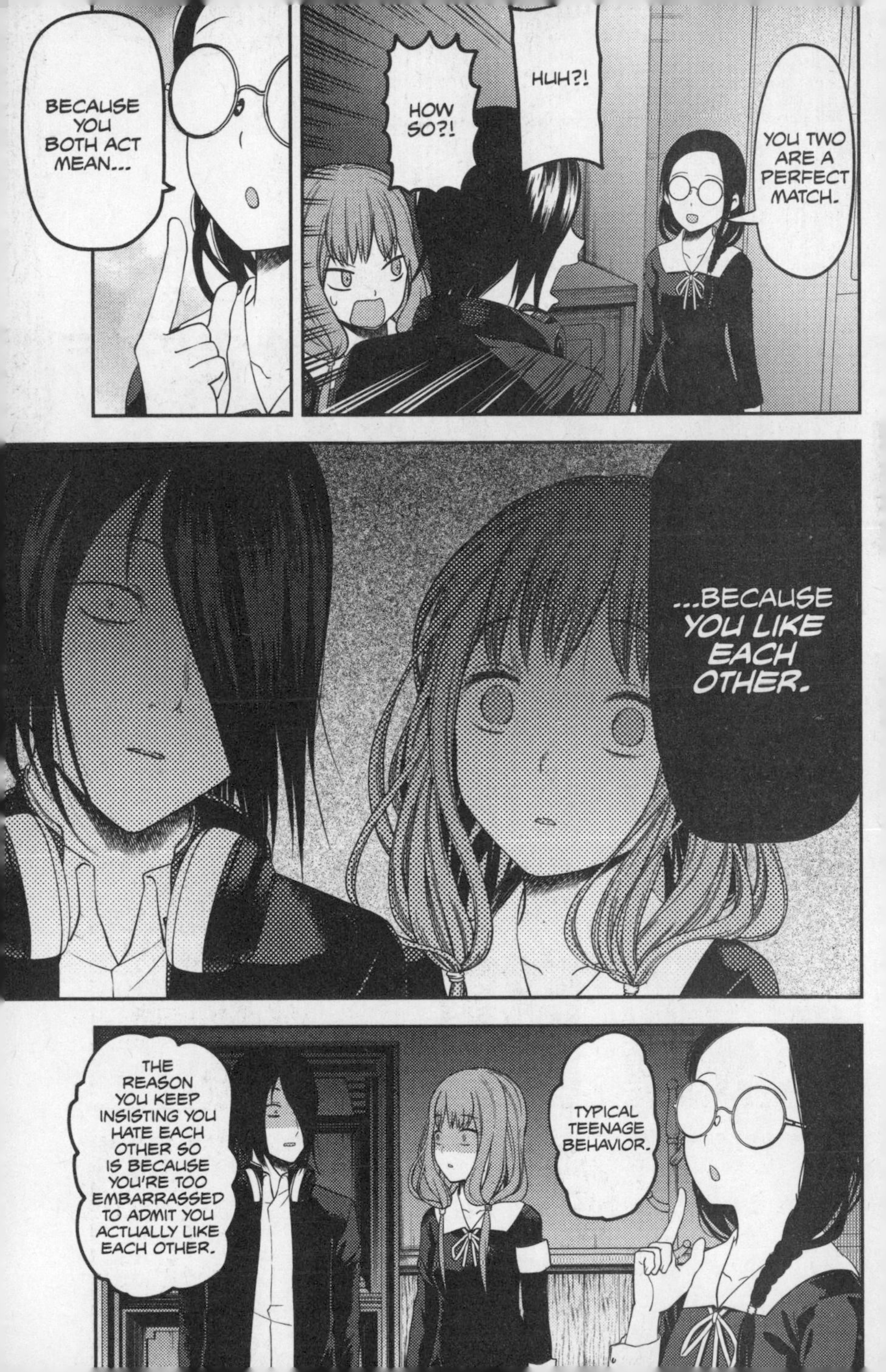
YOU TWO ARE A PERFECT MATCH.
HUH?!
HOW SO?!
BECAUSE YOU BOTH ACT MEAN...
...BECAUSE YOU LIKE EACH OTHER.
TYPICAL TEENAGE BEHAVIOR.
THE REASON YOU KEEP INSISTING YOU HATE EACH OTHER SO IS BECAUSE YOU'RE TOO EMBARRASSED TO ADMIT YOU ACTUALLY LIKE EACH OTHER.

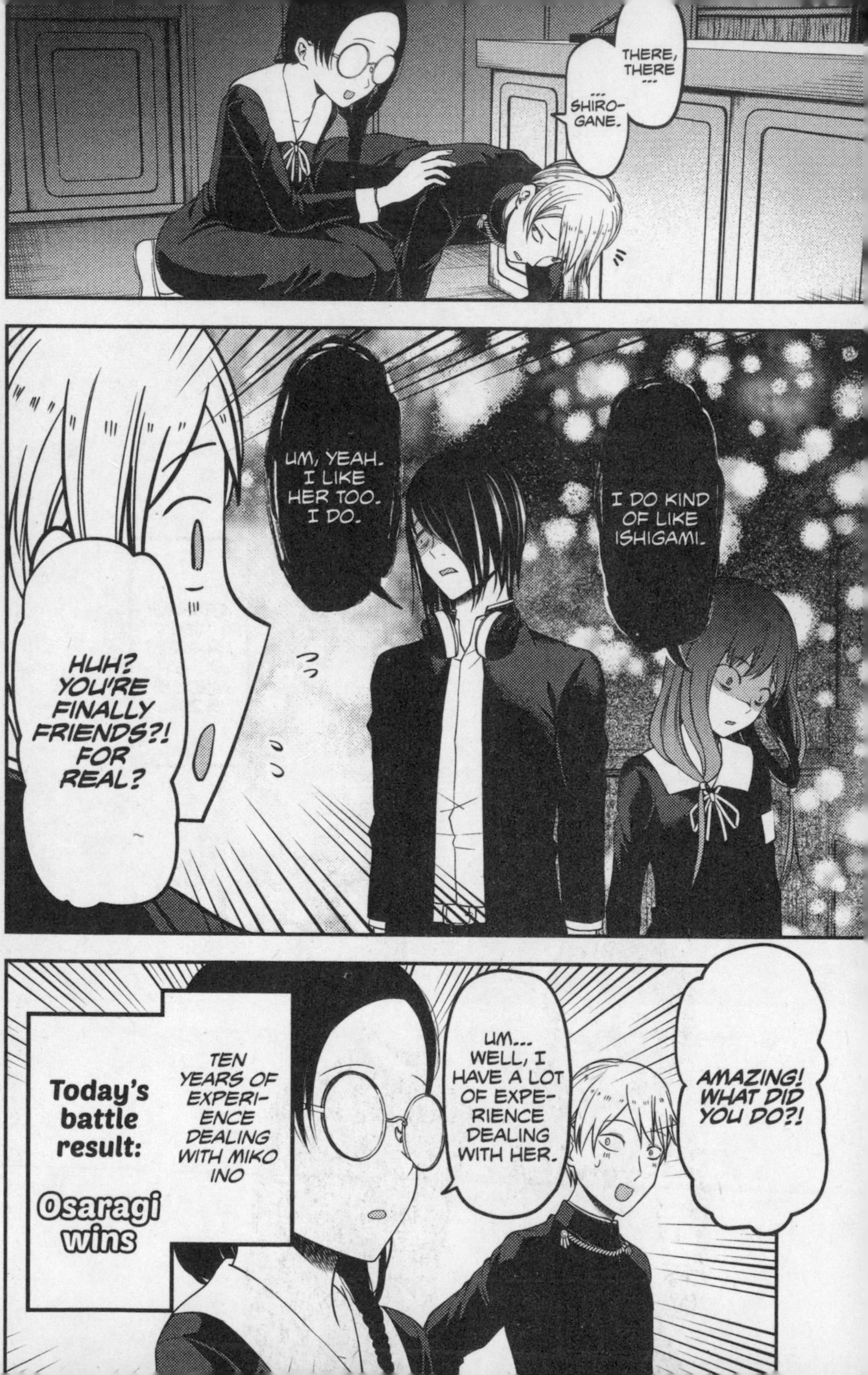
THERE, THERE... SHIRO-GANE.
I DO KIND OF LIKE ISHIGAMI.
UM, YEAH. I LIKE HER TOO. I DO.
HUH? YOU'RE FINALLY FRIENDS?! FOR REAL?
AMAZING! WHAT DID YOU DO?!
UM... WELL, I HAVE A LOT OF EXPE-RIENCE DEALING WITH HER.
TEN YEARS OF EXPERI-ENCE DEALING WITH MIKO INO
Today's battle result:
Osaragi wins

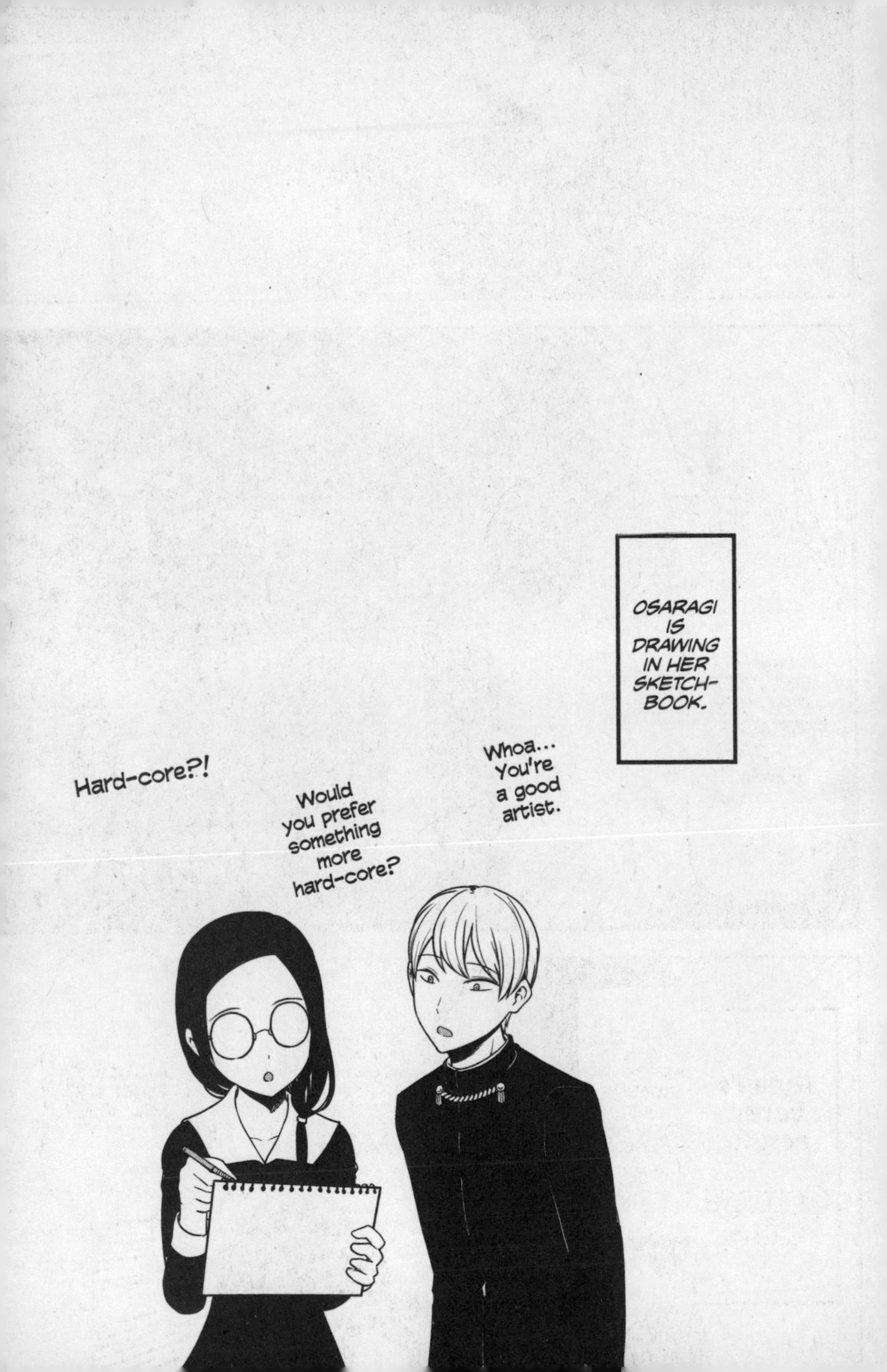
OSARAGI IS DRAWING IN HER SKETCH-BOOK.
Whoa... You're a good artist.
Would you prefer something more hard-core?
Hard-core?!

KAGUYA-SAMA
LOVE IS WAR

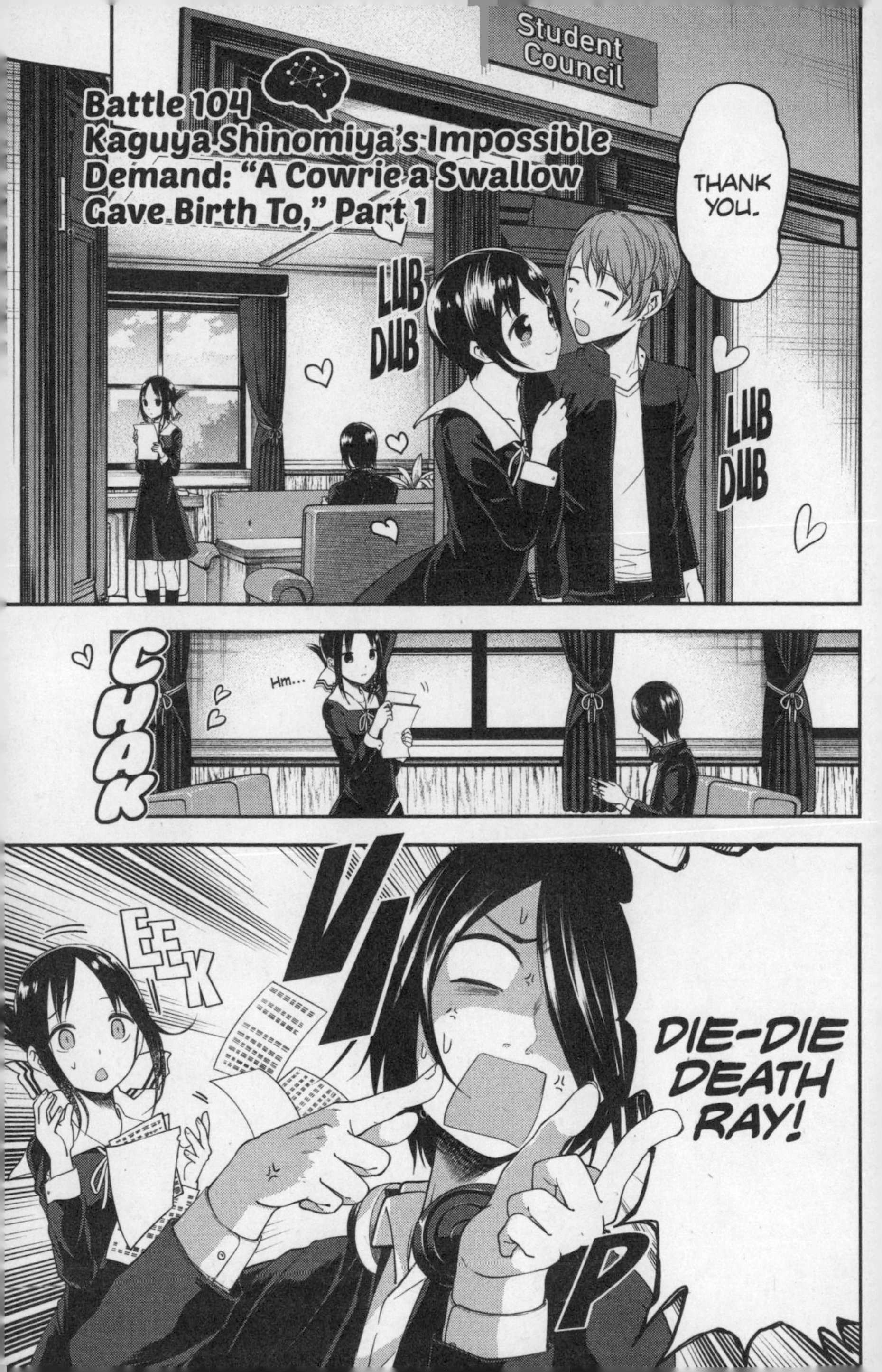
Student Council
THANK YOU.
LUB DUB
Battle 104
Kaguya Shinomiya's Impossible Demand: "A Cowrie a Swallow Gave Birth To," Part 1
LUB DUB
CHAK
Hm...
DIE-DIE DEATH RAY!
EEEK

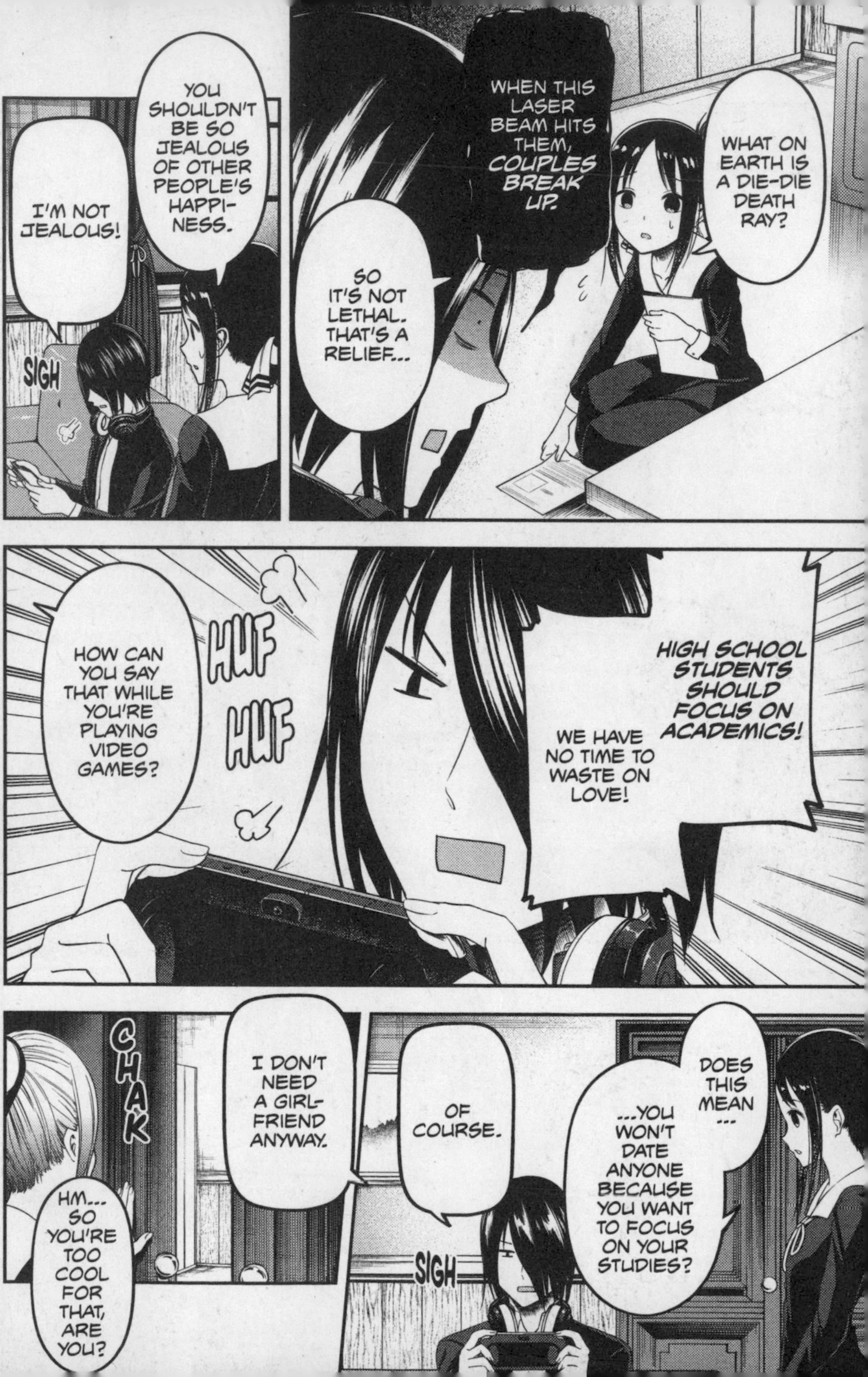

WHAT ON EARTH IS A DIE-DIE DEATH RAY?
WHEN THIS LASER BEAM HITS THEM, COUPLES BREAK UP.
SO IT'S NOT LETHAL. THAT'S A RELIEF...
YOU SHOULDN'T BE SO JEALOUS OF OTHER PEOPLE'S HAPPI-NESS.
I'M NOT JEALOUS!
SIGH
HIGH SCHOOL STUDENTS SHOULD FOCUS ON ACADEMICS!
WE HAVE NO TIME TO WASTE ON LOVE!
HUF
HUF
HOW CAN YOU SAY THAT WHILE YOU'RE PLAYING VIDEO GAMES?
DOES THIS MEAN...
...YOU WON'T DATE ANYONE BECAUSE YOU WANT TO FOCUS ON YOUR STUDIES?
OF COURSE.
SIGH
I DON'T NEED A GIRL-FRIEND ANYWAY.
CHAK
HM... SO YOU'RE TOO COOL FOR THAT, ARE YOU?

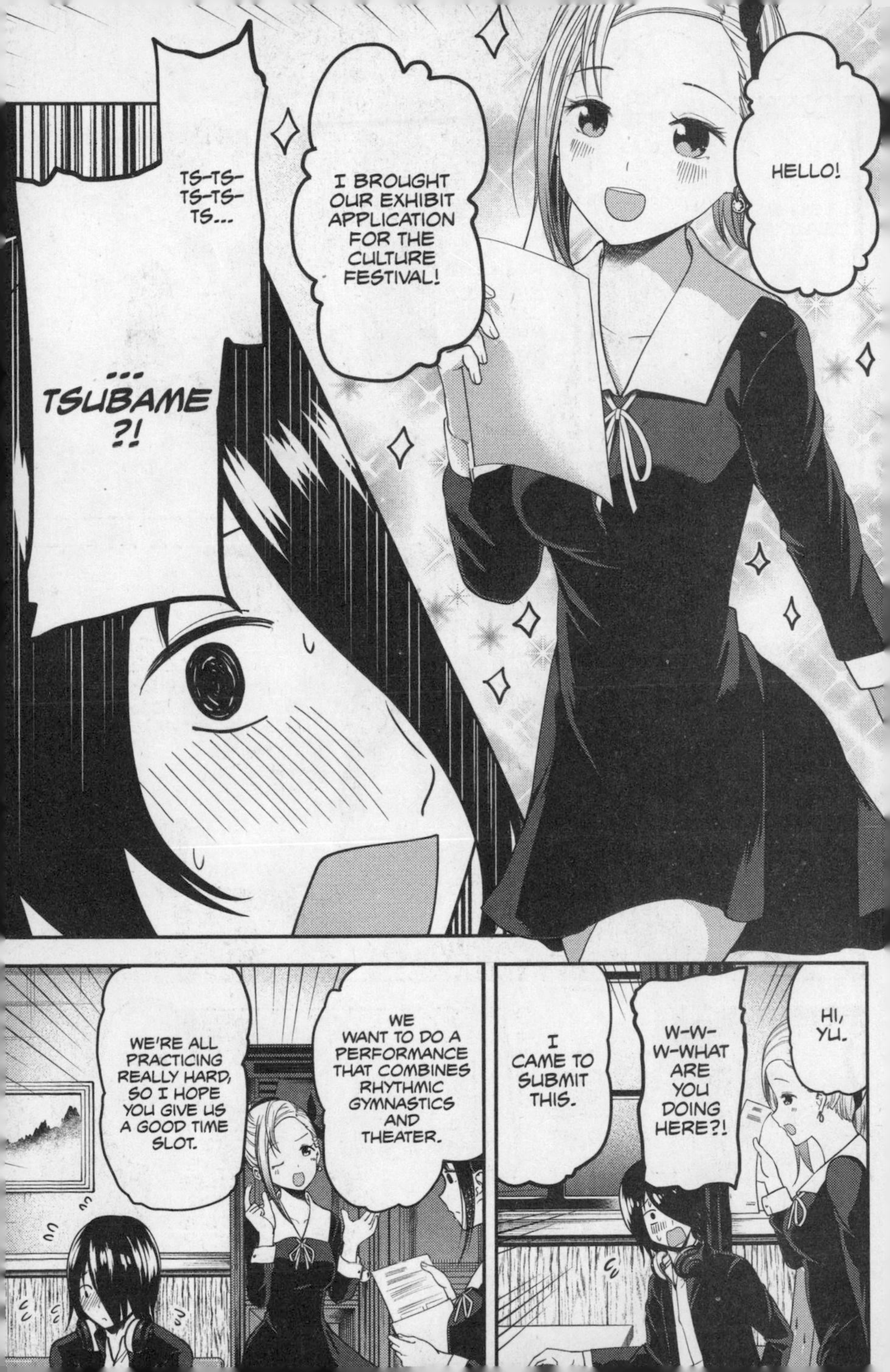
HELLO!
I BROUGHT OUR EXHIBIT APPLICATION FOR THE CULTURE FESTIVAL!
TS-TS-TS-TS-TS...
...TSUBAME?!
HI, YU.
W-W-W-WHAT ARE YOU DOING HERE?!
I CAME TO SUBMIT THIS.
WE WANT TO DO A PERFORMANCE THAT COMBINES RHYTHMIC GYMNASTICS AND THEATER.
WE'RE ALL PRACTICING REALLY HARD, SO I HOPE YOU GIVE US A GOOD TIME SLOT.

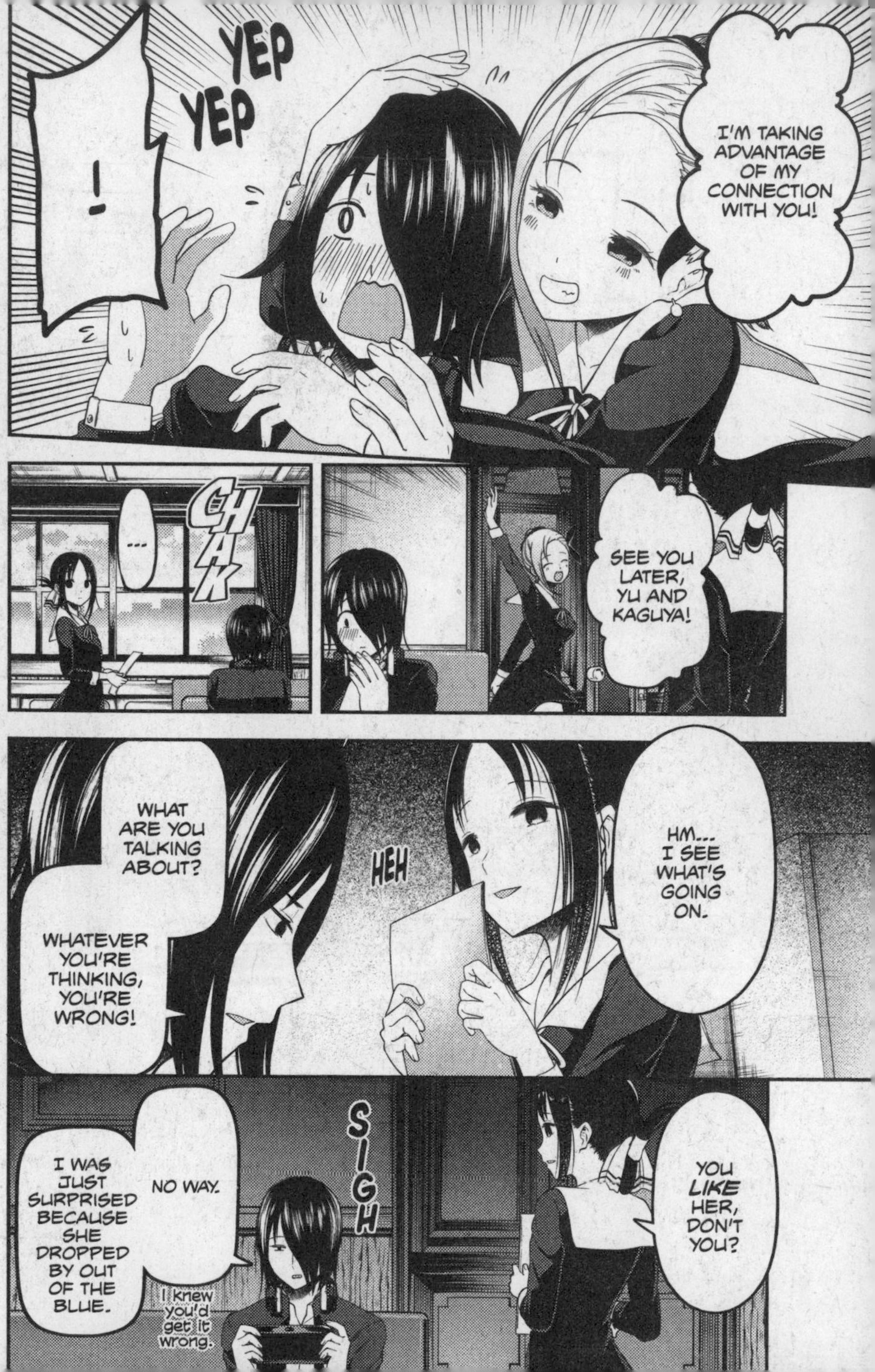
I'M TAKING ADVANTAGE OF MY CONNECTION WITH YOU!
YEP YEP
!
SEE YOU LATER, YU AND KAGUYA!
CHAK
...
HM... I SEE WHAT'S GOING ON.
HEH
WHAT ARE YOU TALKING ABOUT?
WHATEVER YOU'RE THINKING, YOU'RE WRONG!
YOU *LIKE* HER, DON'T YOU?
SIGH
NO WAY.
I WAS JUST SURPRISED BECAUSE SHE DROPPED BY OUT OF THE BLUE.
I knew you'd get it wrong.

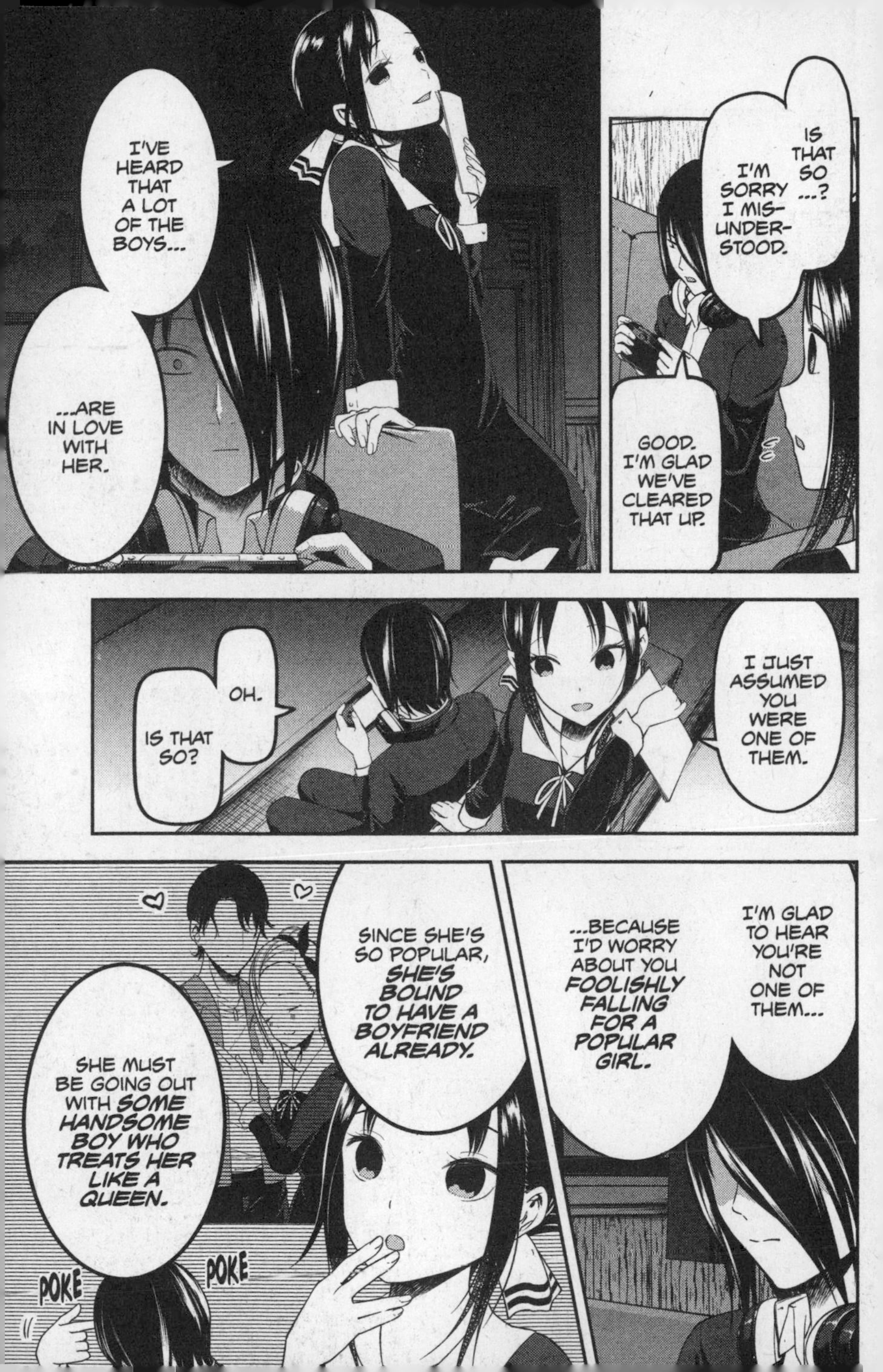
IS THAT SO...?
I'M SORRY I MISUNDERSTOOD.
GOOD. I'M GLAD WE'VE CLEARED THAT UP.
I'VE HEARD THAT A LOT OF THE BOYS...
...ARE IN LOVE WITH HER.
I JUST ASSUMED YOU WERE ONE OF THEM.
OH.
IS THAT SO?
I'M GLAD TO HEAR YOU'RE NOT ONE OF THEM...
...BECAUSE I'D WORRY ABOUT YOU FOOLISHLY FALLING FOR A POPULAR GIRL.
SINCE SHE'S SO POPULAR, SHE'S BOUND TO HAVE A BOYFRIEND ALREADY.
SHE MUST BE GOING OUT WITH SOME HANDSOME BOY WHO TREATS HER LIKE A QUEEN.
POKE
POKE

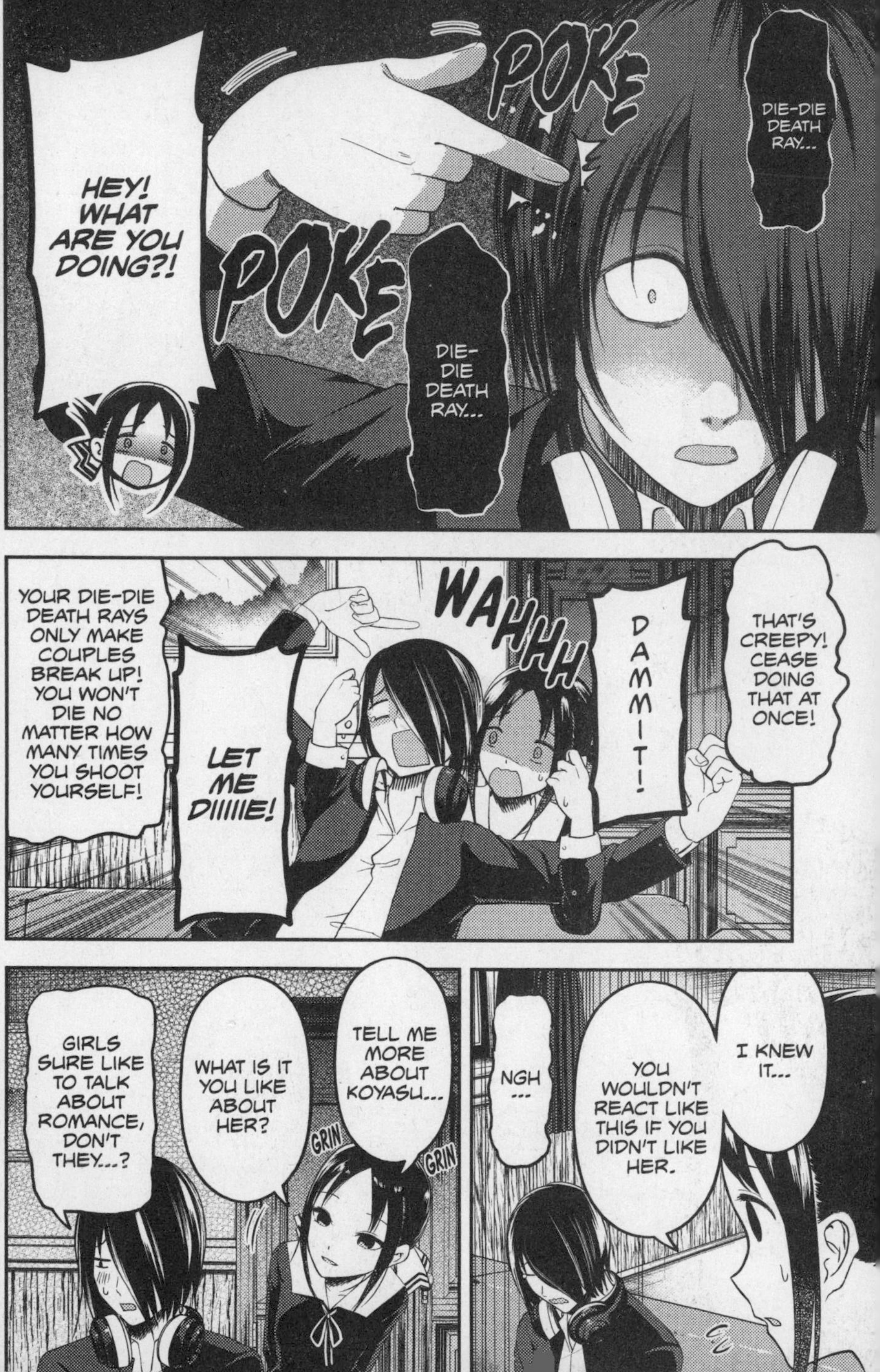
DIE-DIE DEATH RAY...
POKE
DIE-DIE DEATH RAY...
POKE
HEY! WHAT ARE YOU DOING?!
THAT'S CREEPY! CEASE DOING THAT AT ONCE!
DAMMIT!
WAHHHH
LET ME DIIIIIE!
YOUR DIE-DIE DEATH RAYS ONLY MAKE COUPLES BREAK UP! YOU WON'T DIE NO MATTER HOW MANY TIMES YOU SHOOT YOURSELF!
I KNEW IT...
YOU WOULDN'T REACT LIKE THIS IF YOU DIDN'T LIKE HER.
NGH...
TELL ME MORE ABOUT KOYASU...
GRIN
GRIN
WHAT IS IT YOU LIKE ABOUT HER?
GIRLS SURE LIKE TO TALK ABOUT ROMANCE, DON'T THEY...?

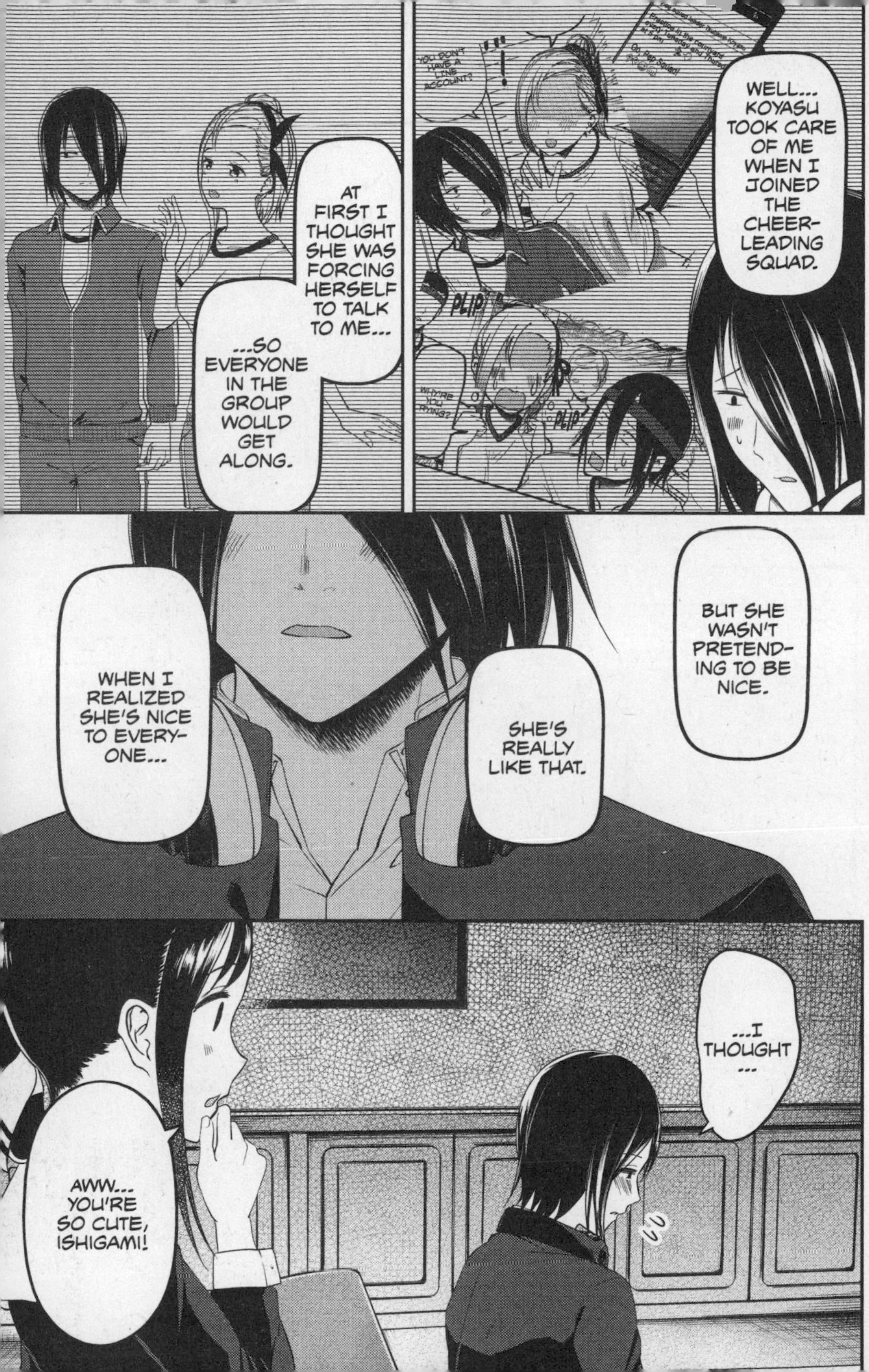
WELL... KOYASU TOOK CARE OF ME WHEN I JOINED THE CHEER-LEADING SQUAD.
Practice in the courtyard every Tuesday and Thursday at 5 pm
Go, Pep Squad!
!!
YOU DON'T HAVE A LINE ACCOUNT?!
PLIP
PLIP
WHY'RE YOU CRYING?
AT FIRST I THOUGHT SHE WAS FORCING HERSELF TO TALK TO ME...
...SO EVERYONE IN THE GROUP WOULD GET ALONG.
BUT SHE WASN'T PRETEND-ING TO BE NICE.
SHE'S REALLY LIKE THAT.
WHEN I REALIZED SHE'S NICE TO EVERY-ONE...
...I THOUGHT ...
AWW... YOU'RE SO CUTE, ISHIGAMI!

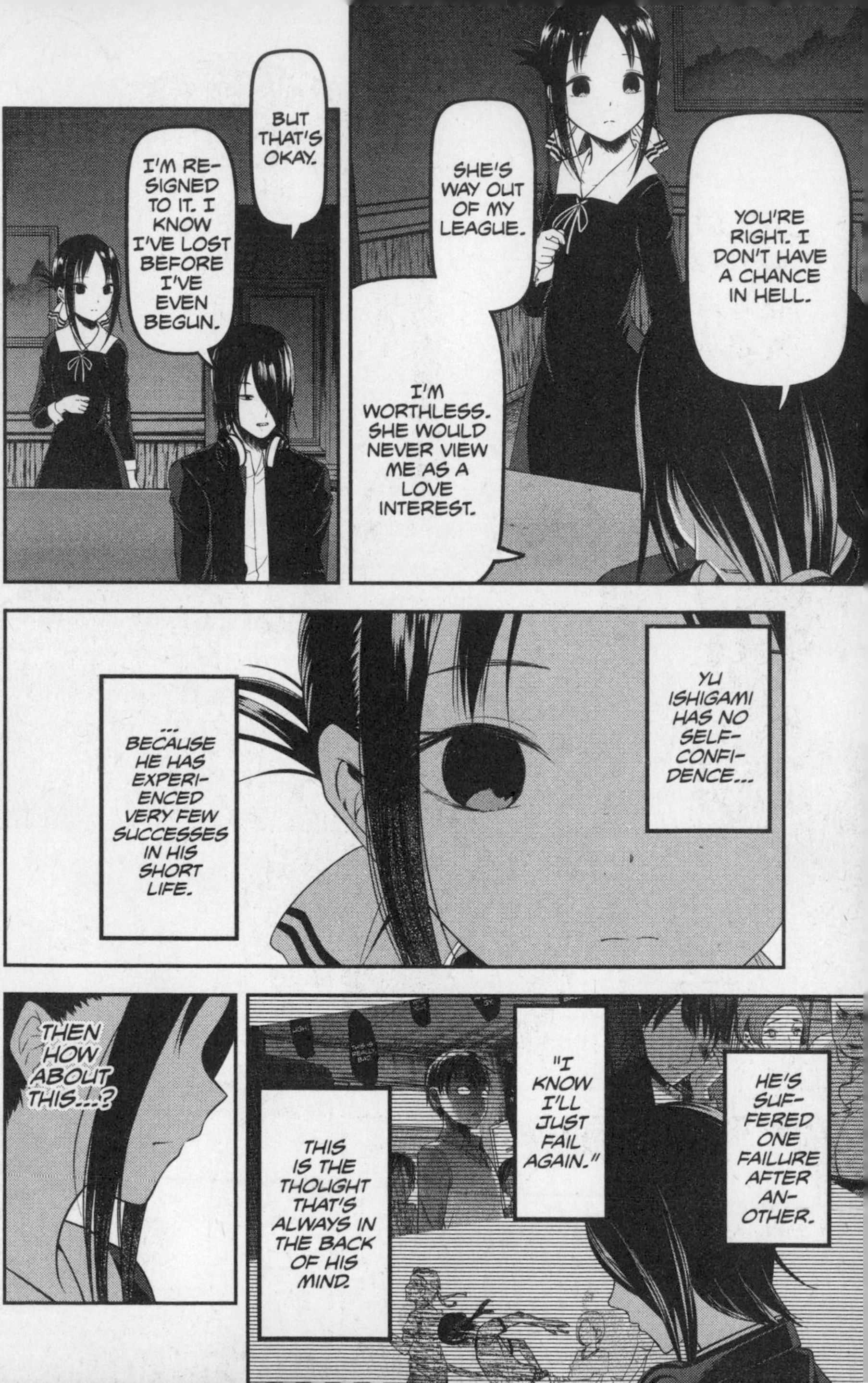
YOU'RE RIGHT. I DON'T HAVE A CHANCE IN HELL.
SHE'S WAY OUT OF MY LEAGUE.
I'M WORTHLESS. SHE WOULD NEVER VIEW ME AS A LOVE INTEREST.
BUT THAT'S OKAY.
I'M RESIGNED TO IT. I KNOW I'VE LOST BEFORE I'VE EVEN BEGUN.
YU ISHIGAMI HAS NO SELF-CONFIDENCE...
...BECAUSE HE HAS EXPERIENCED VERY FEW SUCCESSES IN HIS SHORT LIFE.
HE'S SUFFERED ONE FAILURE AFTER ANOTHER.
"I KNOW I'LL JUST FAIL AGAIN."
THIS IS THE THOUGHT THAT'S ALWAYS IN THE BACK OF HIS MIND.
THEN HOW ABOUT THIS...?

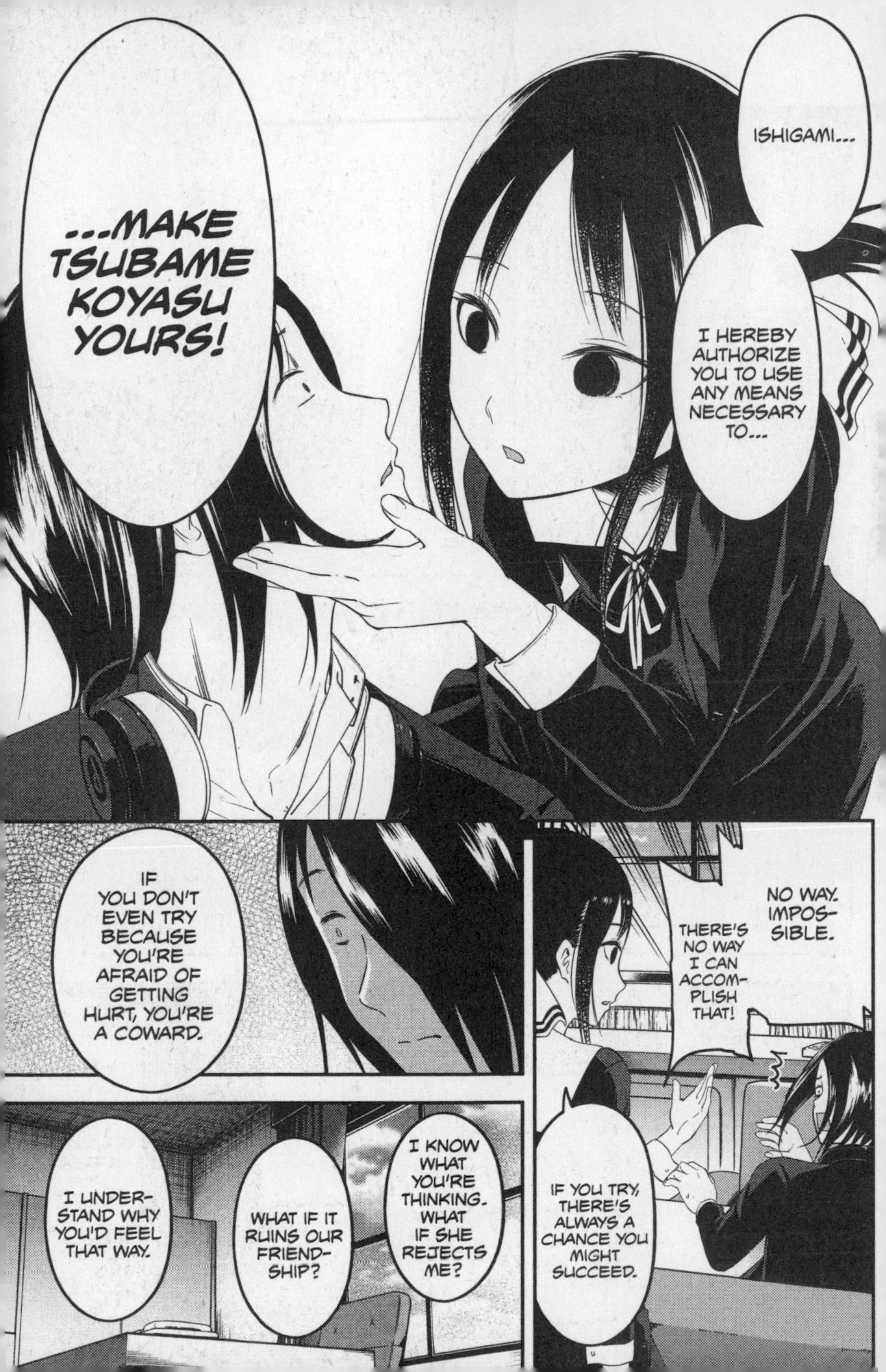
ISHIGAMI...
I HEREBY AUTHORIZE YOU TO USE ANY MEANS NECESSARY TO...
...MAKE TSUBAME KOYASU YOURS!
NO WAY. IMPOSSIBLE.
THERE'S NO WAY I CAN ACCOMPLISH THAT!
IF YOU TRY, THERE'S ALWAYS A CHANCE YOU MIGHT SUCCEED.
IF YOU DON'T EVEN TRY BECAUSE YOU'RE AFRAID OF GETTING HURT, YOU'RE A COWARD.
I KNOW WHAT YOU'RE THINKING. WHAT IF SHE REJECTS ME?
WHAT IF IT RUINS OUR FRIENDSHIP?
I UNDERSTAND WHY YOU'D FEEL THAT WAY.

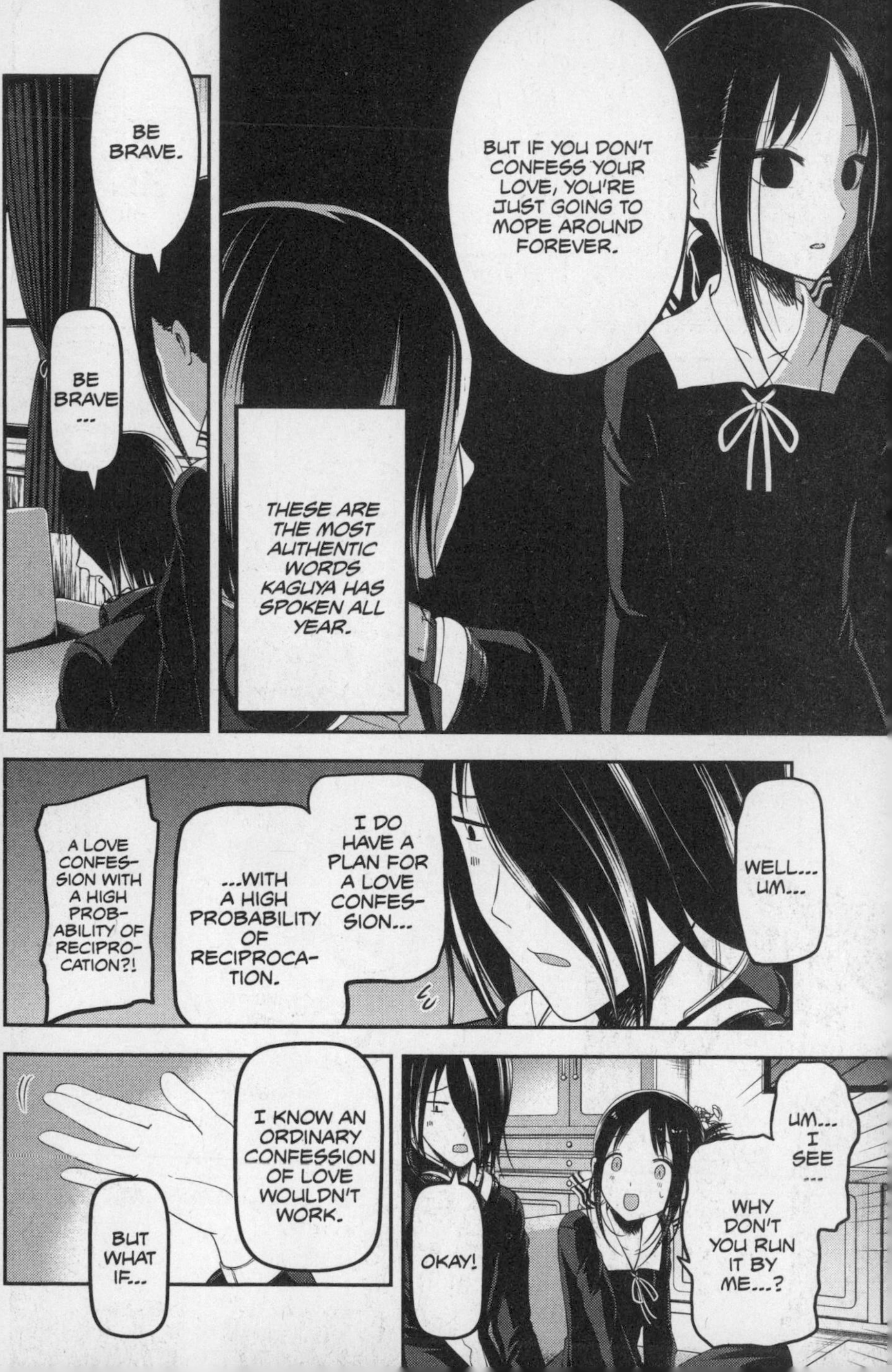
BUT IF YOU DON'T CONFESS YOUR LOVE, YOU'RE JUST GOING TO MOPE AROUND FOREVER.
THESE ARE THE MOST AUTHENTIC WORDS KAGUYA HAS SPOKEN ALL YEAR.
BE BRAVE.
BE BRAVE...
WELL... UM...
I DO HAVE A PLAN FOR A LOVE CONFESSION...
...WITH A HIGH PROBABILITY OF RECIPROCATION.
A LOVE CONFESSION WITH A HIGH PROBABILITY OF RECIPROCATION?!
UM... I SEE...
WHY DON'T YOU RUN IT BY ME...?
OKAY!
I KNOW AN ORDINARY CONFESSION OF LOVE WOULDN'T WORK.
BUT WHAT IF...

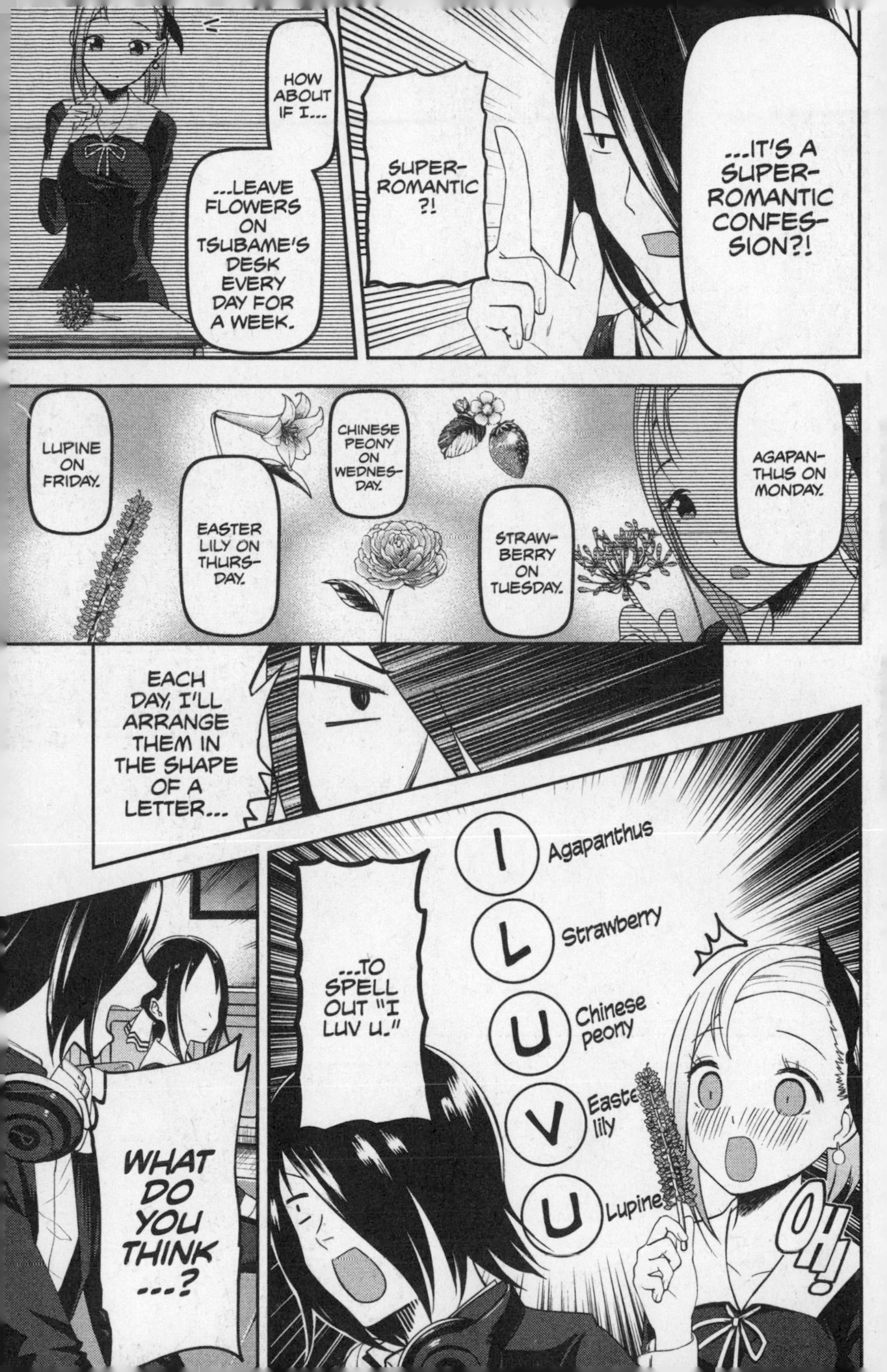

...IT'S A SUPER-ROMANTIC CONFESSION?!
SUPER-ROMANTIC?!
HOW ABOUT IF I...
...LEAVE FLOWERS ON TSUBAME'S DESK EVERY DAY FOR A WEEK.
AGAPANTHUS ON MONDAY.
STRAWBERRY ON TUESDAY.
CHINESE PEONY ON WEDNESDAY.
EASTER LILY ON THURSDAY.
LUPINE ON FRIDAY.
EACH DAY, I'LL ARRANGE THEM IN THE SHAPE OF A LETTER...
I Agapanthus
L Strawberry
U Chinese peony
V Easte lily
U Lupine
...TO SPELL OUT "I LUV U."
OH!
WHAT DO YOU THINK...?

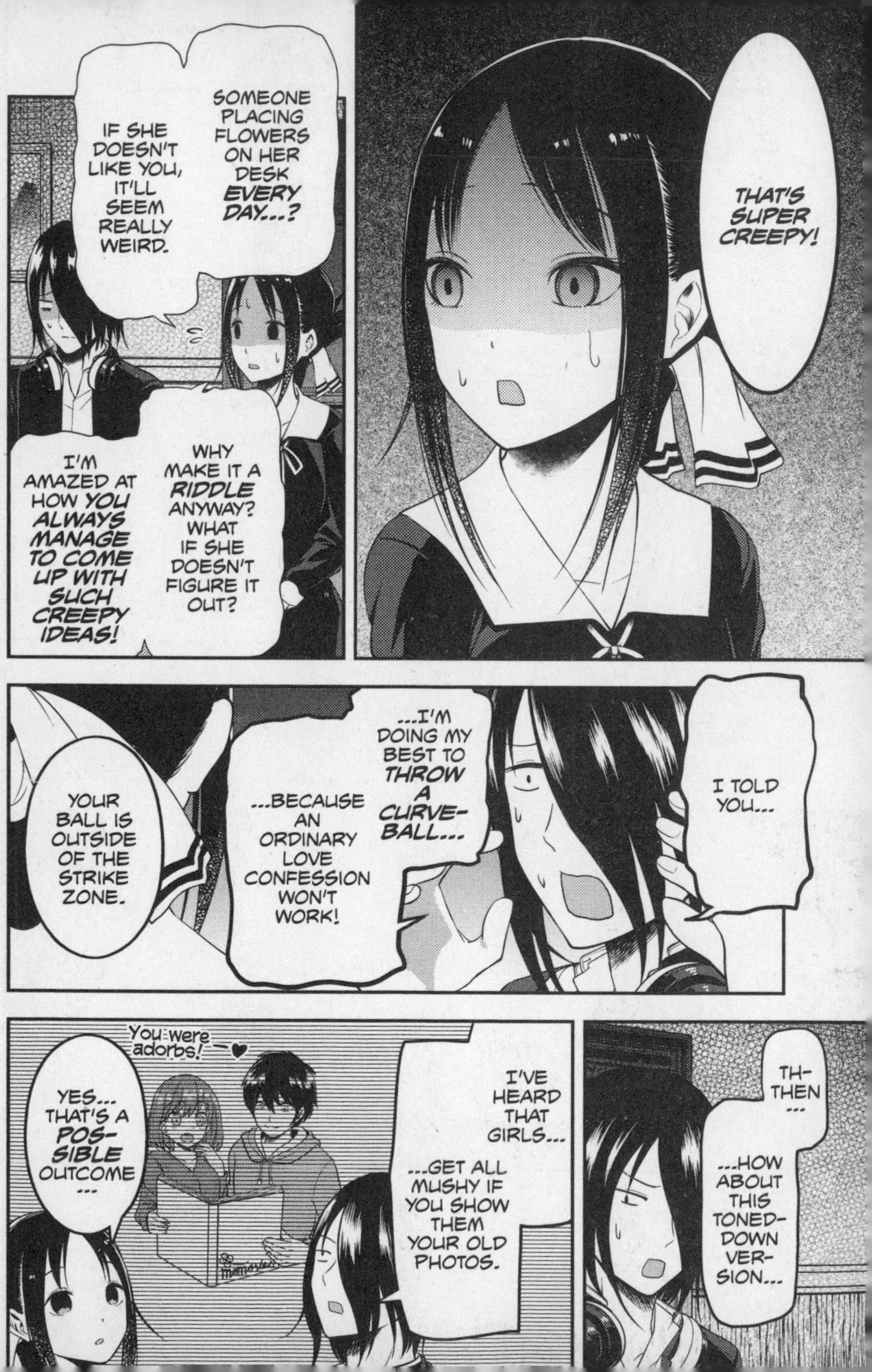
THAT'S SUPER CREEPY!
SOMEONE PLACING FLOWERS ON HER DESK EVERY DAY...?
IF SHE DOESN'T LIKE YOU, IT'LL SEEM REALLY WEIRD.
WHY MAKE IT A RIDDLE ANYWAY? WHAT IF SHE DOESN'T FIGURE IT OUT?
I'M AMAZED AT HOW YOU ALWAYS MANAGE TO COME UP WITH SUCH CREEPY IDEAS!
I TOLD YOU...
...I'M DOING MY BEST TO THROW A CURVE-BALL...
...BECAUSE AN ORDINARY LOVE CONFESSION WON'T WORK!
YOUR BALL IS OUTSIDE OF THE STRIKE ZONE.
TH-THEN...
...HOW ABOUT THIS TONED-DOWN VER-SION...
I'VE HEARD THAT GIRLS...
...GET ALL MUSHY IF YOU SHOW THEM YOUR OLD PHOTOS.
You were adorbs!
YES... THAT'S A POS-SIBLE OUTCOME...

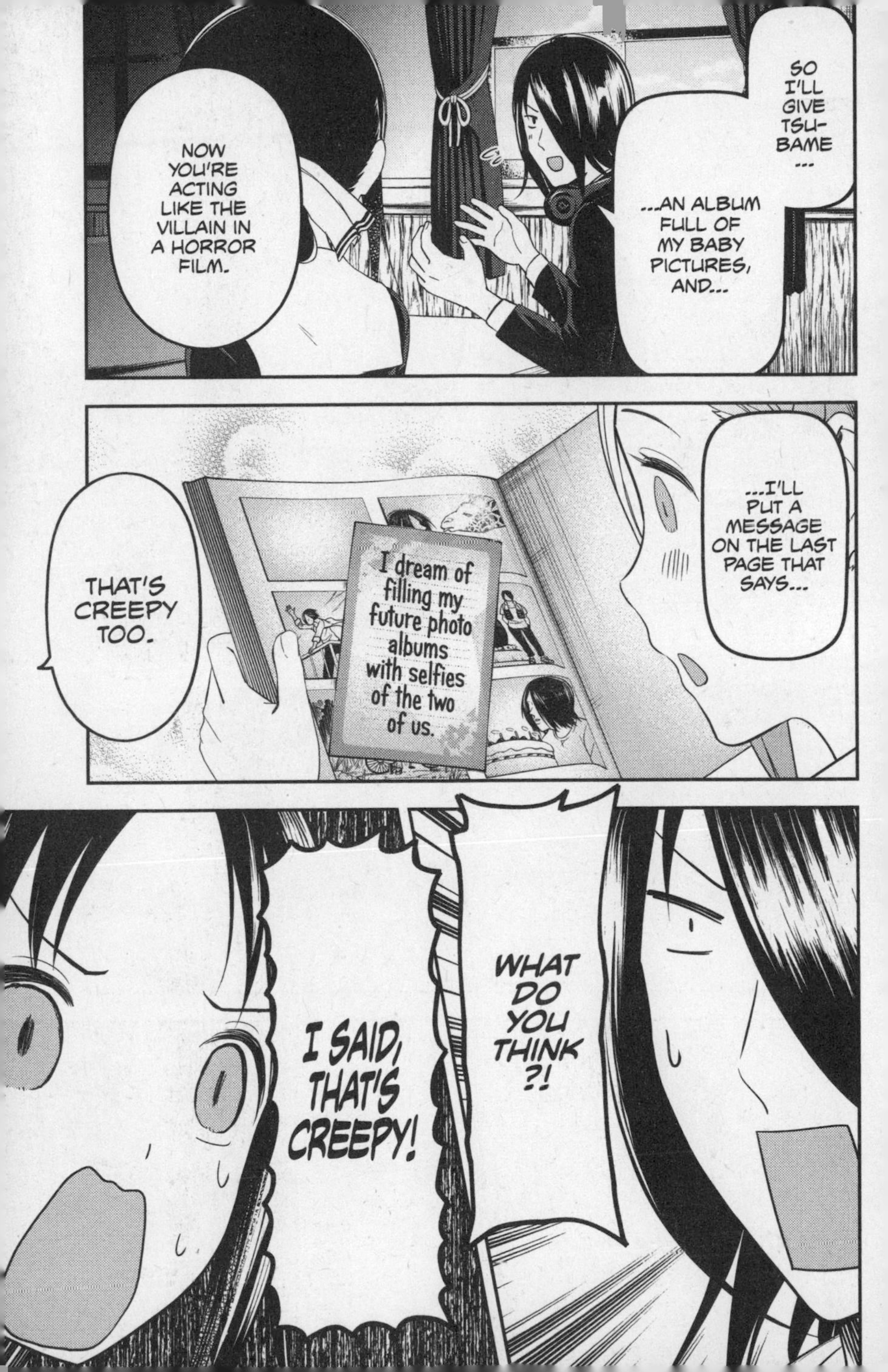
SO I'LL GIVE TSU-BAME...
...AN ALBUM FULL OF MY BABY PICTURES, AND...
NOW YOU'RE ACTING LIKE THE VILLAIN IN A HORROR FILM.
...I'LL PUT A MESSAGE ON THE LAST PAGE THAT SAYS...
I dream of filling my future photo albums with selfies of the two of us.
THAT'S CREEPY TOO.
WHAT DO YOU THINK?!
I SAID, THAT'S CREEPY!

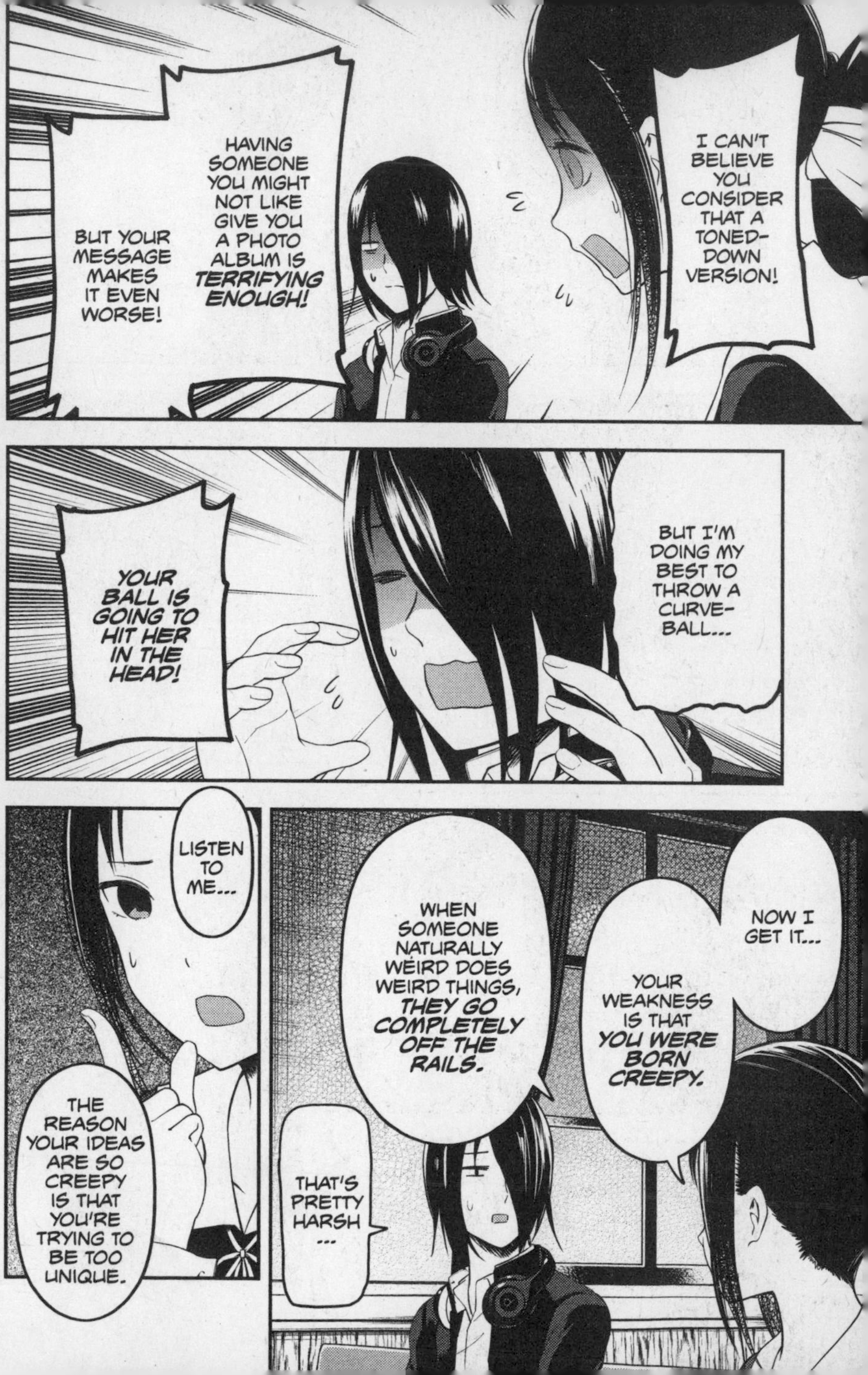
I CAN'T BELIEVE YOU CONSIDER THAT A TONED-DOWN VERSION!
HAVING SOMEONE YOU MIGHT NOT LIKE GIVE YOU A PHOTO ALBUM IS TERRIFYING ENOUGH!
BUT YOUR MESSAGE MAKES IT EVEN WORSE!
BUT I'M DOING MY BEST TO THROW A CURVE-BALL...
YOUR BALL IS GOING TO HIT HER IN THE HEAD!
NOW I GET IT...
YOUR WEAKNESS IS THAT YOU WERE BORN CREEPY.
WHEN SOMEONE NATURALLY WEIRD DOES WEIRD THINGS, THEY GO COMPLETELY OFF THE RAILS.
THAT'S PRETTY HARSH...
LISTEN TO ME...
THE REASON YOUR IDEAS ARE SO CREEPY IS THAT YOU'RE TRYING TO BE TOO UNIQUE.

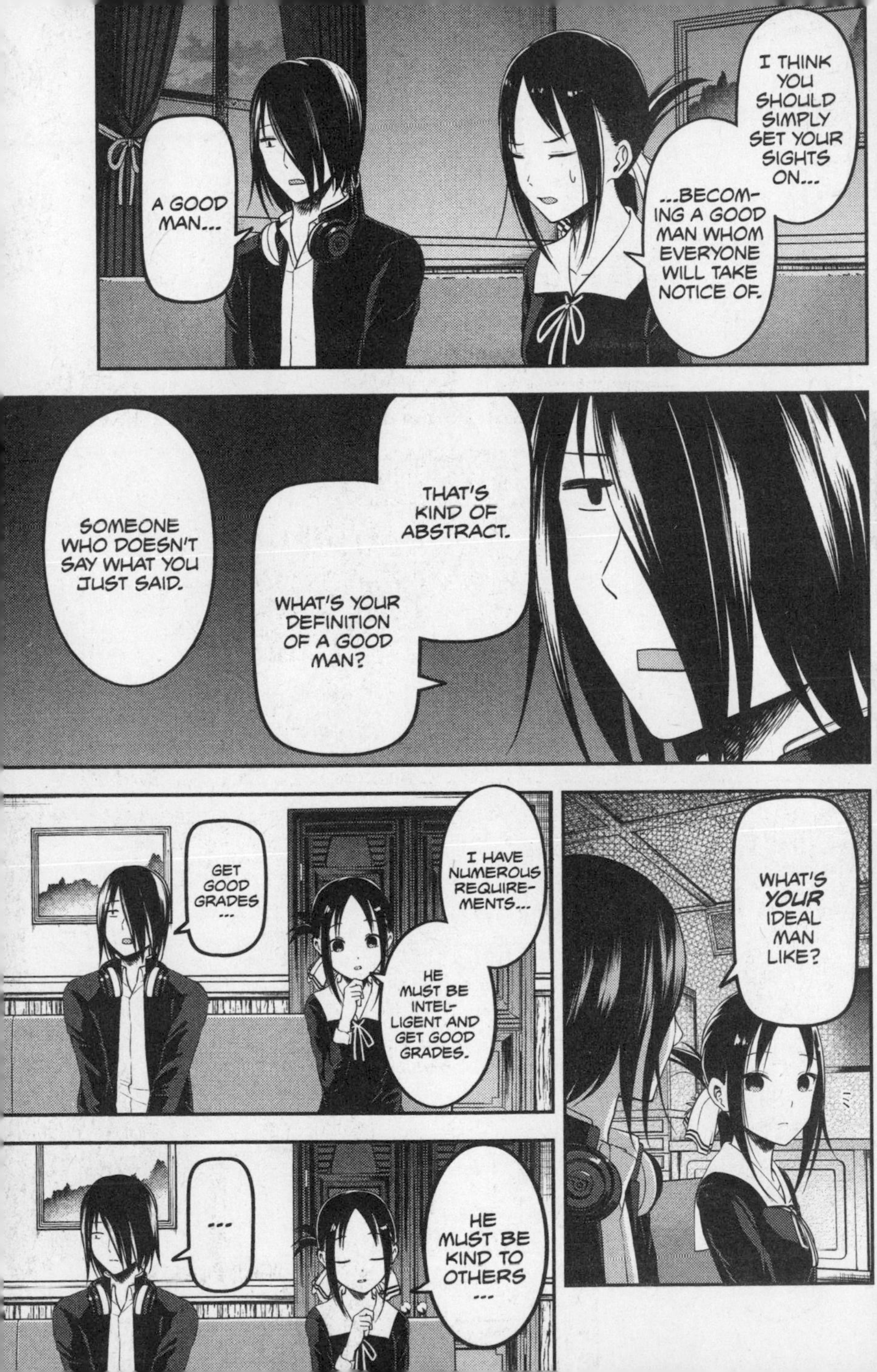
I THINK YOU SHOULD SIMPLY SET YOUR SIGHTS ON...
...BECOMING A GOOD MAN WHOM EVERYONE WILL TAKE NOTICE OF.
A GOOD MAN...
THAT'S KIND OF ABSTRACT.
WHAT'S YOUR DEFINITION OF A GOOD MAN?
SOMEONE WHO DOESN'T SAY WHAT YOU JUST SAID.
WHAT'S *YOUR* IDEAL MAN LIKE?
I HAVE NUMEROUS REQUIREMENTS...
HE MUST BE INTELLIGENT AND GET GOOD GRADES.
GET GOOD GRADES...
HE MUST BE KIND TO OTHERS...
...

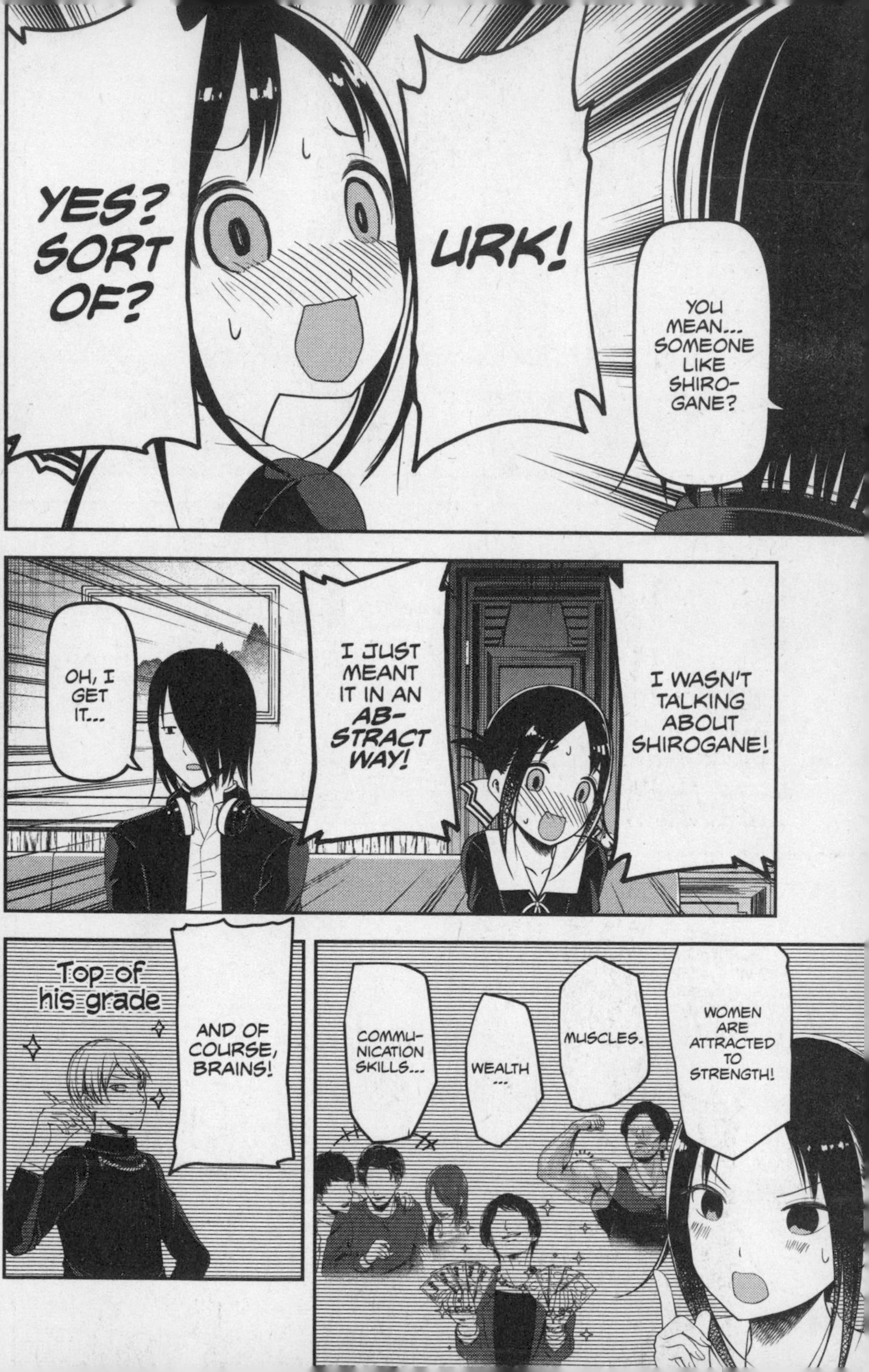
YOU MEAN... SOMEONE LIKE SHIROGANE?
URK!
YES? SORT OF?
I WASN'T TALKING ABOUT SHIROGANE!
I JUST MEANT IT IN AN AB-STRACT WAY!
OH, I GET IT...
WOMEN ARE ATTRACTED TO STRENGTH!
MUSCLES.
WEALTH ...
COMMUNICATION SKILLS...
AND OF COURSE, BRAINS!
Top of his grade

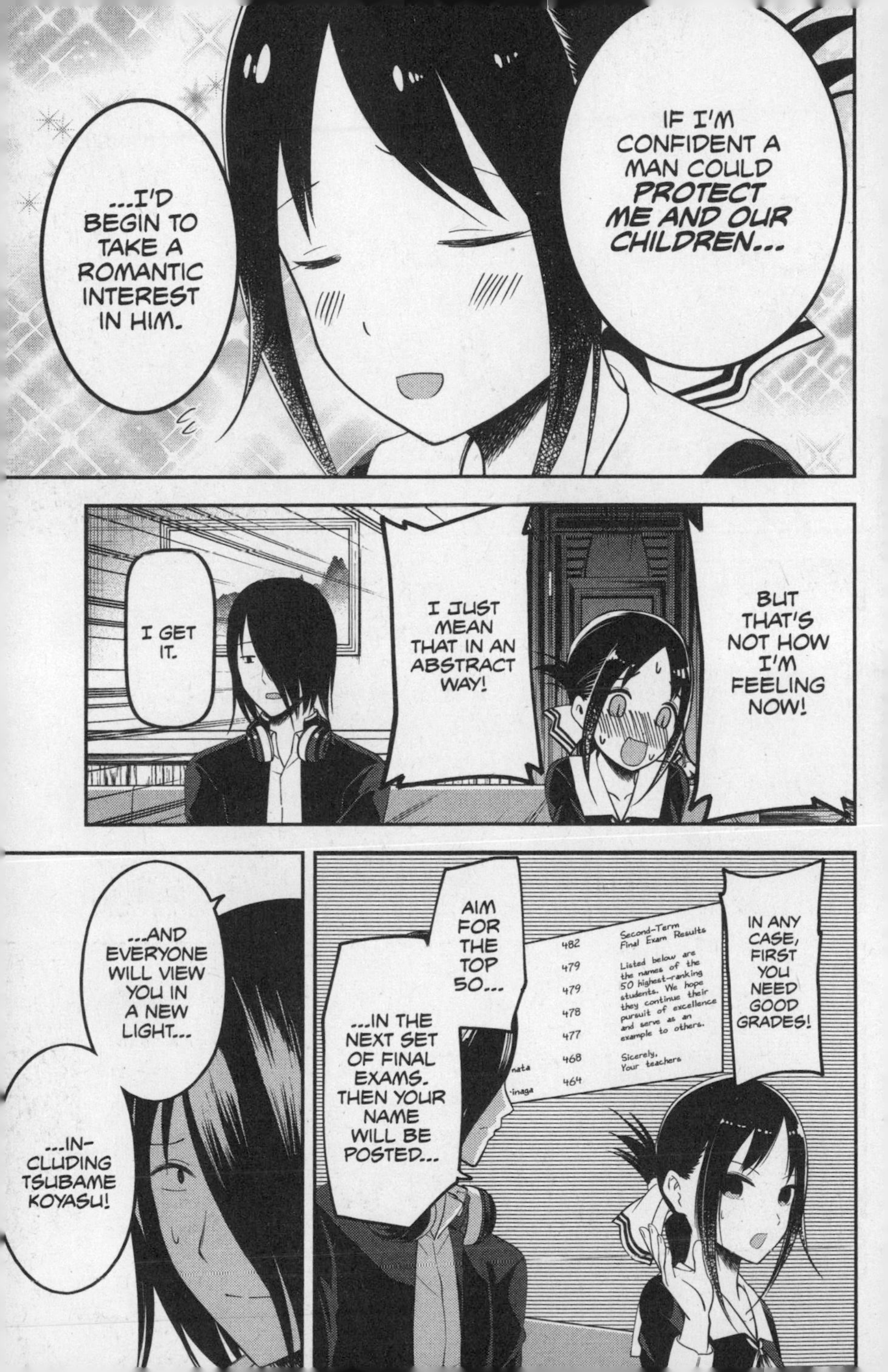
IF I'M CONFIDENT A MAN COULD *PROTECT ME AND OUR CHILDREN...*
...I'D BEGIN TO TAKE A ROMANTIC INTEREST IN HIM.
BUT THAT'S NOT HOW I'M FEELING NOW!
I JUST MEAN THAT IN AN ABSTRACT WAY!
I GET IT.
IN ANY CASE, FIRST YOU NEED GOOD GRADES!
AIM FOR THE TOP 50...
Second-Term Final Exam Results
Listed below are the names of the 50 highest-ranking students. We hope they continue their pursuit of excellence and serve as an example to others.
Sicerely, Your teachers
482
479
479
478
477
468
464
...IN THE NEXT SET OF FINAL EXAMS. THEN YOUR NAME WILL BE POSTED...
...AND EVERYONE WILL VIEW YOU IN A NEW LIGHT...
...IN-CLUDING TSUBAME KOYASU!

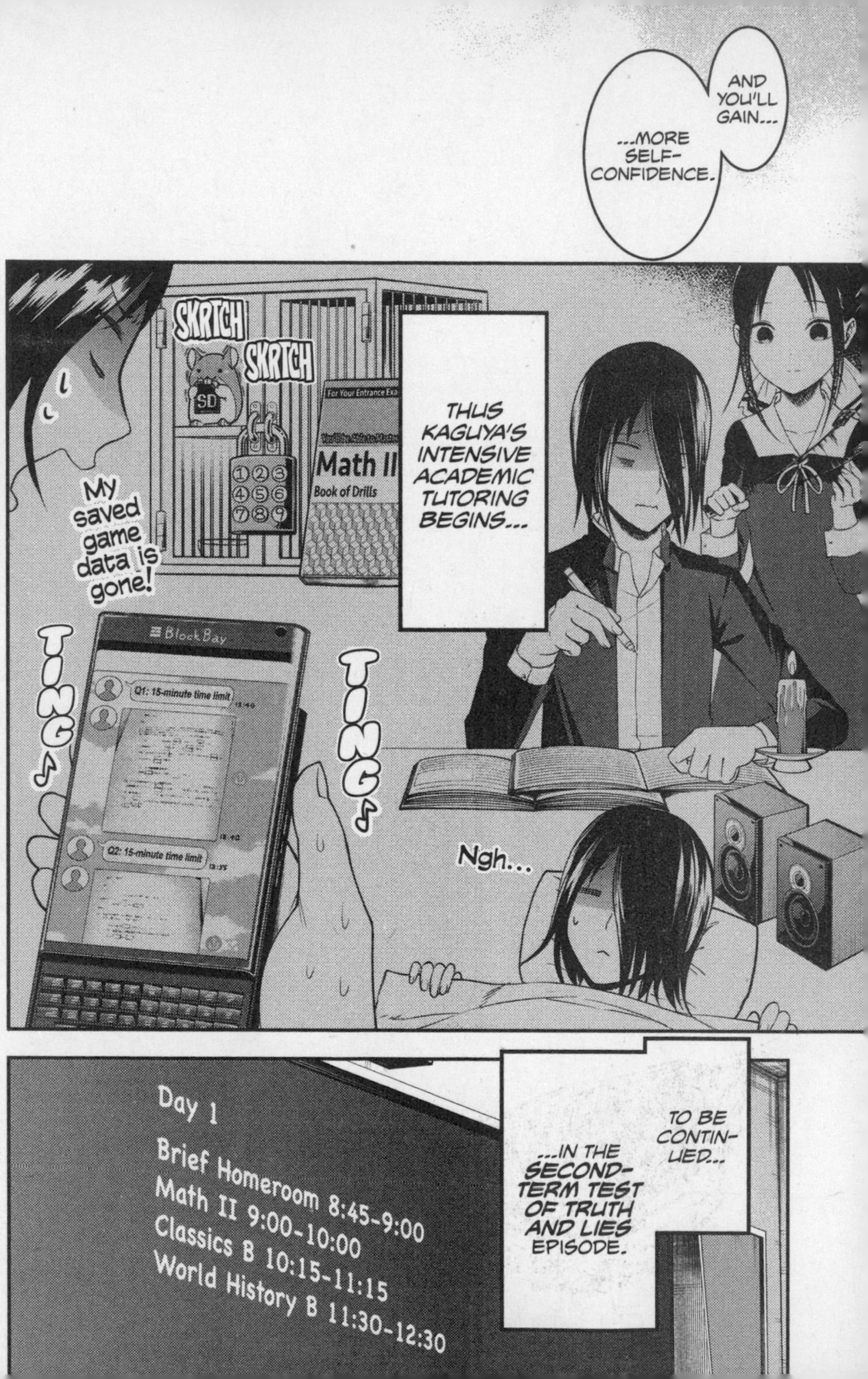
AND YOU'LL GAIN...
...MORE SELF-CONFIDENCE.
THUS KAGUYA'S INTENSIVE ACADEMIC TUTORING BEGINS...
Ngh...
For Your Entrance Exa
Math II
Book of Drills
SKRTCH
SKRTCH
SD
My saved game data is gone!
TING
TING
BlockBay
Q1: 15-minute time limit
Q2: 15-minute time limit
TO BE CONTIN-UED...
...IN THE SECOND-TERM TEST OF TRUTH AND LIES EPISODE.
Day 1
Brief Homeroom 8:45-9:00
Math II 9:00-10:00
Classics B 10:15-11:15
World History B 11:30-12:30

Battle 105
Yu Ishigami Wants to Prove Himself Worthy

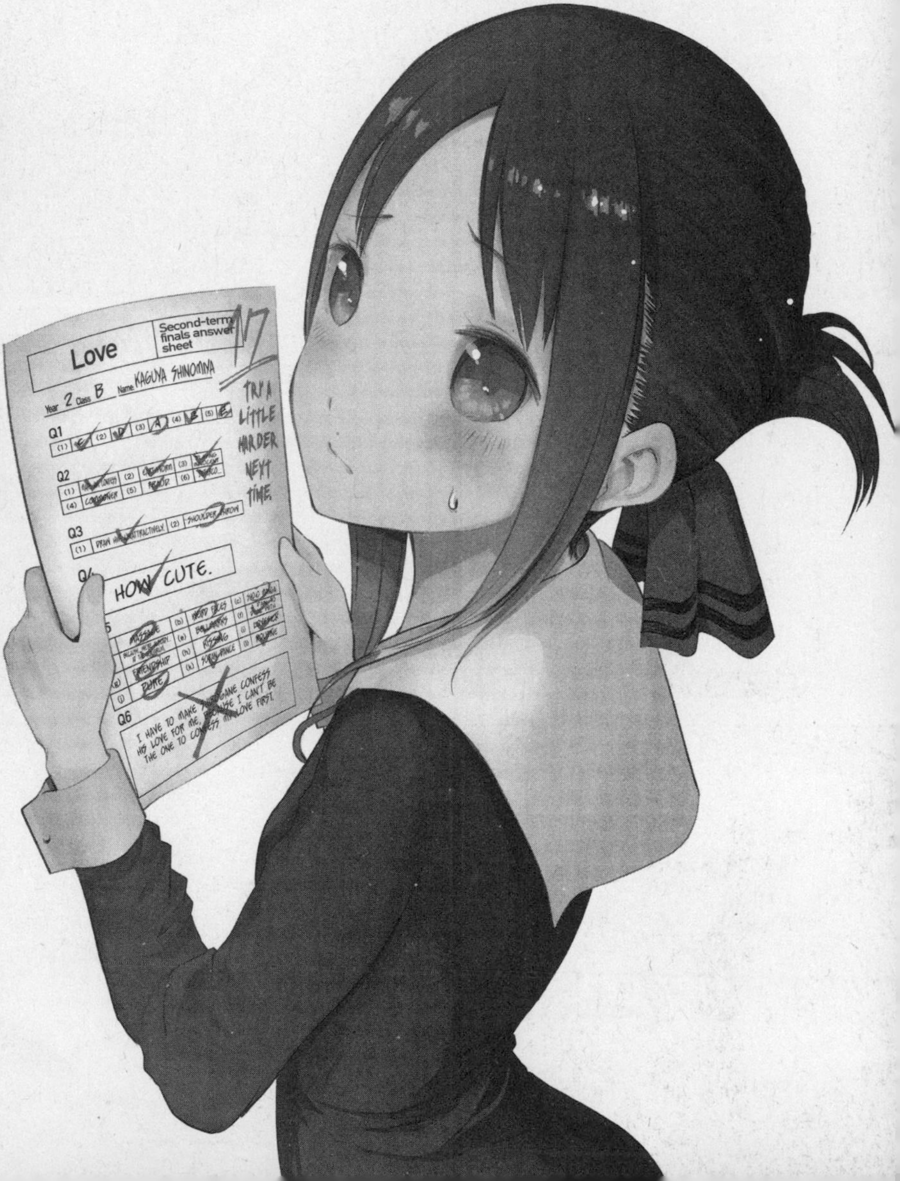
Love
Second-term finals answer sheet
Year 2 Class B Name KAGUYA SHINOMIYA
TRY A LITTLE HARDER NEXT TIME.
Q1
Q2
Q3
HOW CUTE.
Q6

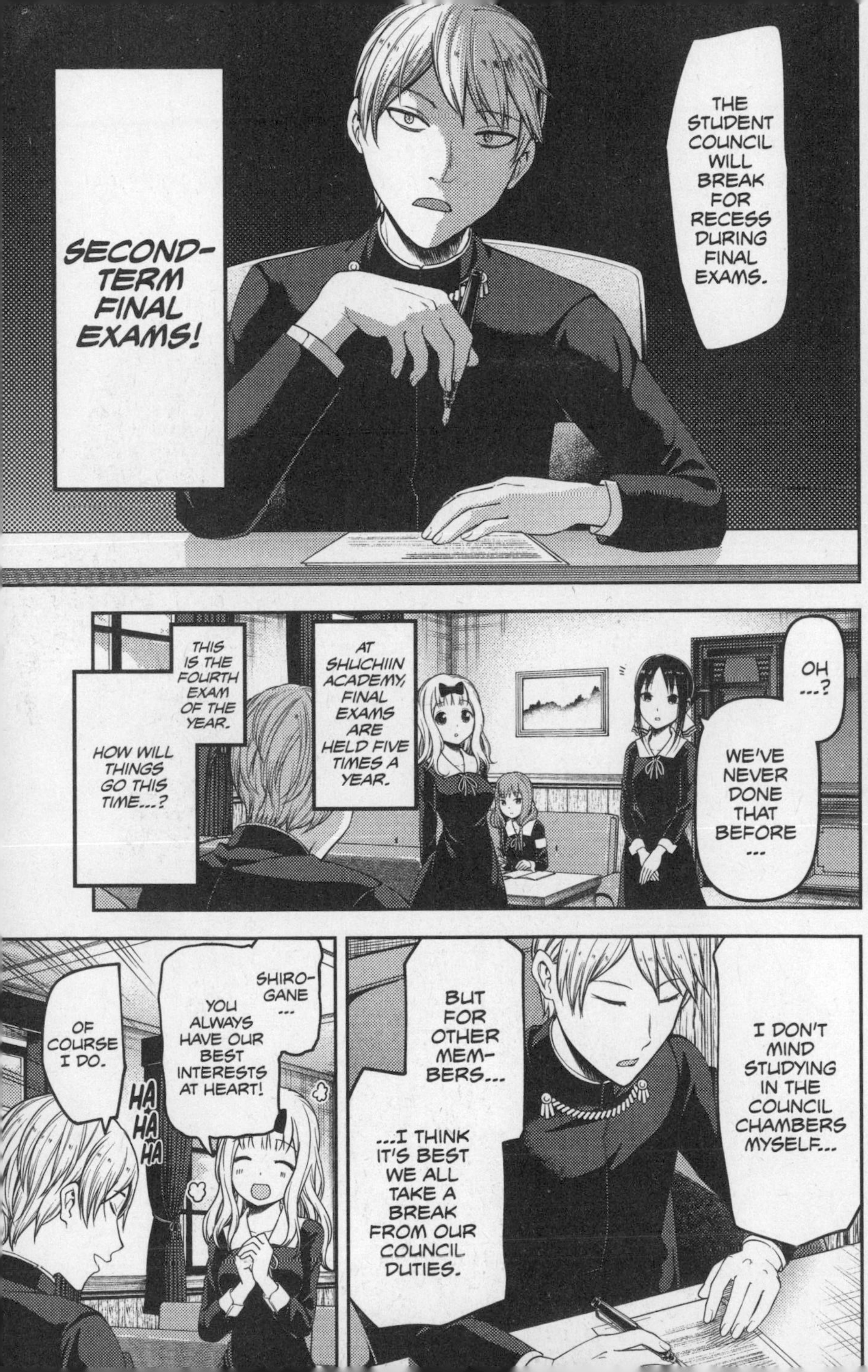
THE STUDENT COUNCIL WILL BREAK FOR RECESS DURING FINAL EXAMS.
SECOND-TERM FINAL EXAMS!
OH...? WE'VE NEVER DONE THAT BEFORE...
AT SHUCHIIN ACADEMY, FINAL EXAMS ARE HELD FIVE TIMES A YEAR.
THIS IS THE FOURTH EXAM OF THE YEAR.
HOW WILL THINGS GO THIS TIME...?
I DON'T MIND STUDYING IN THE COUNCIL CHAMBERS MYSELF...
BUT FOR OTHER MEM-BERS...
...I THINK IT'S BEST WE ALL TAKE A BREAK FROM OUR COUNCIL DUTIES.
SHIRO-GANE... YOU ALWAYS HAVE OUR BEST INTERESTS AT HEART!
HA HA HA
OF COURSE I DO.

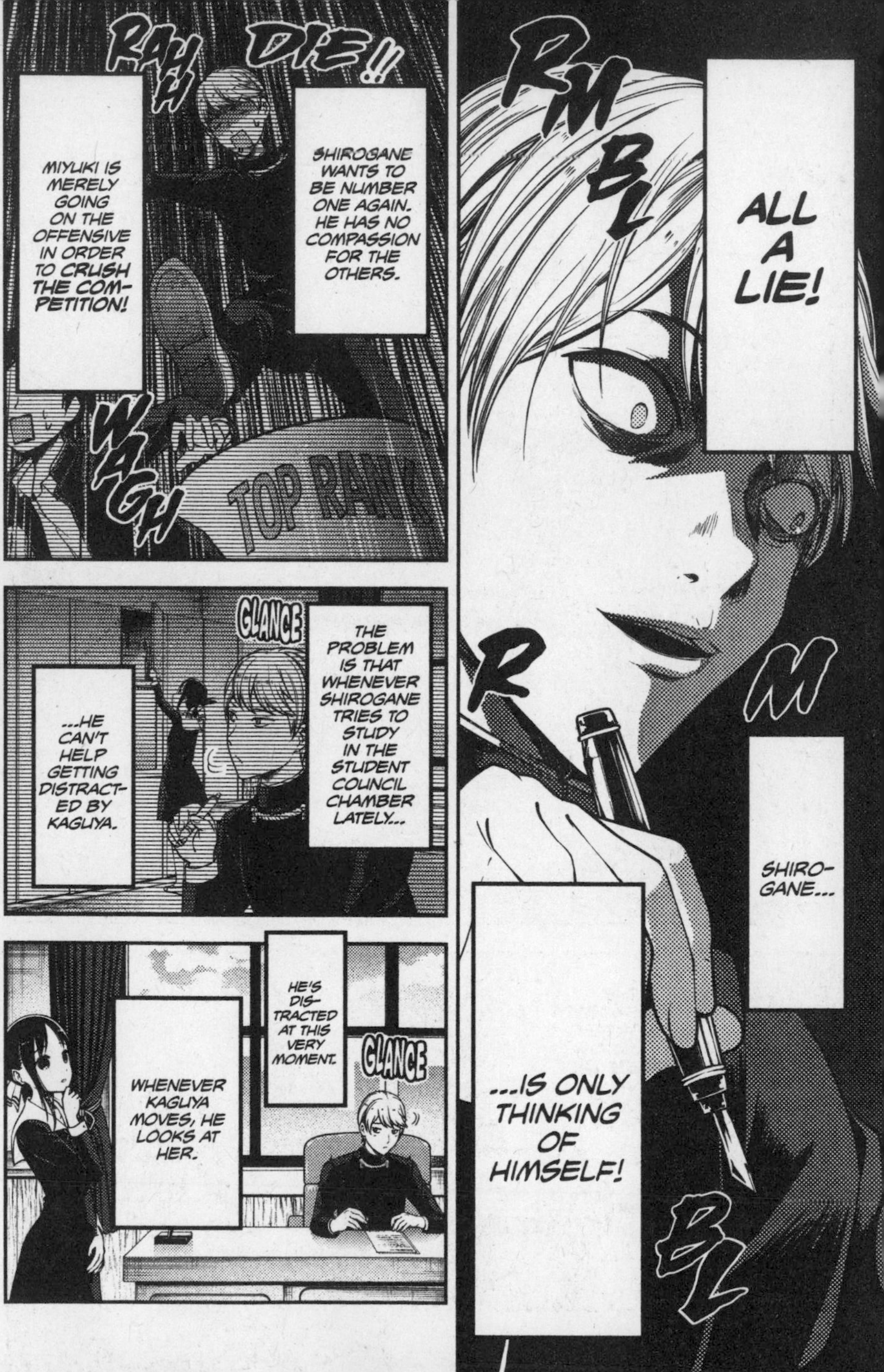
RMBL
ALL A LIE!
SHIROGANE...
...IS ONLY THINKING OF HIMSELF!
RMBL
RAH
DIE!!
SHIROGANE WANTS TO BE NUMBER ONE AGAIN. HE HAS NO COMPASSION FOR THE OTHERS.
MIYUKI IS MERELY GOING ON THE OFFENSIVE IN ORDER TO CRUSH THE COMPETITION!
WAGH
TOP RANKS
GLANCE
THE PROBLEM IS THAT WHENEVER SHIROGANE TRIES TO STUDY IN THE STUDENT COUNCIL CHAMBER LATELY...
...HE CAN'T HELP GETTING DISTRACTED BY KAGUYA.
HE'S DISTRACTED AT THIS VERY MOMENT.
GLANCE
WHENEVER KAGUYA MOVES, HE LOOKS AT HER.

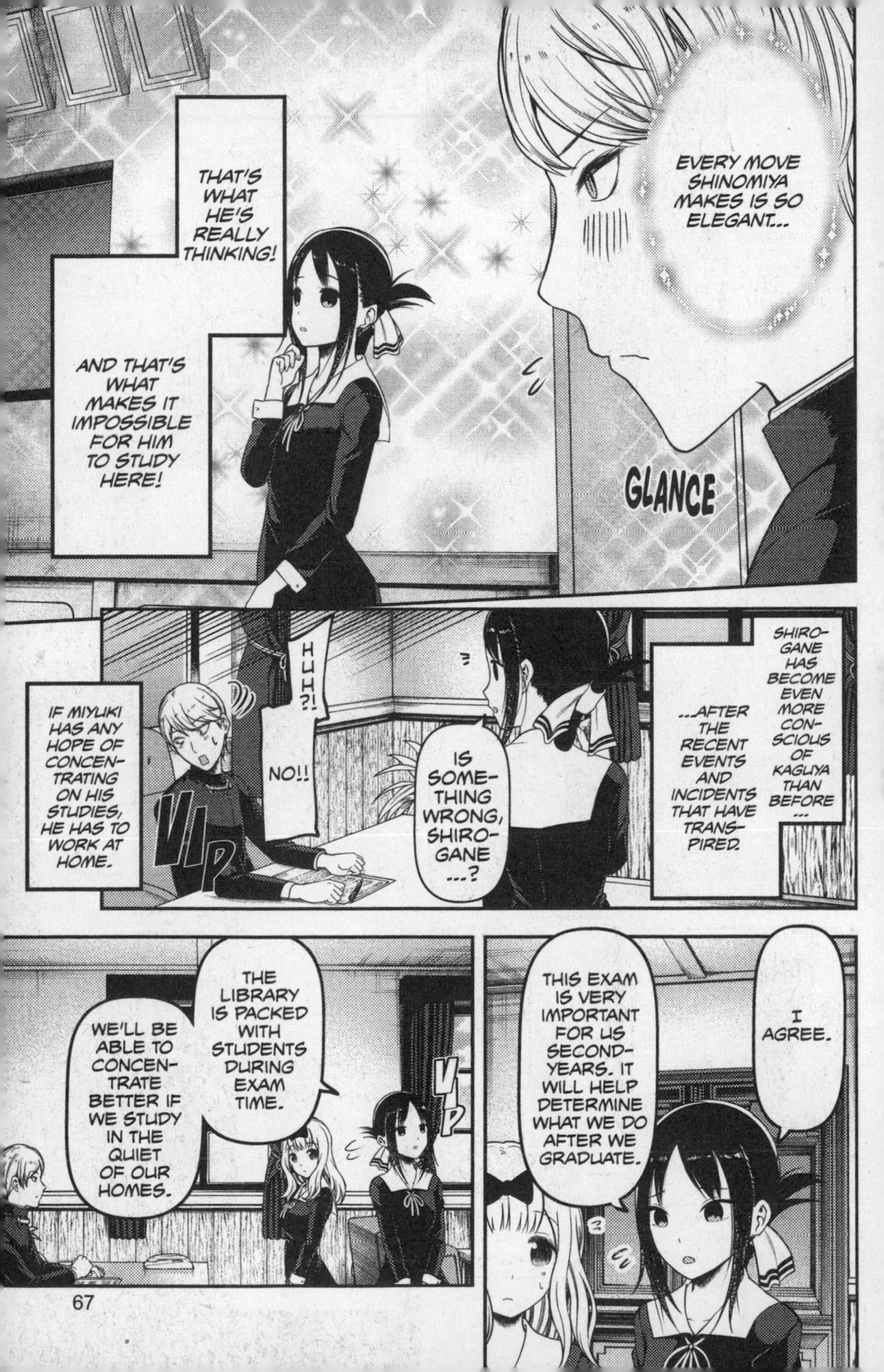
EVERY MOVE SHINOMIYA MAKES IS SO ELEGANT...
GLANCE
THAT'S WHAT HE'S REALLY THINKING!
AND THAT'S WHAT MAKES IT IMPOSSIBLE FOR HIM TO STUDY HERE!
SHIROGANE HAS BECOME EVEN MORE CONSCIOUS OF KAGUYA THAN BEFORE...
...AFTER THE RECENT EVENTS AND INCIDENTS THAT HAVE TRANSPIRED.
IS SOMETHING WRONG, SHIROGANE...?
HUH?!
NO!!
VIP
IF MIYUKI HAS ANY HOPE OF CONCENTRATING ON HIS STUDIES, HE HAS TO WORK AT HOME.
I AGREE.
THIS EXAM IS VERY IMPORTANT FOR US SECOND-YEARS. IT WILL HELP DETERMINE WHAT WE DO AFTER WE GRADUATE.
VIP
THE LIBRARY IS PACKED WITH STUDENTS DURING EXAM TIME.
WE'LL BE ABLE TO CONCENTRATE BETTER IF WE STUDY IN THE QUIET OF OUR HOMES.

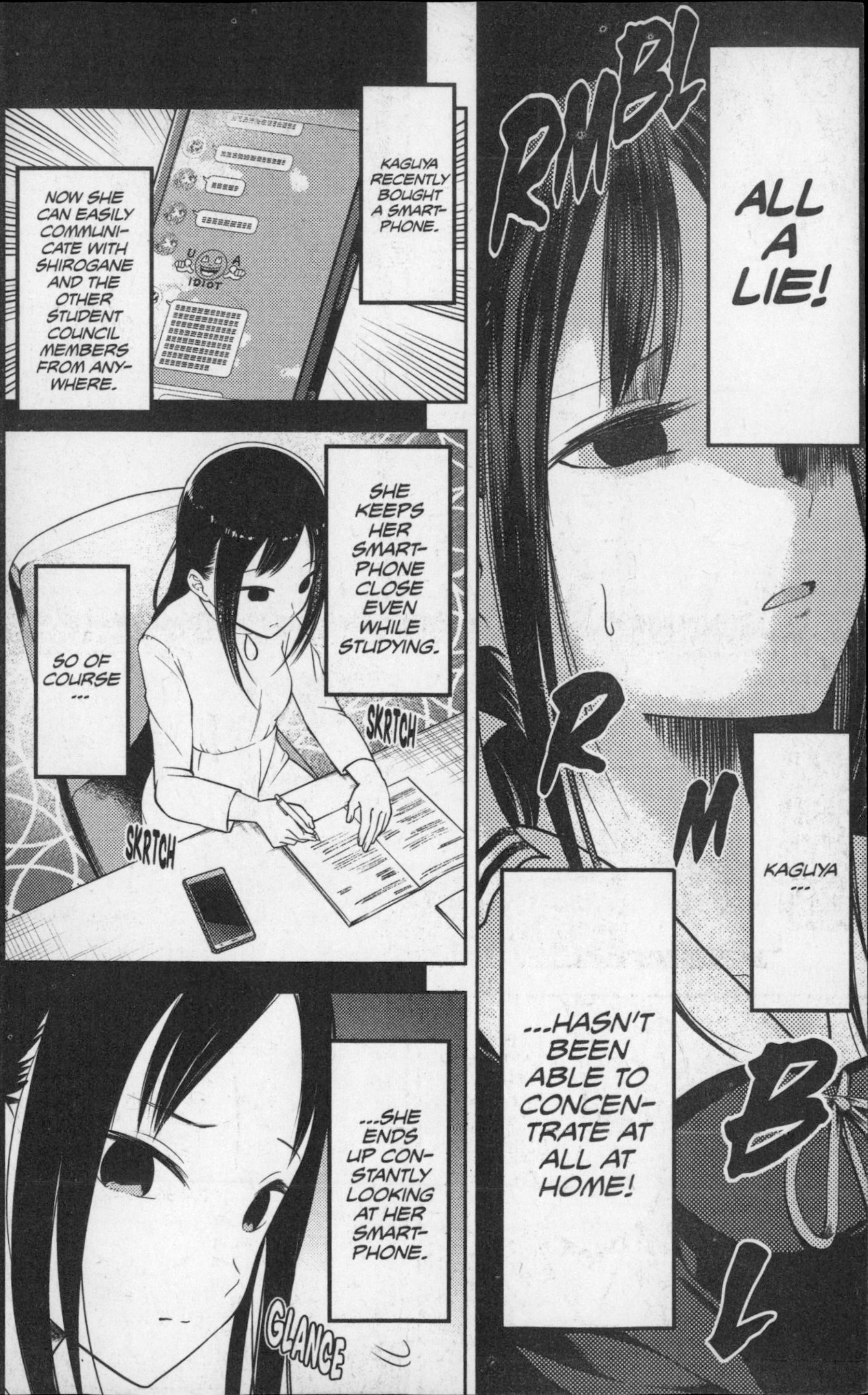
RMBL
ALL A LIE!
KAGUYA...
...HASN'T BEEN ABLE TO CONCENTRATE AT ALL AT HOME!
RRMBL
KAGUYA RECENTLY BOUGHT A SMARTPHONE.
NOW SHE CAN EASILY COMMUNICATE WITH SHIROGANE AND THE OTHER STUDENT COUNCIL MEMBERS FROM ANYWHERE.
U
A
IDIOT
SHE KEEPS HER SMARTPHONE CLOSE EVEN WHILE STUDYING.
SKRTCH
SO OF COURSE...
SKRTCH
...SHE ENDS UP CONSTANTLY LOOKING AT HER SMARTPHONE.
GLANCE

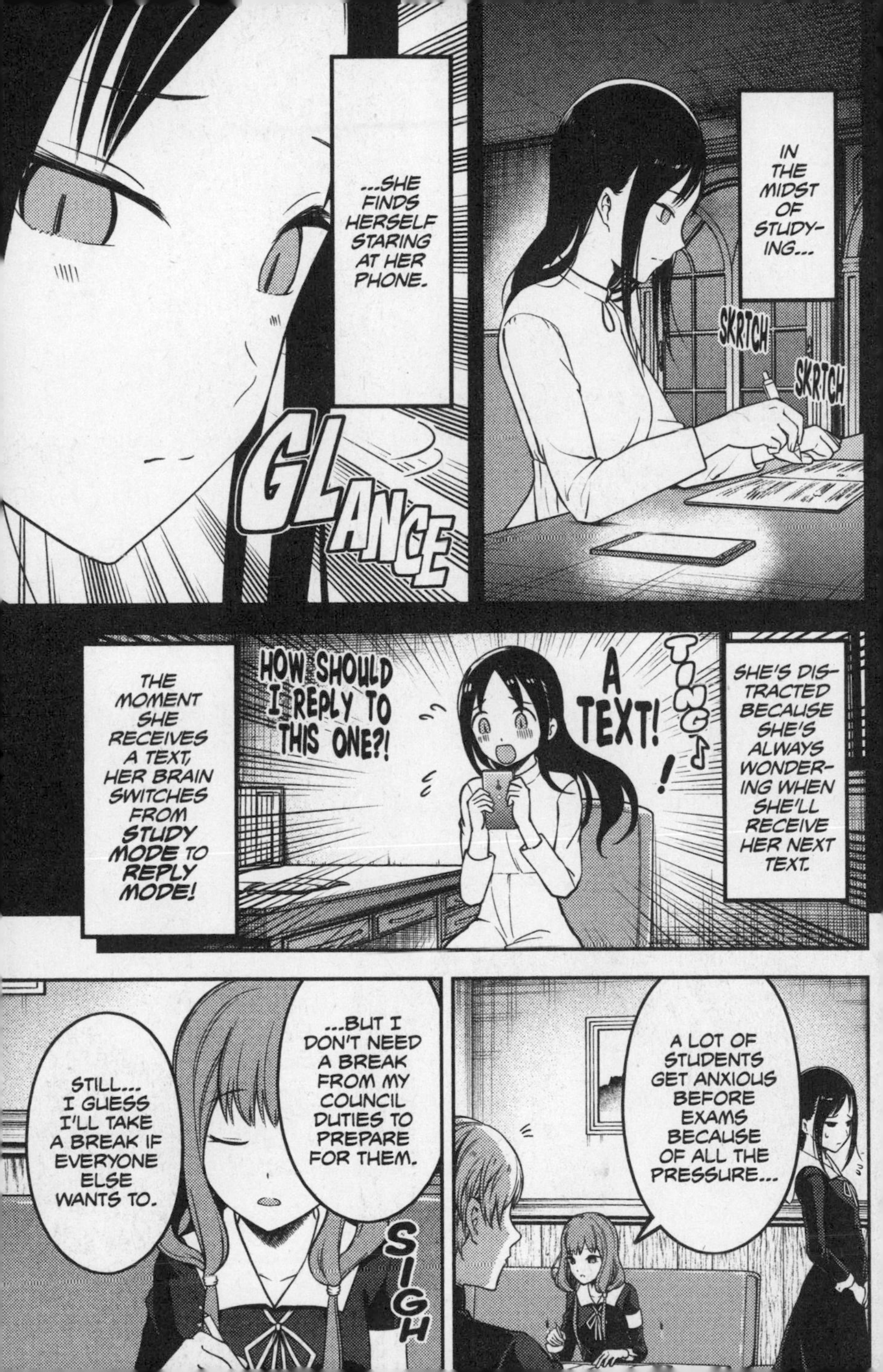
IN THE MIDST OF STUDYING...
SKRTCH
SKRTCH
...SHE FINDS HERSELF STARING AT HER PHONE.
GLANCE
SHE'S DISTRACTED BECAUSE SHE'S ALWAYS WONDERING WHEN SHE'LL RECEIVE HER NEXT TEXT.
TING♪
!
A TEXT!
HOW SHOULD I REPLY TO THIS ONE?!
THE MOMENT SHE RECEIVES A TEXT, HER BRAIN SWITCHES FROM STUDY MODE TO REPLY MODE!
A LOT OF STUDENTS GET ANXIOUS BEFORE EXAMS BECAUSE OF ALL THE PRESSURE...
...BUT I DON'T NEED A BREAK FROM MY COUNCIL DUTIES TO PREPARE FOR THEM.
STILL... I GUESS I'LL TAKE A BREAK IF EVERYONE ELSE WANTS TO.
SIGH

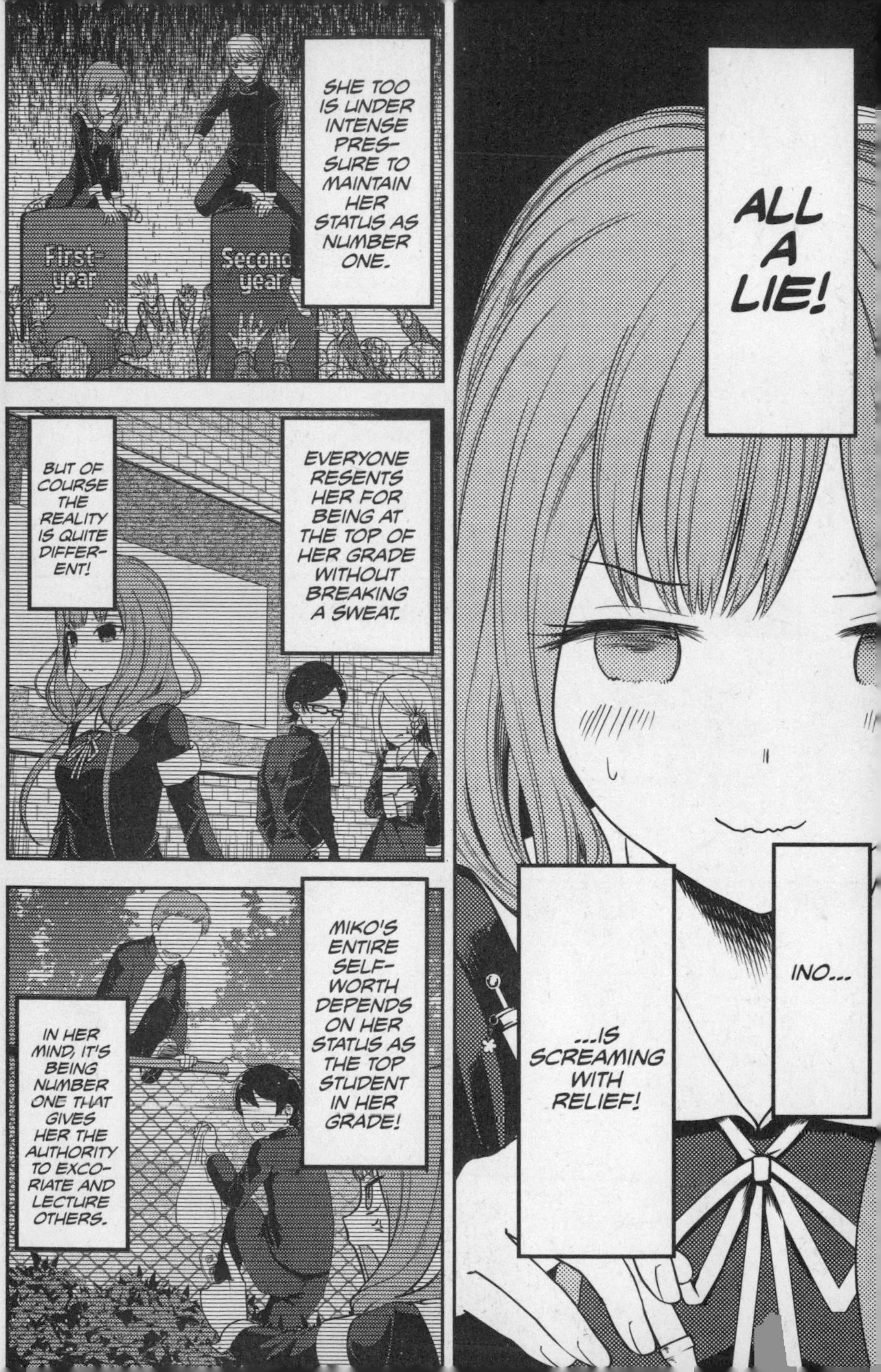
ALL A LIE!
INO...
...IS SCREAMING WITH RELIEF!
SHE TOO IS UNDER INTENSE PRES-SURE TO MAINTAIN HER STATUS AS NUMBER ONE.
Second-year
First-year
EVERYONE RESENTS HER FOR BEING AT THE TOP OF HER GRADE WITHOUT BREAKING A SWEAT.
BUT OF COURSE THE REALITY IS QUITE DIFFER-ENT!
MIKO'S ENTIRE SELF-WORTH DEPENDS ON HER STATUS AS THE TOP STUDENT IN HER GRADE!
IN HER MIND, IT'S BEING NUMBER ONE THAT GIVES HER THE AUTHORITY TO EXCO-RIATE AND LECTURE OTHERS.

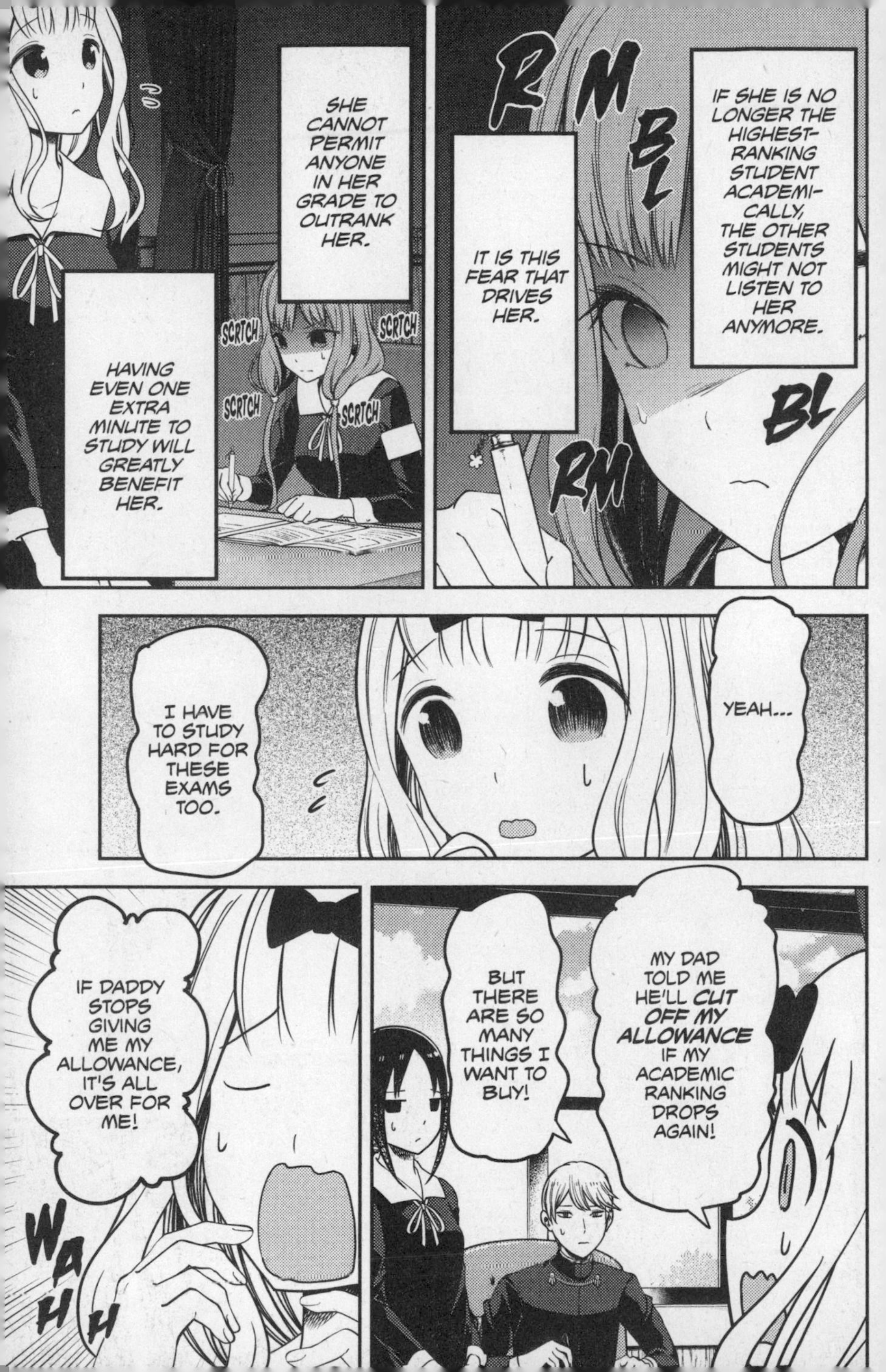
RMBL
IF SHE IS NO LONGER THE HIGHEST-RANKING STUDENT ACADEMICALLY, THE OTHER STUDENTS MIGHT NOT LISTEN TO HER ANYMORE.
IT IS THIS FEAR THAT DRIVES HER.
BL
RM
SHE CANNOT PERMIT ANYONE IN HER GRADE TO OUTRANK HER.
SCRTCH
SCRTCH
SCRTCH
SCRTCH
HAVING EVEN ONE EXTRA MINUTE TO STUDY WILL GREATLY BENEFIT HER.
YEAH...
I HAVE TO STUDY HARD FOR THESE EXAMS TOO.
MY DAD TOLD ME HE'LL *CUT OFF MY ALLOWANCE* IF MY ACADEMIC RANKING DROPS AGAIN!
BUT THERE ARE SO MANY THINGS I WANT TO BUY!
IF DADDY STOPS GIVING ME MY ALLOWANCE, IT'S ALL OVER FOR ME!
WAHH

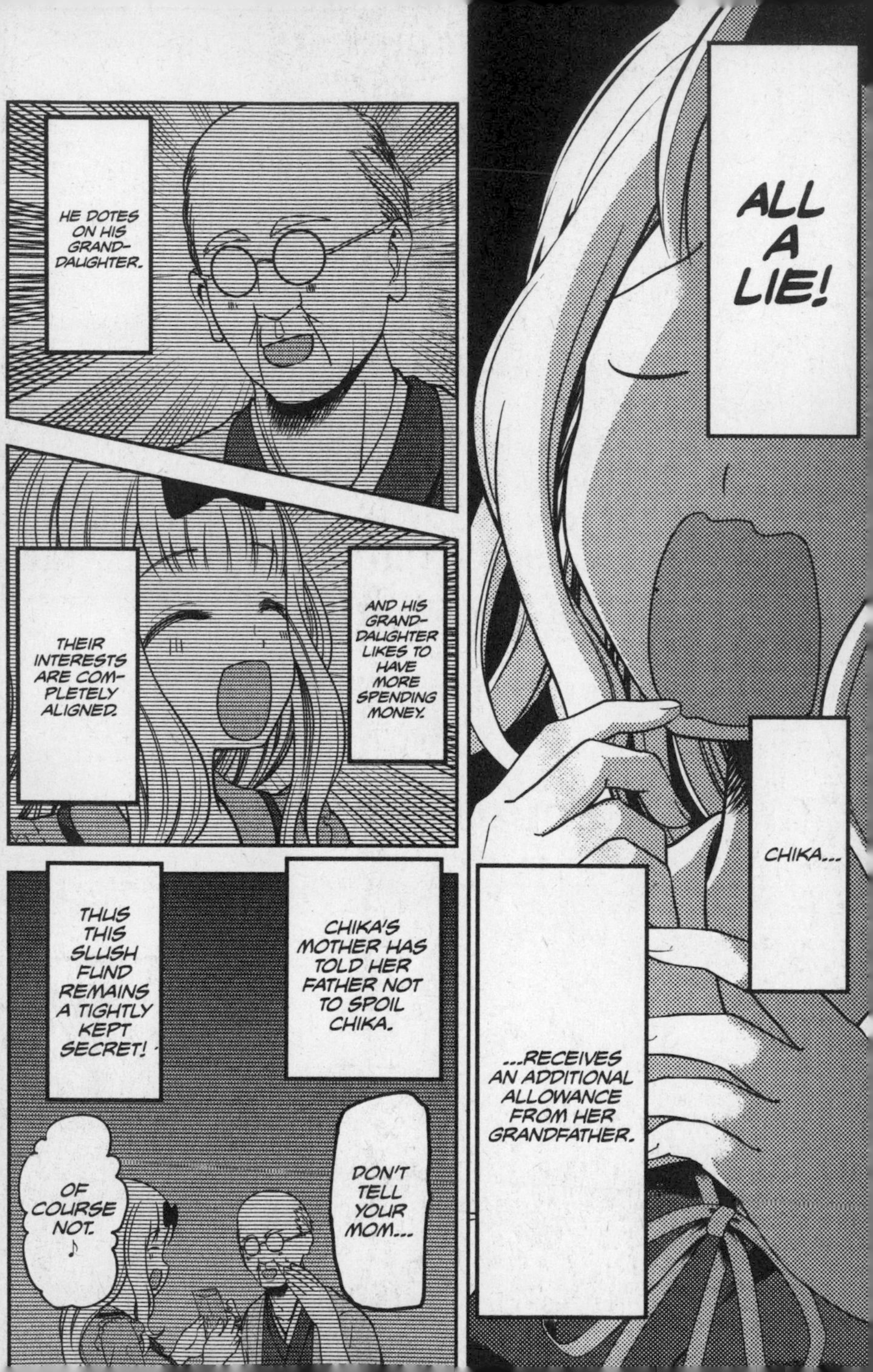
ALL A LIE!
CHIKA...
...RECEIVES AN ADDITIONAL ALLOWANCE FROM HER GRANDFATHER.
HE DOTES ON HIS GRAND-DAUGHTER.
AND HIS GRAND-DAUGHTER LIKES TO HAVE MORE SPENDING MONEY.
THEIR INTERESTS ARE COM-PLETELY ALIGNED.
CHIKA'S MOTHER HAS TOLD HER FATHER NOT TO SPOIL CHIKA.
THUS THIS SLUSH FUND REMAINS A TIGHTLY KEPT SECRET!
DON'T TELL YOUR MOM...
OF COURSE NOT. ♪

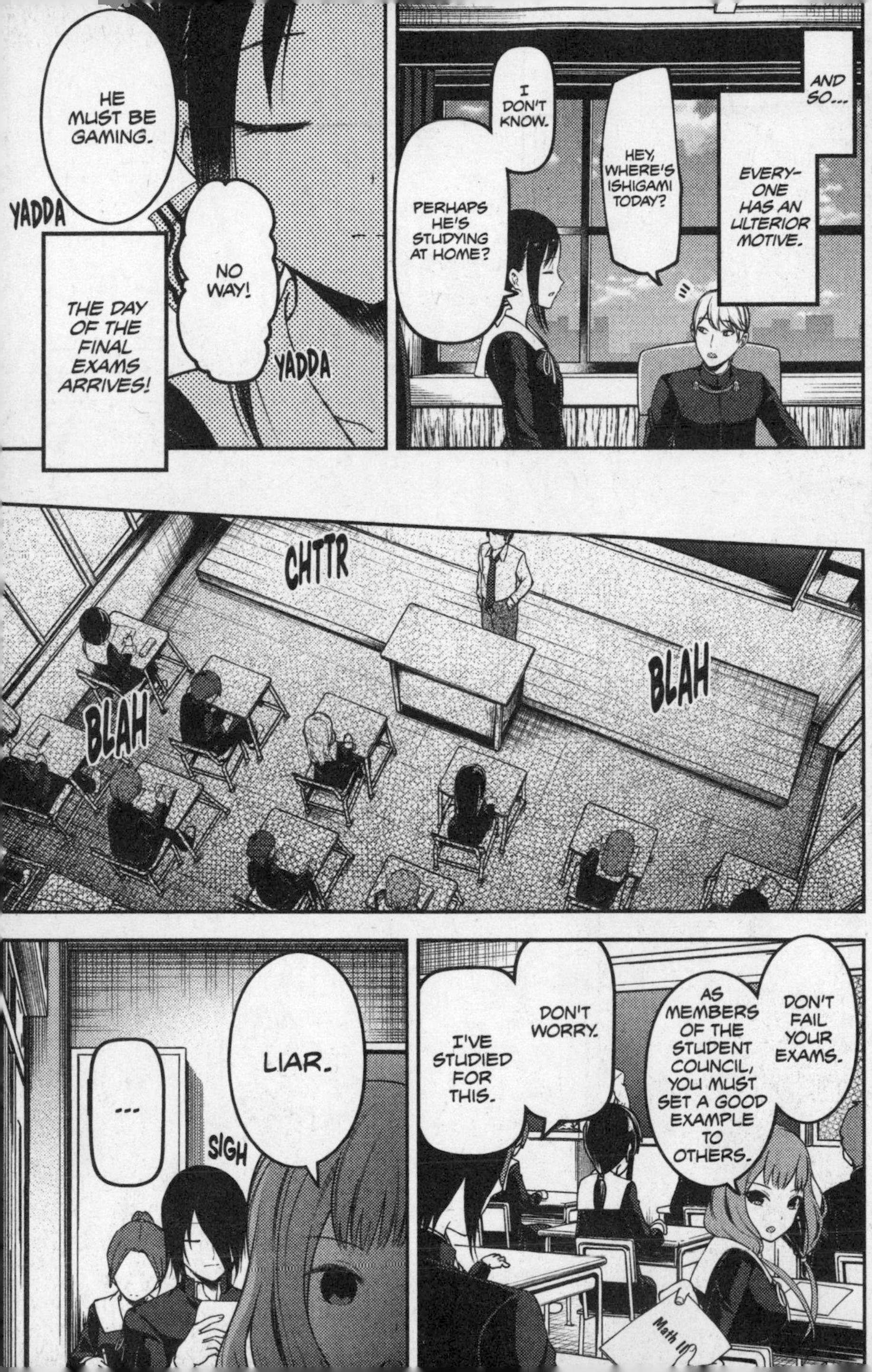
AND SO...
EVERYONE HAS AN ULTERIOR MOTIVE.
HEY, WHERE'S ISHIGAMI TODAY?
I DON'T KNOW.
PERHAPS HE'S STUDYING AT HOME?
NO WAY!
YADDA
HE MUST BE GAMING.
YADDA
THE DAY OF THE FINAL EXAMS ARRIVES!
CHTTR
BLAH
BLAH
DON'T FAIL YOUR EXAMS.
AS MEMBERS OF THE STUDENT COUNCIL, YOU MUST SET A GOOD EXAMPLE TO OTHERS.
DON'T WORRY.
I'VE STUDIED FOR THIS.
Math II
LIAR.
...
SIGH

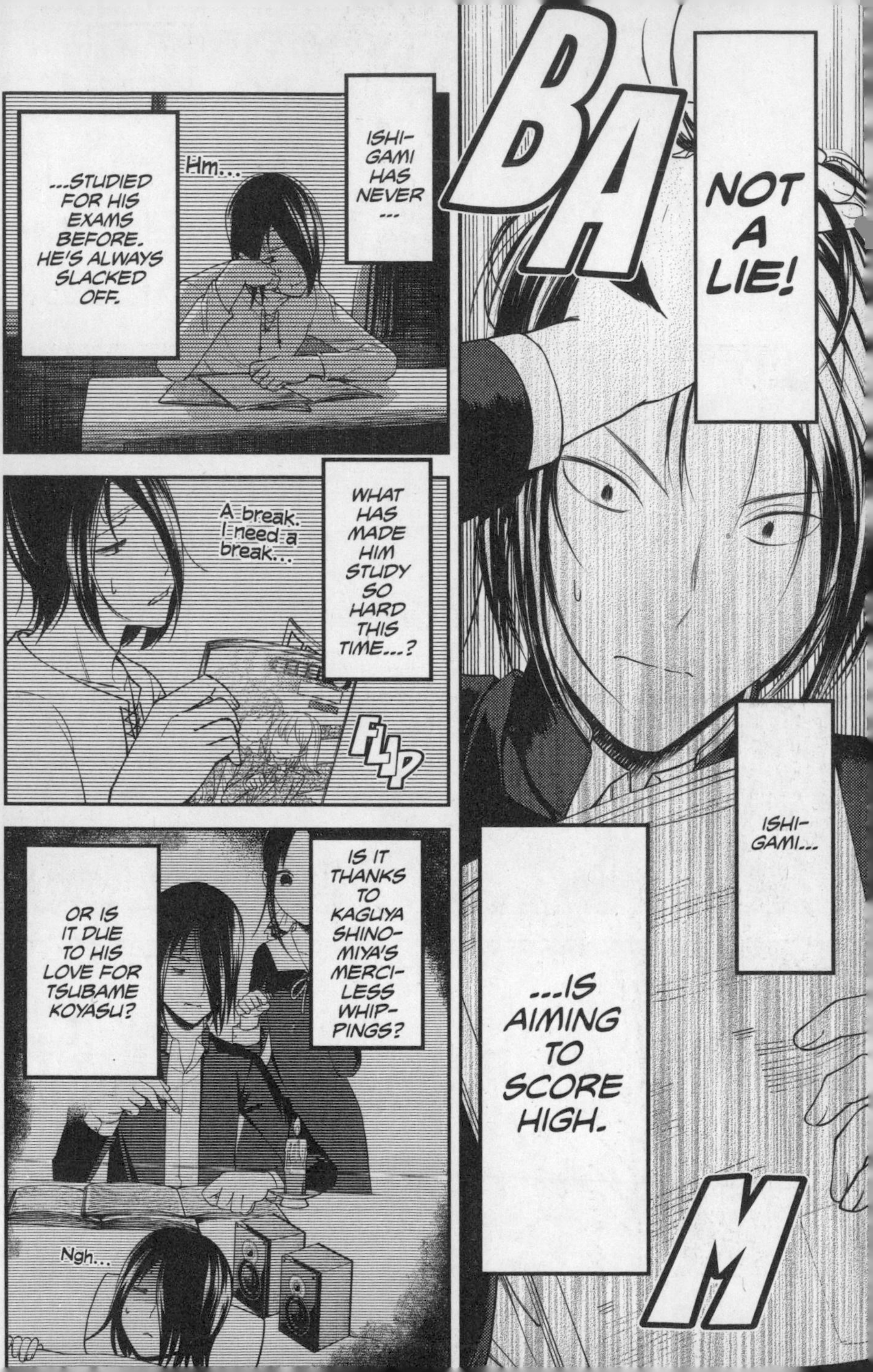
BA
NOT A LIE!
M
ISHI-GAMI...
...IS AIMING TO SCORE HIGH.
ISHI-GAMI HAS NEVER...
...STUDIED FOR HIS EXAMS BEFORE. HE'S ALWAYS SLACKED OFF.
Hm...
WHAT HAS MADE HIM STUDY SO HARD THIS TIME...?
A break. I need a break...
FLIP
IS IT THANKS TO KAGUYA SHINOMIYA'S MERCILESS WHIPPINGS?
OR IS IT DUE TO HIS LOVE FOR TSUBAME KOYASU?
Ngh...

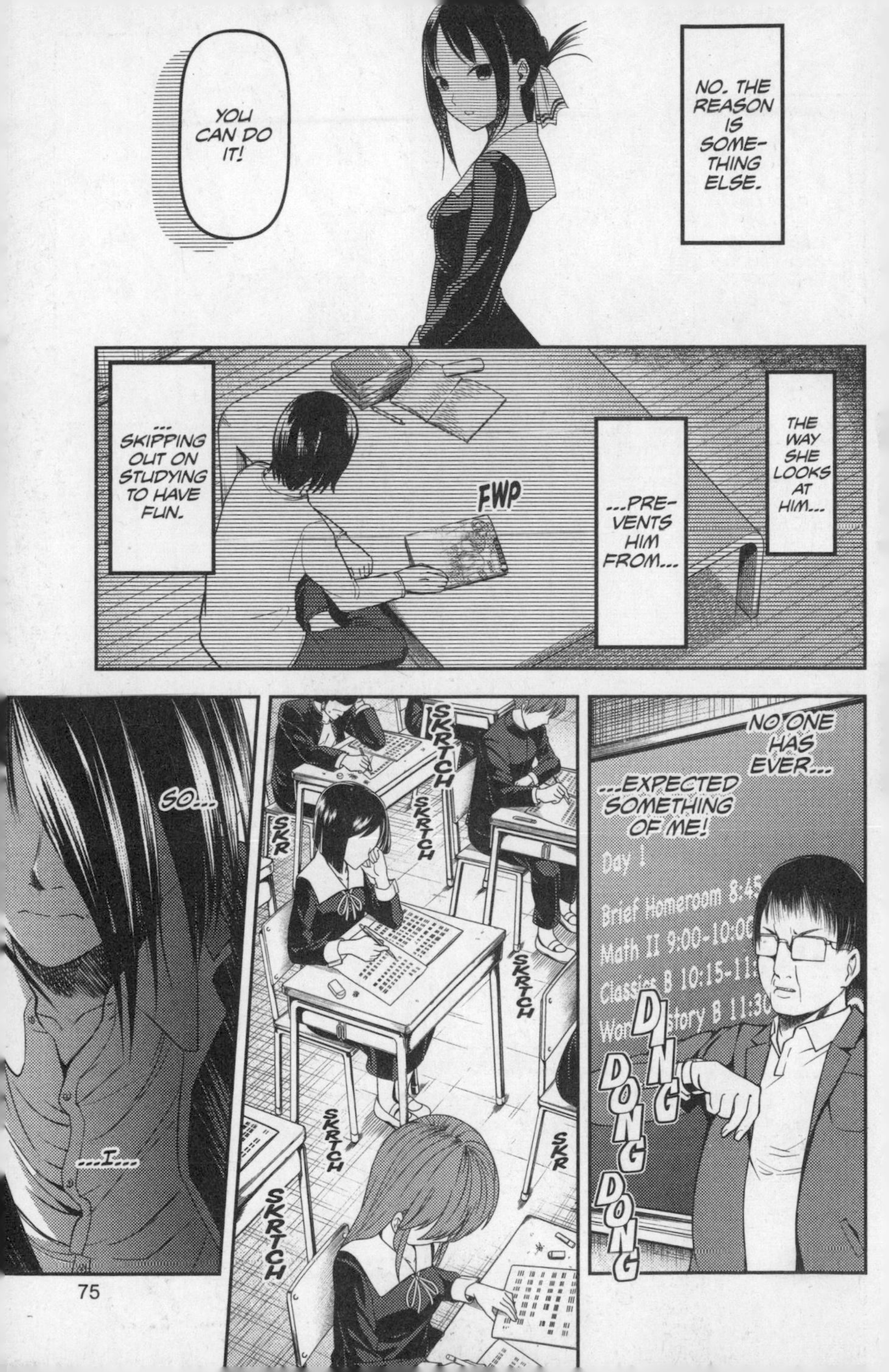
NO. THE REASON IS SOMETHING ELSE.
YOU CAN DO IT!
THE WAY SHE LOOKS AT HIM...
...PREVENTS HIM FROM...
FWP
...SKIPPING OUT ON STUDYING TO HAVE FUN.
NO ONE HAS EVER...
...EXPECTED SOMETHING OF ME!
Day 1
Brief Homeroom 8:45
Math II 9:00-10:00
Classics B 10:15-11:
World History B 11:30
DING DONG DING DONG
SKRTCH
SKRTCH
SKR
SKRTCH
SKR
SKRTCH
SKRTCH
SO...
...I...

...DON'T WANT TO LET HER DOWN!

VP

#1	Miko Ino	482
#2	Daisuke Izumo	479
#2	Shizuka Son	479
#4	Yayuyo Abe	478
#5	Kei Takashiro	477
#6	Megumi Numata	468
#7	Atsushi Morinaga	464

Second-Term Final Exam Results

Listed below are the names of the 50 highest-ranking students. We hope they continue their pursuit of excellence and serve as an example to others.

Sincerely,
Your teachers

#50	Hidetaka Tomioka	417
#49	Korom... ...nui	412
#48	Rei C...	41...
#47	Anthony Jhabi	
#46	Tomonari Shindo	
#44	Momo Uemi	
#44	Sora Ide	
	Chihiro Hayash...	

YADDA YADDA
YADDA YADDA
YADDA YADDA

YOUR NAME ISN'T ON THE LIST.

I ALREADY KNEW WHEN I GRADED MY OWN TESTS...

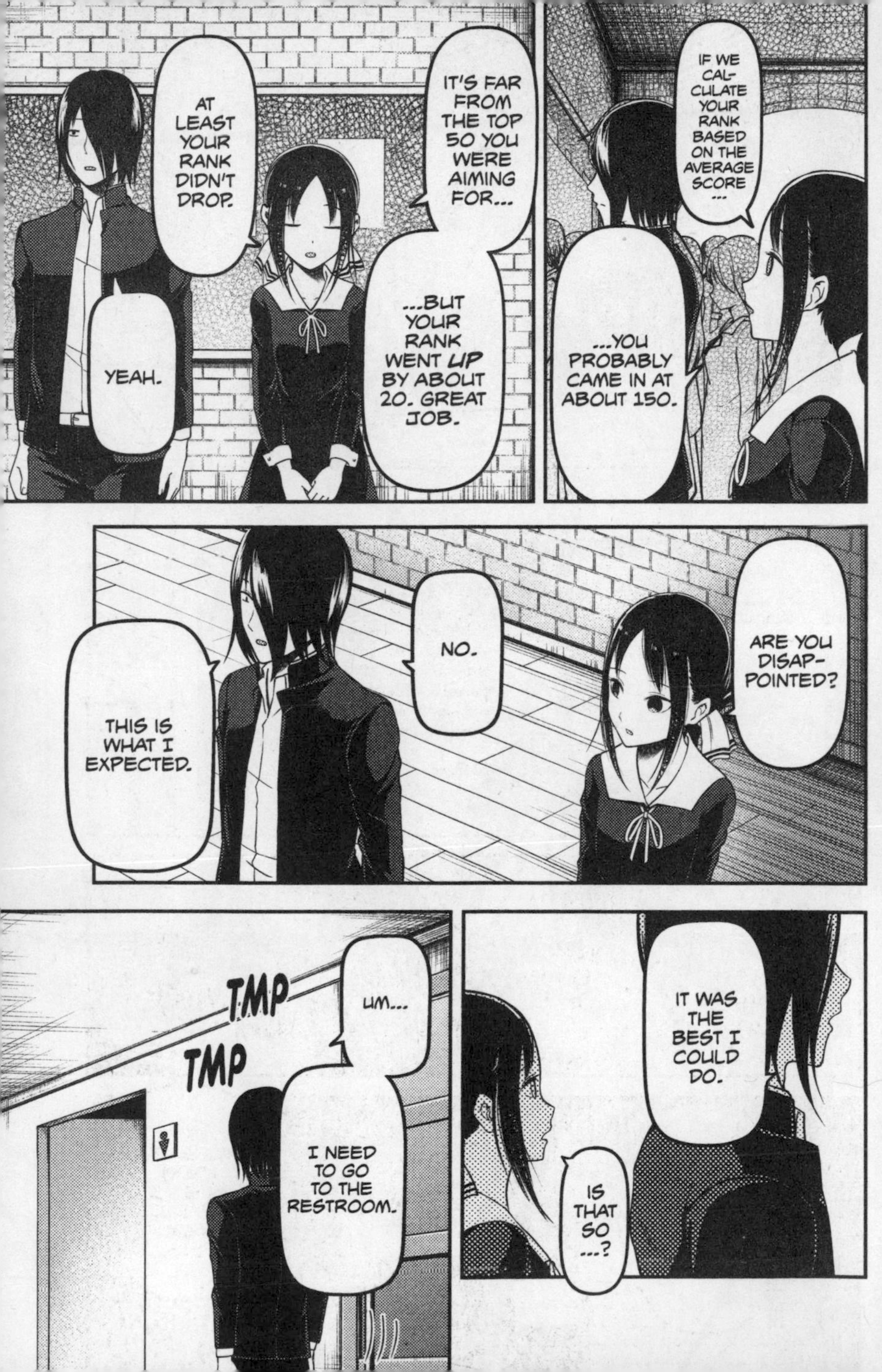
IF WE CALCULATE YOUR RANK BASED ON THE AVERAGE SCORE ...
...YOU PROBABLY CAME IN AT ABOUT 150.
IT'S FAR FROM THE TOP 50 YOU WERE AIMING FOR...
...BUT YOUR RANK WENT *UP* BY ABOUT 20. GREAT JOB.
AT LEAST YOUR RANK DIDN'T DROP.
YEAH.
ARE YOU DISAPPOINTED?
NO.
THIS IS WHAT I EXPECTED.
IT WAS THE BEST I COULD DO.
IS THAT SO ...?
UM...
TMP
TMP
I NEED TO GO TO THE RESTROOM.

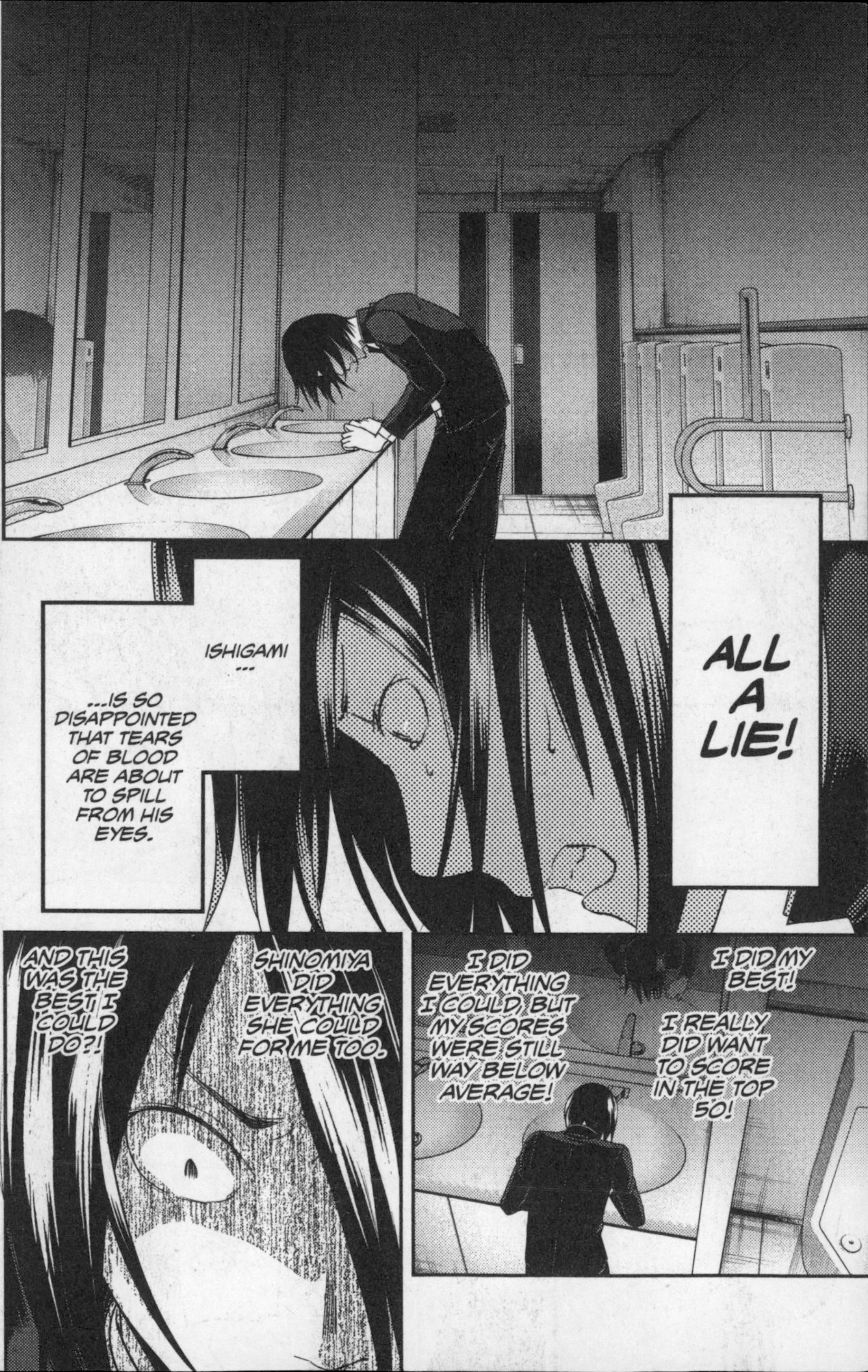
ALL A LIE!
ISHIGAMI...
...IS SO DISAPPOINTED THAT TEARS OF BLOOD ARE ABOUT TO SPILL FROM HIS EYES.
I DID MY BEST!
I REALLY DID WANT TO SCORE IN THE TOP 50!
I DID EVERYTHING I COULD, BUT MY SCORES WERE STILL WAY BELOW AVERAGE!
SHINOMIYA DID EVERYTHING SHE COULD FOR ME TOO.
AND THIS WAS THE BEST I COULD DO?!

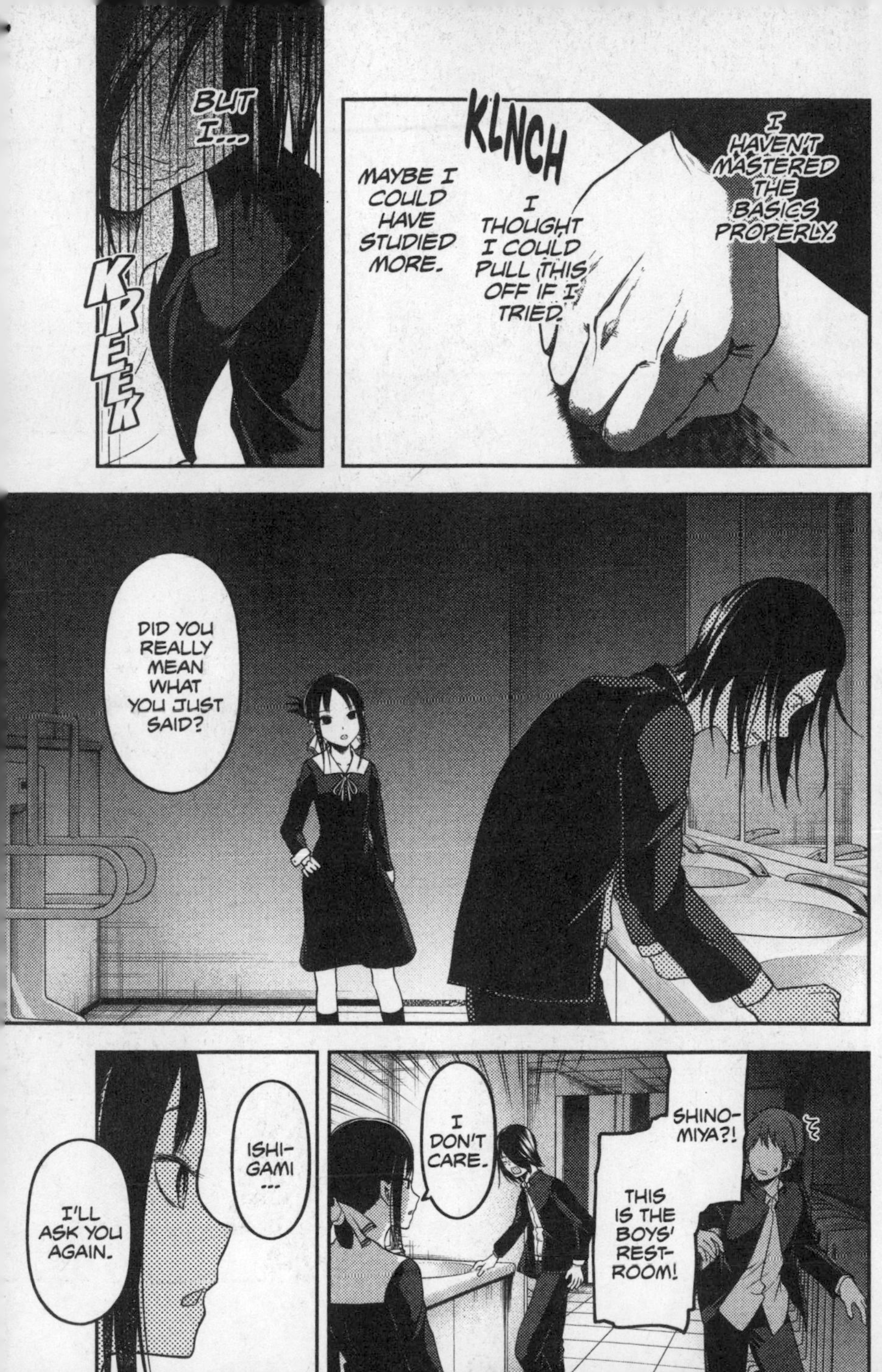
I HAVEN'T MASTERED THE BASICS PROPERLY.
KLNCH
I THOUGHT I COULD PULL THIS OFF IF I TRIED.
MAYBE I COULD HAVE STUDIED MORE.
BUT I...
KREEK
DID YOU REALLY MEAN WHAT YOU JUST SAID?
SHINO-MIYA?!
THIS IS THE BOYS' REST-ROOM!
I DON'T CARE.
ISHI-GAMI...
I'LL ASK YOU AGAIN.

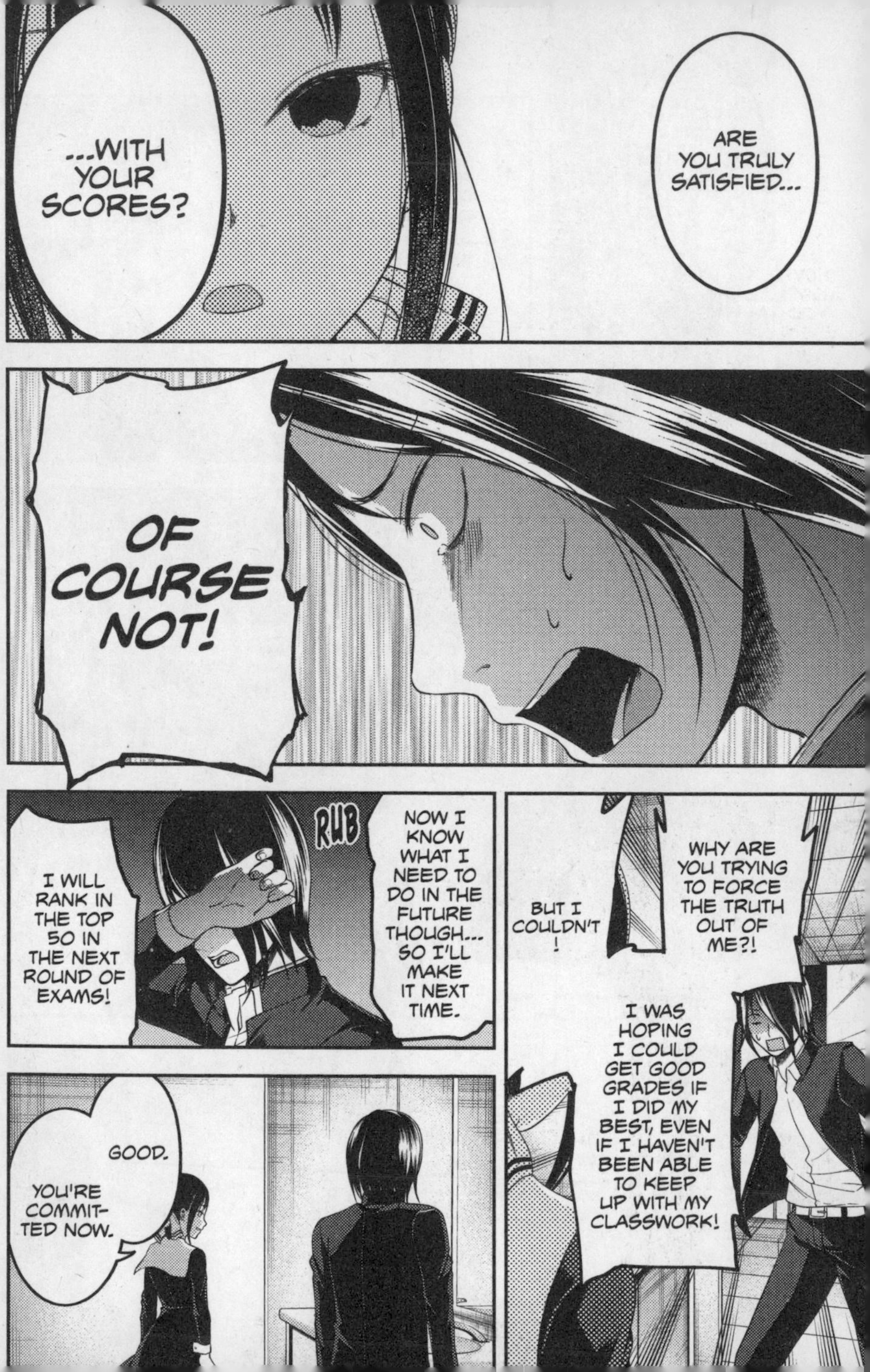
ARE YOU TRULY SATISFIED...
...WITH YOUR SCORES?
OF COURSE NOT!
WHY ARE YOU TRYING TO FORCE THE TRUTH OUT OF ME?!
I WAS HOPING I COULD GET GOOD GRADES IF I DID MY BEST, EVEN IF I HAVEN'T BEEN ABLE TO KEEP UP WITH MY CLASSWORK!
BUT I COULDN'T!
RUB
NOW I KNOW WHAT I NEED TO DO IN THE FUTURE THOUGH... SO I'LL MAKE IT NEXT TIME.
I WILL RANK IN THE TOP 50 IN THE NEXT ROUND OF EXAMS!
GOOD.
YOU'RE COMMITTED NOW.

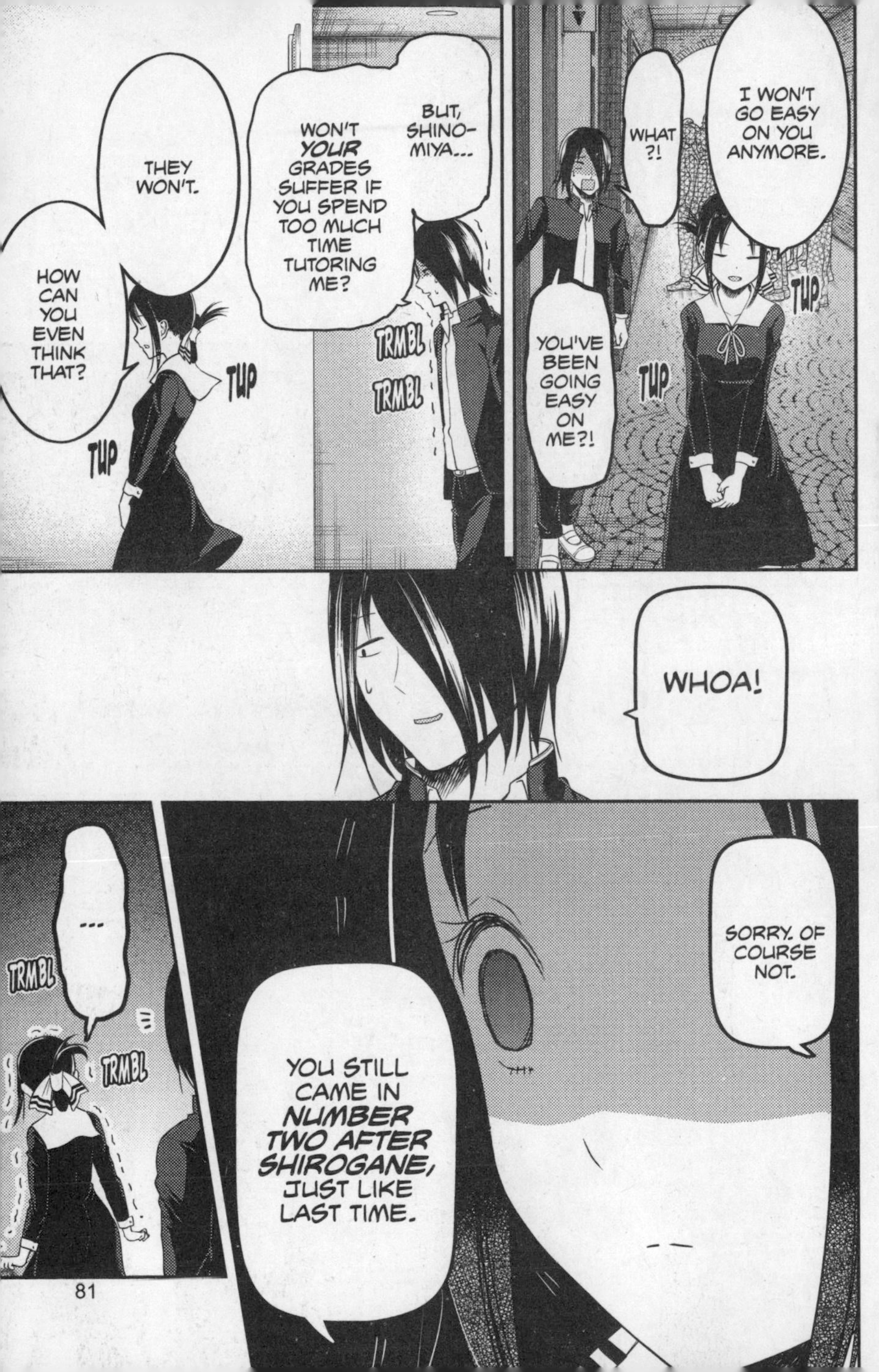
I WON'T GO EASY ON YOU ANYMORE.
WHAT?!
TUP
YOU'VE BEEN GOING EASY ON ME?!
TUP
BUT, SHINO-MIYA...
WON'T YOUR GRADES SUFFER IF YOU SPEND TOO MUCH TIME TUTORING ME?
TRMBL
TRMBL
THEY WON'T.
HOW CAN YOU EVEN THINK THAT?
TUP
TUP
WHOA!
SORRY. OF COURSE NOT.
YOU STILL CAME IN NUMBER TWO AFTER SHIROGANE, JUST LIKE LAST TIME.
...
TRMBL
TRMBL

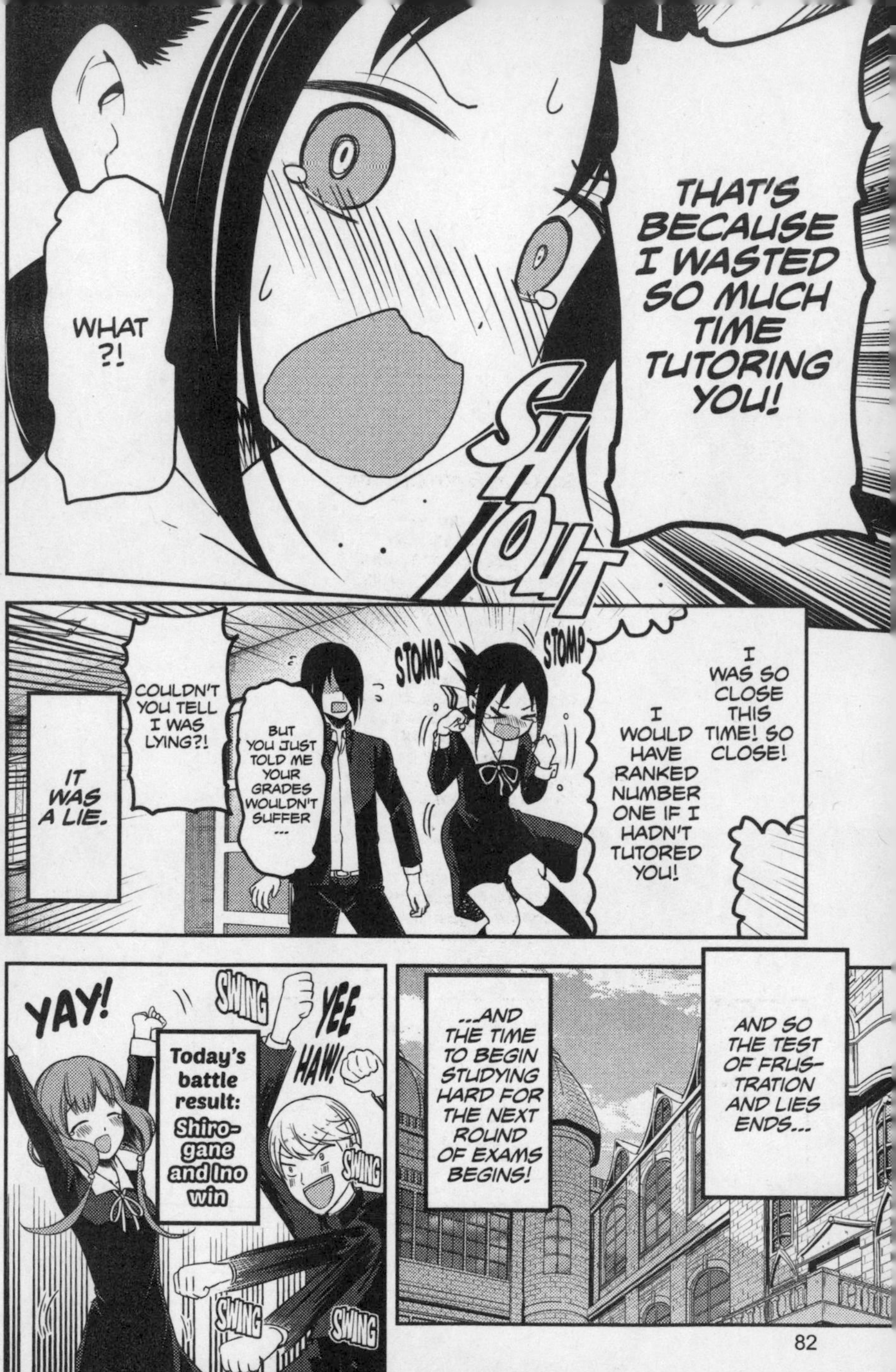
THAT'S BECAUSE I WASTED SO MUCH TIME TUTORING YOU!
SHOUT
WHAT?!
I WAS SO CLOSE THIS TIME! SO CLOSE!
I WOULD HAVE RANKED NUMBER ONE IF I HADN'T TUTORED YOU!
STOMP
STOMP
BUT YOU JUST TOLD ME YOUR GRADES WOULDN'T SUFFER...
COULDN'T YOU TELL I WAS LYING?!
IT WAS A LIE.
AND SO THE TEST OF FRUS-TRATION AND LIES ENDS...
...AND THE TIME TO BEGIN STUDYING HARD FOR THE NEXT ROUND OF EXAMS BEGINS!
YEE HAW!
SWING
YAY!
Today's battle result: Shiro-gane and Ino win
SWING
SWING
SWING

Second-Term Grades

First-Years:
Miko Ino #1 → #1
Makky Senhai #10 → #8
Rei Onodera #37 → #48
Kobachi Osaragi #160 → #151
Yu Ishigami #177 → #152

Second-Years:
Miyuki Shirogane #1 → #1
Kaguya Shinomiya #2 → #2
Maki Shijo #3 → #3
Saburo Toyosaki #6 → #5
Go Kazamatsuri #11 → #13
Nagisa Kashiwagi #7 → #27
Chika Fujiwara #101 → #111
Ai Hayasaka #114 → #114
Kashiwagi's boyfriend #84 → #34

Third-Years:
Squad leader Kazeno #4 → #4
Tsubame Koyasu #8 → #7
Megako #174 → #176

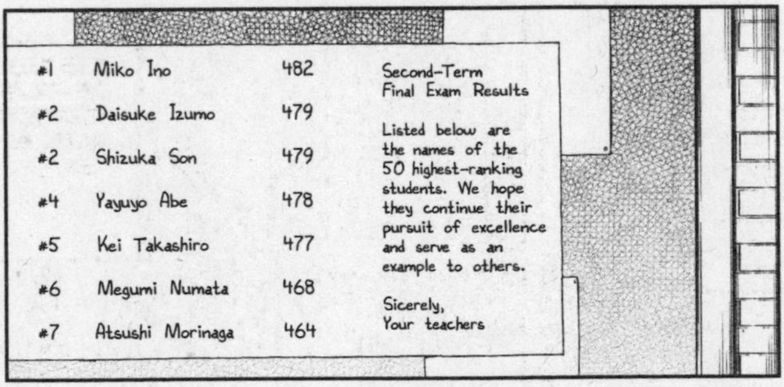

#1	Miko Ino	482
#2	Daisuke Izumo	479
#2	Shizuka Son	479
#4	Yayuyo Abe	478
#5	Kei Takashiro	477
#6	Megumi Numata	468
#7	Atsushi Morinaga	464

Second-Term
Final Exam Results

Listed below are
the names of the
50 highest-ranking
students. We hope
they continue their
pursuit of excellence
and serve as an
example to others.

Sicerely,
Your teachers

KAGUYA-SAMA
LOVE IS WAR

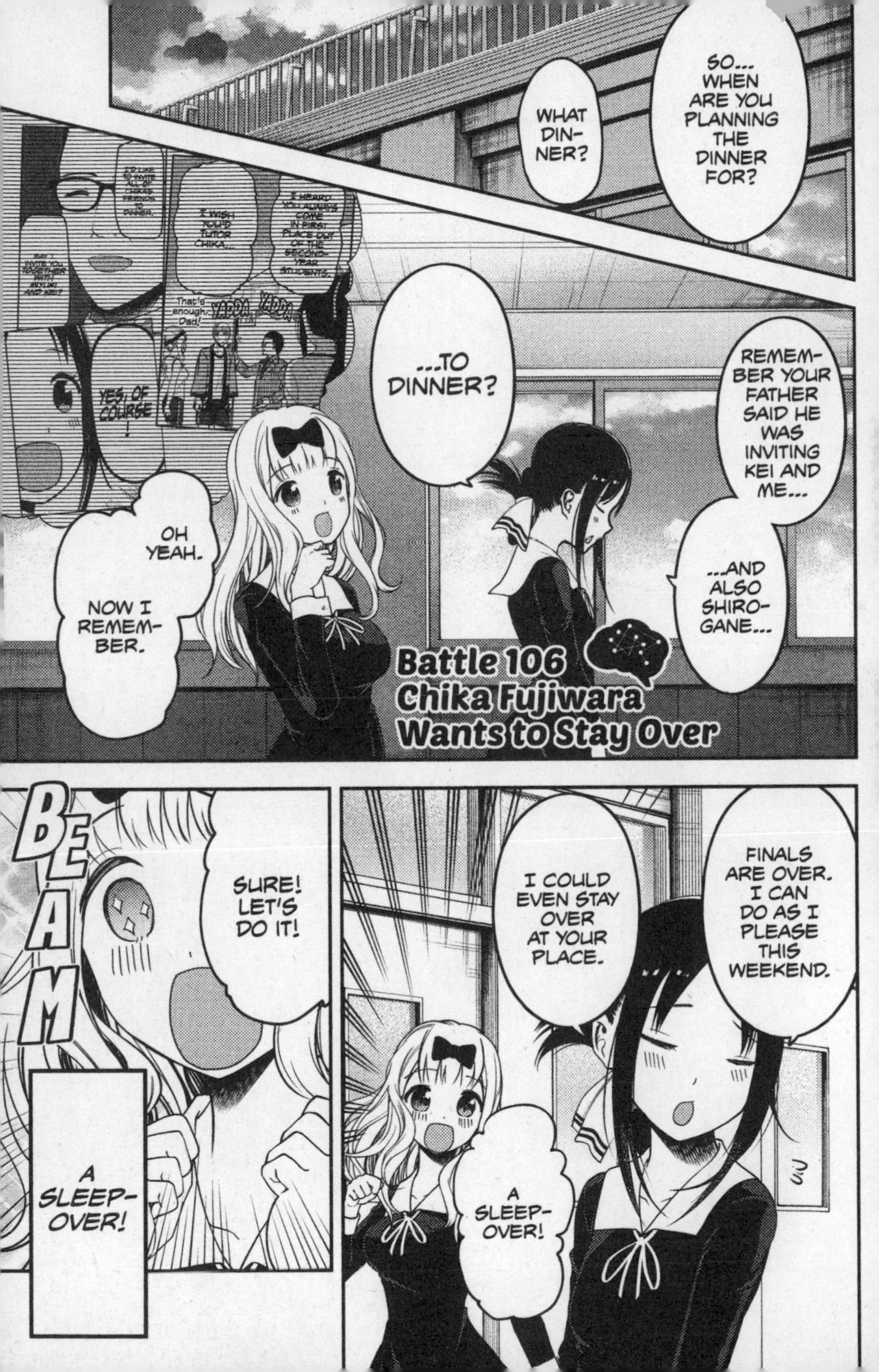
SO... WHEN ARE YOU PLANNING THE DINNER FOR?
WHAT DINNER?
REMEMBER YOUR FATHER SAID HE WAS INVITING KEI AND ME...
...AND ALSO SHIROGANE...
...TO DINNER?
I HEARD YOU ALWAYS COME IN FIRST PLACE OUT OF THE SECOND-YEAR STUDENTS.
I WISH YOU'D TUTOR CHIKA...
That's enough, Dad!
YADDA
YADDA
I'D LIKE TO INVITE ALL OF CHIKA'S FRIENDS TO DINNER.
MAY I INVITE YOU TOGETHER WITH MIYUKI AND KEI?
YES, OF COURSE!
OH YEAH.
NOW I REMEMBER.
Battle 106
Chika Fujiwara Wants to Stay Over
FINALS ARE OVER. I CAN DO AS I PLEASE THIS WEEKEND.
I COULD EVEN STAY OVER AT YOUR PLACE.
A SLEEPOVER!
SURE! LET'S DO IT!
BEAM
A SLEEPOVER!

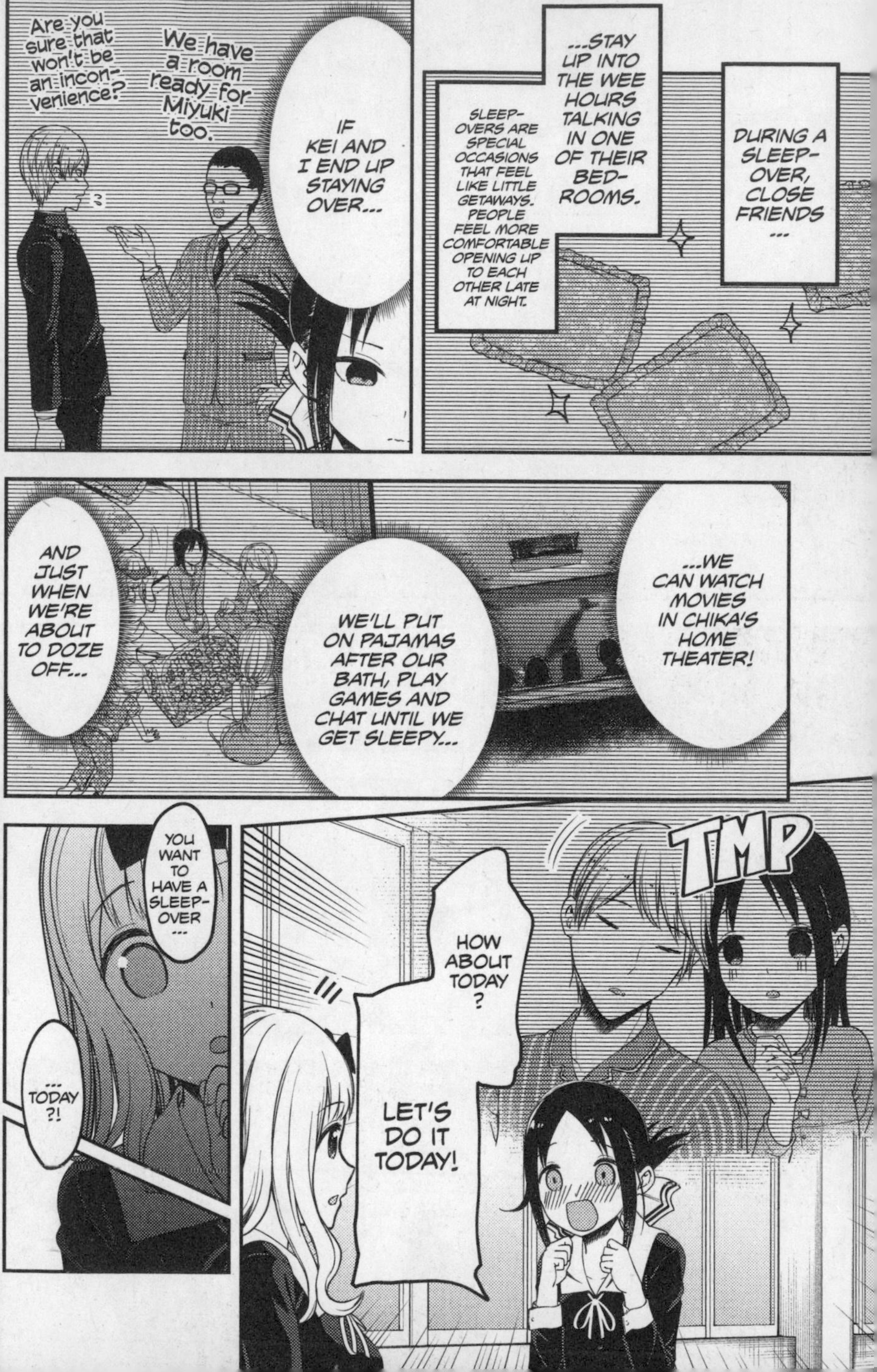
DURING A SLEEP-OVER, CLOSE FRIENDS...
...STAY UP INTO THE WEE HOURS TALKING IN ONE OF THEIR BED-ROOMS.
SLEEP-OVERS ARE SPECIAL OCCASIONS THAT FEEL LIKE LITTLE GETAWAYS. PEOPLE FEEL MORE COMFORTABLE OPENING UP TO EACH OTHER LATE AT NIGHT.
IF KEI AND I END UP STAYING OVER...
We have a room ready for Miyuki too.
Are you sure that won't be an incon-venience?
...WE CAN WATCH MOVIES IN CHIKA'S HOME THEATER!
WE'LL PUT ON PAJAMAS AFTER OUR BATH, PLAY GAMES AND CHAT UNTIL WE GET SLEEPY...
AND JUST WHEN WE'RE ABOUT TO DOZE OFF...
TMP
HOW ABOUT TODAY?
LET'S DO IT TODAY!
YOU WANT TO HAVE A SLEEP-OVER...
...TODAY?!

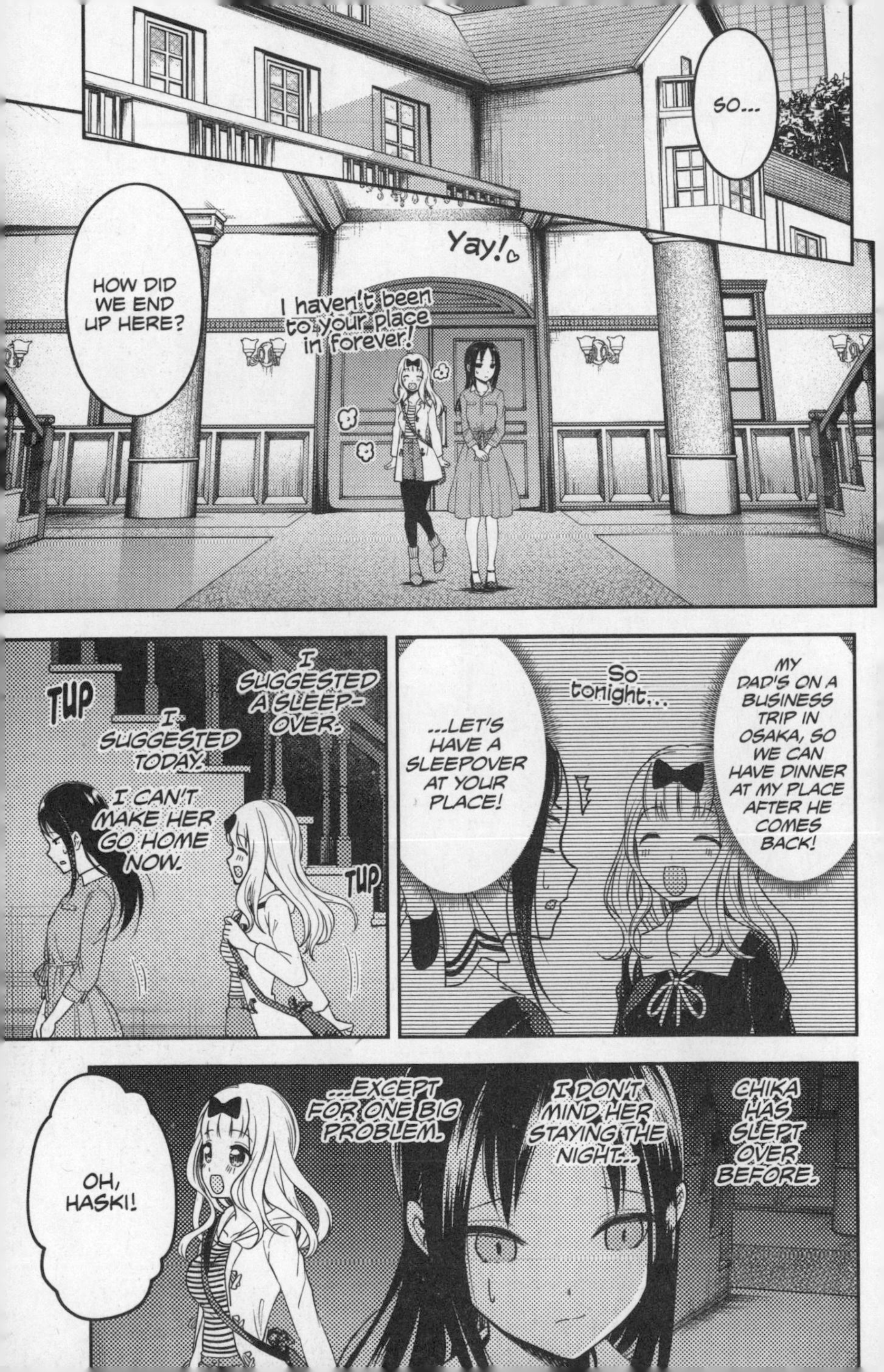
SO...
HOW DID WE END UP HERE?
Yay!♡
I haven't been to your place in forever!
MY DAD'S ON A BUSINESS TRIP IN OSAKA, SO WE CAN HAVE DINNER AT MY PLACE AFTER HE COMES BACK!
So tonight...
...LET'S HAVE A SLEEPOVER AT YOUR PLACE!
I SUGGESTED A SLEEP-OVER.
TUP
I SUGGESTED TODAY.
I CAN'T MAKE HER GO HOME NOW.
TUP
CHIKA HAS SLEPT OVER BEFORE.
I DON'T MIND HER STAYING THE NIGHT...
...EXCEPT FOR ONE BIG PROBLEM.
OH, HASKI!

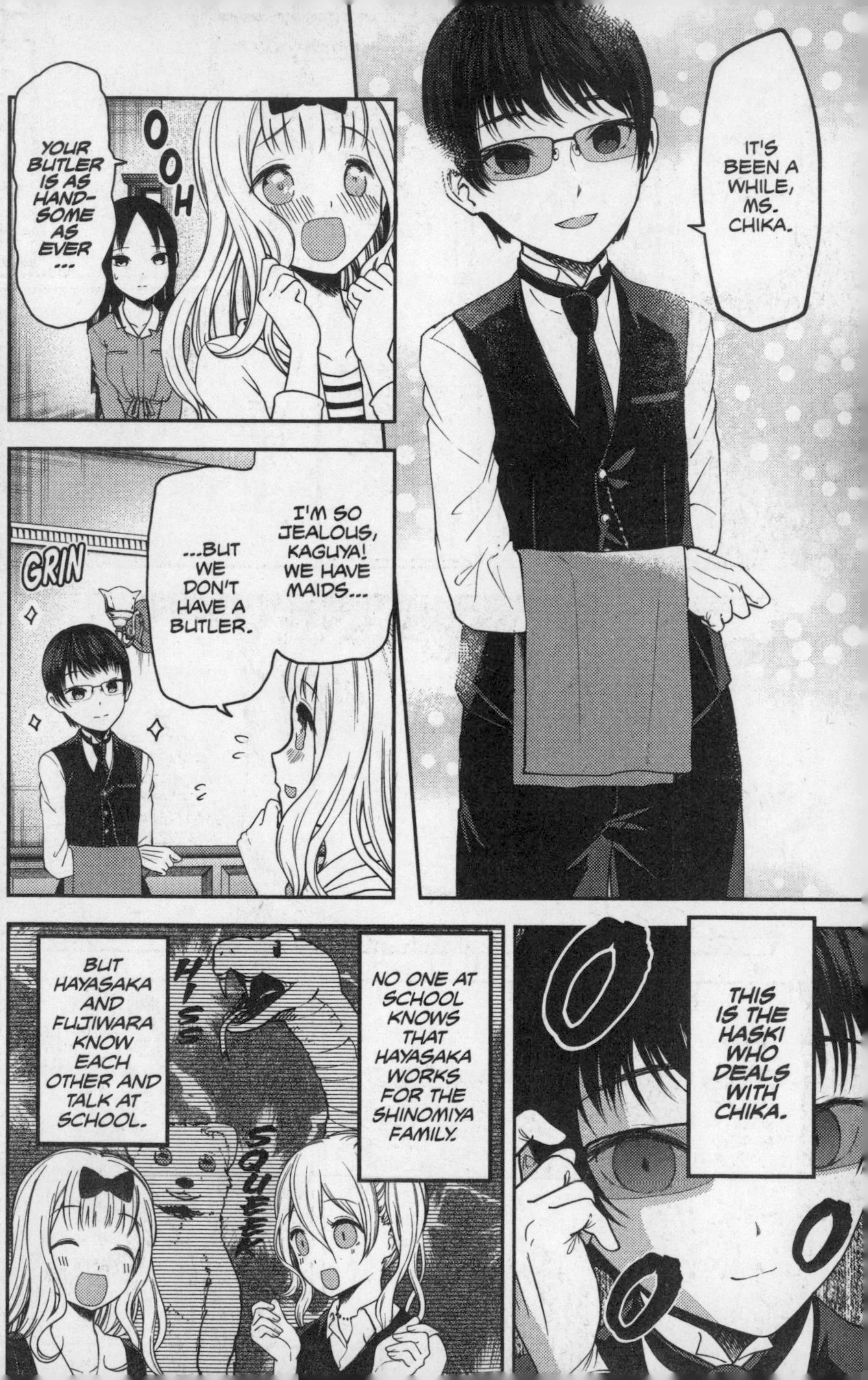
IT'S BEEN A WHILE, MS. CHIKA.
OOH
YOUR BUTLER IS AS HANDSOME AS EVER...
I'M SO JEALOUS, KAGUYA! WE HAVE MAIDS...
...BUT WE DON'T HAVE A BUTLER.
GRIN
THIS IS THE HASKI WHO DEALS WITH CHIKA.
NO ONE AT SCHOOL KNOWS THAT HAYASAKA WORKS FOR THE SHINOMIYA FAMILY.
BUT HAYASAKA AND FUJIWARA KNOW EACH OTHER AND TALK AT SCHOOL.
HISS
SQUEEK

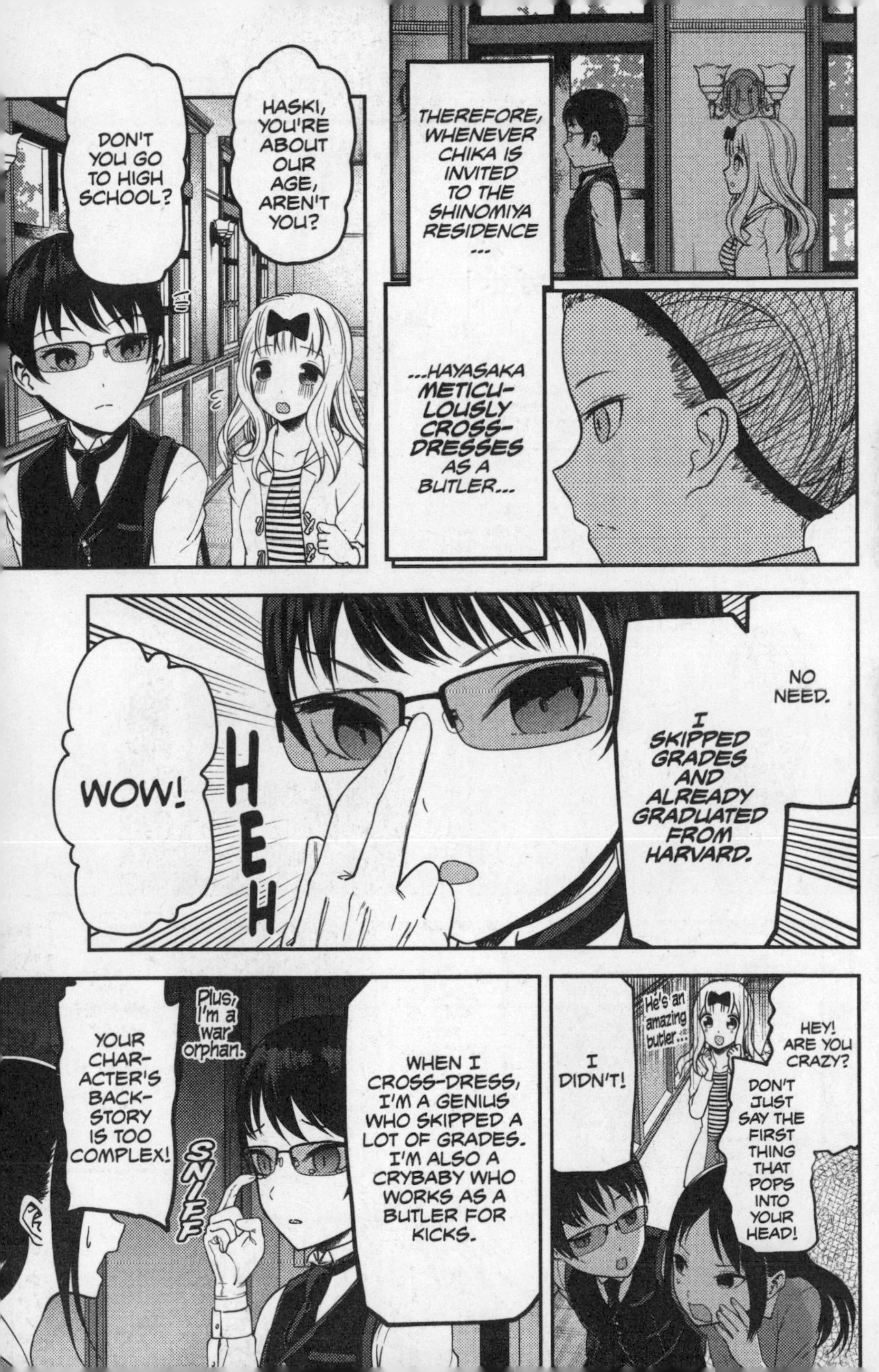
THEREFORE, WHENEVER CHIKA IS INVITED TO THE SHINOMIYA RESIDENCE ...
...HAYASAKA METICULOUSLY CROSS-DRESSES AS A BUTLER...
HASKI, YOU'RE ABOUT OUR AGE, AREN'T YOU?
DON'T YOU GO TO HIGH SCHOOL?
NO NEED.
I SKIPPED GRADES AND ALREADY GRADUATED FROM HARVARD.
HEH
WOW!
HEY! ARE YOU CRAZY?
DON'T JUST SAY THE FIRST THING THAT POPS INTO YOUR HEAD!
He's an amazing butler...
I DIDN'T!
WHEN I CROSS-DRESS, I'M A GENIUS WHO SKIPPED A LOT OF GRADES. I'M ALSO A CRYBABY WHO WORKS AS A BUTLER FOR KICKS.
Plus, I'm a war orphan.
SNIFF
YOUR CHARACTER'S BACKSTORY IS TOO COMPLEX!

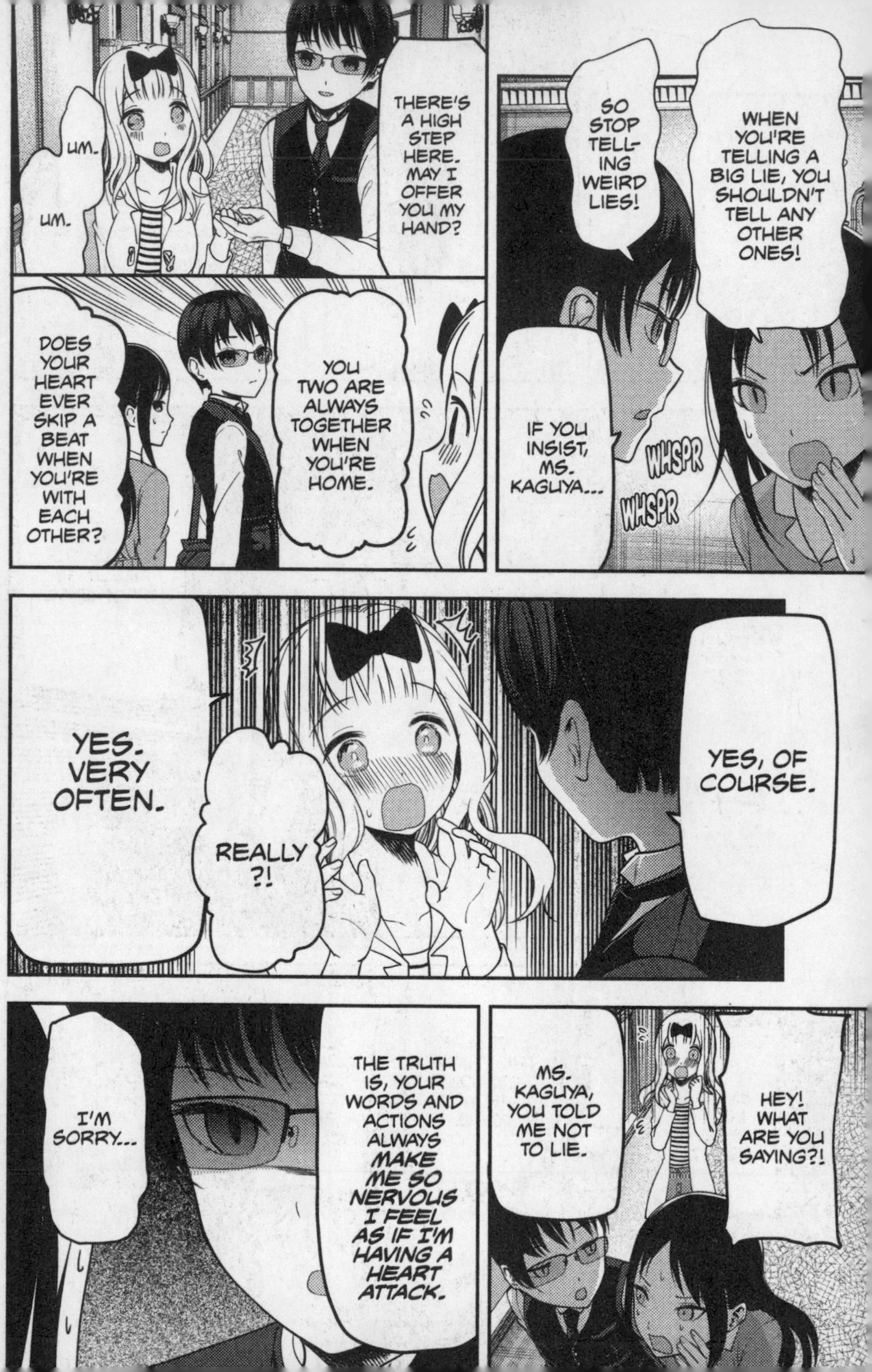
WHEN YOU'RE TELLING A BIG LIE, YOU SHOULDN'T TELL ANY OTHER ONES!
SO STOP TELLING WEIRD LIES!
IF YOU INSIST, MS. KAGUYA...
WHSPR
WHSPR
THERE'S A HIGH STEP HERE. MAY I OFFER YOU MY HAND?
UM.
UM.
YOU TWO ARE ALWAYS TOGETHER WHEN YOU'RE HOME.
DOES YOUR HEART EVER SKIP A BEAT WHEN YOU'RE WITH EACH OTHER?
YES, OF COURSE.
REALLY?!
YES. VERY OFTEN.
HEY! WHAT ARE YOU SAYING?!
MS. KAGUYA, YOU TOLD ME NOT TO LIE.
THE TRUTH IS, YOUR WORDS AND ACTIONS ALWAYS *MAKE ME SO NERVOUS I FEEL AS IF I'M HAVING A HEART ATTACK.*
I'M SORRY...

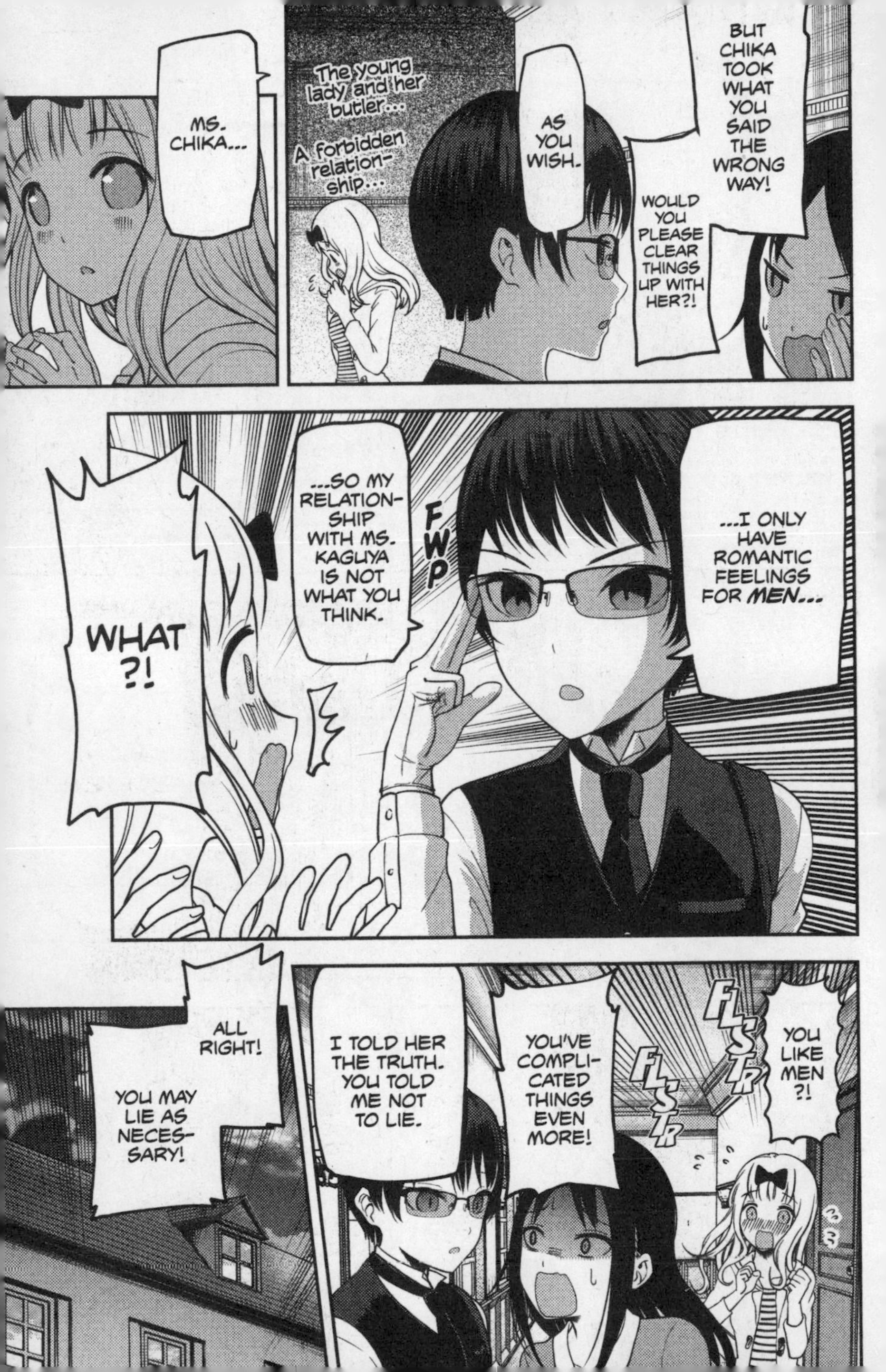
BUT CHIKA TOOK WHAT YOU SAID THE WRONG WAY!
WOULD YOU PLEASE CLEAR THINGS UP WITH HER?!
AS YOU WISH.
The young lady and her butler...
A forbidden relationship...
MS. CHIKA...
...I ONLY HAVE ROMANTIC FEELINGS FOR MEN...
FWP
...SO MY RELATIONSHIP WITH MS. KAGUYA IS NOT WHAT YOU THINK.
WHAT ?!
YOU LIKE MEN ?!
FLSTR
FLSTR
YOU'VE COMPLICATED THINGS EVEN MORE!
I TOLD HER THE TRUTH. YOU TOLD ME NOT TO LIE.
ALL RIGHT!
YOU MAY LIE AS NECESSARY!

THE EVENING PASSES WITHOUT FURTHER INCIDENT.

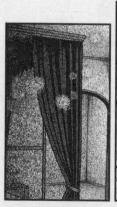

AND THEN IT'S *PAJAMA* PARTY TIME!

GULP

IS THAT SO?

...I FEEL LIKE SOMETHING'S UP WITH THE GUYS!

...AND THAT'S WHY...

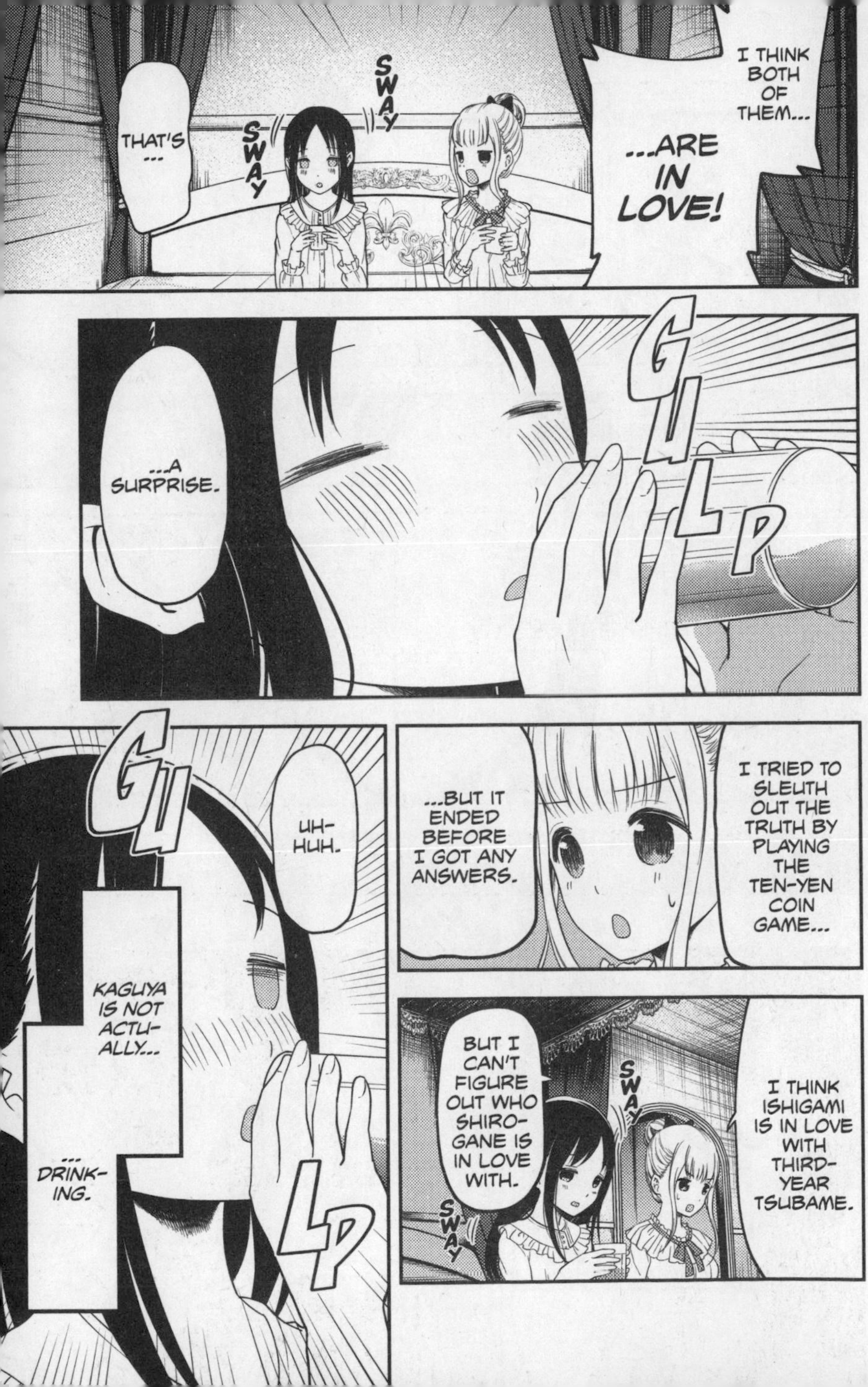
I THINK BOTH OF THEM...
...ARE IN LOVE!
SWAY
SWAY
THAT'S ...
GULP
...A SURPRISE.
I TRIED TO SLEUTH OUT THE TRUTH BY PLAYING THE TEN-YEN COIN GAME...
...BUT IT ENDED BEFORE I GOT ANY ANSWERS.
I THINK ISHIGAMI IS IN LOVE WITH THIRD-YEAR TSUBAME.
SWAY
BUT I CAN'T FIGURE OUT WHO SHIRO-GANE IS IN LOVE WITH.
SWAY
UH-HUH.
GULP
KAGUYA IS NOT ACTU-ALLY...
...DRINK-ING.

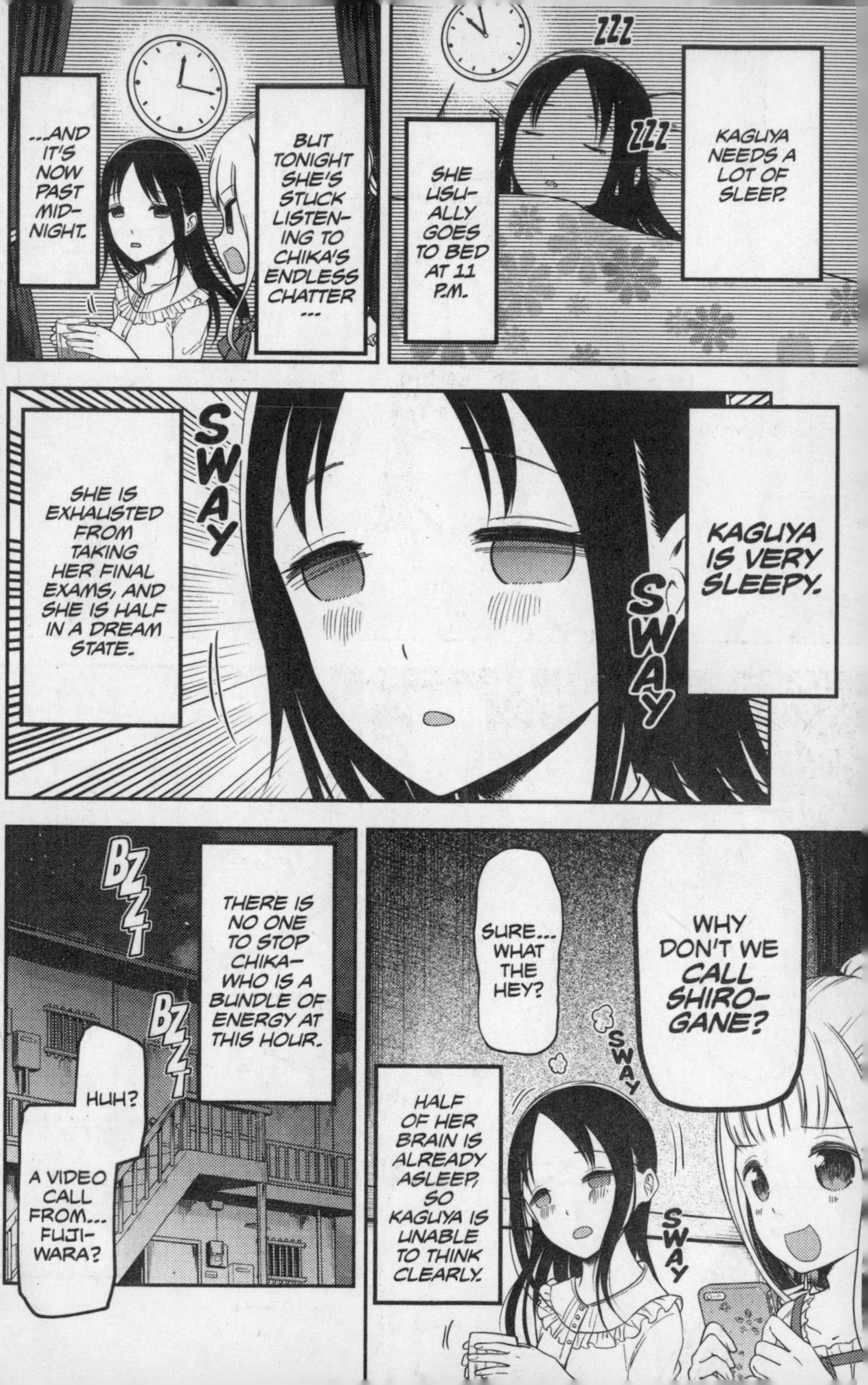
ZZZ
KAGUYA NEEDS A LOT OF SLEEP.
ZZZ
SHE USUALLY GOES TO BED AT 11 P.M.
BUT TONIGHT SHE'S STUCK LISTENING TO CHIKA'S ENDLESS CHATTER...
...AND IT'S NOW PAST MIDNIGHT.
KAGUYA IS VERY SLEEPY.
SWAY
SWAY
SHE IS EXHAUSTED FROM TAKING HER FINAL EXAMS, AND SHE IS HALF IN A DREAM STATE.
WHY DON'T WE CALL SHIROGANE?
SURE... WHAT THE HEY?
SWAY
HALF OF HER BRAIN IS ALREADY ASLEEP, SO KAGUYA IS UNABLE TO THINK CLEARLY.
SWAY
BZZT
THERE IS NO ONE TO STOP CHIKA—WHO IS A BUNDLE OF ENERGY AT THIS HOUR.
BZZT
HUH?
A VIDEO CALL FROM... FUJIWARA?

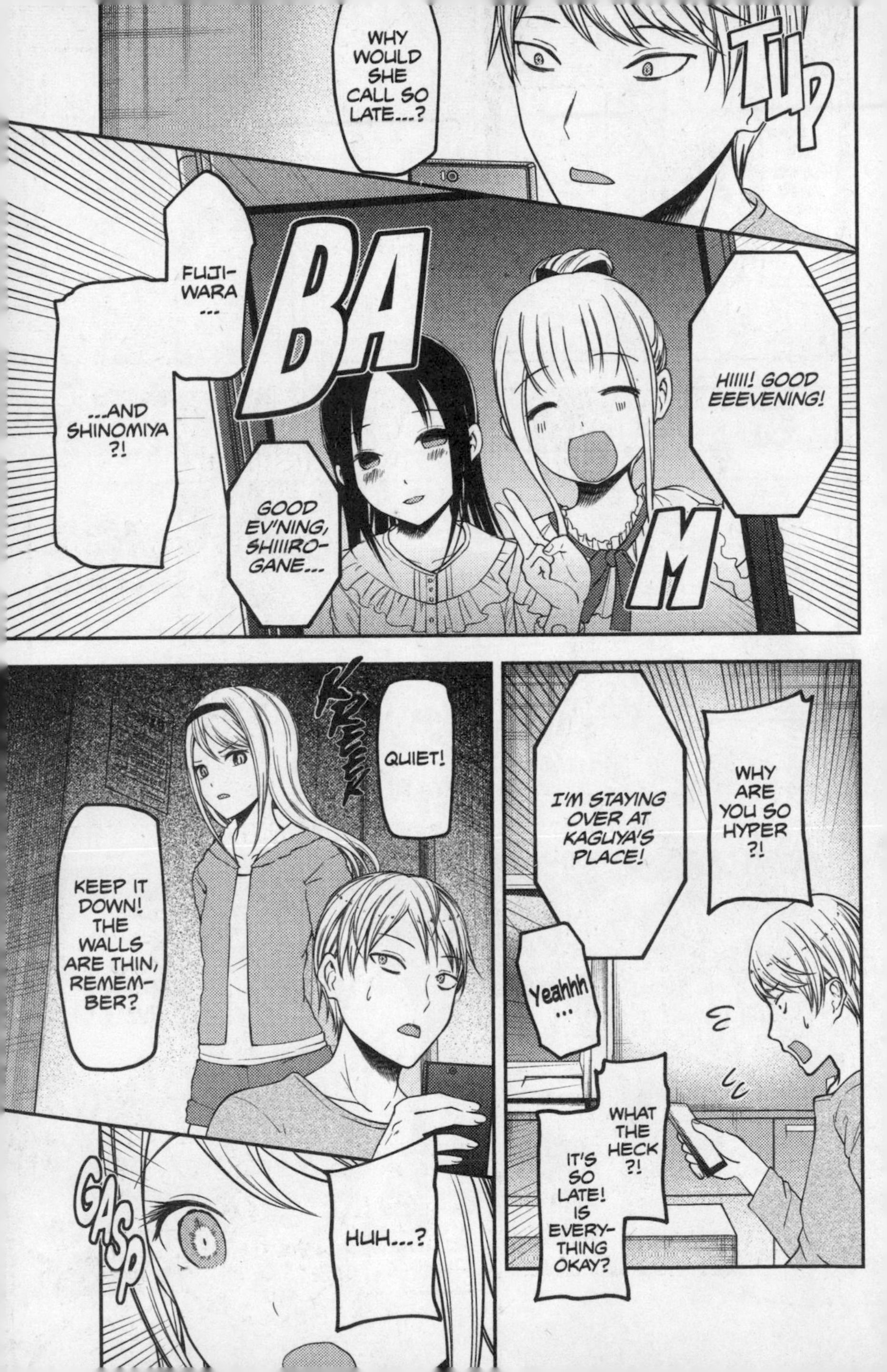
TUP
WHY WOULD SHE CALL SO LATE...?
BAM
HIIII! GOOD EEEVENING!
GOOD EV'NING, SHIIIRO-GANE...
FUJI-WARA...
...AND SHINOMIYA ?!
WHY ARE YOU SO HYPER ?!
I'M STAYING OVER AT KAGUYA'S PLACE!
Yeahhh...
WHAT THE HECK ?!
IT'S SO LATE! IS EVERY-THING OKAY?
QUIET!
KEEP IT DOWN! THE WALLS ARE THIN, REMEM-BER?
GASP
HUH...?

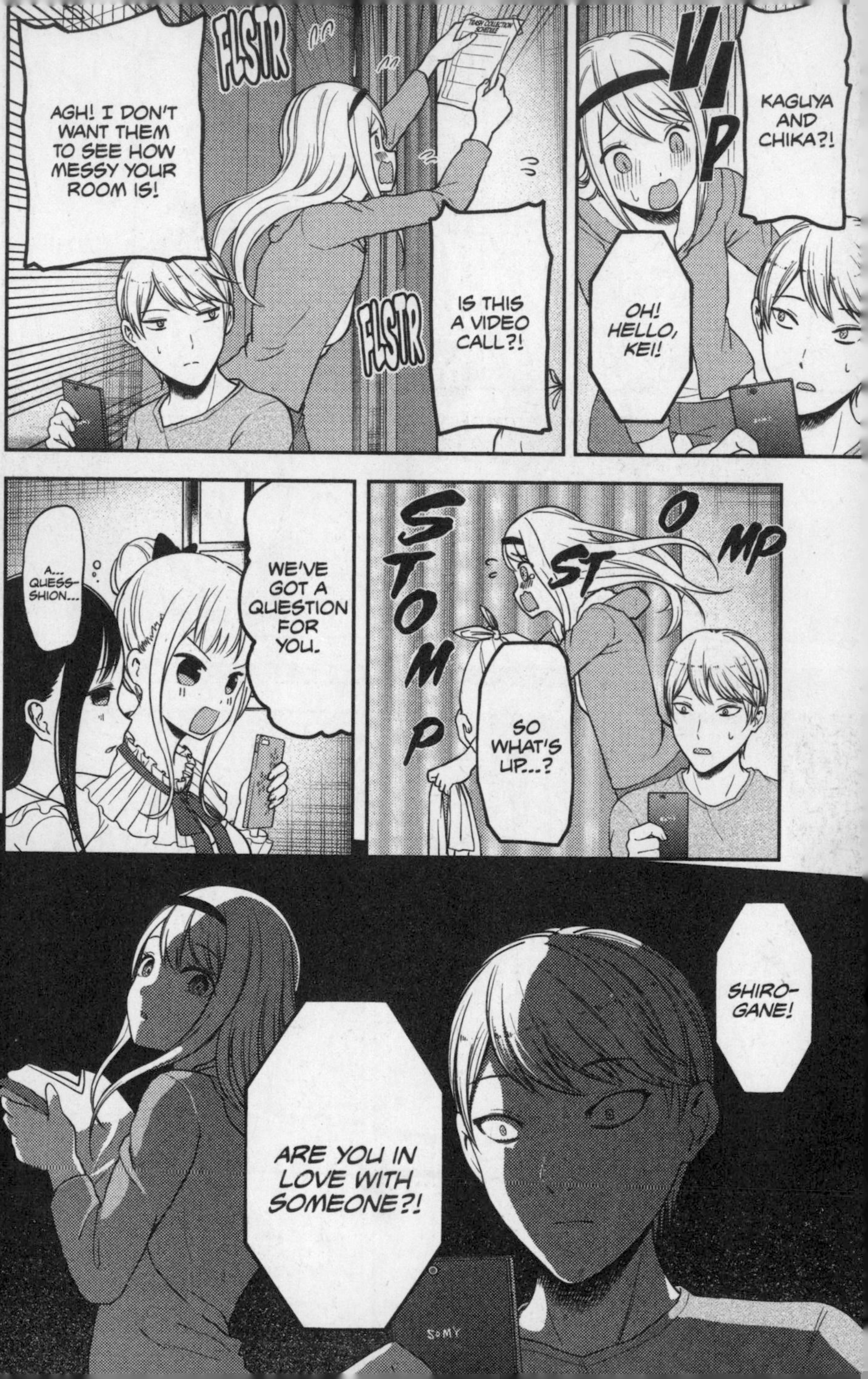
KAGUYA AND CHIKA?!
VIP
OH! HELLO, KEI!
IS THIS A VIDEO CALL?!
FLSTR
AGH! I DON'T WANT THEM TO SEE HOW MESSY YOUR ROOM IS!
FLSTR
TRASH COLLECTION SCHEDULE
STOMP
STOMP
SO WHAT'S UP...?
WE'VE GOT A QUESTION FOR YOU.
A... QUESS-SHION...
SHIRO-GANE!
ARE YOU IN LOVE WITH SOMEONE?!
SOMY

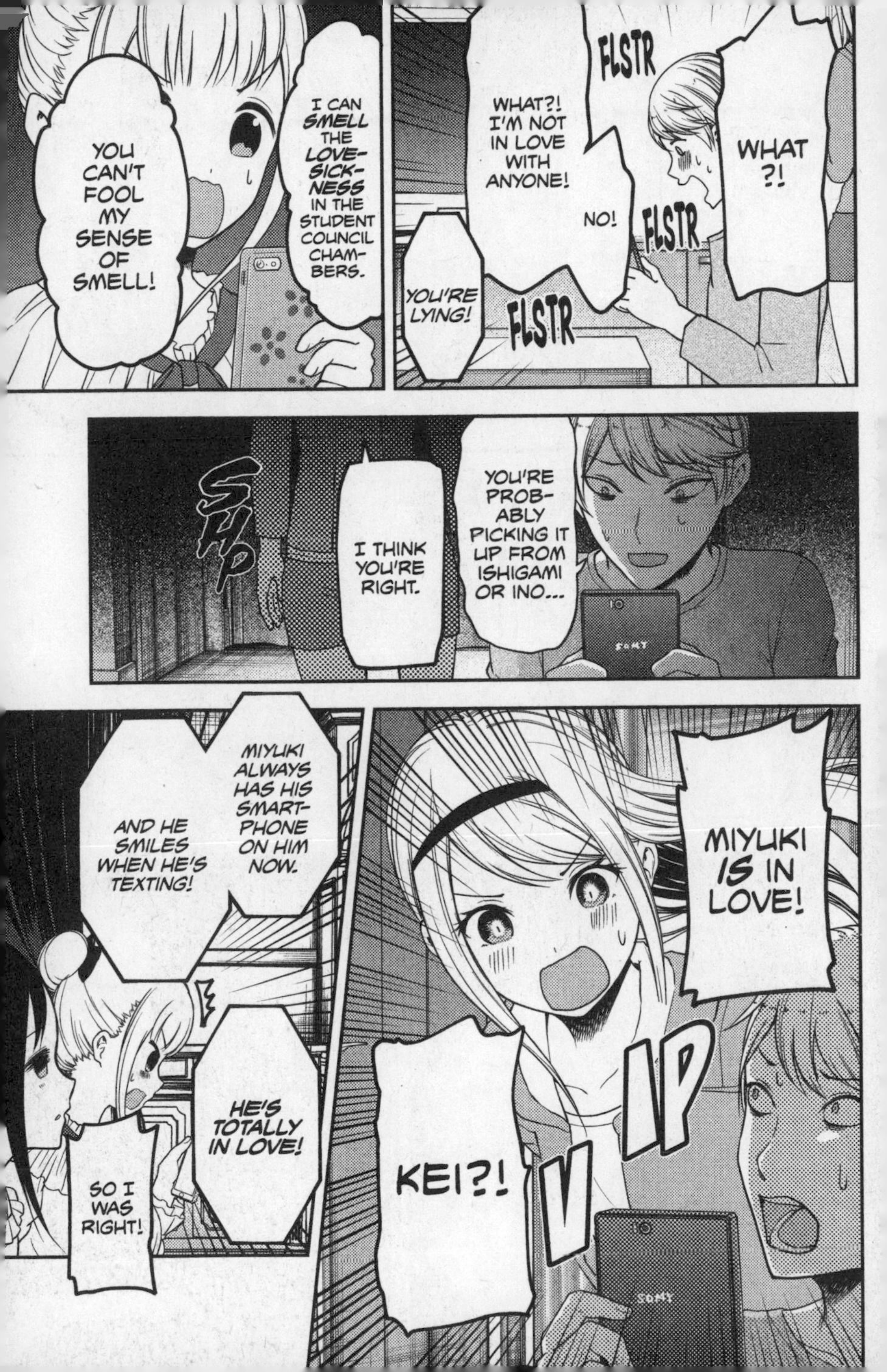
FLSTR
WHAT?!
WHAT?! I'M NOT IN LOVE WITH ANYONE!
NO!
FLSTR
YOU'RE LYING!
FLSTR
I CAN SMELL THE LOVE-SICKNESS IN THE STUDENT COUNCIL CHAMBERS.
YOU CAN'T FOOL MY SENSE OF SMELL!
YOU'RE PROBABLY PICKING IT UP FROM ISHIGAMI OR INO...
I THINK YOU'RE RIGHT.
SHP
MIYUKI IS IN LOVE!
VIP
KEI?!
MIYUKI ALWAYS HAS HIS SMARTPHONE ON HIM NOW.
AND HE SMILES WHEN HE'S TEXTING!
HE'S TOTALLY IN LOVE!
SO I WAS RIGHT!

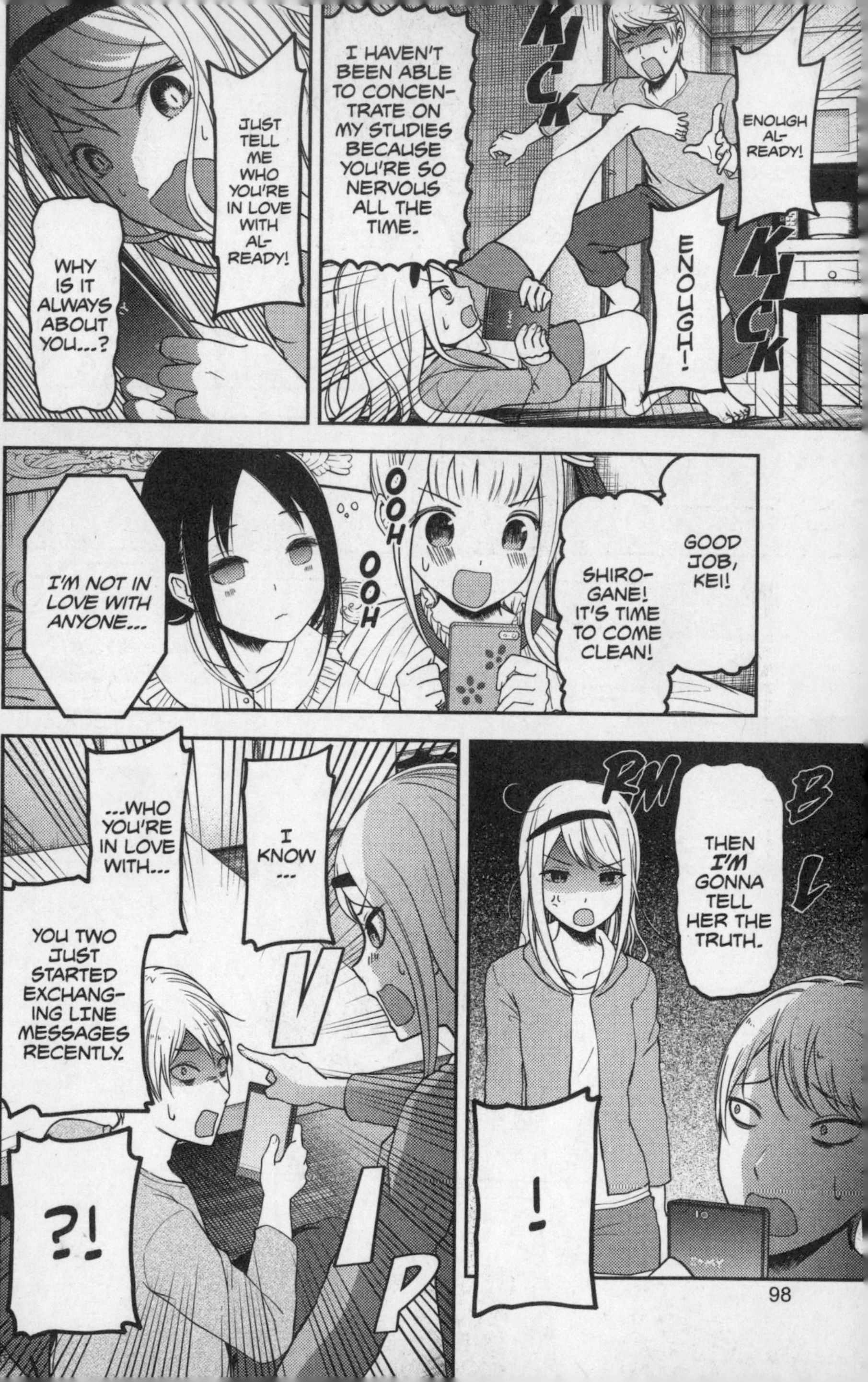
ENOUGH AL-READY!
KICK
I HAVEN'T BEEN ABLE TO CONCEN-TRATE ON MY STUDIES BECAUSE YOU'RE SO NERVOUS ALL THE TIME.
ENOUGH!
KICK
JUST TELL ME WHO YOU'RE IN LOVE WITH AL-READY!
WHY IS IT ALWAYS ABOUT YOU...?
GOOD JOB, KEI!
SHIRO-GANE! IT'S TIME TO COME CLEAN!
OOOH
OOOH
I'M NOT IN LOVE WITH ANYONE...
RMBL
THEN I'M GONNA TELL HER THE TRUTH.
!
I KNOW...
...WHO YOU'RE IN LOVE WITH...
YOU TWO JUST STARTED EXCHANG-ING LINE MESSAGES RECENTLY.
VIP
?!

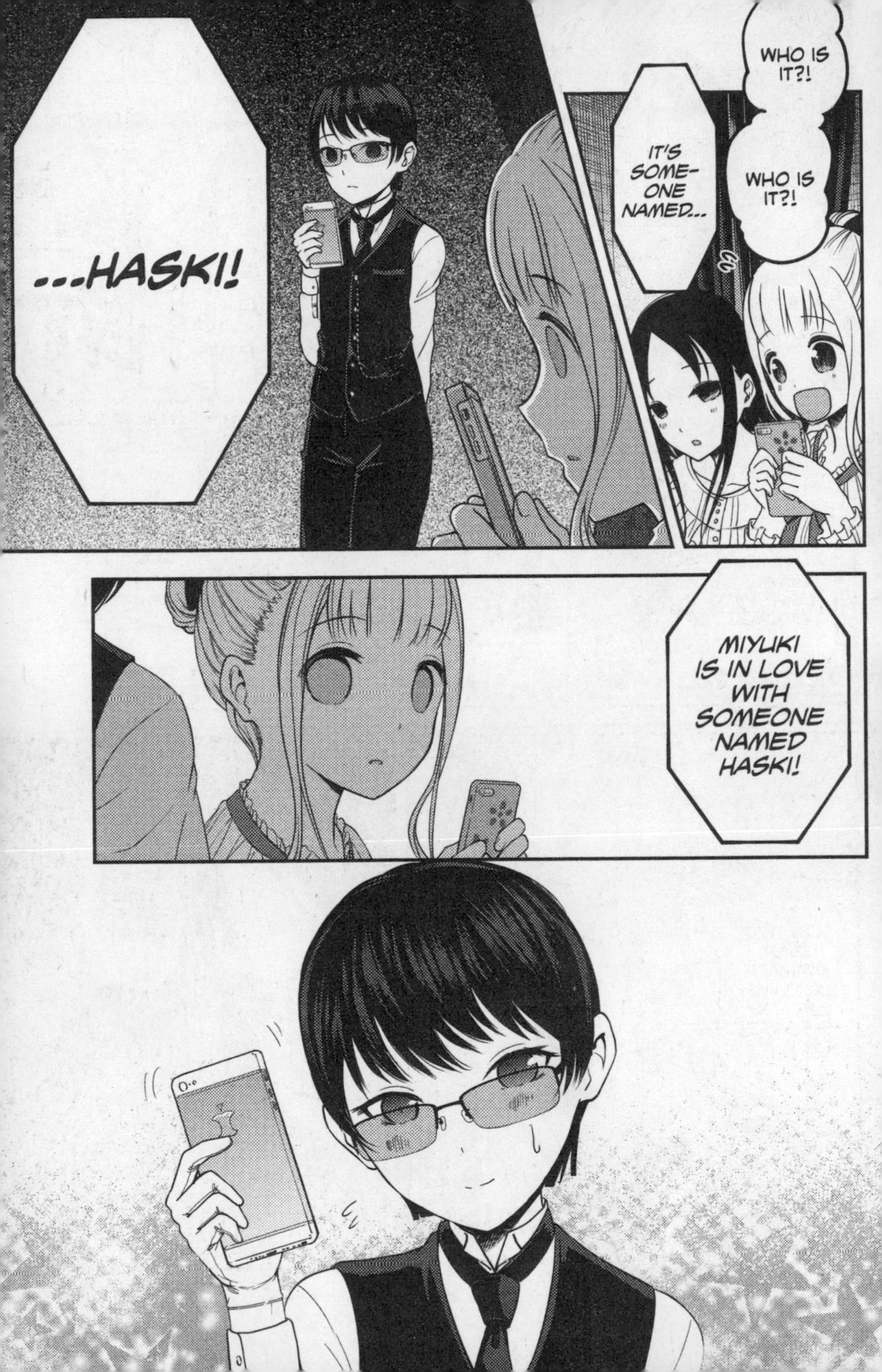
WHO IS IT?!
WHO IS IT?!
IT'S SOME-ONE NAMED...
...HASKI!
MIYUKI IS IN LOVE WITH SOMEONE NAMED HASKI!

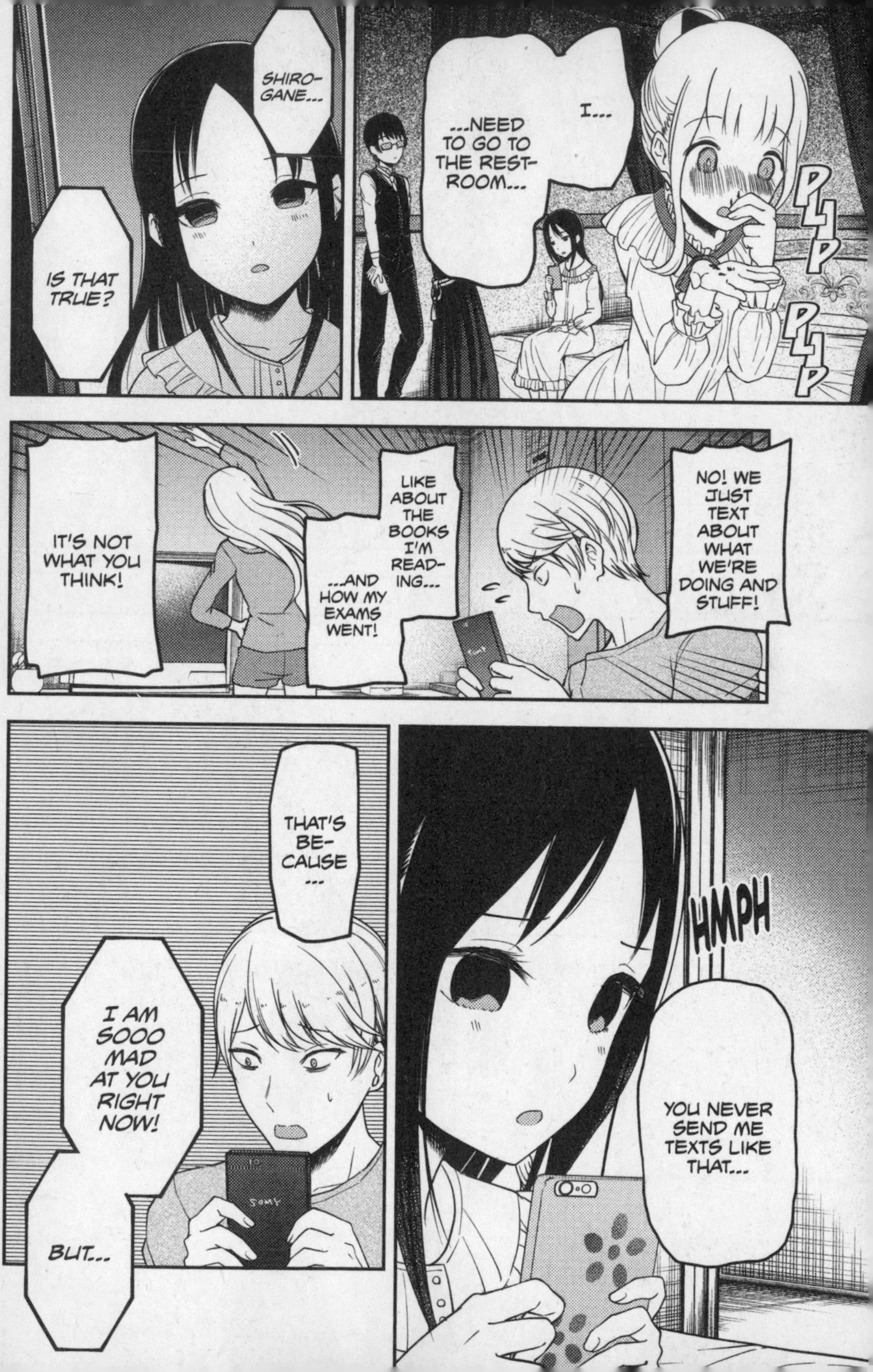
I...
...NEED TO GO TO THE REST-ROOM...
PLIP
PLIP
PLIP
SHIRO-GANE...
IS THAT TRUE?
NO! WE JUST TEXT ABOUT WHAT WE'RE DOING AND STUFF!
LIKE ABOUT THE BOOKS I'M READ-ING...
...AND HOW MY EXAMS WENT!
IT'S NOT WHAT YOU THINK!
HMPH
YOU NEVER SEND ME TEXTS LIKE THAT...
THAT'S BE-CAUSE...
I AM SOOO MAD AT YOU RIGHT NOW!
BUT...

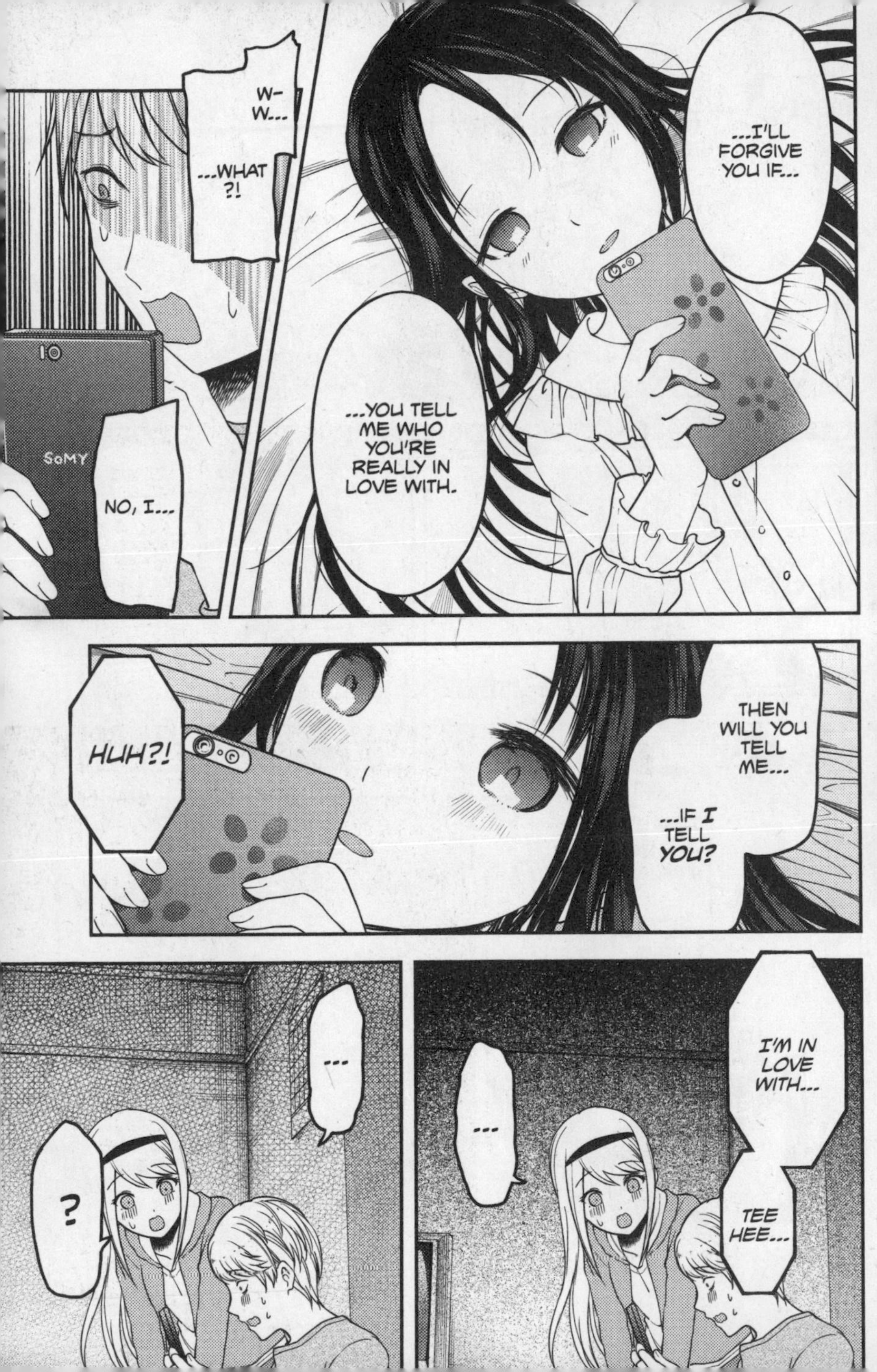
...I'LL FORGIVE YOU IF...
...YOU TELL ME WHO YOU'RE REALLY IN LOVE WITH.
W- W...
...WHAT?!
SoMY
NO, I...
THEN WILL YOU TELL ME...
...IF I TELL YOU?
HUH?!
I'M IN LOVE WITH...
TEE HEE...
...
...
?

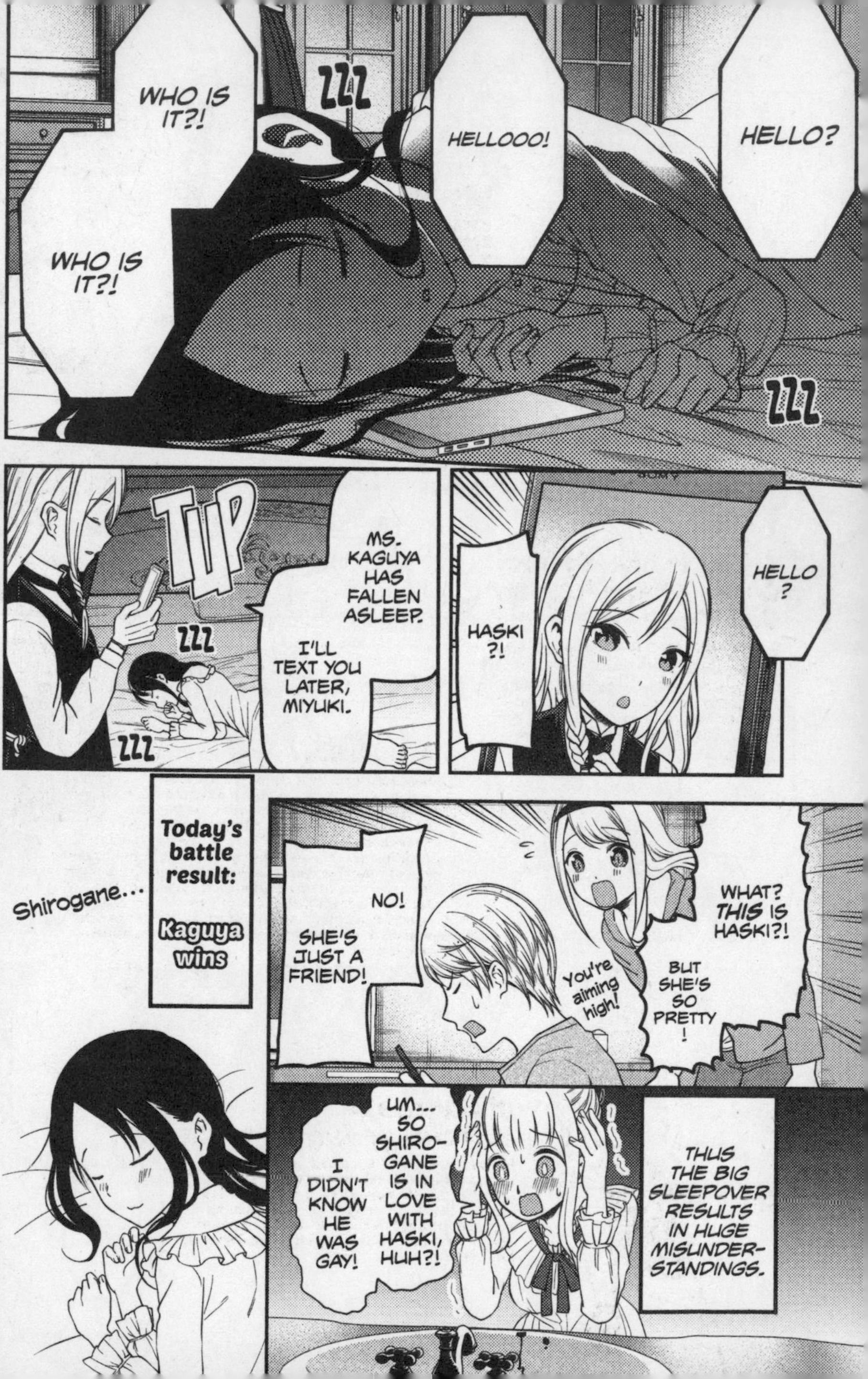
HELLO?
HELLOOO!
ZZZ
WHO IS IT?!
WHO IS IT?!
ZZZ
HELLO?
HASKI?!
MS. KAGUYA HAS FALLEN ASLEEP.
I'LL TEXT YOU LATER, MIYUKI.
TUP
ZZZ
ZZZ
WHAT? THIS IS HASKI?!
BUT SHE'S SO PRETTY!
You're aiming high!
NO!
SHE'S JUST A FRIEND!
THUS THE BIG SLEEPOVER RESULTS IN HUGE MISUNDER-STANDINGS.
UM... SO SHIRO-GANE IS IN LOVE WITH HASKI, HUH?!
I DIDN'T KNOW HE WAS GAY!
Today's battle result:
Kaguya wins
Shirogane...

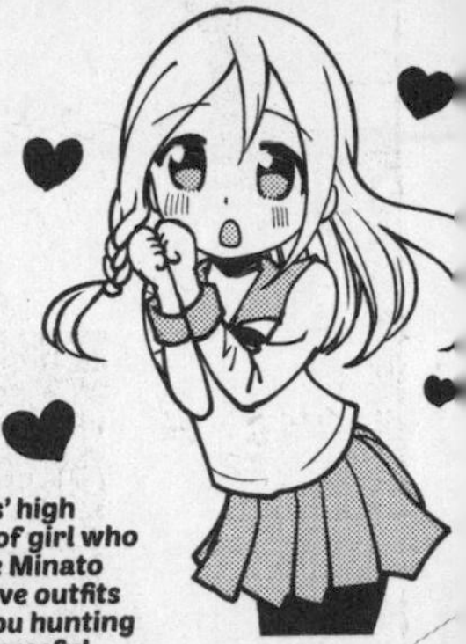

Ms. Haski

A well-bred daughter who lives in Yamate, Naka Ward, Yokohama City.

Her backstory: *Bored at her all-girls' high school, she pretends to be the type of girl who lives in the extravagantly expensive Minato Ward of Tokyo, dressing in suggestive outfits and frequenting Roppongi and Azabu hunting for men. Her exploits have been successful. Currently, she wants her relationship with a man she just met to get serious.*

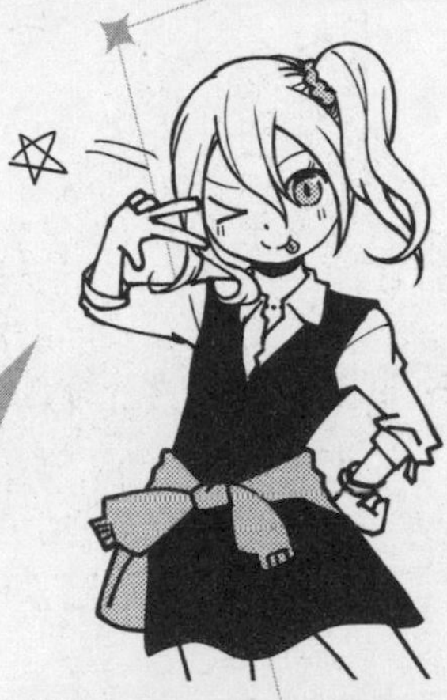

Ai Hayasaka: School Camouflage Popular Girl Mode

A lively girl who loves fashion and breaking school rules.

Her backstory: *She works part-time to buy clothes and accessories. She's so busy she doesn't have time for fun with friends. She has never dated anyone.*

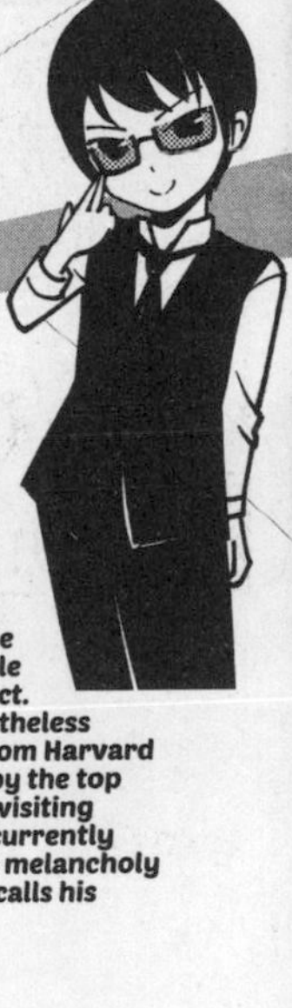

Mr. Haski

His backstory: *He is the descendant of an Irish family that emigrated during the potato famine and ended up in the Middle East. His parents died in a military conflict. He wound up in an orphanage but nevertheless excelled academically and graduated from Harvard in less than four years. He was scouted by the top brass of a business conglomerate while visiting Japan, his grandfather's homeland. He currently works as a butler, mostly for a lark. He's melancholy and dissolves into tears whenever he recalls his tragic past...*

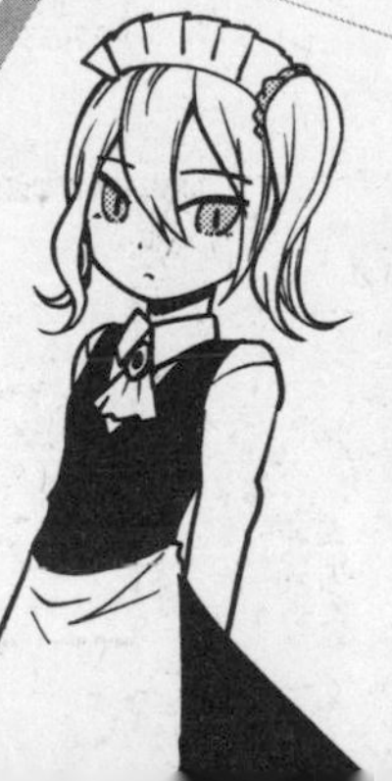

Ai Hayasaka: Shinomiya Family Mode

Her backstory: *She is a levelheaded maid who performs all her duties impeccably. She sometimes rebels against her mistress's self-centeredness. She talks back to her mistress but also showers her with love and affection. The two are more like sisters than mistress and servant.*

KAGUYA-SAMA
LOVE IS WAR

Battle 107
Chika Fujiwara Wants to Beat a Rhythm

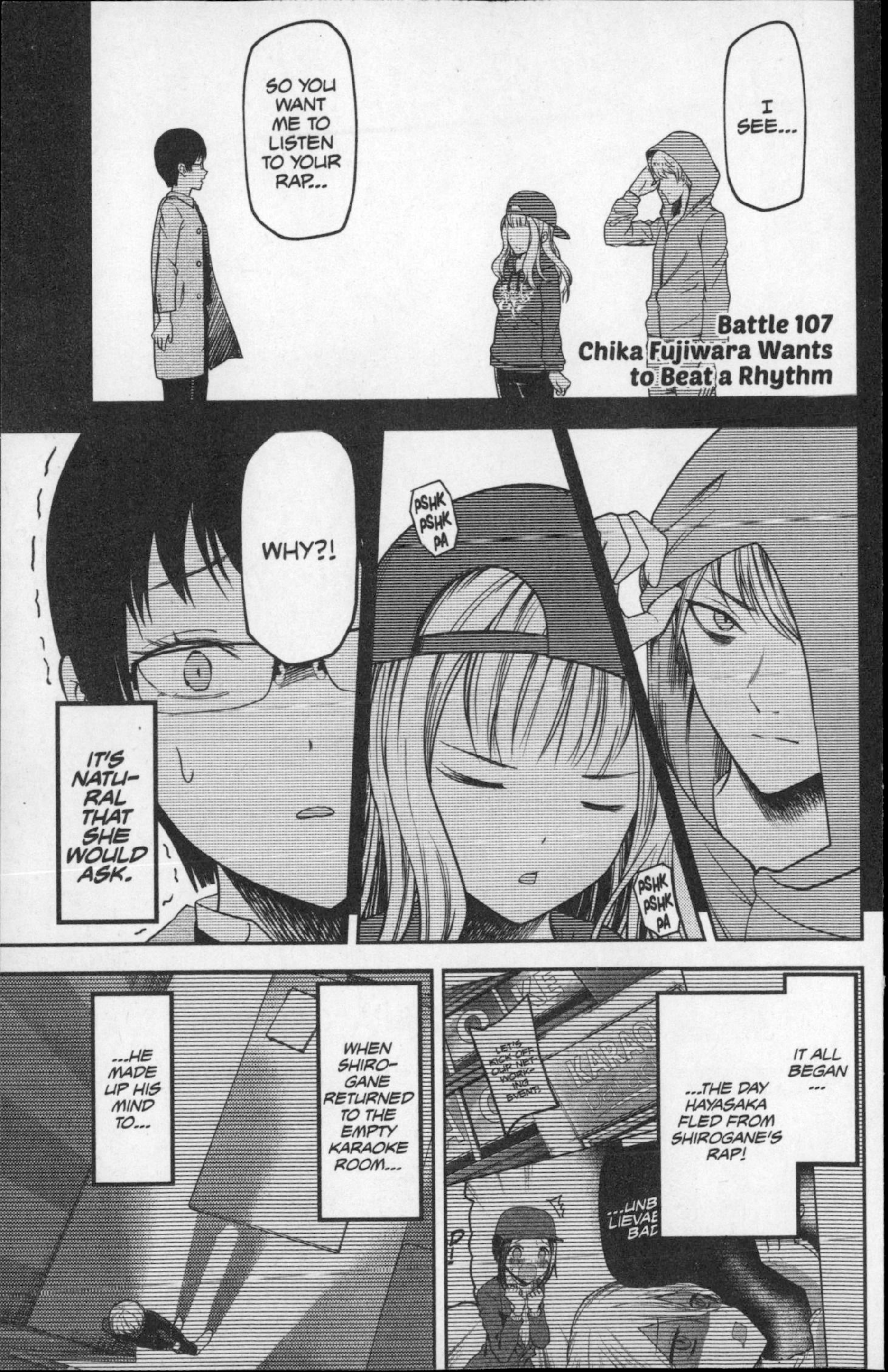
I SEE...
SO YOU WANT ME TO LISTEN TO YOUR RAP...
PSHK PSHK PA
PSHK PSHK PA
WHY?!
IT'S NATURAL THAT SHE WOULD ASK.
IT ALL BEGAN...
...THE DAY HAYASAKA FLED FROM SHIROGANE'S RAP!
LET'S KICK OFF OUR NETWORKING EVENT!
WHEN SHIROGANE RETURNED TO THE EMPTY KARAOKE ROOM...
...HE MADE UP HIS MIND TO...

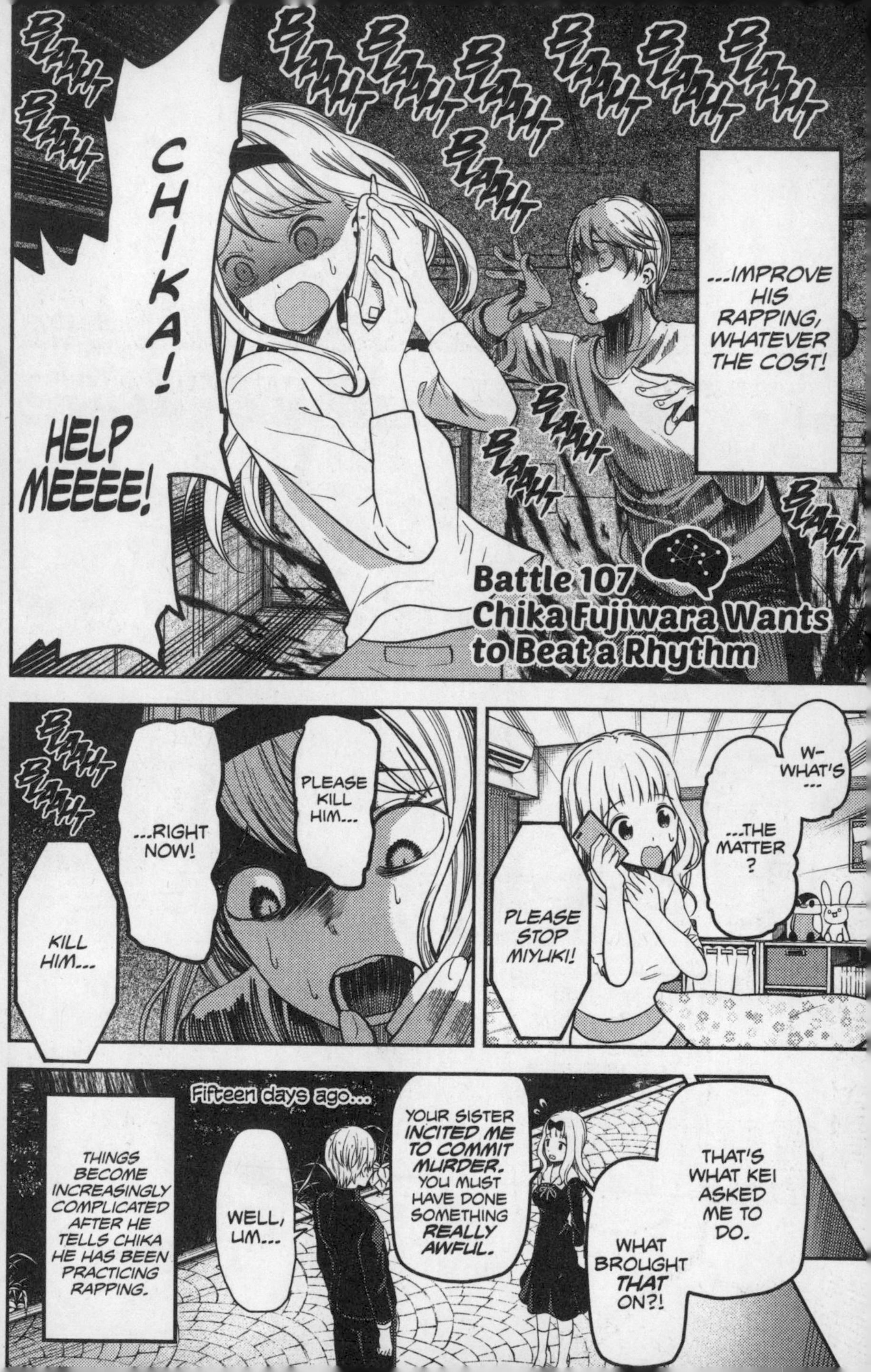
BLAAH BLAAH BLAAH BLAAH BLAAH BLAAH BLAAH
...IMPROVE HIS RAPPING, WHATEVER THE COST!
BLAAH BLAAH
Battle 107 Chika Fujiwara Wants to Beat a Rhythm
BLAAH BLAAH
CHIKA!
HELP MEEEEE!
BLAAH BLAAH
W- WHAT'S...
...THE MATTER?
PLEASE STOP MIYUKI!
PLEASE KILL HIM...
...RIGHT NOW!
KILL HIM...
BLAAH BLAAH
THAT'S WHAT KEI ASKED ME TO DO.
WHAT BROUGHT THAT ON?!
YOUR SISTER INCITED ME TO COMMIT MURDER. YOU MUST HAVE DONE SOMETHING REALLY AWFUL.
Fifteen days ago...
WELL, UM...
THINGS BECOME INCREASINGLY COMPLICATED AFTER HE TELLS CHIKA HE HAS BEEN PRACTICING RAPPING.

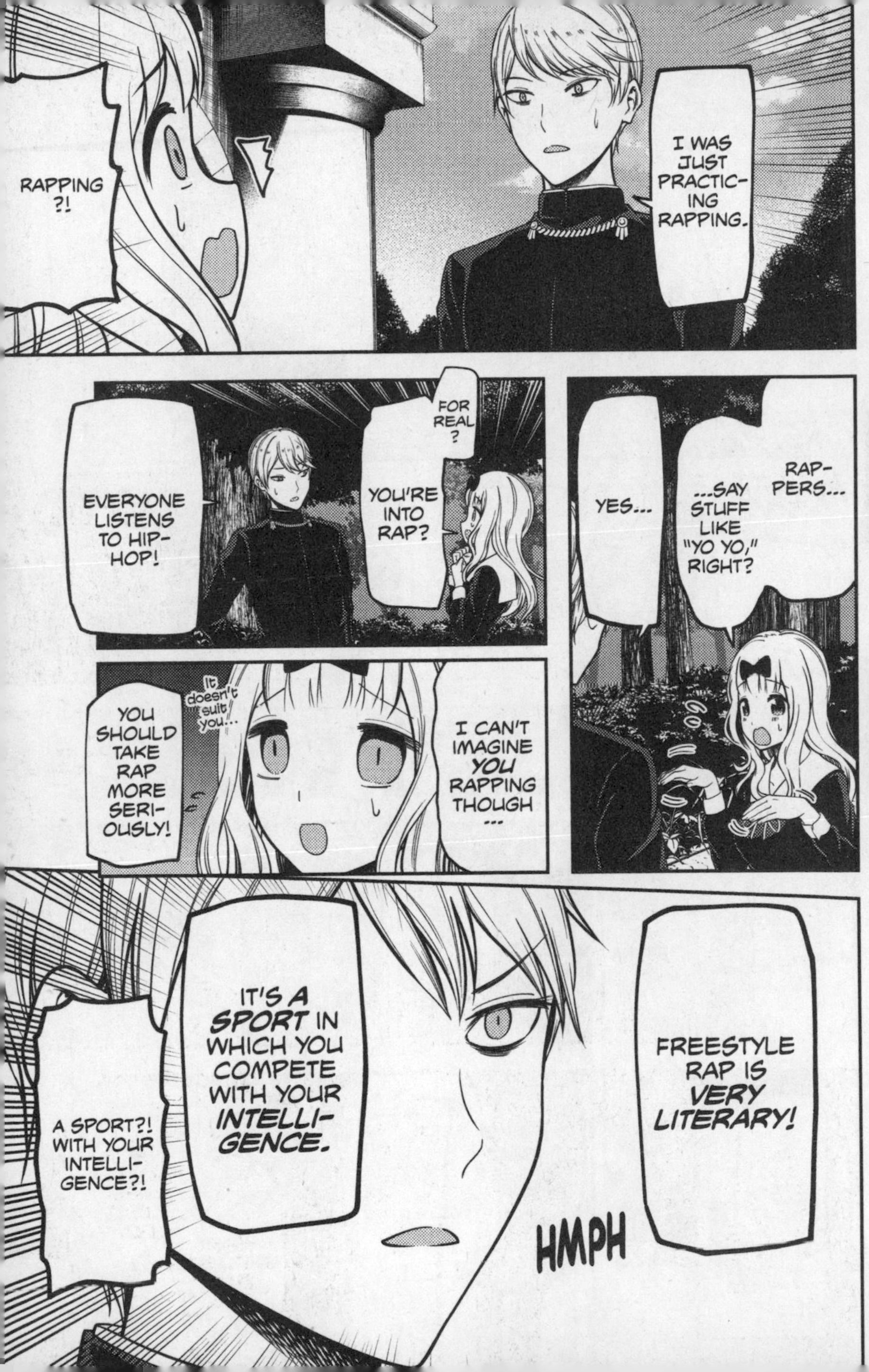
I WAS JUST PRACTICING RAPPING.
RAPPING?!
RAPPERS...
...SAY STUFF LIKE "YO YO," RIGHT?
YES...
FOR REAL?
YOU'RE INTO RAP?
EVERYONE LISTENS TO HIP-HOP!
I CAN'T IMAGINE YOU RAPPING THOUGH...
It doesn't suit you...
YOU SHOULD TAKE RAP MORE SERIOUSLY!
FREESTYLE RAP IS VERY LITERARY!
HMPH
IT'S A SPORT IN WHICH YOU COMPETE WITH YOUR INTELLIGENCE.
A SPORT?! WITH YOUR INTELLIGENCE?!

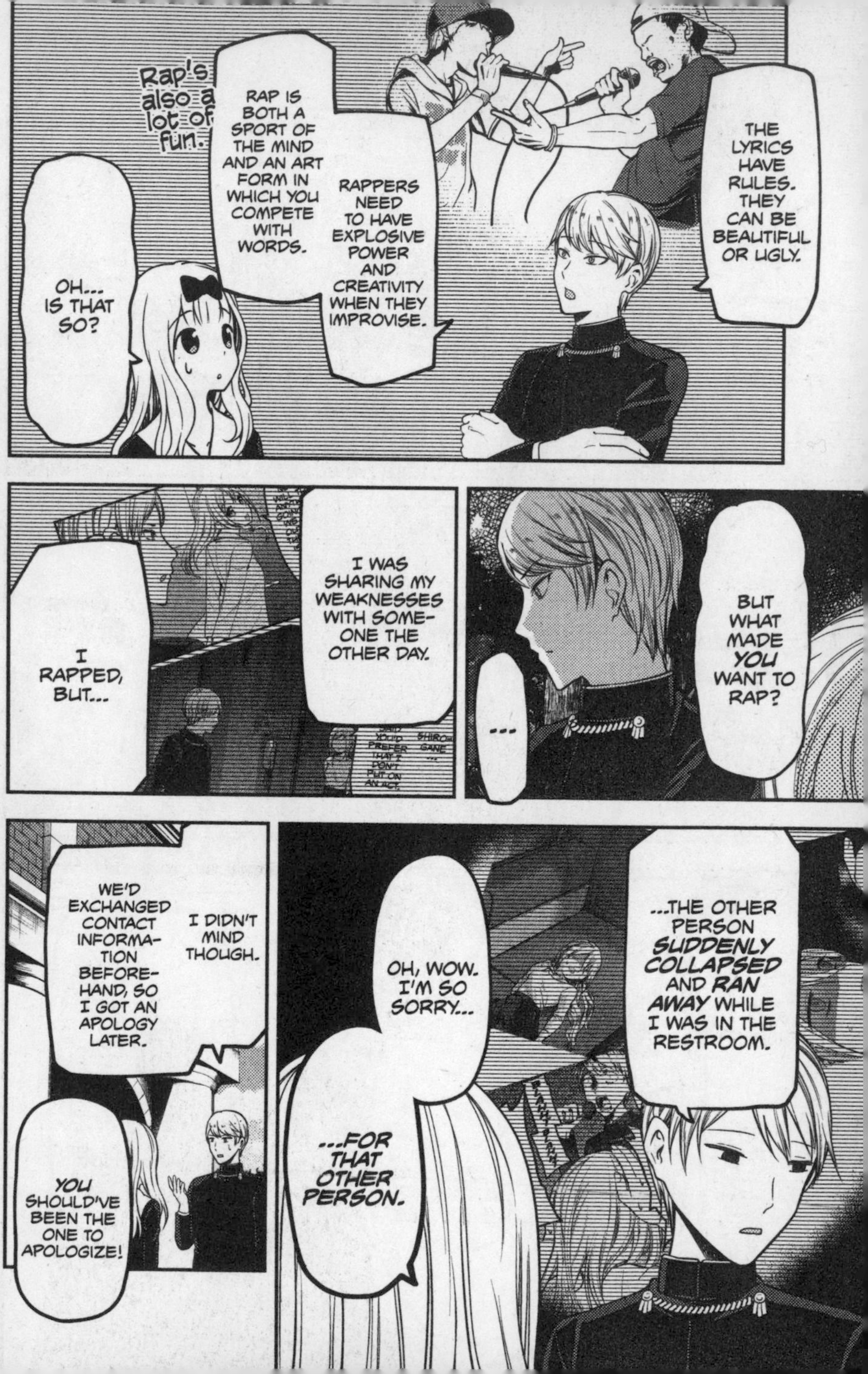
THE LYRICS HAVE RULES. THEY CAN BE BEAUTIFUL OR UGLY.
RAP IS BOTH A SPORT OF THE MIND AND AN ART FORM IN WHICH YOU COMPETE WITH WORDS.
RAPPERS NEED TO HAVE EXPLOSIVE POWER AND CREATIVITY WHEN THEY IMPROVISE.
Rap's also a lot of fun.
OH... IS THAT SO?
BUT WHAT MADE *YOU* WANT TO RAP?
...
I WAS SHARING MY WEAKNESSES WITH SOME-ONE THE OTHER DAY.
SHIRO-GANE...
YOU'D PREFER THAT I DON'T PUT ON AN ACT.
I RAPPED, BUT...
...THE OTHER PERSON *SUDDENLY COLLAPSED* AND *RAN AWAY* WHILE I WAS IN THE RESTROOM.
OH, WOW. I'M SO SORRY...
...FOR THAT OTHER PERSON.
I DIDN'T MIND THOUGH.
WE'D EXCHANGED CONTACT INFORMA-TION BEFORE-HAND, SO I GOT AN APOLOGY LATER.
YOU SHOULD'VE BEEN THE ONE TO APOLOGIZE!

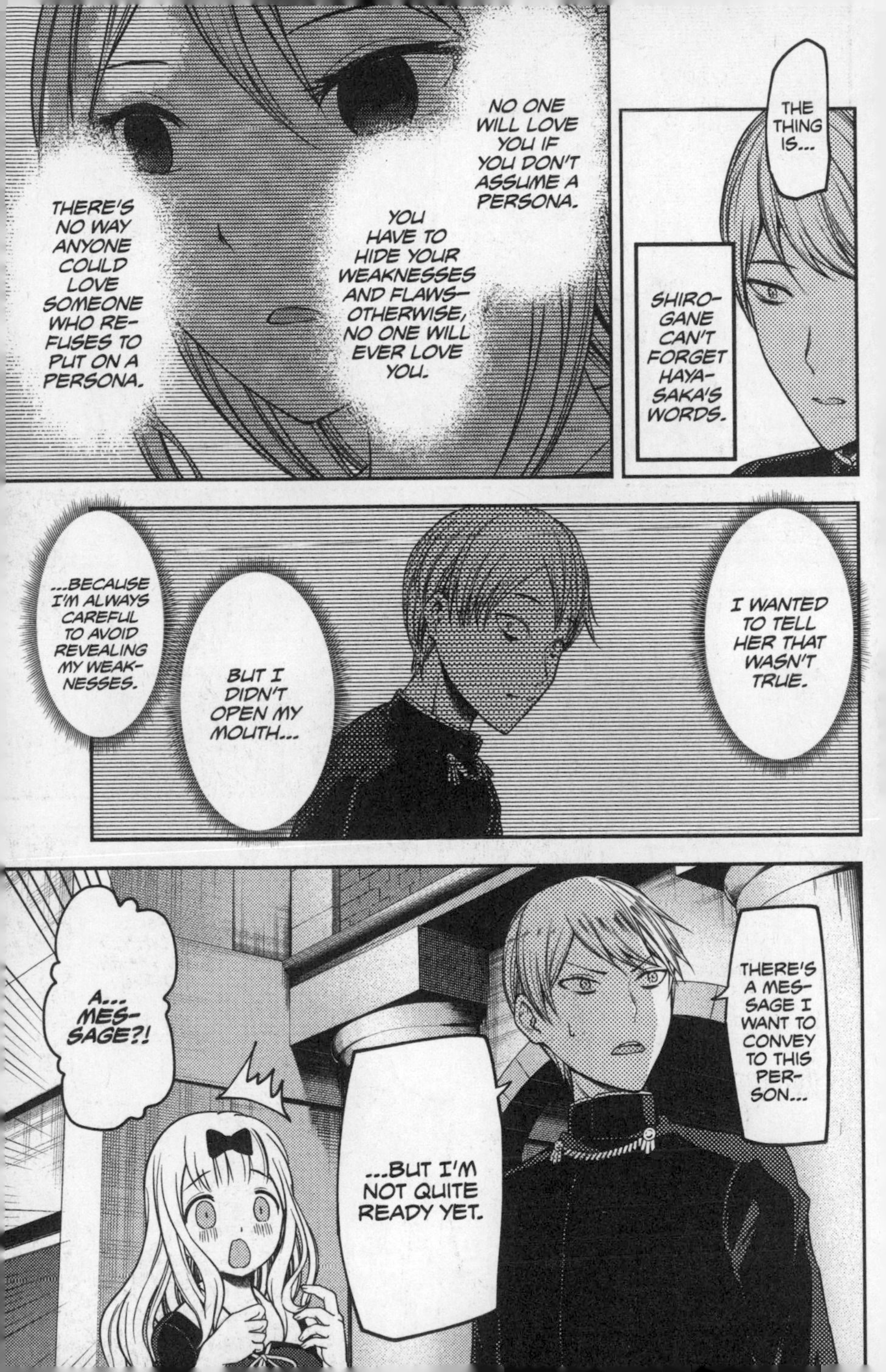
THE THING IS...
SHIRO-GANE CAN'T FORGET HAYA-SAKA'S WORDS.
NO ONE WILL LOVE YOU IF YOU DON'T ASSUME A PERSONA.
YOU HAVE TO HIDE YOUR WEAKNESSES AND FLAWS—OTHERWISE, NO ONE WILL EVER LOVE YOU.
THERE'S NO WAY ANYONE COULD LOVE SOMEONE WHO RE-FUSES TO PUT ON A PERSONA.
I WANTED TO TELL HER THAT WASN'T TRUE.
BUT I DIDN'T OPEN MY MOUTH...
...BECAUSE I'M ALWAYS CAREFUL TO AVOID REVEALING MY WEAK-NESSES.
THERE'S A MES-SAGE I WANT TO CONVEY TO THIS PER-SON...
...BUT I'M NOT QUITE READY YET.
A... MES-SAGE?!

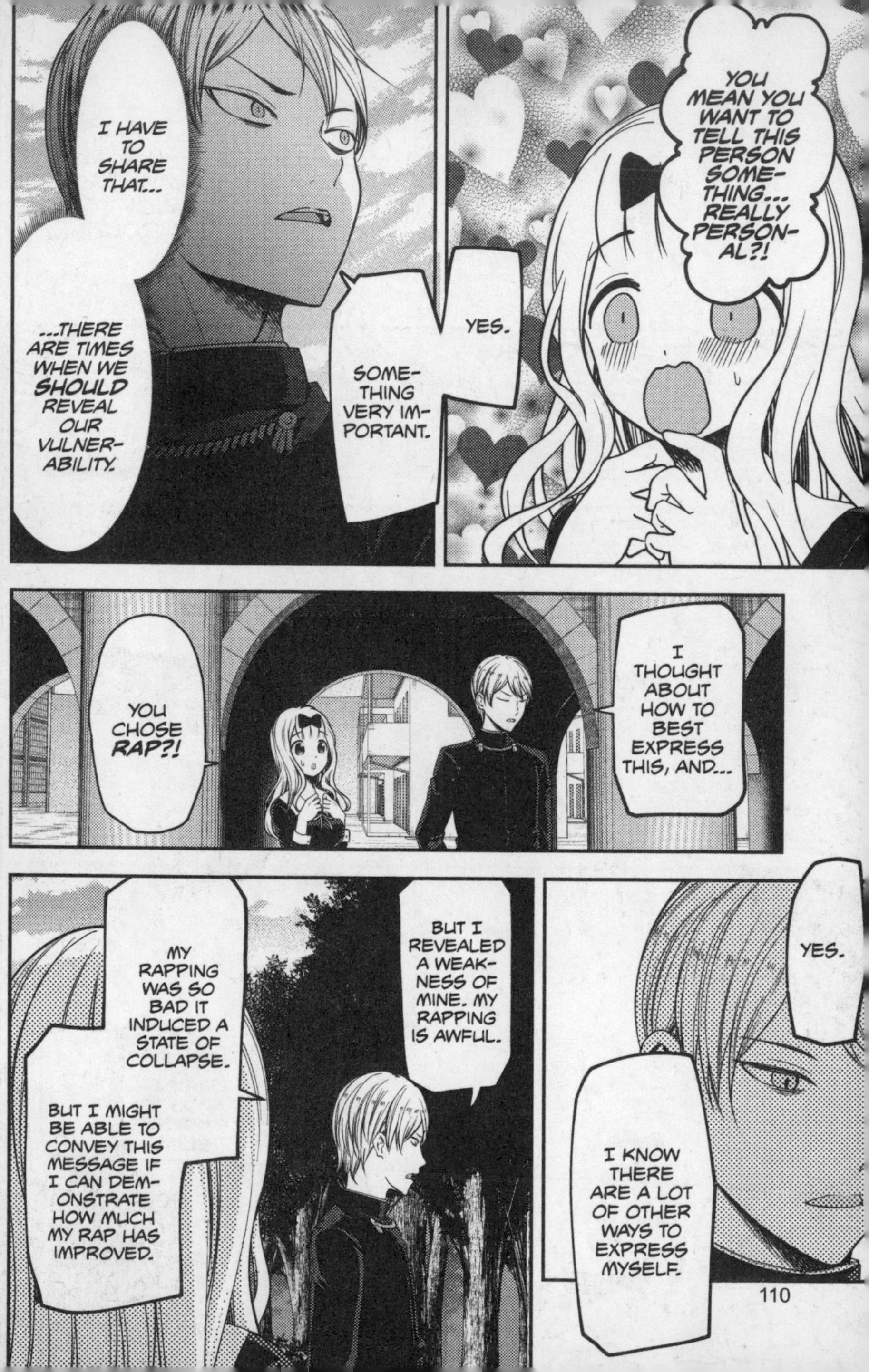
YOU MEAN YOU WANT TO TELL THIS PERSON SOMETHING... REALLY PERSONAL?!
YES.
SOMETHING VERY IMPORTANT.
I HAVE TO SHARE THAT...
...THERE ARE TIMES WHEN WE SHOULD REVEAL OUR VULNERABILITY.
I THOUGHT ABOUT HOW TO BEST EXPRESS THIS, AND...
YOU CHOSE RAP?!
YES.
I KNOW THERE ARE A LOT OF OTHER WAYS TO EXPRESS MYSELF.
BUT I REVEALED A WEAKNESS OF MINE. MY RAPPING IS AWFUL.
MY RAPPING WAS SO BAD IT INDUCED A STATE OF COLLAPSE.
BUT I MIGHT BE ABLE TO CONVEY THIS MESSAGE IF I CAN DEMONSTRATE HOW MUCH MY RAP HAS IMPROVED.

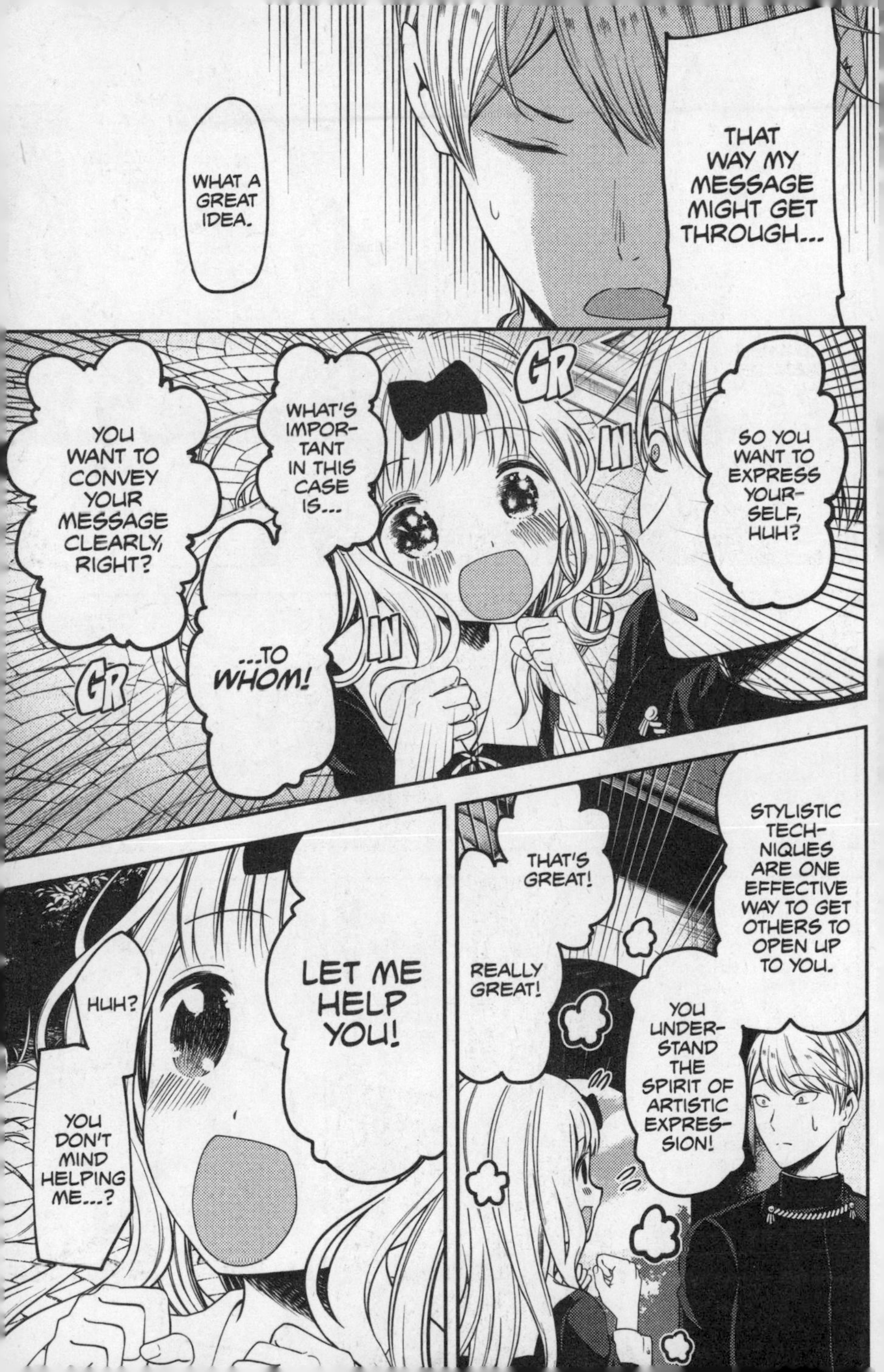
THAT WAY MY MESSAGE MIGHT GET THROUGH...
WHAT A GREAT IDEA.
SO YOU WANT TO EXPRESS YOURSELF, HUH?
GR IN
WHAT'S IMPORTANT IN THIS CASE IS...
YOU WANT TO CONVEY YOUR MESSAGE CLEARLY, RIGHT?
...TO WHOM!
GR IN
STYLISTIC TECHNIQUES ARE ONE EFFECTIVE WAY TO GET OTHERS TO OPEN UP TO YOU.
THAT'S GREAT!
REALLY GREAT!
YOU UNDERSTAND THE SPIRIT OF ARTISTIC EXPRESSION!
LET ME HELP YOU!
HUH?
YOU DON'T MIND HELPING ME...?

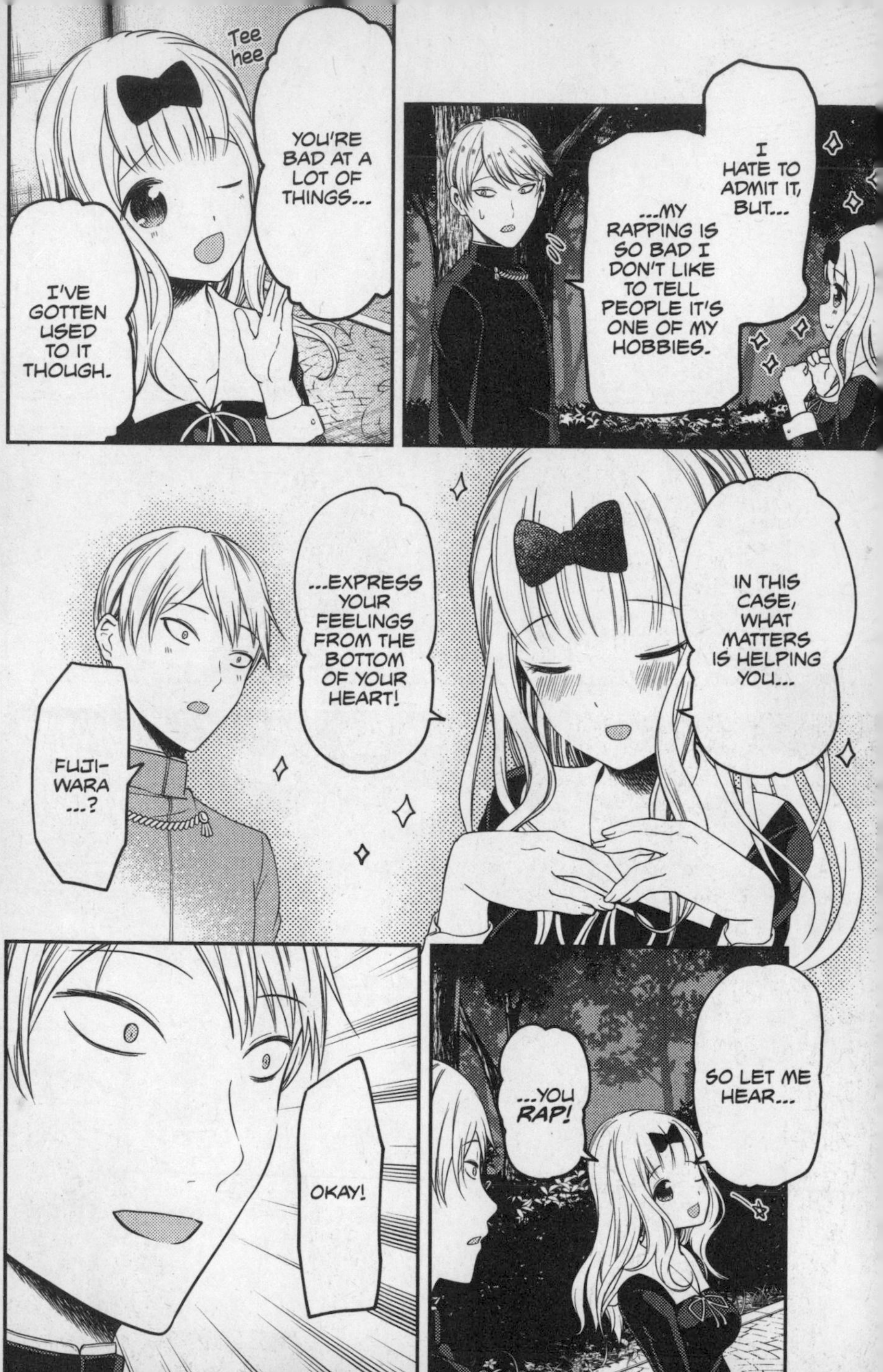
I HATE TO ADMIT IT, BUT...
...MY RAPPING IS SO BAD I DON'T LIKE TO TELL PEOPLE IT'S ONE OF MY HOBBIES.
Tee hee
YOU'RE BAD AT A LOT OF THINGS...
I'VE GOTTEN USED TO IT THOUGH.
IN THIS CASE, WHAT MATTERS IS HELPING YOU...
...EXPRESS YOUR FEELINGS FROM THE BOTTOM OF YOUR HEART!
FUJI-WARA...?
SO LET ME HEAR...
...YOU RAP!
OKAY!

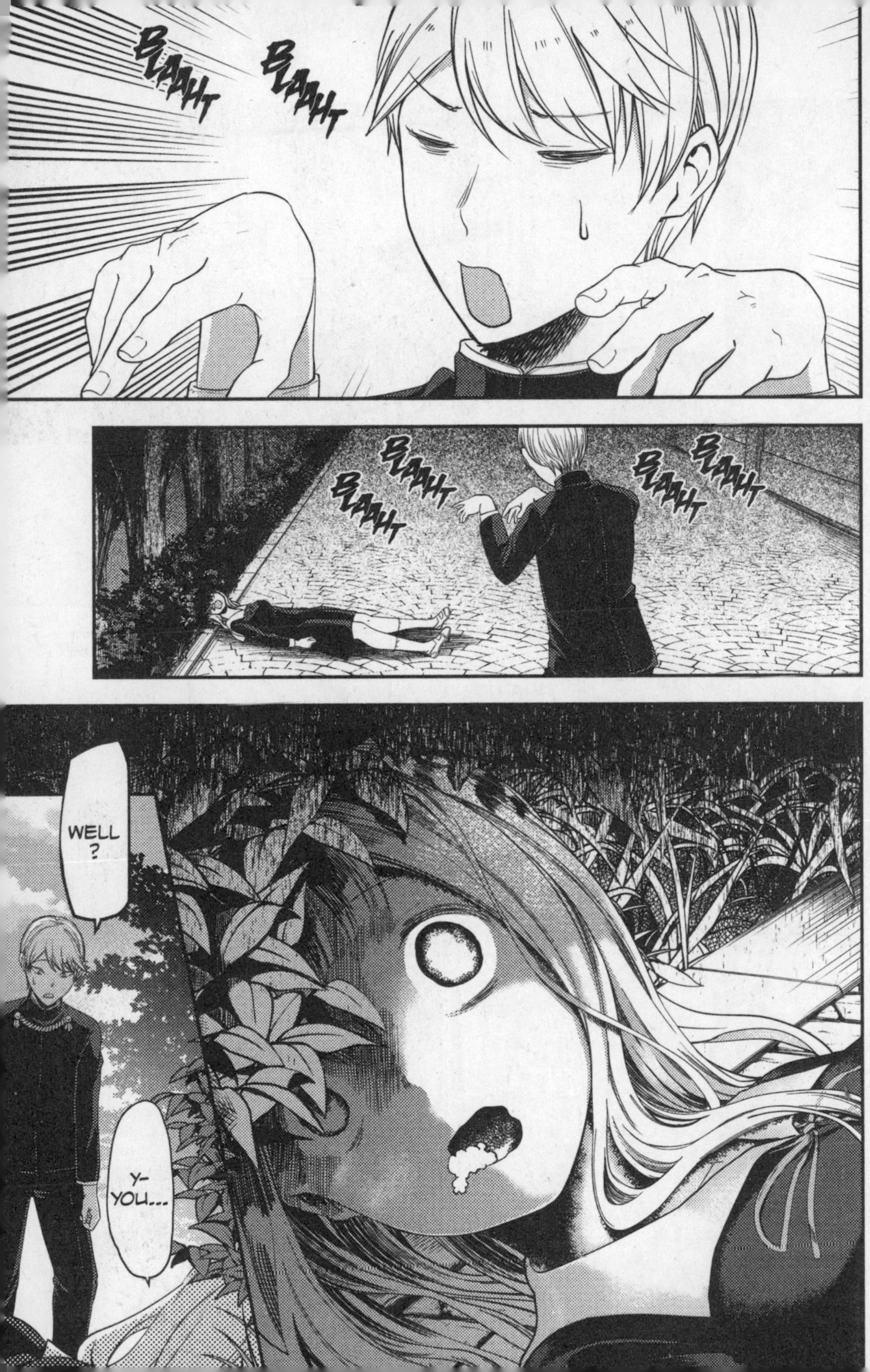
BLAAHT
BLAAHT
BLAAHT
BLAAHT
BLAAHT
BLAAHT
WELL?
Y-YOU...

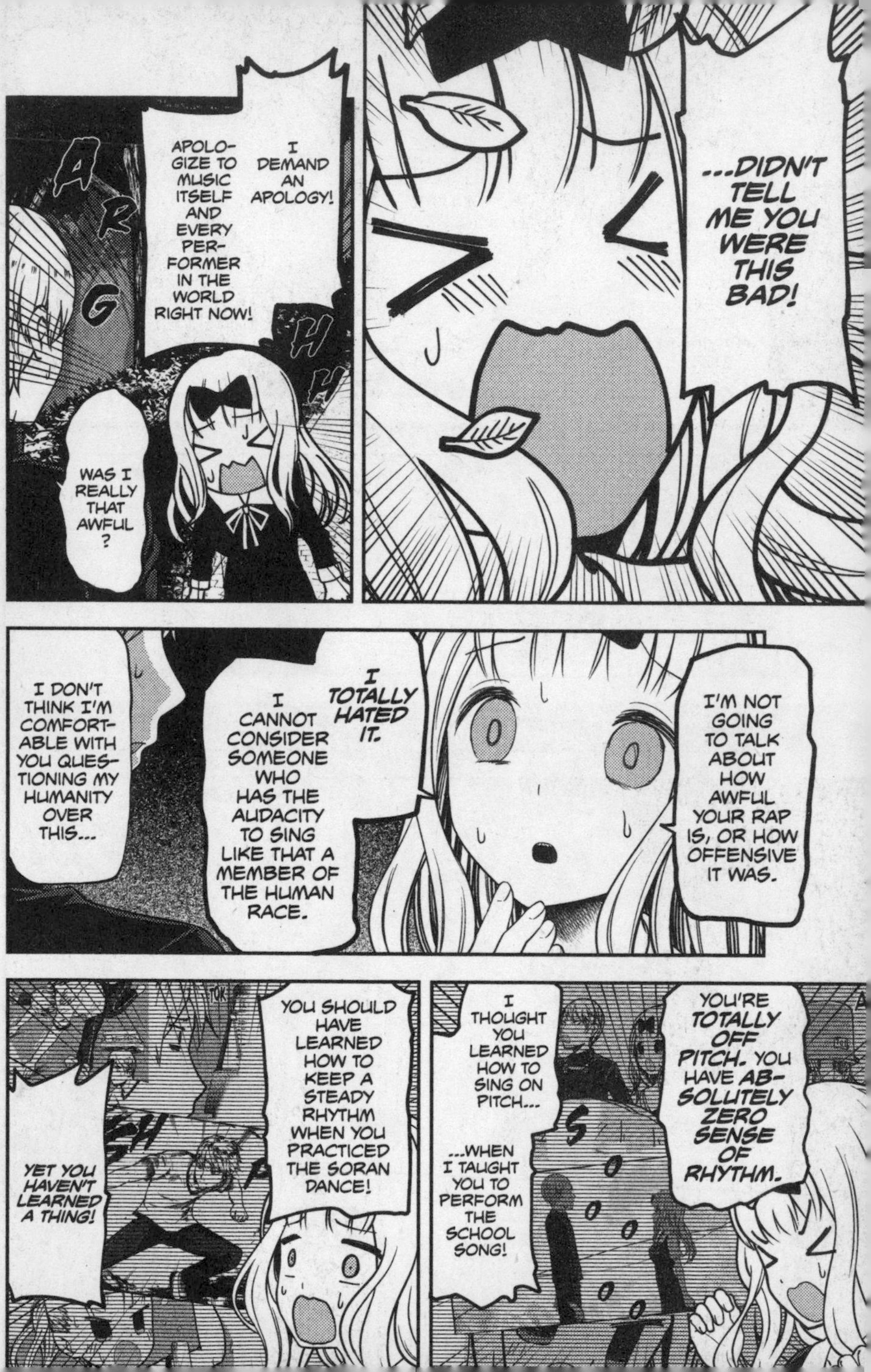
...DIDN'T TELL ME YOU WERE THIS BAD!
I DEMAND AN APOLOGY!
APOLOGIZE TO MUSIC ITSELF AND EVERY PERFORMER IN THE WORLD RIGHT NOW!
WAS I REALLY THAT AWFUL?
I'M NOT GOING TO TALK ABOUT HOW AWFUL YOUR RAP IS, OR HOW OFFENSIVE IT WAS.
I TOTALLY HATED IT.
I CANNOT CONSIDER SOMEONE WHO HAS THE AUDACITY TO SING LIKE THAT A MEMBER OF THE HUMAN RACE.
I DON'T THINK I'M COMFORTABLE WITH YOU QUESTIONING MY HUMANITY OVER THIS...
YOU'RE TOTALLY OFF PITCH. YOU HAVE ABSOLUTELY ZERO SENSE OF RHYTHM.
I THOUGHT YOU LEARNED HOW TO SING ON PITCH...
...WHEN I TAUGHT YOU TO PERFORM THE SCHOOL SONG!
YOU SHOULD HAVE LEARNED HOW TO KEEP A STEADY RHYTHM WHEN YOU PRACTICED THE SORAN DANCE!
YET YOU HAVEN'T LEARNED A THING!

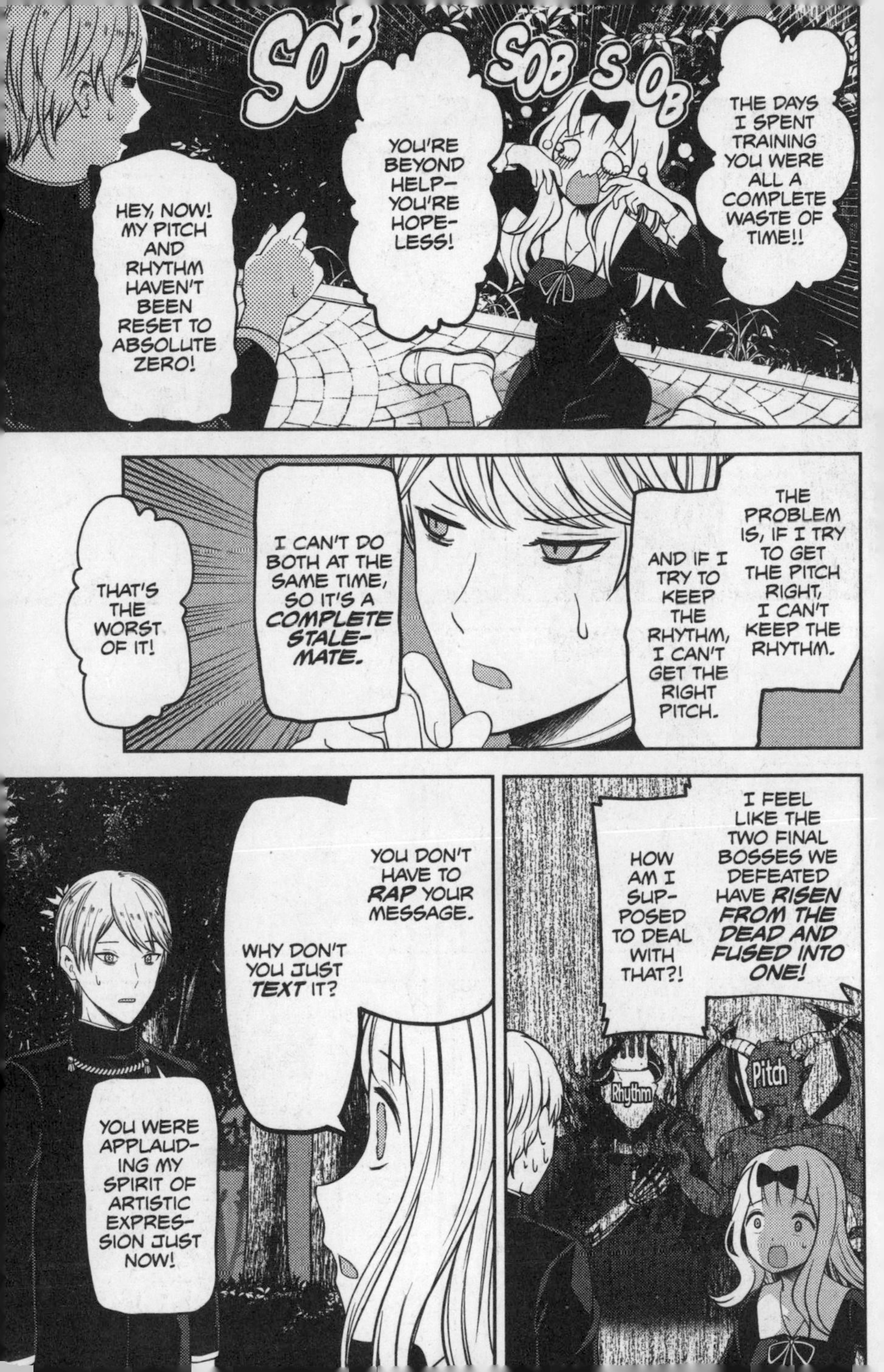
THE DAYS I SPENT TRAINING YOU WERE ALL A COMPLETE WASTE OF TIME!!
SOB S OB
SOB
YOU'RE BEYOND HELP—YOU'RE HOPELESS!
SOB
HEY, NOW! MY PITCH AND RHYTHM HAVEN'T BEEN RESET TO ABSOLUTE ZERO!
THE PROBLEM IS, IF I TRY TO GET THE PITCH RIGHT, I CAN'T KEEP THE RHYTHM.
AND IF I TRY TO KEEP THE RHYTHM, I CAN'T GET THE RIGHT PITCH.
I CAN'T DO BOTH AT THE SAME TIME, SO IT'S A *COMPLETE STALEMATE.*
THAT'S THE WORST OF IT!
I FEEL LIKE THE TWO FINAL BOSSES WE DEFEATED HAVE *RISEN FROM THE DEAD AND FUSED INTO ONE!*
HOW AM I SUPPOSED TO DEAL WITH THAT?!
Pitch
Rhythm
YOU DON'T HAVE TO *RAP* YOUR MESSAGE.
WHY DON'T YOU JUST *TEXT* IT?
YOU WERE APPLAUDING MY SPIRIT OF ARTISTIC EXPRESSION JUST NOW!

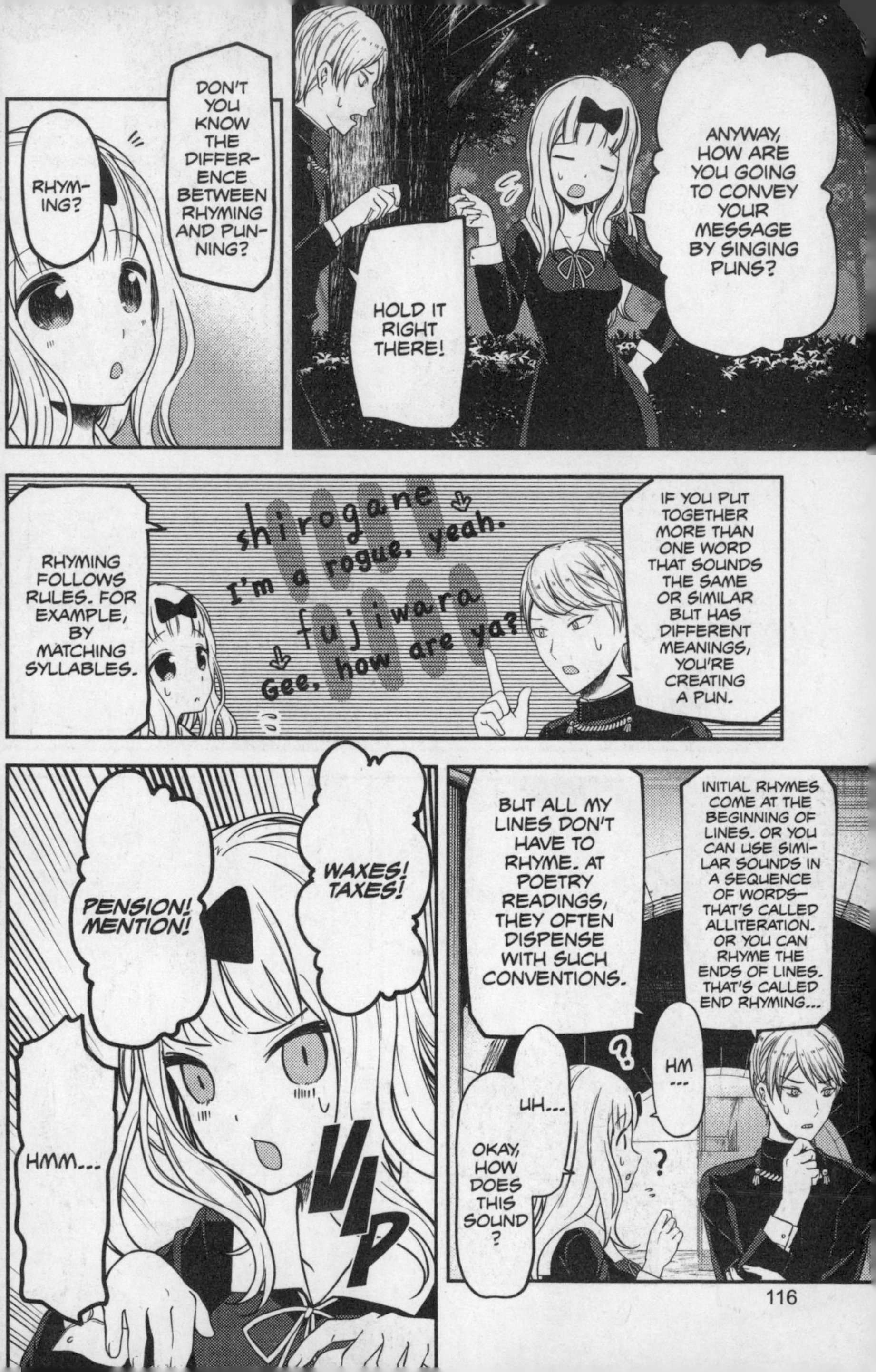
ANYWAY, HOW ARE YOU GOING TO CONVEY YOUR MESSAGE BY SINGING PUNS?
HOLD IT RIGHT THERE!
DON'T YOU KNOW THE DIFFERENCE BETWEEN RHYMING AND PUNNING?
RHYMING?
IF YOU PUT TOGETHER MORE THAN ONE WORD THAT SOUNDS THE SAME OR SIMILAR BUT HAS DIFFERENT MEANINGS, YOU'RE CREATING A PUN.
shirogane
I'm a rogue, yeah.
fujiwara
Gee, how are ya?
RHYMING FOLLOWS RULES. FOR EXAMPLE, BY MATCHING SYLLABLES.
INITIAL RHYMES COME AT THE BEGINNING OF LINES. OR YOU CAN USE SIMILAR SOUNDS IN A SEQUENCE OF WORDS—THAT'S CALLED ALLITERATION. OR YOU CAN RHYME THE ENDS OF LINES. THAT'S CALLED END RHYMING...
BUT ALL MY LINES DON'T HAVE TO RHYME. AT POETRY READINGS, THEY OFTEN DISPENSE WITH SUCH CONVENTIONS.
HM...
UH...
OKAY, HOW DOES THIS SOUND?
WAXES! TAXES!
PENSION! MENTION!
HMM...

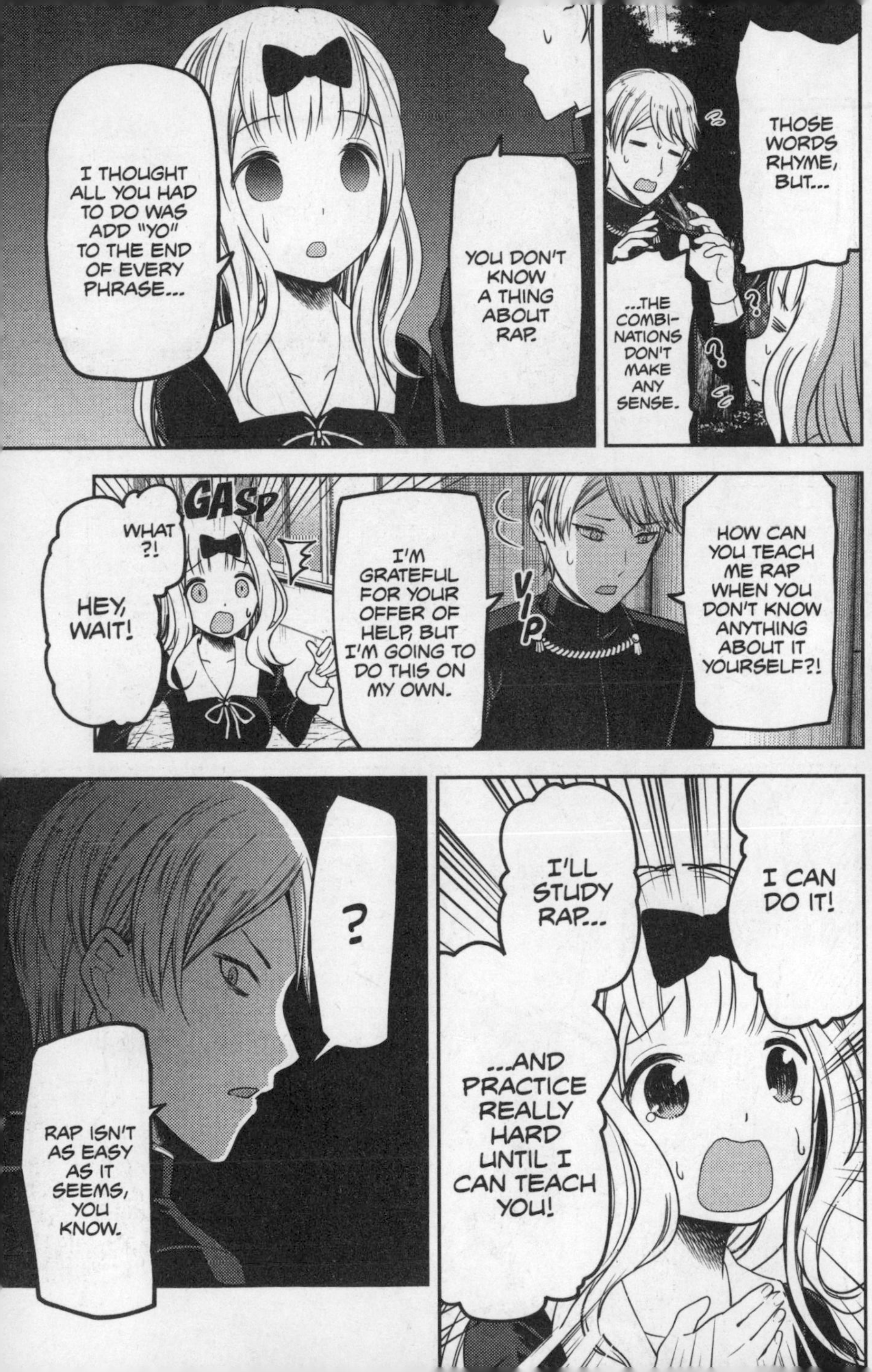
THOSE WORDS RHYME, BUT...
...THE COMBINATIONS DON'T MAKE ANY SENSE.
YOU DON'T KNOW A THING ABOUT RAP.
I THOUGHT ALL YOU HAD TO DO WAS ADD "YO" TO THE END OF EVERY PHRASE...
HOW CAN YOU TEACH ME RAP WHEN YOU DON'T KNOW ANYTHING ABOUT IT YOURSELF?!
VIP
I'M GRATEFUL FOR YOUR OFFER OF HELP, BUT I'M GOING TO DO THIS ON MY OWN.
GASP
WHAT?!
HEY, WAIT!
I CAN DO IT!
I'LL STUDY RAP...
...AND PRACTICE REALLY HARD UNTIL I CAN TEACH YOU!
?
RAP ISN'T AS EASY AS IT SEEMS, YOU KNOW.

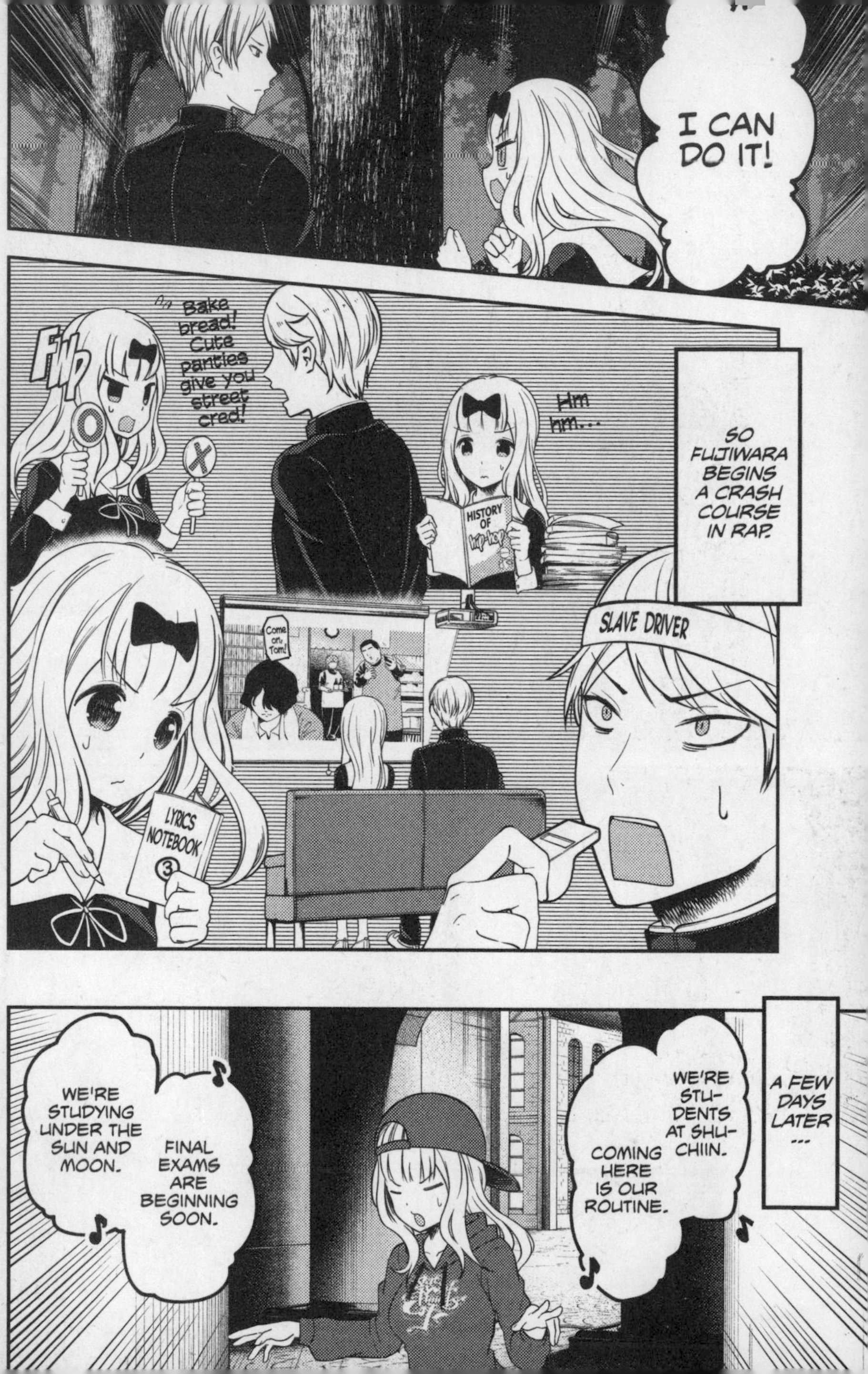
I CAN DO IT!
SO FUJIWARA BEGINS A CRASH COURSE IN RAP.
SLAVE DRIVER
Hm hm...
HISTORY OF hip-hop
Bake bread! Cute panties give you street cred!
FWP
Come on, Tom!
LYRICS NOTEBOOK 3
A FEW DAYS LATER...
WE'RE STUDENTS AT SHUCHIIN.
COMING HERE IS OUR ROUTINE.
WE'RE STUDYING UNDER THE SUN AND MOON.
FINAL EXAMS ARE BEGINNING SOON.

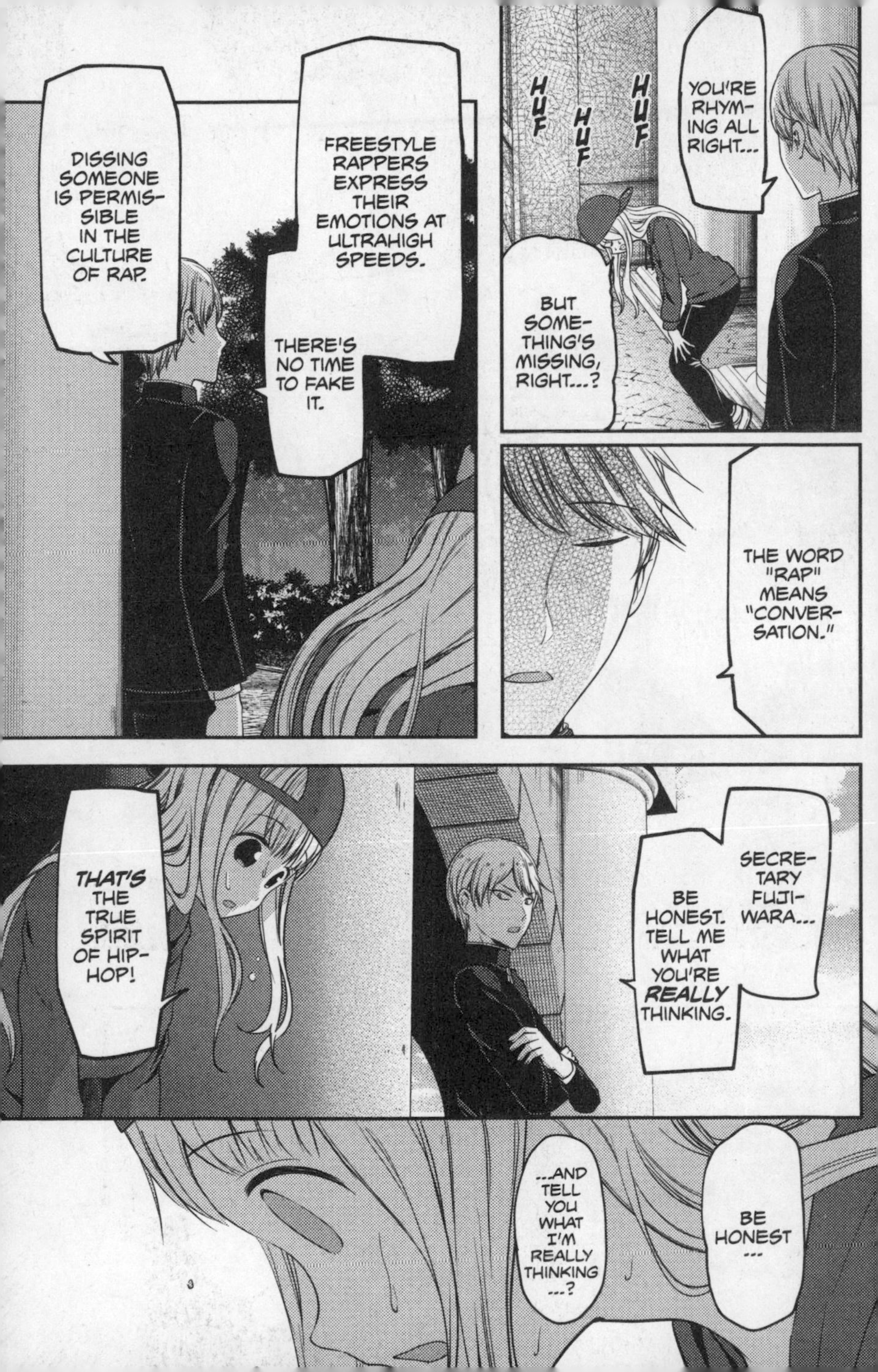
YOU'RE RHYMING ALL RIGHT...
HUF HUF HUF
BUT SOMETHING'S MISSING, RIGHT...?
THE WORD "RAP" MEANS "CONVERSATION."
FREESTYLE RAPPERS EXPRESS THEIR EMOTIONS AT ULTRAHIGH SPEEDS.
THERE'S NO TIME TO FAKE IT.
DISSING SOMEONE IS PERMISSIBLE IN THE CULTURE OF RAP.
SECRETARY FUJIWARA...
BE HONEST. TELL ME WHAT YOU'RE *REALLY* THINKING.
THAT'S THE TRUE SPIRIT OF HIP-HOP!
BE HONEST...
...AND TELL YOU WHAT I'M REALLY THINKING...?

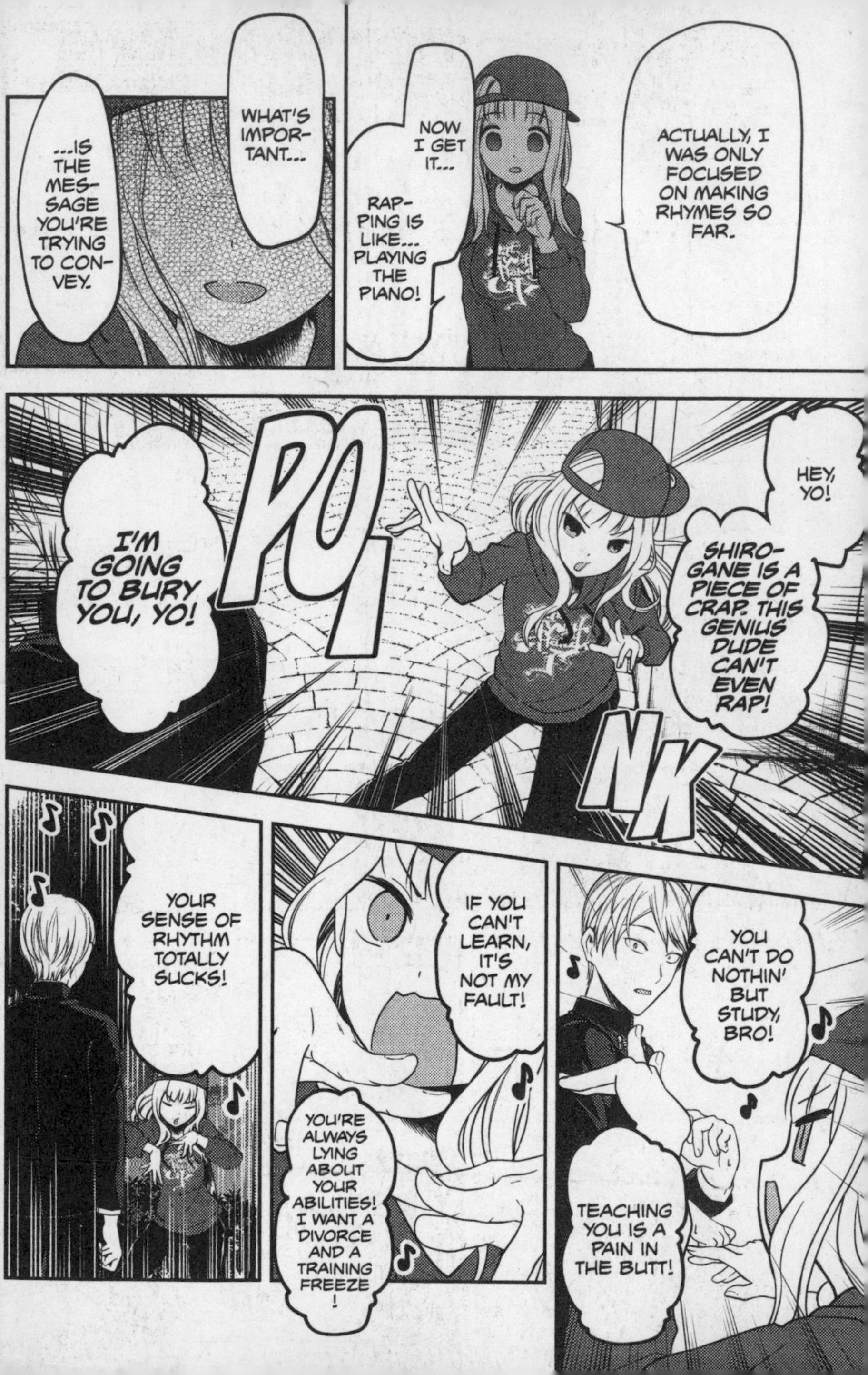
ACTUALLY, I WAS ONLY FOCUSED ON MAKING RHYMES SO FAR.
NOW I GET IT...
RAPPING IS LIKE... PLAYING THE PIANO!
WHAT'S IMPORTANT...
...IS THE MESSAGE YOU'RE TRYING TO CONVEY.
HEY, YO!
SHIROGANE IS A PIECE OF CRAP. THIS GENIUS DUDE CAN'T EVEN RAP!
PONK
I'M GOING TO BURY YOU, YO!
YOU CAN'T DO NOTHIN' BUT STUDY, BRO!
TEACHING YOU IS A PAIN IN THE BUTT!
IF YOU CAN'T LEARN, IT'S NOT MY FAULT!
YOU'RE ALWAYS LYING ABOUT YOUR ABILITIES! I WANT A DIVORCE AND A TRAINING FREEZE!
YOUR SENSE OF RHYTHM TOTALLY SUCKS!

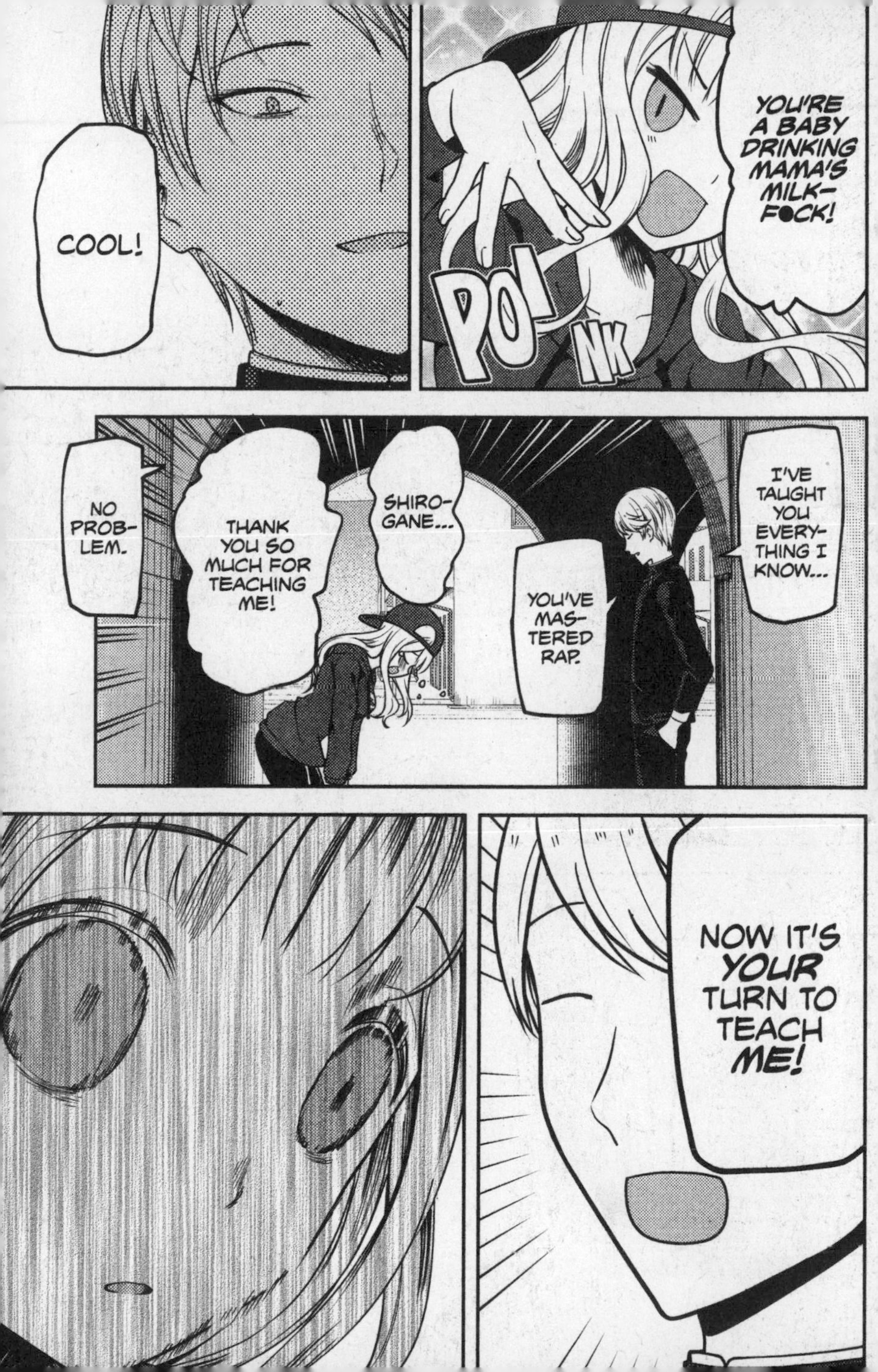
YOU'RE A BABY DRINKING MAMA'S MILK-F●CK!
POINK
COOL!
I'VE TAUGHT YOU EVERY-THING I KNOW...
YOU'VE MAS-TERED RAP.
SHIRO-GANE...
THANK YOU SO MUCH FOR TEACHING ME!
NO PROB-LEM.
NOW IT'S *YOUR* TURN TO TEACH *ME!*

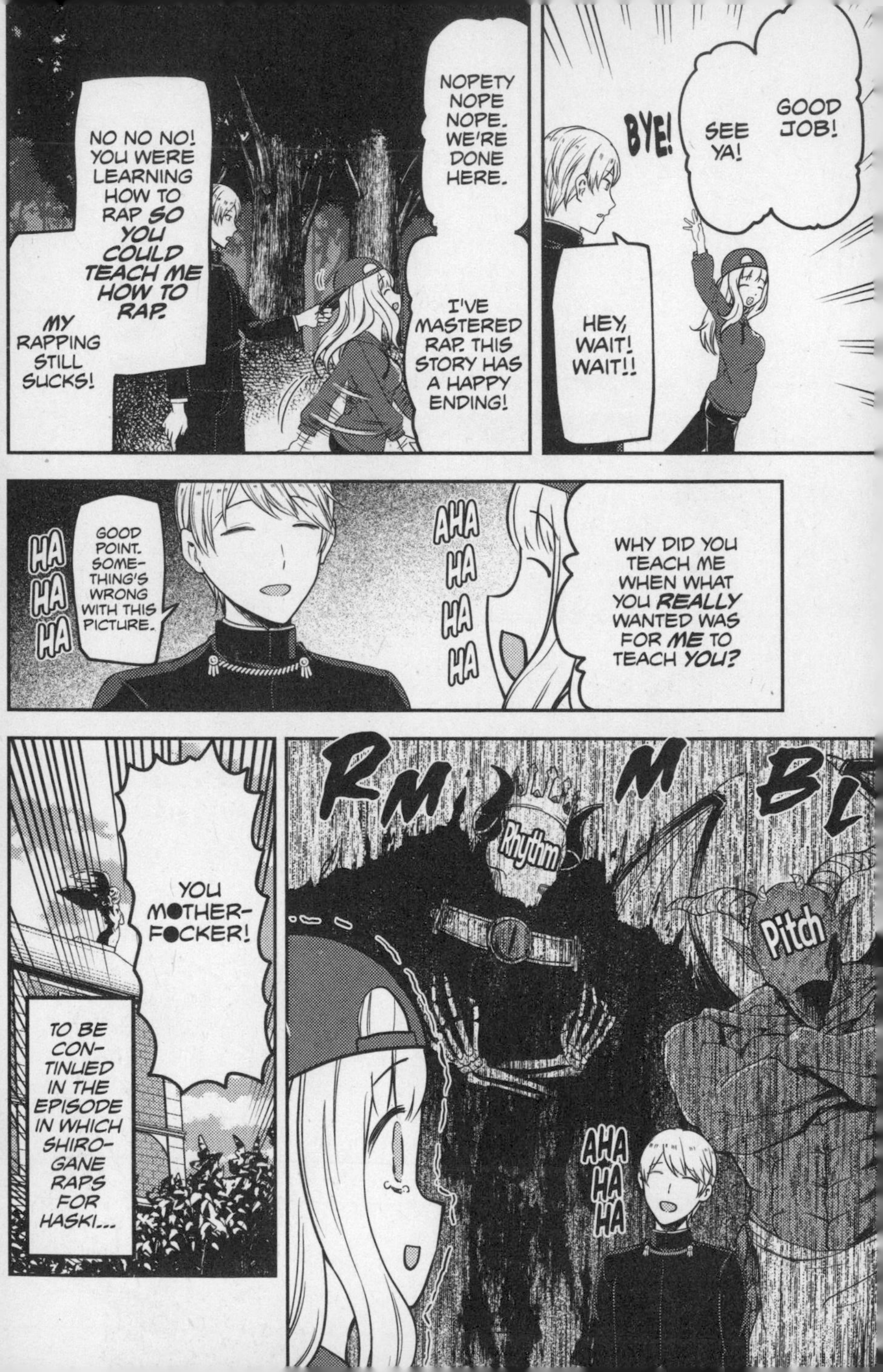
GOOD JOB!
SEE YA!
BYE!
HEY, WAIT! WAIT!!
NOPETY NOPE NOPE. WE'RE DONE HERE.
I'VE MASTERED RAP. THIS STORY HAS A HAPPY ENDING!
NO NO NO! YOU WERE LEARNING HOW TO RAP SO YOU COULD TEACH ME HOW TO RAP.
MY RAPPING STILL SUCKS!
WHY DID YOU TEACH ME WHEN WHAT YOU REALLY WANTED WAS FOR ME TO TEACH YOU?
AHA HA HA HA
HA HA HA
GOOD POINT. SOMETHING'S WRONG WITH THIS PICTURE.
RM M BL
Rhythm
Pitch
AHA HA HA
YOU M●THER-F●CKER!
TO BE CONTINUED IN THE EPISODE IN WHICH SHIROGANE RAPS FOR HASKI...

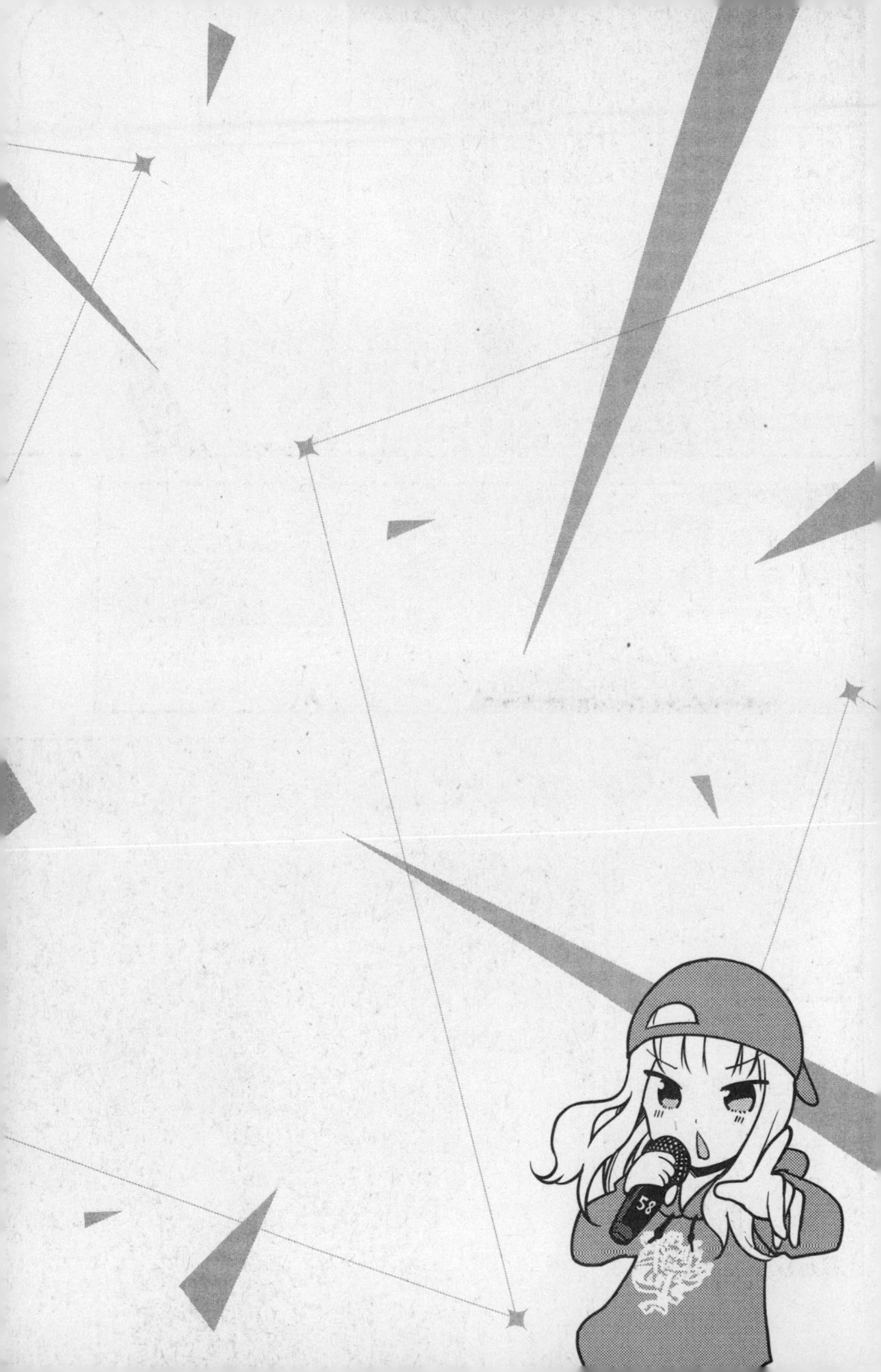
58

KAGUYA-SAMA

LOVE IS WAR

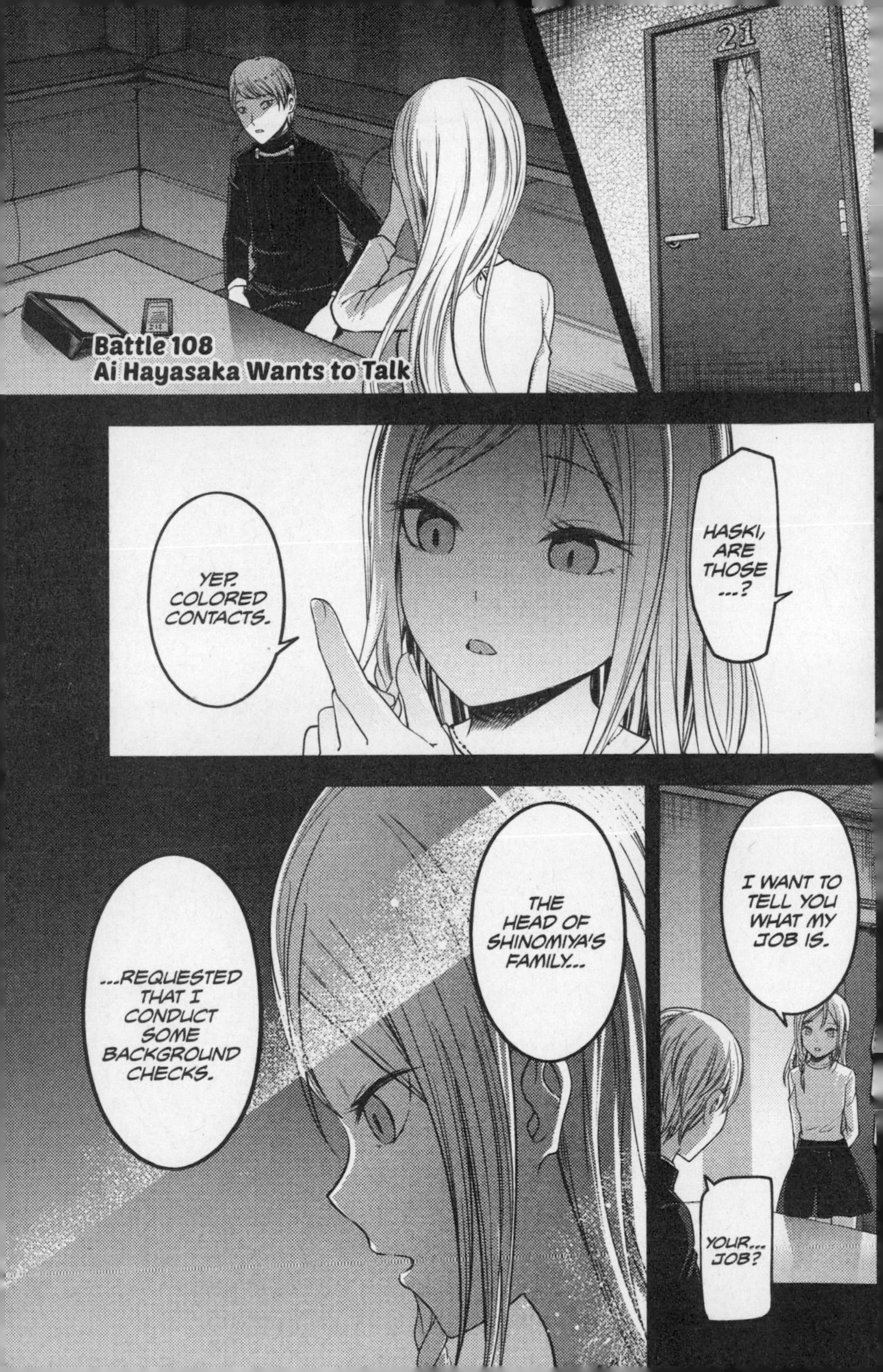
21
Battle 108
Ai Hayasaka Wants to Talk
HASKI, ARE THOSE ...?
YEP. COLORED CONTACTS.
I WANT TO TELL YOU WHAT MY JOB IS.
YOUR... JOB?
THE HEAD OF SHINOMIYA'S FAMILY...
...REQUESTED THAT I CONDUCT SOME BACKGROUND CHECKS.

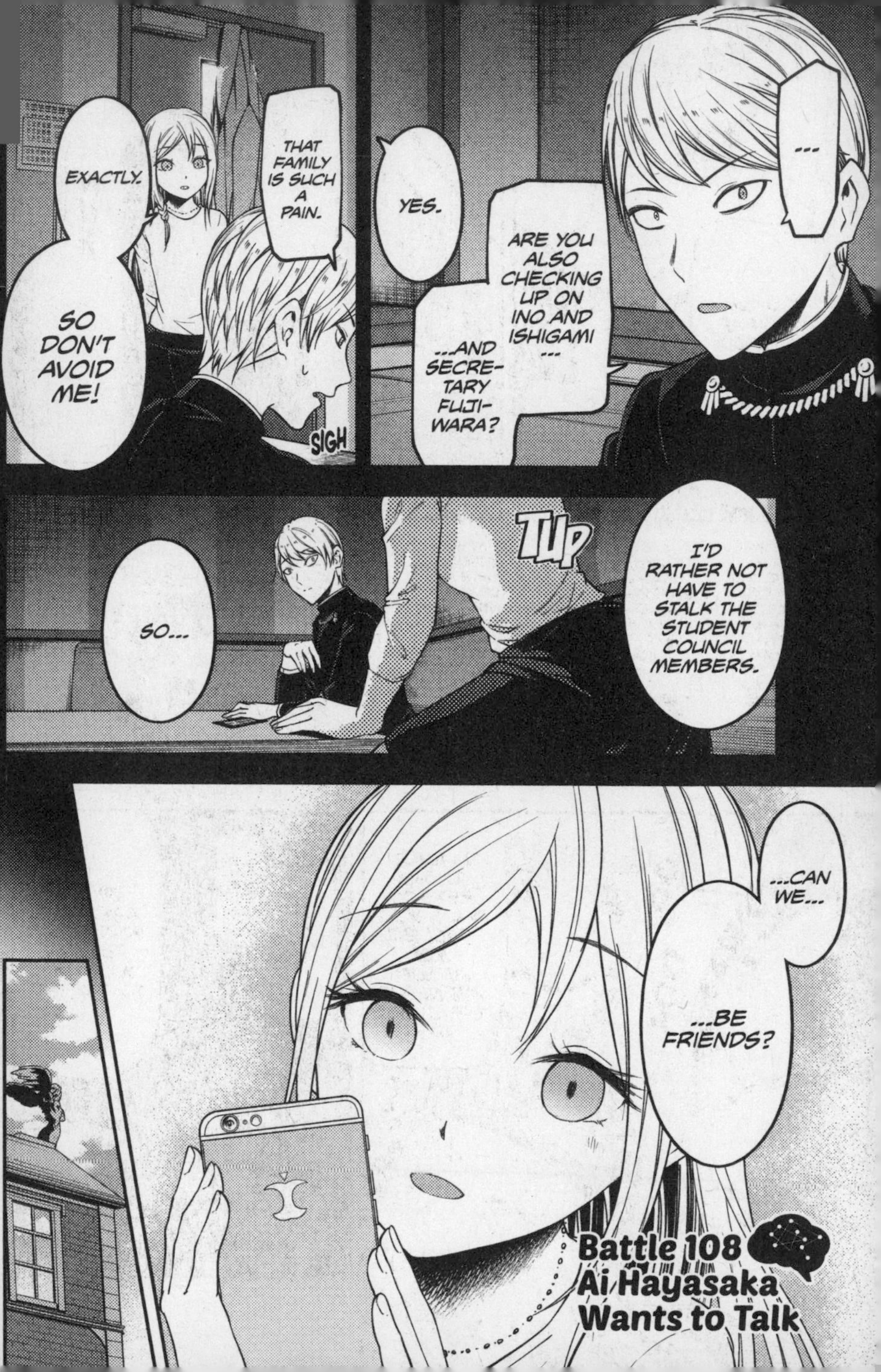
...
ARE YOU ALSO CHECKING UP ON INO AND ISHIGAMI...
...AND SECRETARY FUJIWARA?
YES.
THAT FAMILY IS SUCH A PAIN.
EXACTLY.
SO DON'T AVOID ME!
SIGH
TUP
I'D RATHER NOT HAVE TO STALK THE STUDENT COUNCIL MEMBERS.
SO...
...CAN WE...
...BE FRIENDS?

Battle 108 Ai Hayasaka Wants to Talk

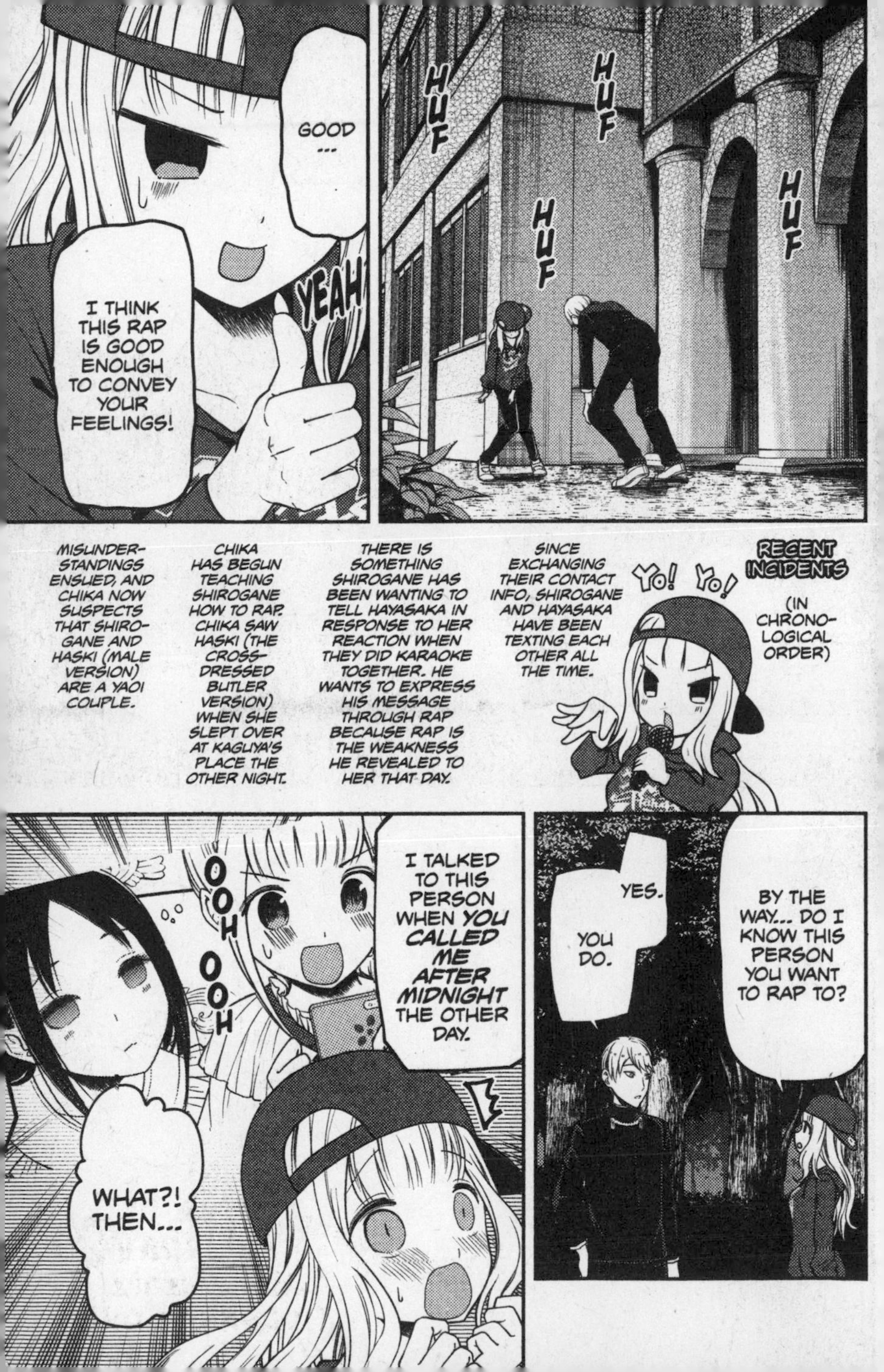
HUF HUF
HUF HUF
GOOD...
YEAH
I THINK THIS RAP IS GOOD ENOUGH TO CONVEY YOUR FEELINGS!
RECENT INCIDENTS
(IN CHRONOLOGICAL ORDER)
YO! YO!
SINCE EXCHANGING THEIR CONTACT INFO, SHIROGANE AND HAYASAKA HAVE BEEN TEXTING EACH OTHER ALL THE TIME.
THERE IS SOMETHING SHIROGANE HAS BEEN WANTING TO TELL HAYASAKA IN RESPONSE TO HER REACTION WHEN THEY DID KARAOKE TOGETHER. HE WANTS TO EXPRESS HIS MESSAGE THROUGH RAP BECAUSE RAP IS THE WEAKNESS HE REVEALED TO HER THAT DAY.
CHIKA HAS BEGUN TEACHING SHIROGANE HOW TO RAP. CHIKA SAW HASKI (THE CROSS-DRESSED BUTLER VERSION) WHEN SHE SLEPT OVER AT KAGUYA'S PLACE THE OTHER NIGHT.
MISUNDERSTANDINGS ENSUED, AND CHIKA NOW SUSPECTS THAT SHIROGANE AND HASKI (MALE VERSION) ARE A YAOI COUPLE.
BY THE WAY... DO I KNOW THIS PERSON YOU WANT TO RAP TO?
YES.
YOU DO.
I TALKED TO THIS PERSON WHEN YOU CALLED ME AFTER MIDNIGHT THE OTHER DAY.
OOH
OOH
WHAT?! THEN...

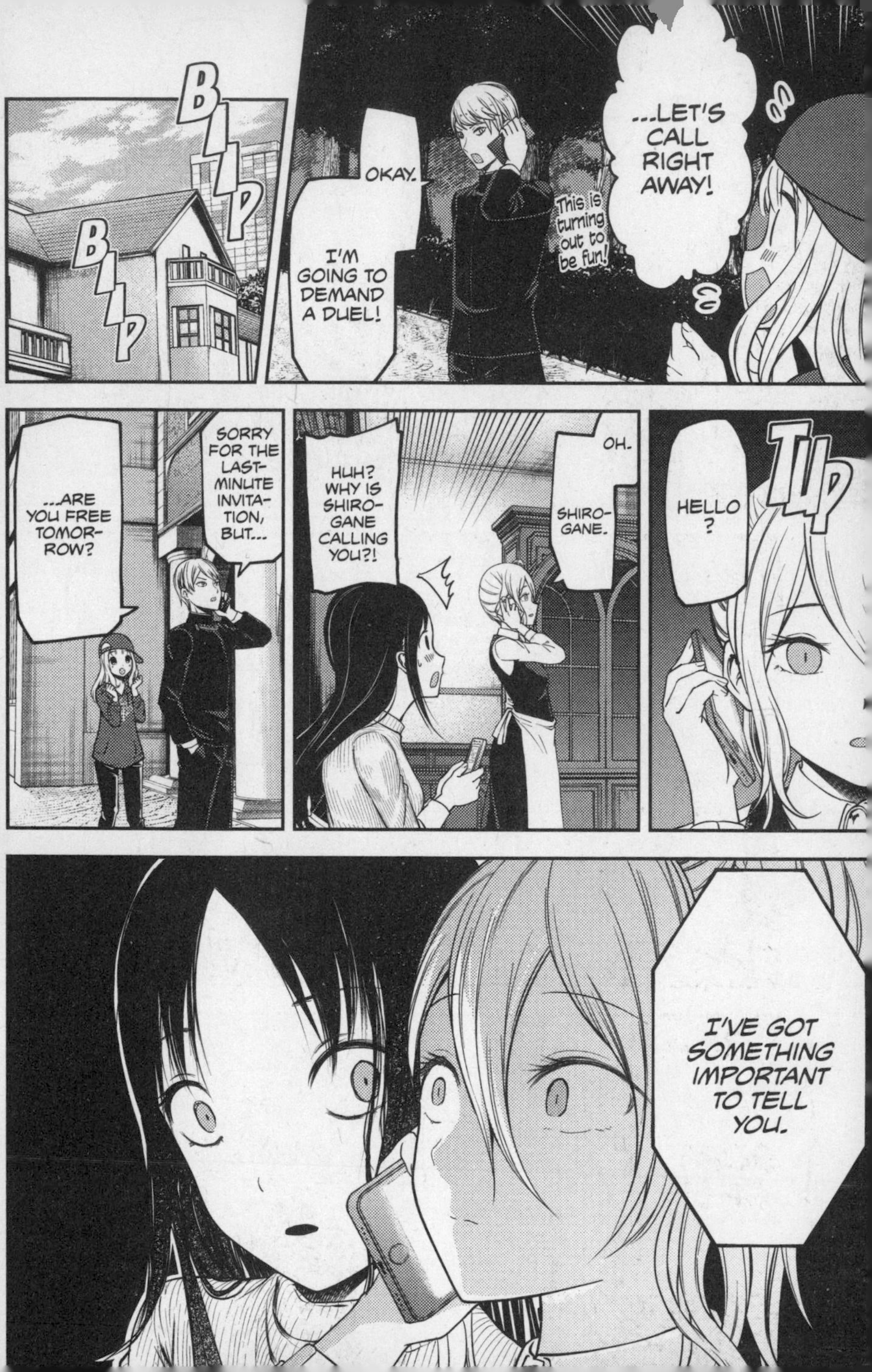
...LET'S CALL RIGHT AWAY!
This is turning out to be fun!
OKAY.
I'M GOING TO DEMAND A DUEL!
BIIP
BIIP
TUP
HELLO?
OH.
SHIRO-GANE.
HUH? WHY IS SHIRO-GANE CALLING YOU?!
SORRY FOR THE LAST-MINUTE INVITA-TION, BUT...
...ARE YOU FREE TOMOR-ROW?
I'VE GOT SOMETHING IMPORTANT TO TELL YOU.

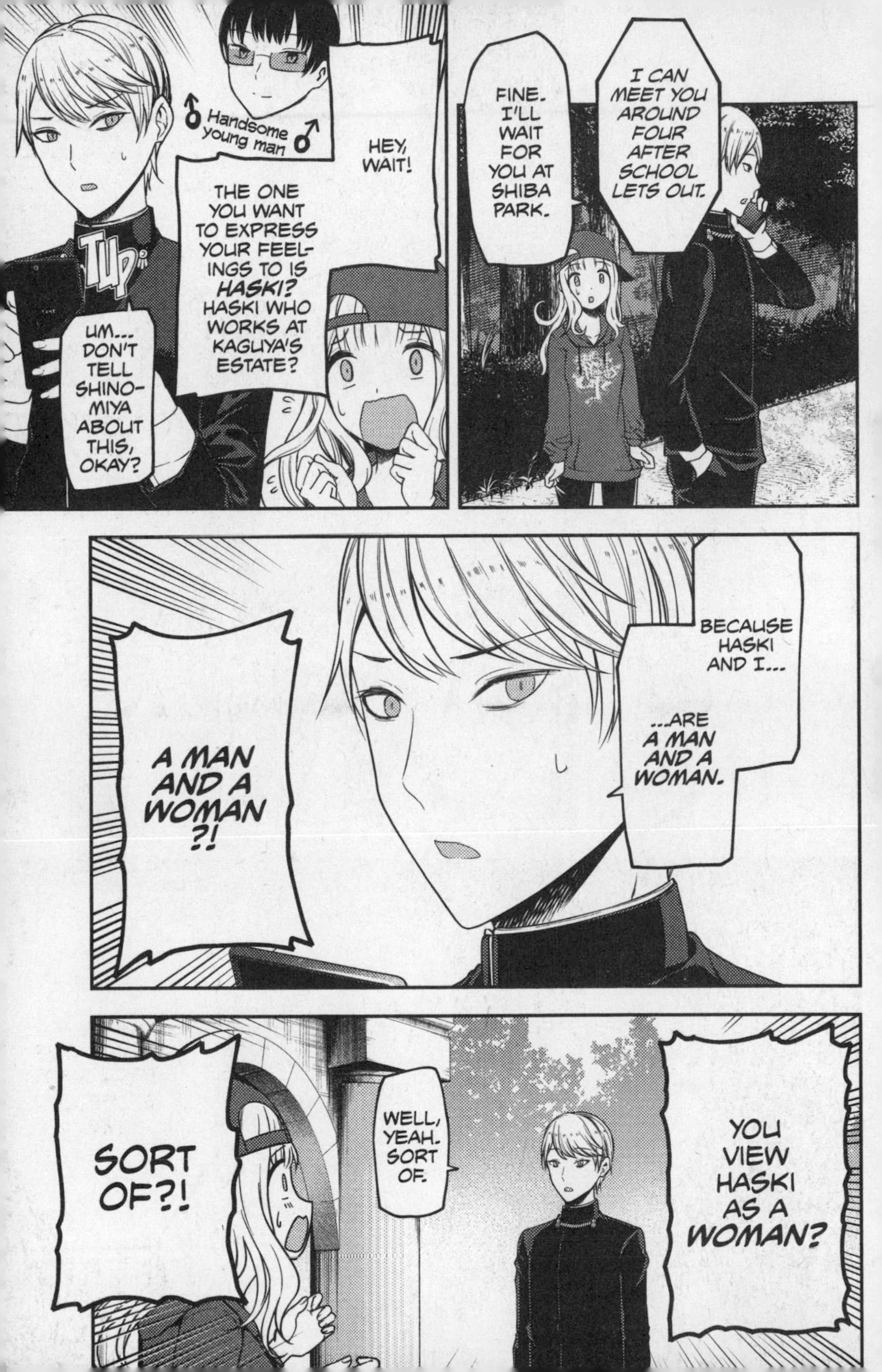
I CAN MEET YOU AROUND FOUR AFTER SCHOOL LETS OUT.
FINE. I'LL WAIT FOR YOU AT SHIBA PARK.
HEY, WAIT!
THE ONE YOU WANT TO EXPRESS YOUR FEEL-INGS TO IS *HASKI?* HASKI WHO WORKS AT KAGUYA'S ESTATE?
♂ Handsome young man ♂
UM... DON'T TELL SHINO-MIYA ABOUT THIS, OKAY?
BECAUSE HASKI AND I...
...ARE *A MAN AND A WOMAN.*
A MAN AND A WOMAN ?!
YOU VIEW HASKI AS A *WOMAN?*
WELL, YEAH. SORT OF.
SORT OF?!

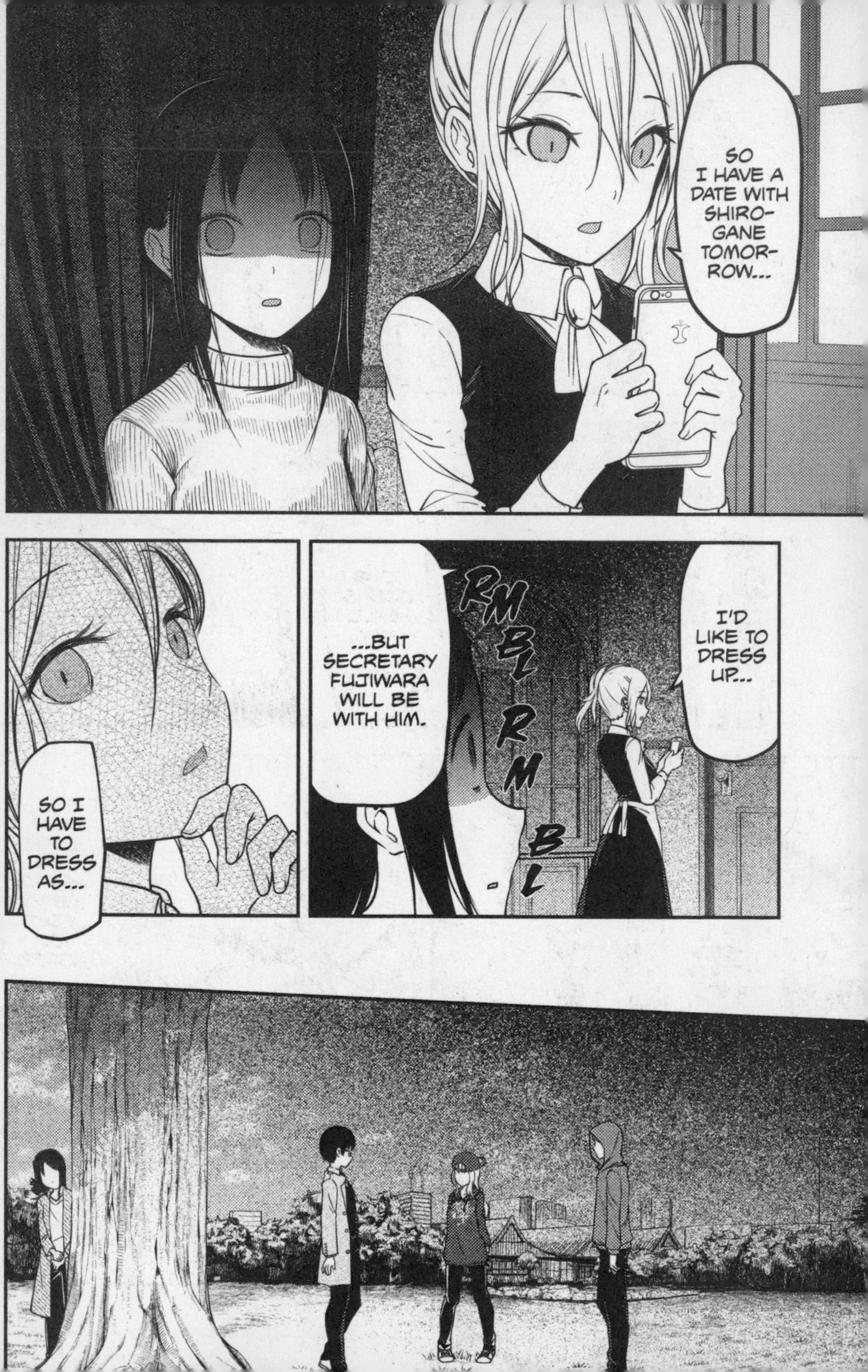
SO I HAVE A DATE WITH SHIRO-GANE TOMOR-ROW...
I'D LIKE TO DRESS UP...
...BUT SECRETARY FUJIWARA WILL BE WITH HIM.
RMBL RMBL
SO I HAVE TO DRESS AS...

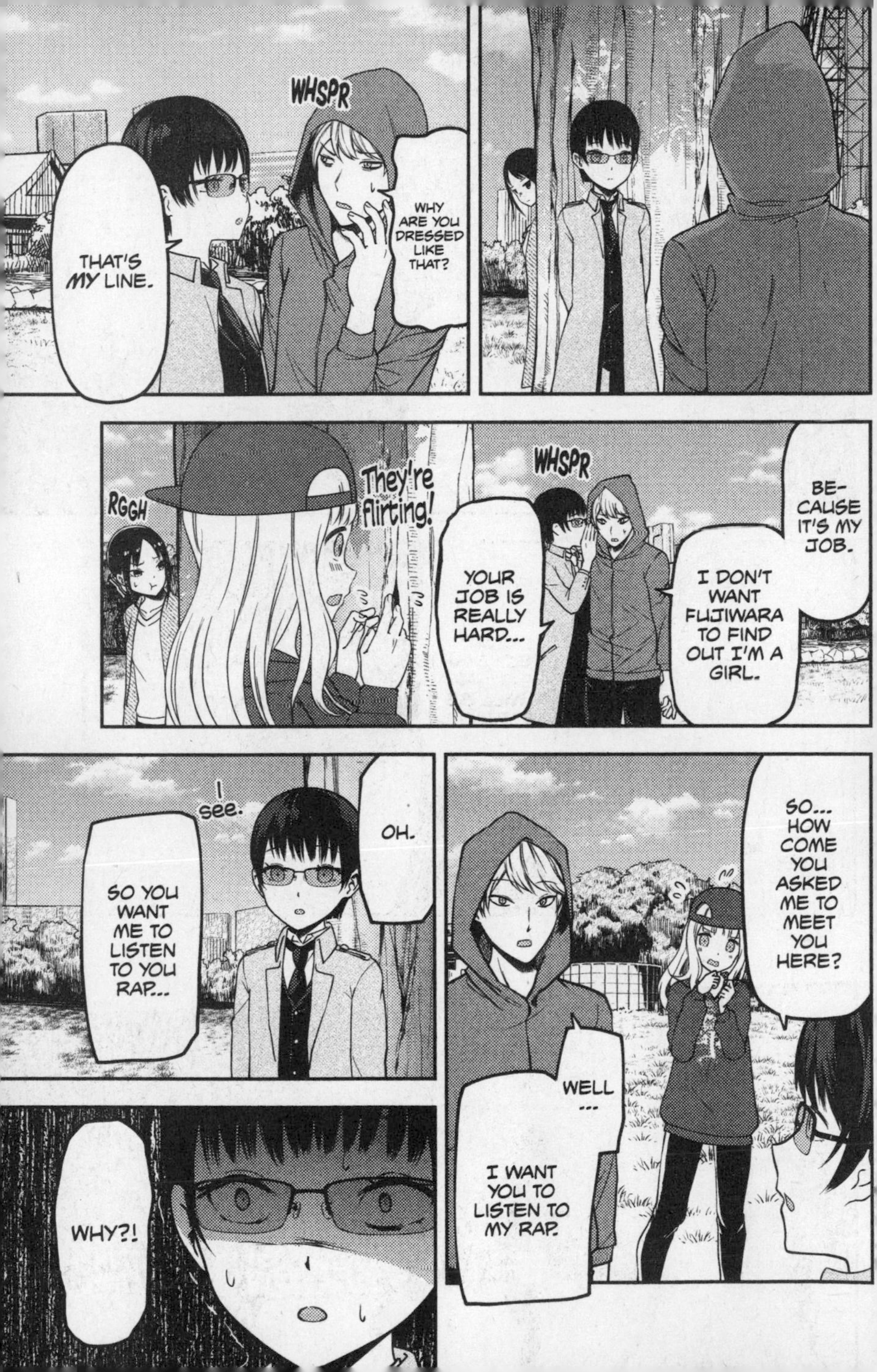
WHSPR
WHY ARE YOU DRESSED LIKE THAT?
THAT'S MY LINE.
BE-CAUSE IT'S MY JOB.
I DON'T WANT FUJIWARA TO FIND OUT I'M A GIRL.
WHSPR
YOUR JOB IS REALLY HARD...
They're flirting!
RGGH
SO... HOW COME YOU ASKED ME TO MEET YOU HERE?
WELL...
I WANT YOU TO LISTEN TO MY RAP.
OH.
I see.
SO YOU WANT ME TO LISTEN TO YOU RAP...
WHY?!

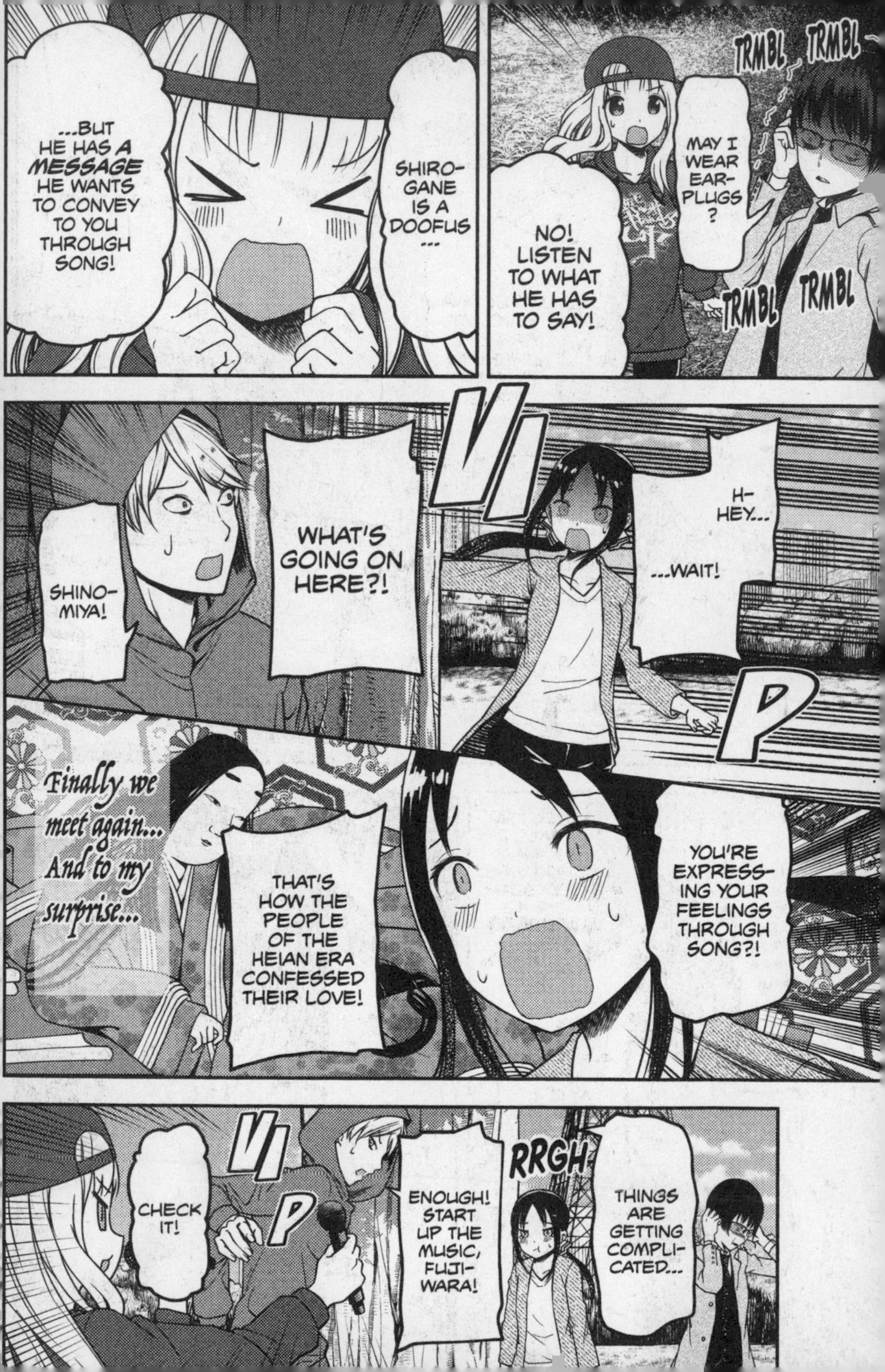
TRMBL TRMBL
MAY I WEAR EAR-PLUGS?
NO! LISTEN TO WHAT HE HAS TO SAY!
TRMBL TRMBL
SHIRO-GANE IS A DOOFUS...
...BUT HE HAS A *MESSAGE* HE WANTS TO CONVEY TO YOU THROUGH SONG!
VI
H-HEY...
...WAIT!
P
WHAT'S GOING ON HERE?!
SHINO-MIYA!
YOU'RE EXPRESS-ING YOUR FEELINGS THROUGH SONG?!
THAT'S HOW THE PEOPLE OF THE HEIAN ERA CONFESSED THEIR LOVE!
Finally we meet again... And to my surprise...
THINGS ARE GETTING COMPLI-CATED...
RRGH
ENOUGH! START UP THE MUSIC, FUJI-WARA!
VI
P
CHECK IT!

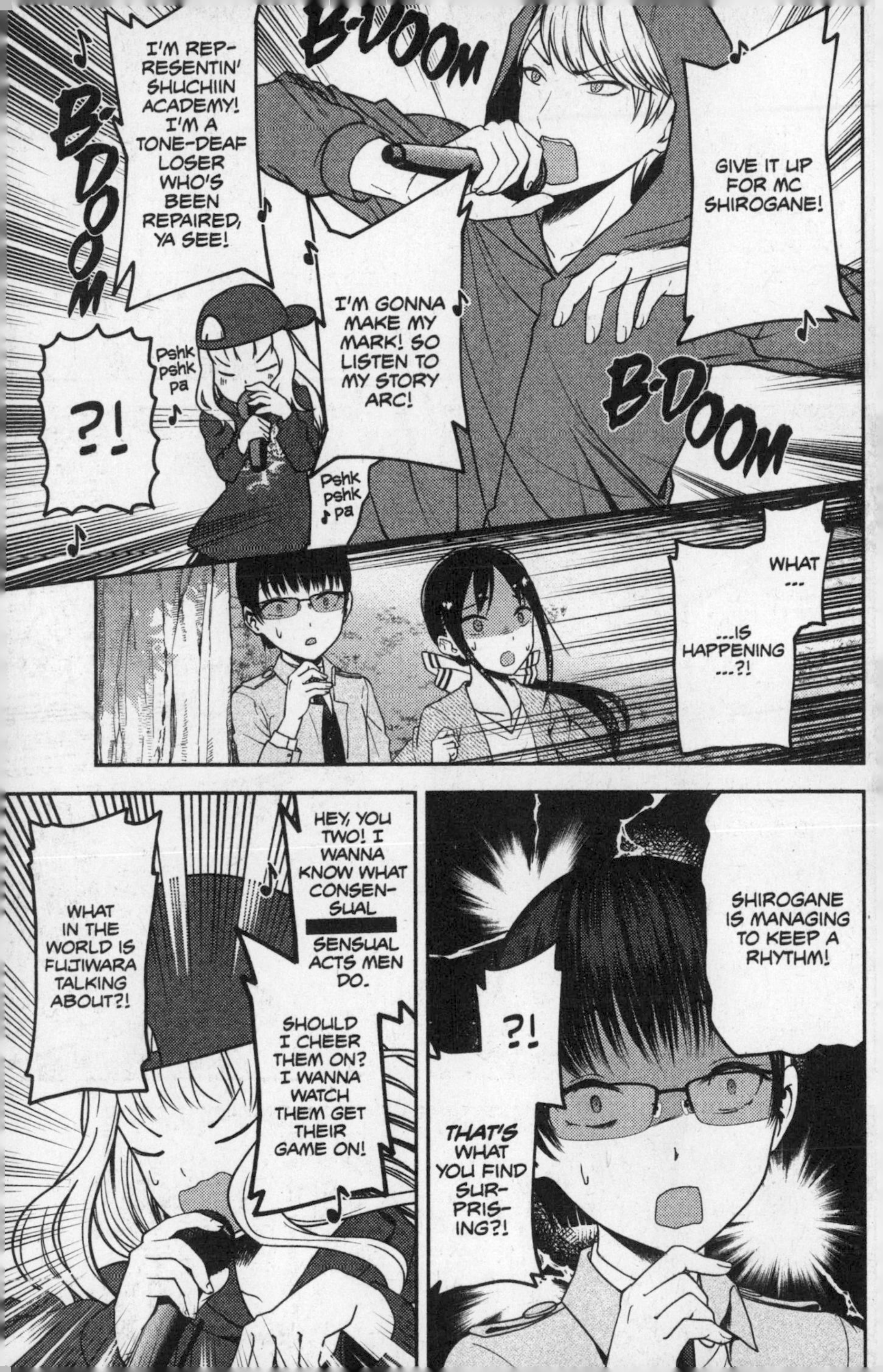
B-VOOM
GIVE IT UP FOR MC SHIROGANE!
B-DOOM
I'M REPRESENTIN' SHUCHIIN ACADEMY! I'M A TONE-DEAF LOSER WHO'S BEEN REPAIRED, YA SEE!
B-DOOM
I'M GONNA MAKE MY MARK! SO LISTEN TO MY STORY ARC!
Pshk pshk pa
?!
Pshk pshk pa
WHAT ---
---IS HAPPENING ---?!
SHIROGANE IS MANAGING TO KEEP A RHYTHM!
?!
THAT'S WHAT YOU FIND SURPRISING?!
HEY, YOU TWO! I WANNA KNOW WHAT CONSENSUAL [redacted] SENSUAL ACTS MEN DO.
SHOULD I CHEER THEM ON? I WANNA WATCH THEM GET THEIR GAME ON!
WHAT IN THE WORLD IS FUJIWARA TALKING ABOUT?!

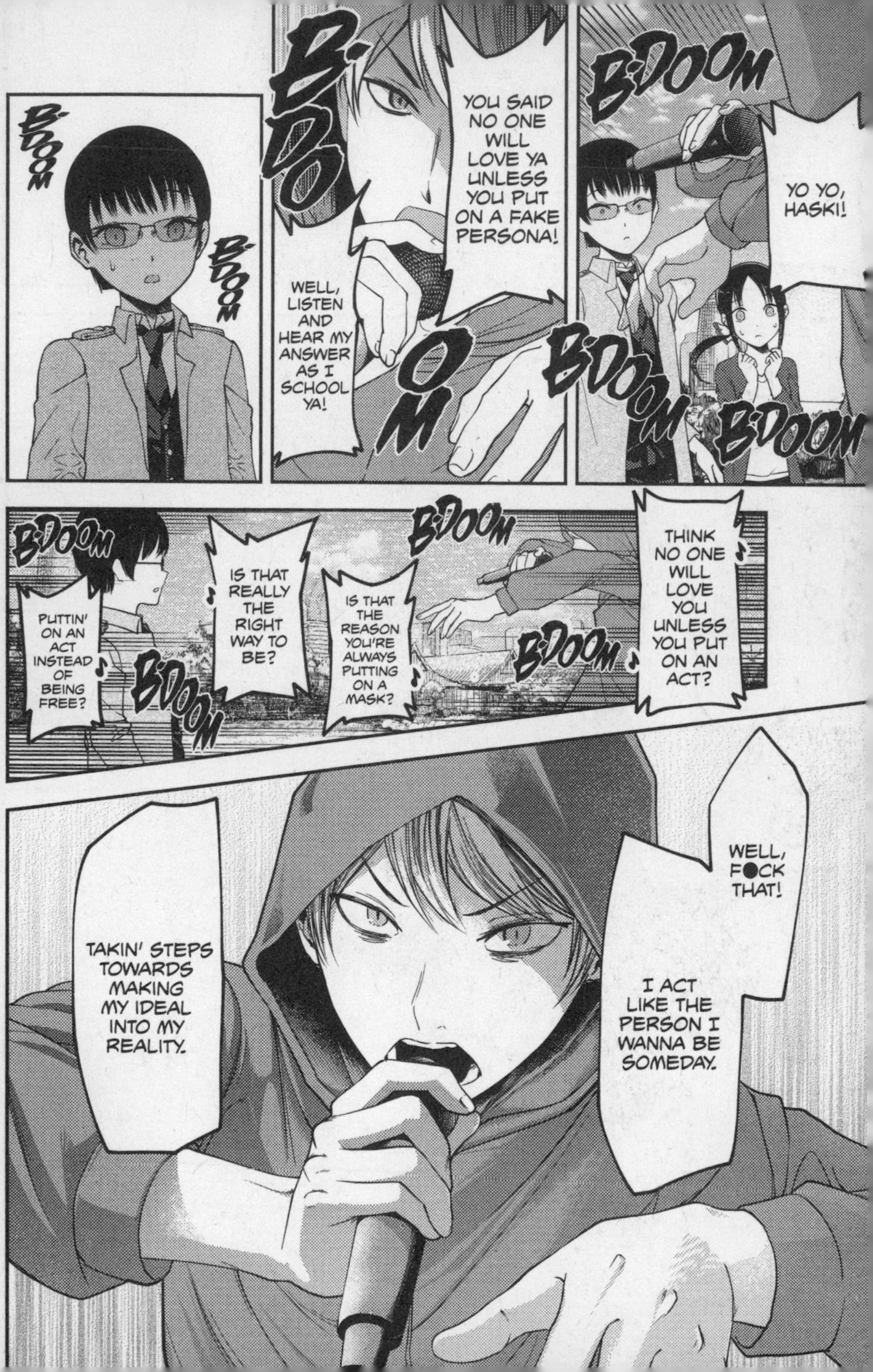
B-DOOM
YO YO, HASKI!
B-DOOM
B-DOOM
B-DOOOM
YOU SAID NO ONE WILL LOVE YA UNLESS YOU PUT ON A FAKE PERSONA!
WELL, LISTEN AND HEAR MY ANSWER AS I SCHOOL YA!
B-DOOM
B-DOOM
THINK NO ONE WILL LOVE YOU UNLESS YOU PUT ON AN ACT?
B-DOOM
B-DOOM
IS THAT THE REASON YOU'RE ALWAYS PUTTING ON A MASK?
IS THAT REALLY THE RIGHT WAY TO BE?
B-DOOM
PUTTIN' ON AN ACT INSTEAD OF BEING FREE?
B-DOOM
WELL, F●CK THAT!
I ACT LIKE THE PERSON I WANNA BE SOMEDAY.
TAKIN' STEPS TOWARDS MAKING MY IDEAL INTO MY REALITY.

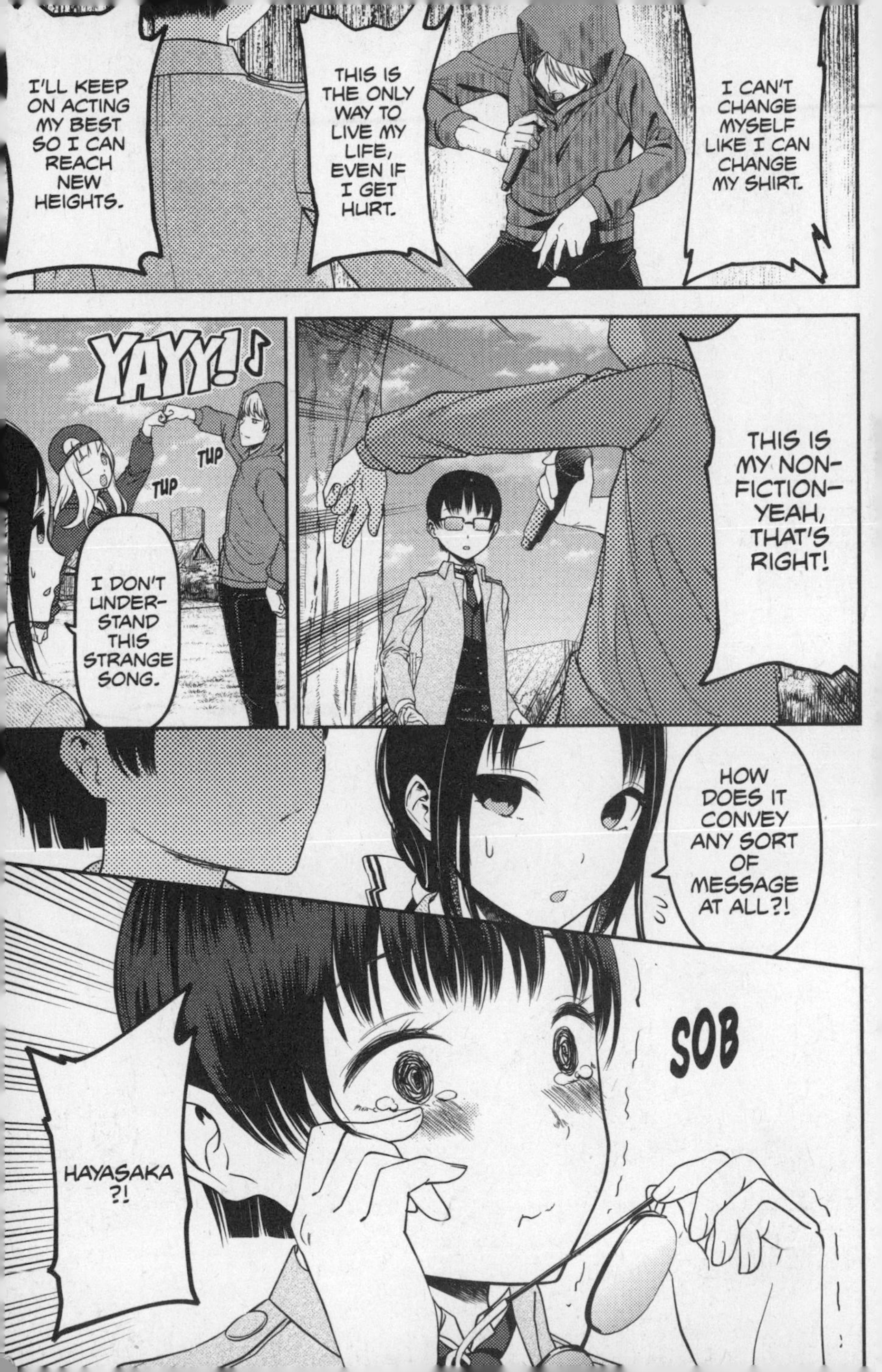
I CAN'T CHANGE MYSELF LIKE I CAN CHANGE MY SHIRT.
THIS IS THE ONLY WAY TO LIVE MY LIFE, EVEN IF I GET HURT.
I'LL KEEP ON ACTING MY BEST SO I CAN REACH NEW HEIGHTS.
THIS IS MY NON-FICTION—YEAH, THAT'S RIGHT!
YAYY! ♪
TUP
TUP
I DON'T UNDER-STAND THIS STRANGE SONG.
HOW DOES IT CONVEY ANY SORT OF MESSAGE AT ALL?!
SOB
HAYASAKA?!

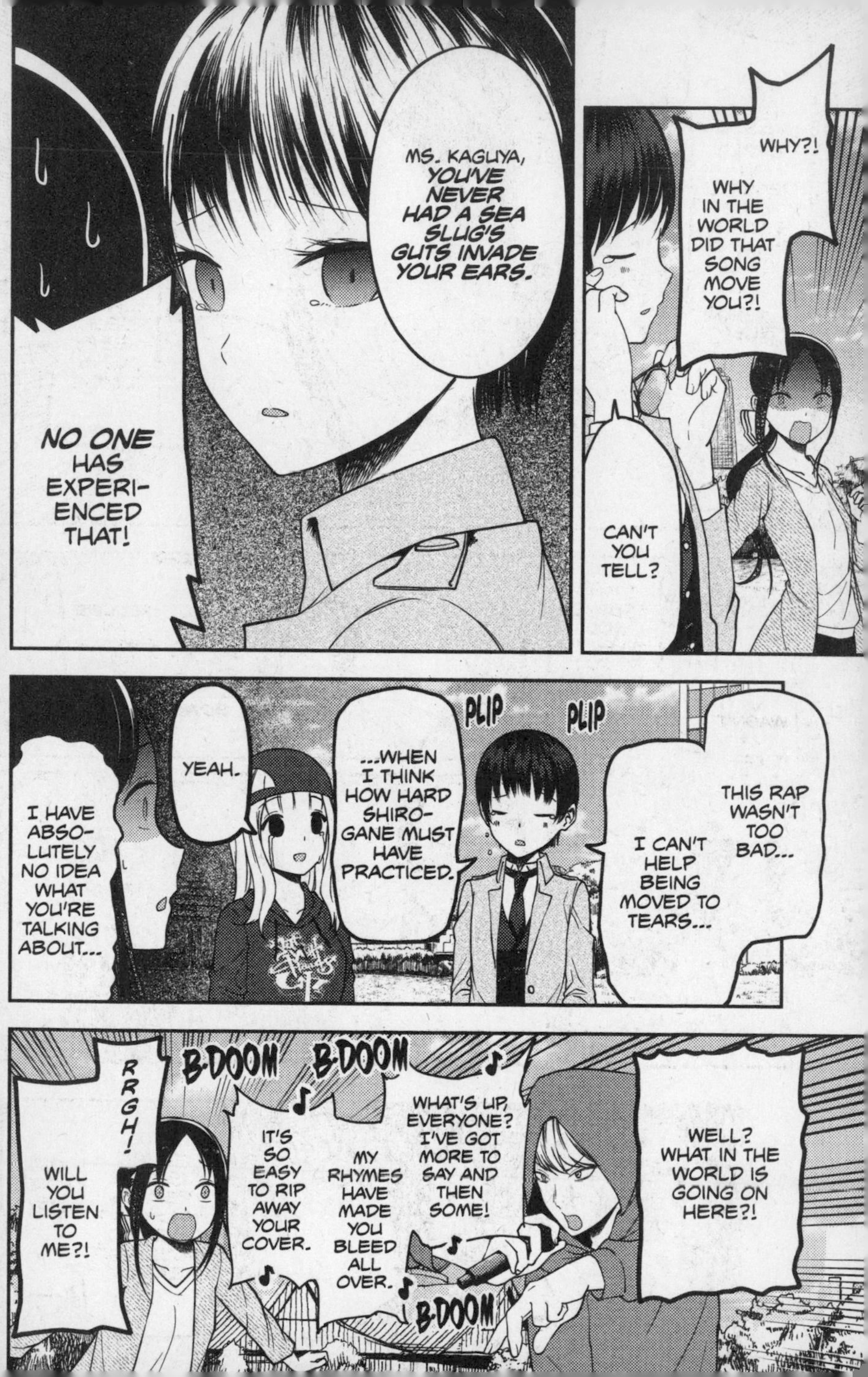
WHY?!
WHY IN THE WORLD DID THAT SONG MOVE YOU?!
CAN'T YOU TELL?
MS. KAGUYA, YOU'VE NEVER HAD A SEA SLUG'S GUTS INVADE YOUR EARS.
NO ONE HAS EXPERIENCED THAT!
THIS RAP WASN'T TOO BAD...
I CAN'T HELP BEING MOVED TO TEARS...
PLIP
PLIP
...WHEN I THINK HOW HARD SHIROGANE MUST HAVE PRACTICED.
YEAH.
I HAVE ABSOLUTELY NO IDEA WHAT YOU'RE TALKING ABOUT...
WELL? WHAT IN THE WORLD IS GOING ON HERE?!
B-DOOM
B-DOOM
WHAT'S UP, EVERYONE? I'VE GOT MORE TO SAY AND THEN SOME!
MY RHYMES HAVE MADE YOU BLEED ALL OVER.
IT'S SO EASY TO RIP AWAY YOUR COVER.
B-DOOM
RRGH!
WILL YOU LISTEN TO ME?!

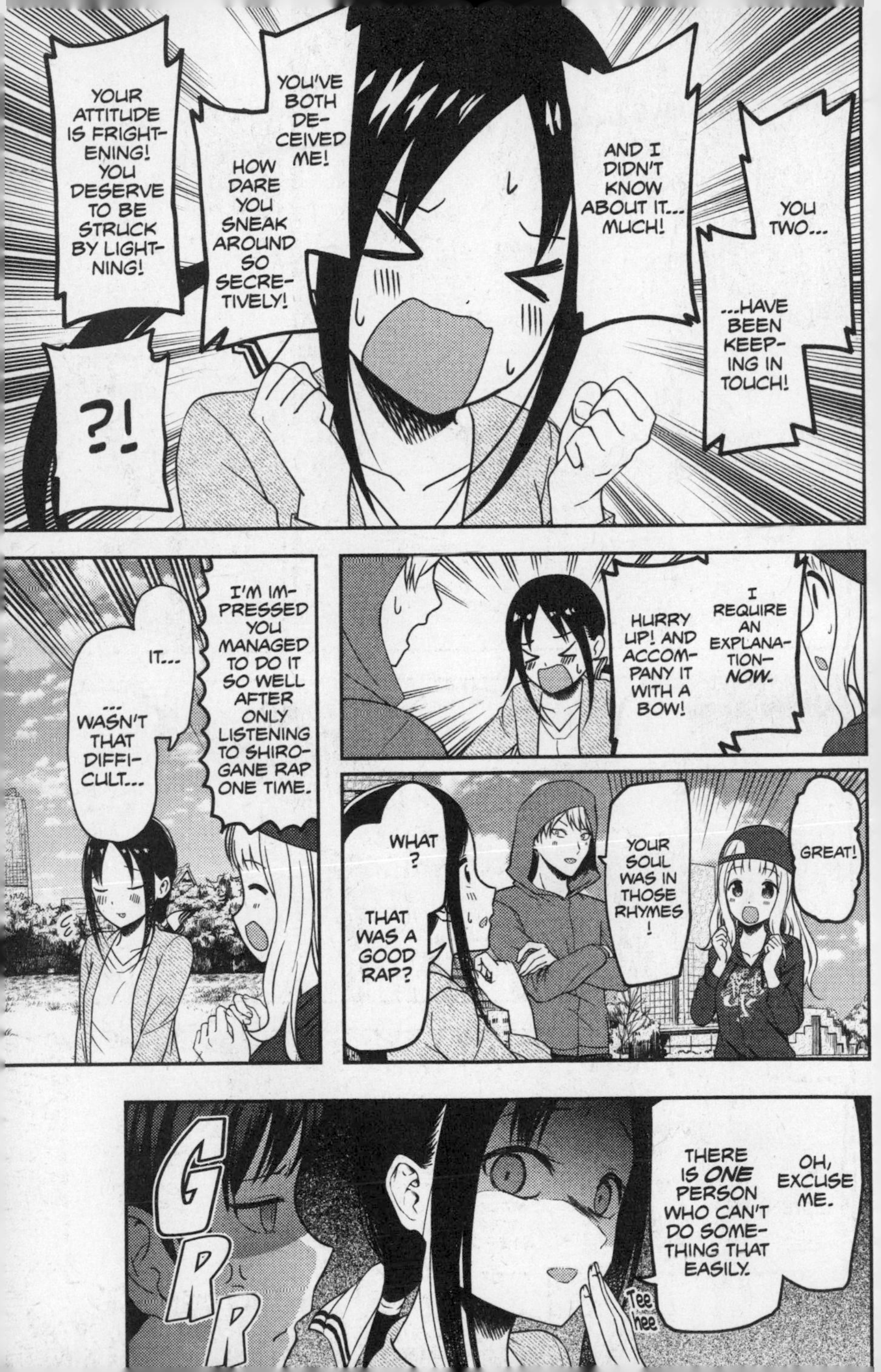
YOU TWO...
...HAVE BEEN KEEPING IN TOUCH!
AND I DIDN'T KNOW ABOUT IT... MUCH!
YOU'VE BOTH DECEIVED ME!
HOW DARE YOU SNEAK AROUND SO SECRETIVELY!
YOUR ATTITUDE IS FRIGHTENING! YOU DESERVE TO BE STRUCK BY LIGHTNING!
?!
I REQUIRE AN EXPLANATION—*NOW.*
HURRY UP! AND ACCOMPANY IT WITH A BOW!
GREAT!
YOUR SOUL WAS IN THOSE RHYMES!
WHAT? THAT WAS A GOOD RAP?
I'M IMPRESSED YOU MANAGED TO DO IT SO WELL AFTER ONLY LISTENING TO SHIROGANE RAP ONE TIME.
IT...
...WASN'T THAT DIFFICULT...
OH, EXCUSE ME.
THERE IS *ONE* PERSON WHO CAN'T DO SOMETHING THAT EASILY.
Tee hee
GRR

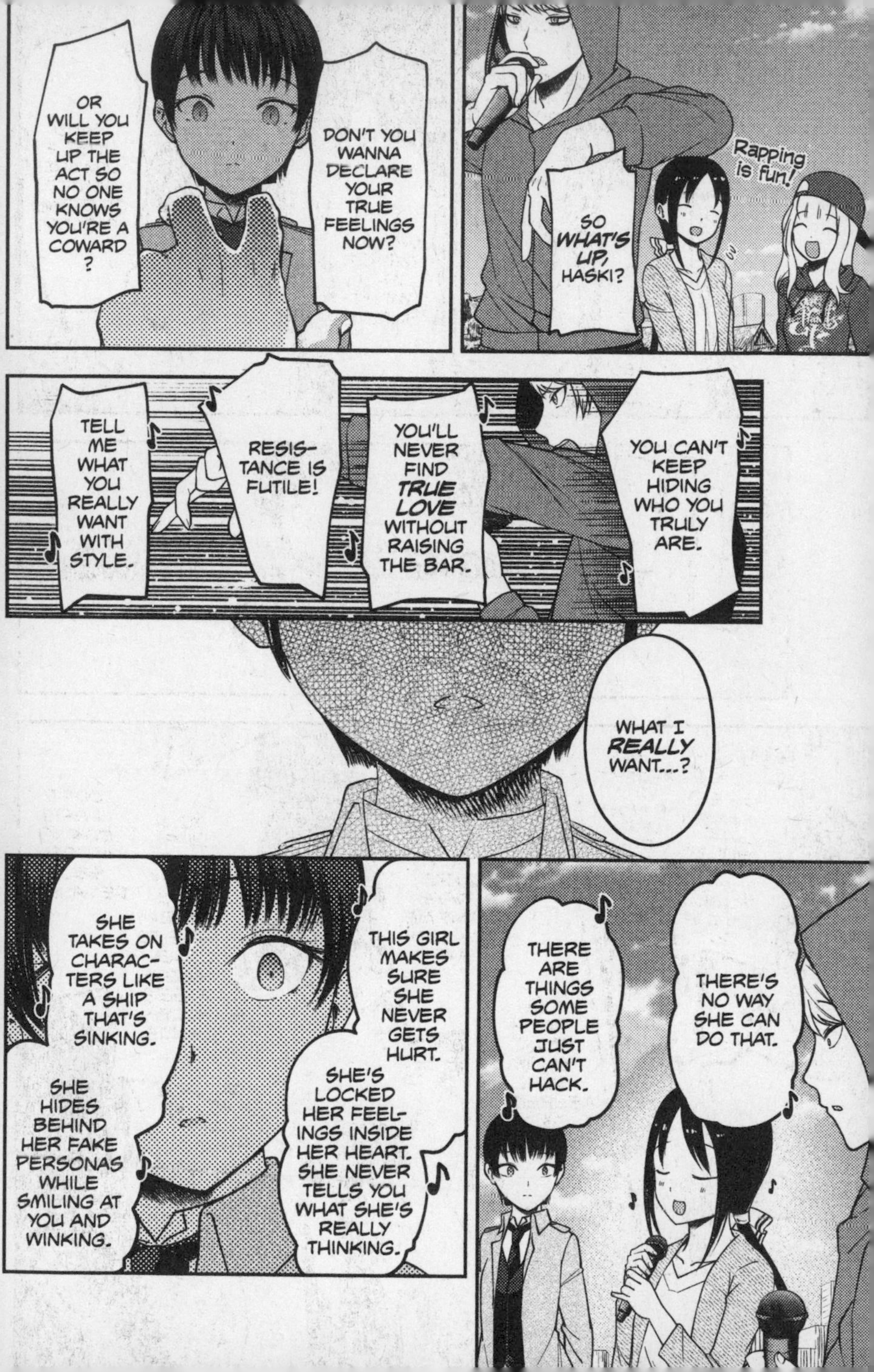
Rapping is fun!
SO *WHAT'S UP*, HASKI?
DON'T YOU WANNA DECLARE YOUR TRUE FEELINGS NOW?
OR WILL YOU KEEP UP THE ACT SO NO ONE KNOWS YOU'RE A COWARD?
YOU CAN'T KEEP HIDING WHO YOU TRULY ARE.
YOU'LL NEVER FIND *TRUE LOVE* WITHOUT RAISING THE BAR.
RESIS-TANCE IS FUTILE!
TELL ME WHAT YOU REALLY WANT WITH STYLE.
WHAT I *REALLY* WANT...?
THERE'S NO WAY SHE CAN DO THAT.
THERE ARE THINGS SOME PEOPLE JUST CAN'T HACK.
THIS GIRL MAKES SURE SHE NEVER GETS HURT.
SHE TAKES ON CHARAC-TERS LIKE A SHIP THAT'S SINKING.
SHE'S LOCKED HER FEEL-INGS INSIDE HER HEART. SHE NEVER TELLS YOU WHAT SHE'S REALLY THINKING.
SHE HIDES BEHIND HER FAKE PERSONAS WHILE SMILING AT YOU AND WINKING.

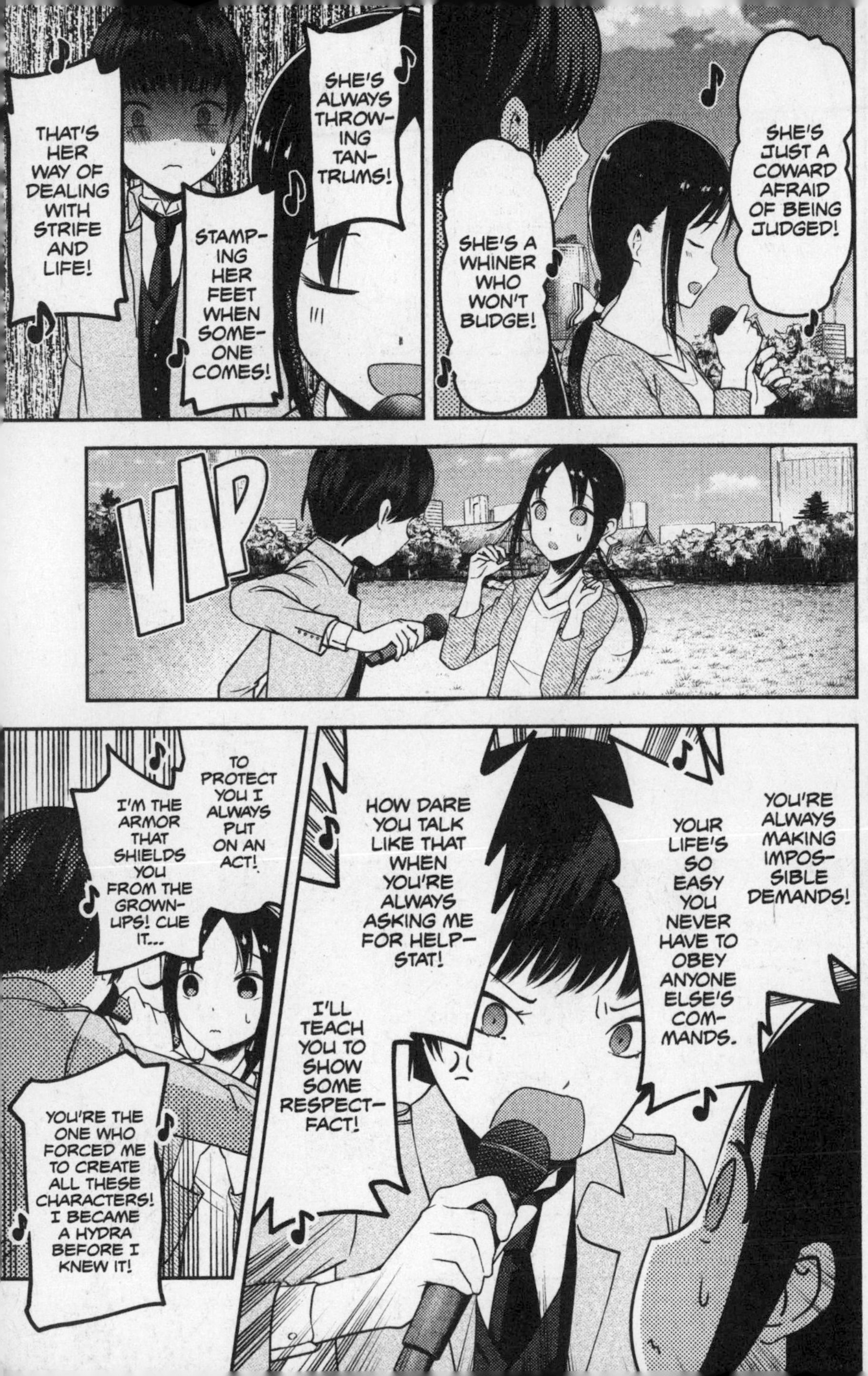
SHE'S JUST A COWARD AFRAID OF BEING JUDGED!
SHE'S A WHINER WHO WON'T BUDGE!
SHE'S ALWAYS THROWING TANTRUMS!
STAMPING HER FEET WHEN SOMEONE COMES!
THAT'S HER WAY OF DEALING WITH STRIFE AND LIFE!
VIP
YOU'RE ALWAYS MAKING IMPOSSIBLE DEMANDS!
YOUR LIFE'S SO EASY YOU NEVER HAVE TO OBEY ANYONE ELSE'S COMMANDS.
HOW DARE YOU TALK LIKE THAT WHEN YOU'RE ALWAYS ASKING ME FOR HELP-STAT!
I'LL TEACH YOU TO SHOW SOME RESPECT-FACT!
TO PROTECT YOU I ALWAYS PUT ON AN ACT!
I'M THE ARMOR THAT SHIELDS YOU FROM THE GROWN-UPS! CUE IT...
YOU'RE THE ONE WHO FORCED ME TO CREATE ALL THESE CHARACTERS! I BECAME A HYDRA BEFORE I KNEW IT!

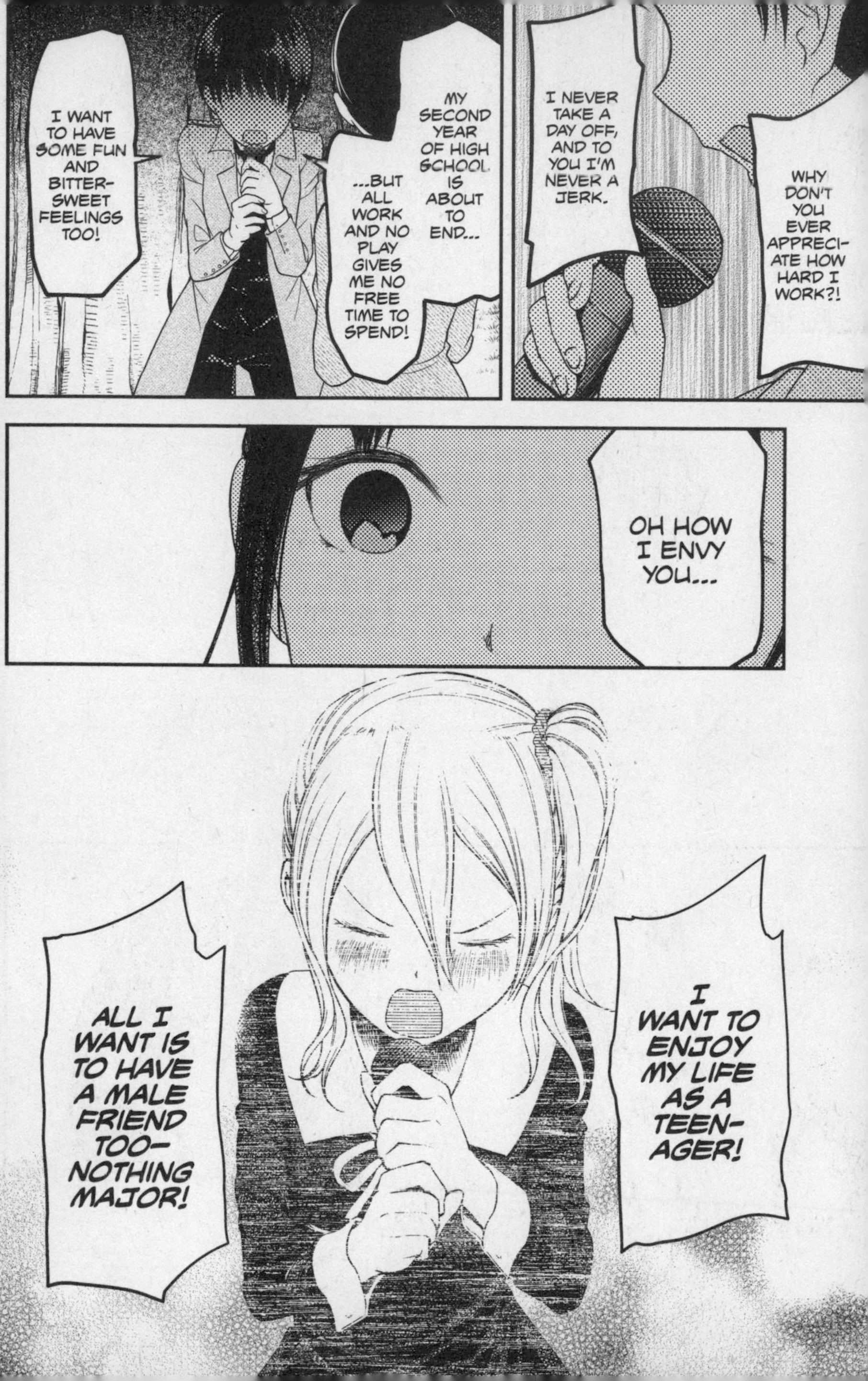

WHY DON'T YOU EVER APPRECIATE HOW HARD I WORK?!
I NEVER TAKE A DAY OFF, AND TO YOU I'M NEVER A JERK.
MY SECOND YEAR OF HIGH SCHOOL IS ABOUT TO END...
...BUT ALL WORK AND NO PLAY GIVES ME NO FREE TIME TO SPEND!
I WANT TO HAVE SOME FUN AND BITTER-SWEET FEELINGS TOO!
OH HOW I ENVY YOU...
I WANT TO ENJOY MY LIFE AS A TEEN-AGER!
ALL I WANT IS TO HAVE A MALE FRIEND TOO—NOTHING MAJOR!

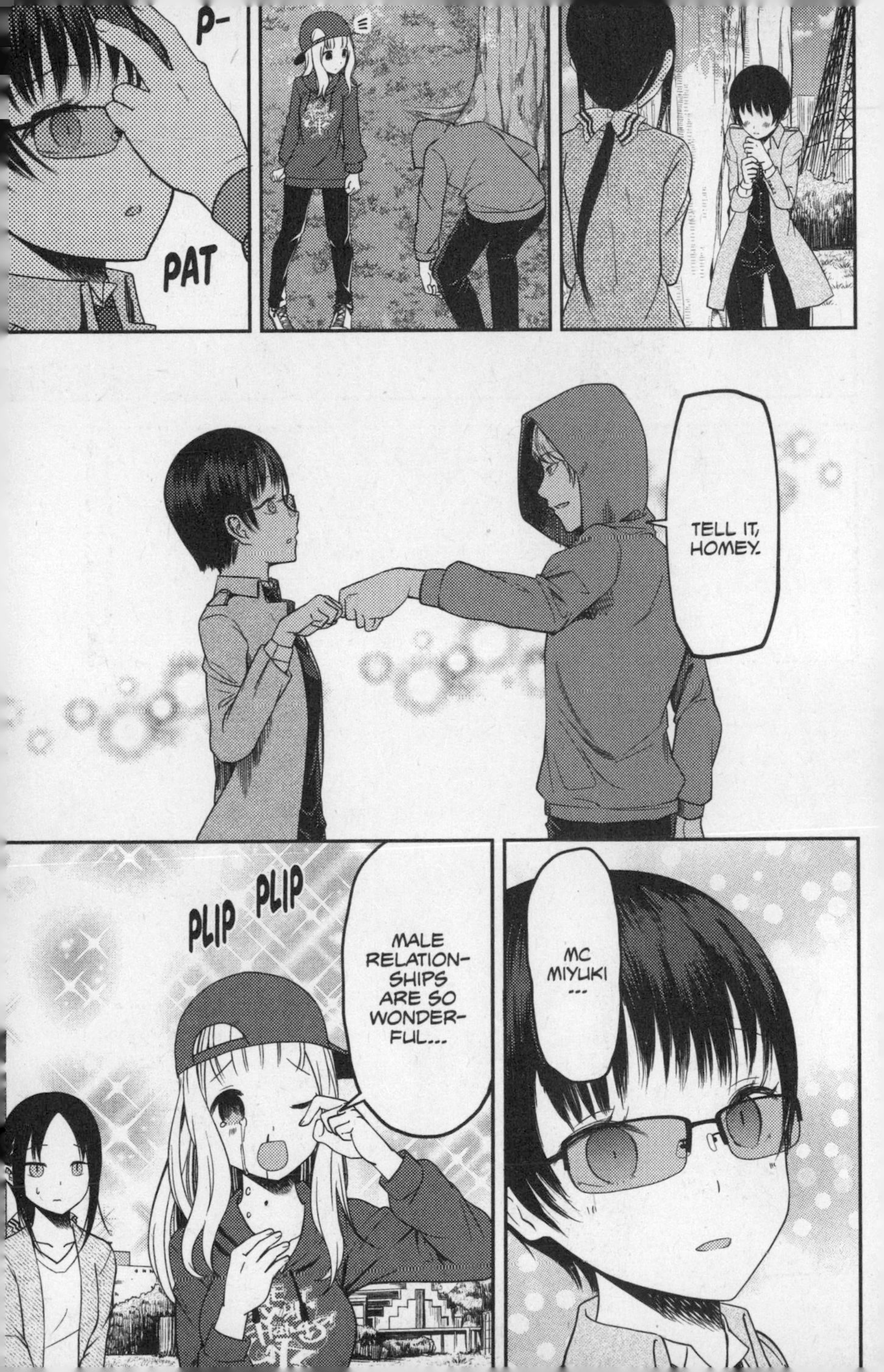
P-
PAT
TELL IT, HOMEY.
MC MIYUKI...
PLIP PLIP
MALE RELATIONSHIPS ARE SO WONDERFUL...

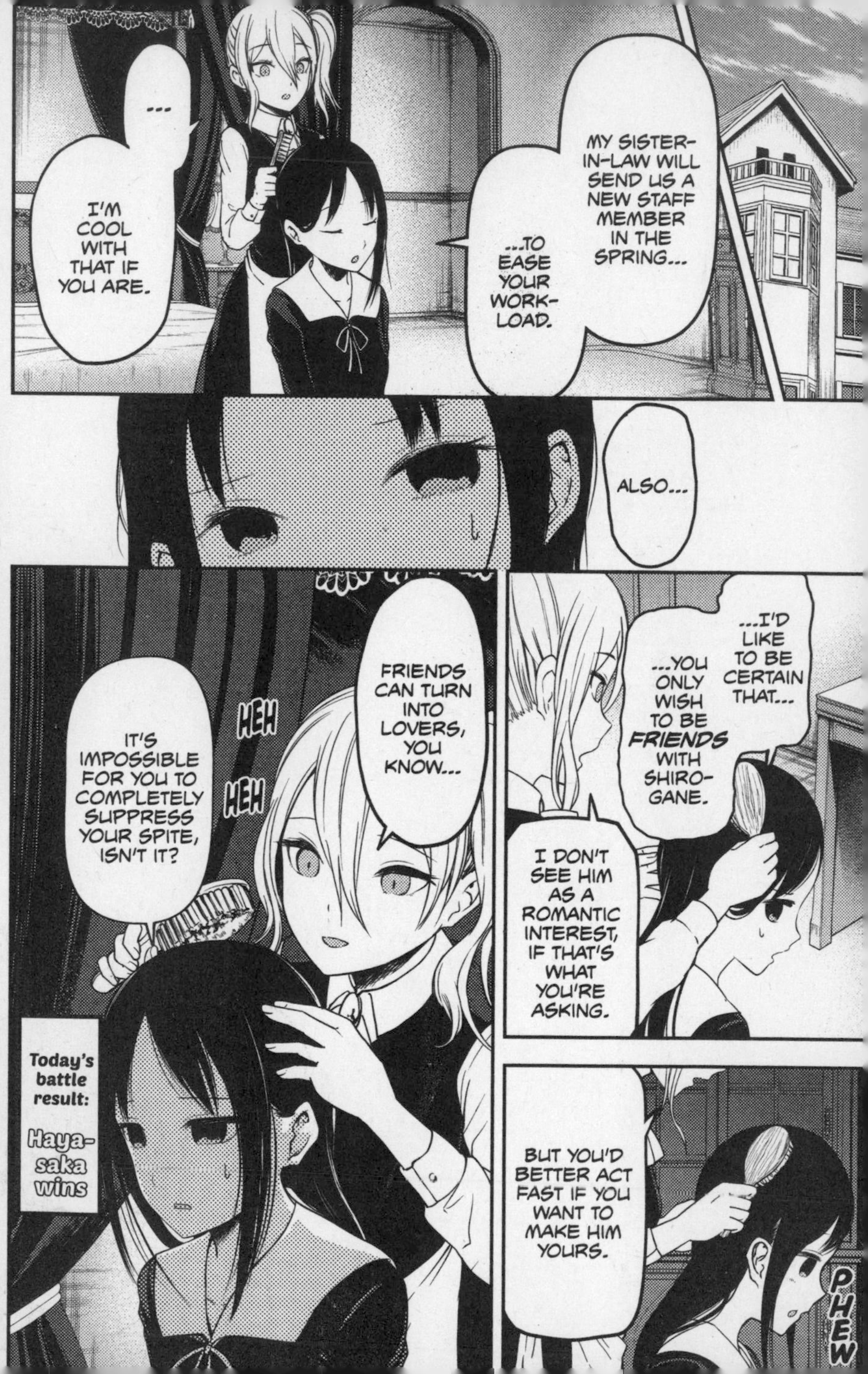
MY SISTER-IN-LAW WILL SEND US A NEW STAFF MEMBER IN THE SPRING...
...TO EASE YOUR WORK-LOAD.
...
I'M COOL WITH THAT IF YOU ARE.
ALSO...
...I'D LIKE TO BE CERTAIN THAT...
...YOU ONLY WISH TO BE FRIENDS WITH SHIRO-GANE.
I DON'T SEE HIM AS A ROMANTIC INTEREST, IF THAT'S WHAT YOU'RE ASKING.
BUT YOU'D BETTER ACT FAST IF YOU WANT TO MAKE HIM YOURS.
PHEW
FRIENDS CAN TURN INTO LOVERS, YOU KNOW...
HEH
HEH
IT'S IMPOSSIBLE FOR YOU TO COMPLETELY SUPPRESS YOUR SPITE, ISN'T IT?
Today's battle result:
Haya-saka wins

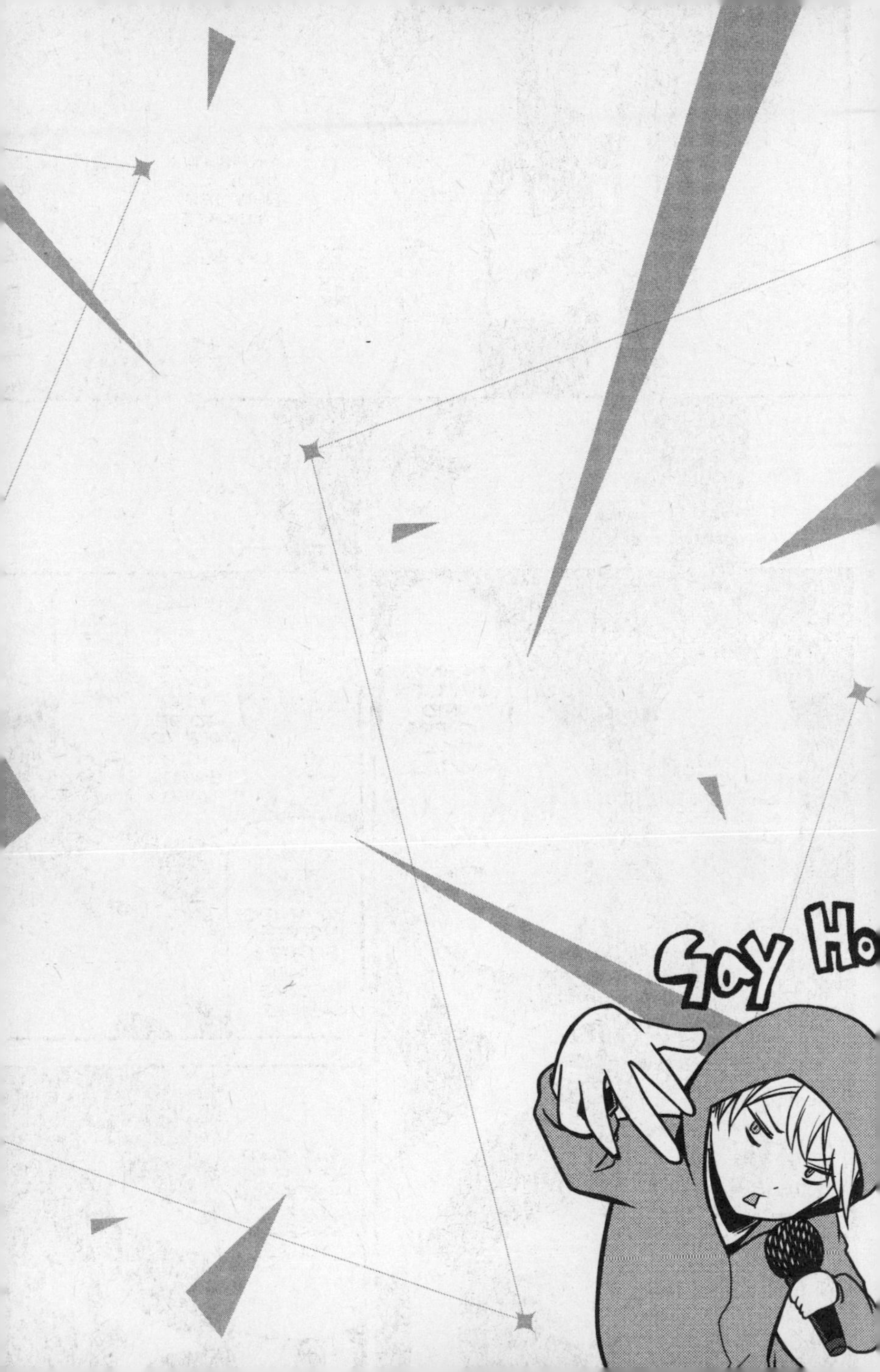
Say Ho

KAGUYA-SAMA
LOVE IS WAR

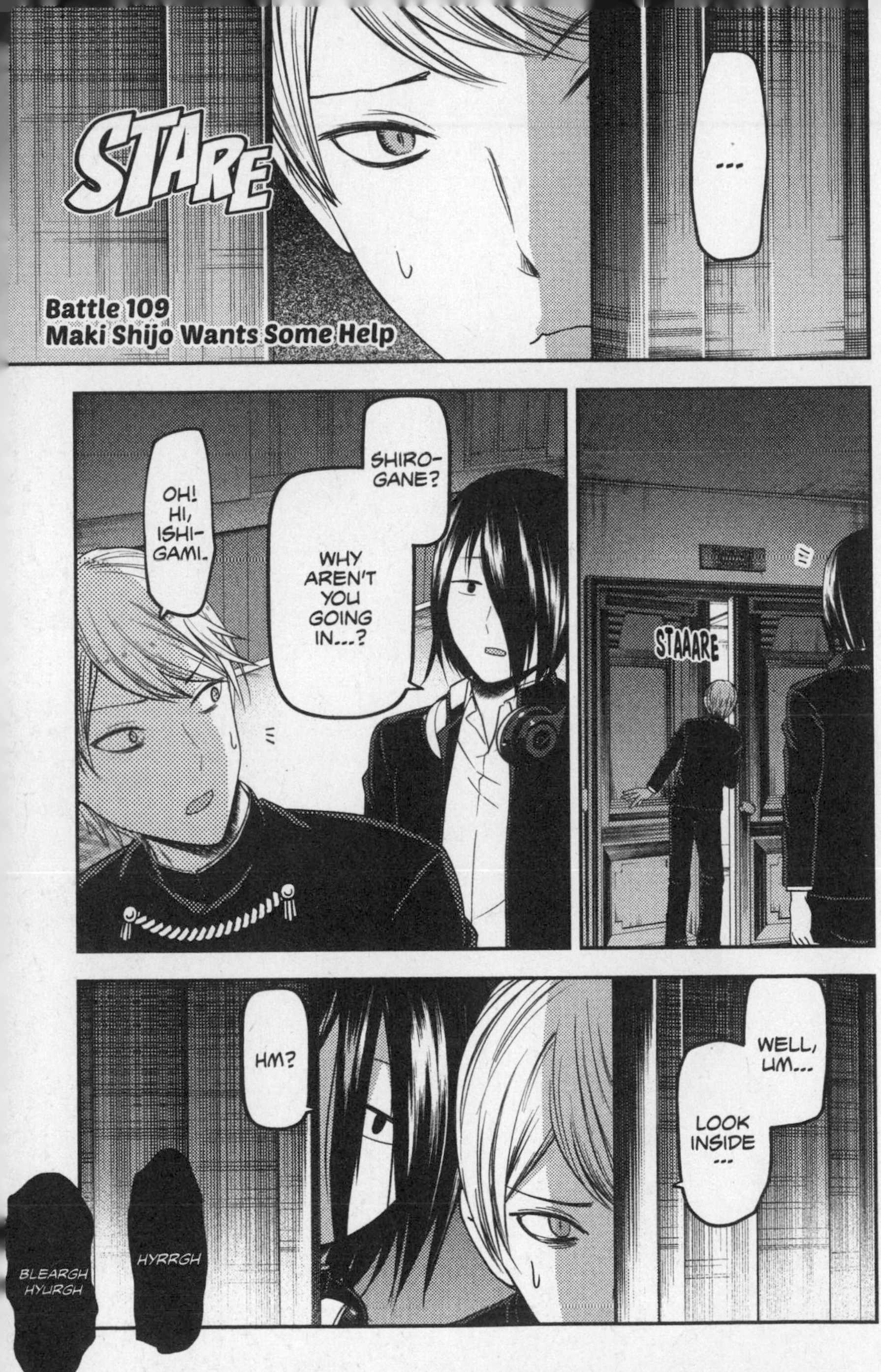
...
STARE
Battle 109
Maki Shijo Wants Some Help
STAAARE
SHIRO-GANE?
WHY AREN'T YOU GOING IN...?
OH! HI, ISHI-GAMI.
WELL, UM...
LOOK INSIDE ...
HM?
HYRRGH
BLEARGH HYURGH

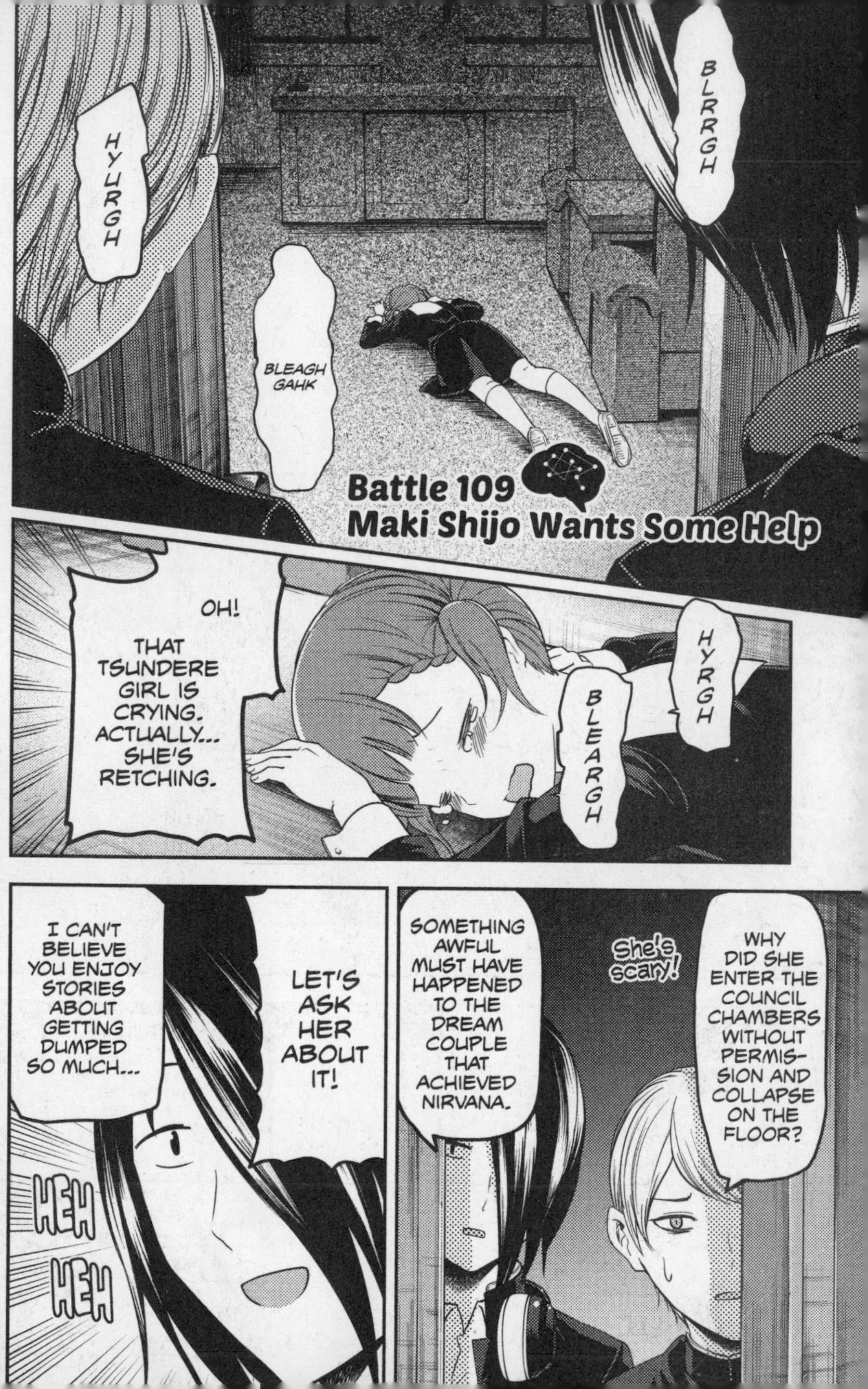
BLRRGH
BLEAGH GAHK
HYURGH
Battle 109
Maki Shijo Wants Some Help
HYRGH
BLEARGH
OH!
THAT TSUNDERE GIRL IS CRYING. ACTUALLY... SHE'S RETCHING.
WHY DID SHE ENTER THE COUNCIL CHAMBERS WITHOUT PERMISSION AND COLLAPSE ON THE FLOOR?
She's scary!
SOMETHING AWFUL MUST HAVE HAPPENED TO THE DREAM COUPLE THAT ACHIEVED NIRVANA.
LET'S ASK HER ABOUT IT!
I CAN'T BELIEVE YOU ENJOY STORIES ABOUT GETTING DUMPED SO MUCH...
HEH
HEH

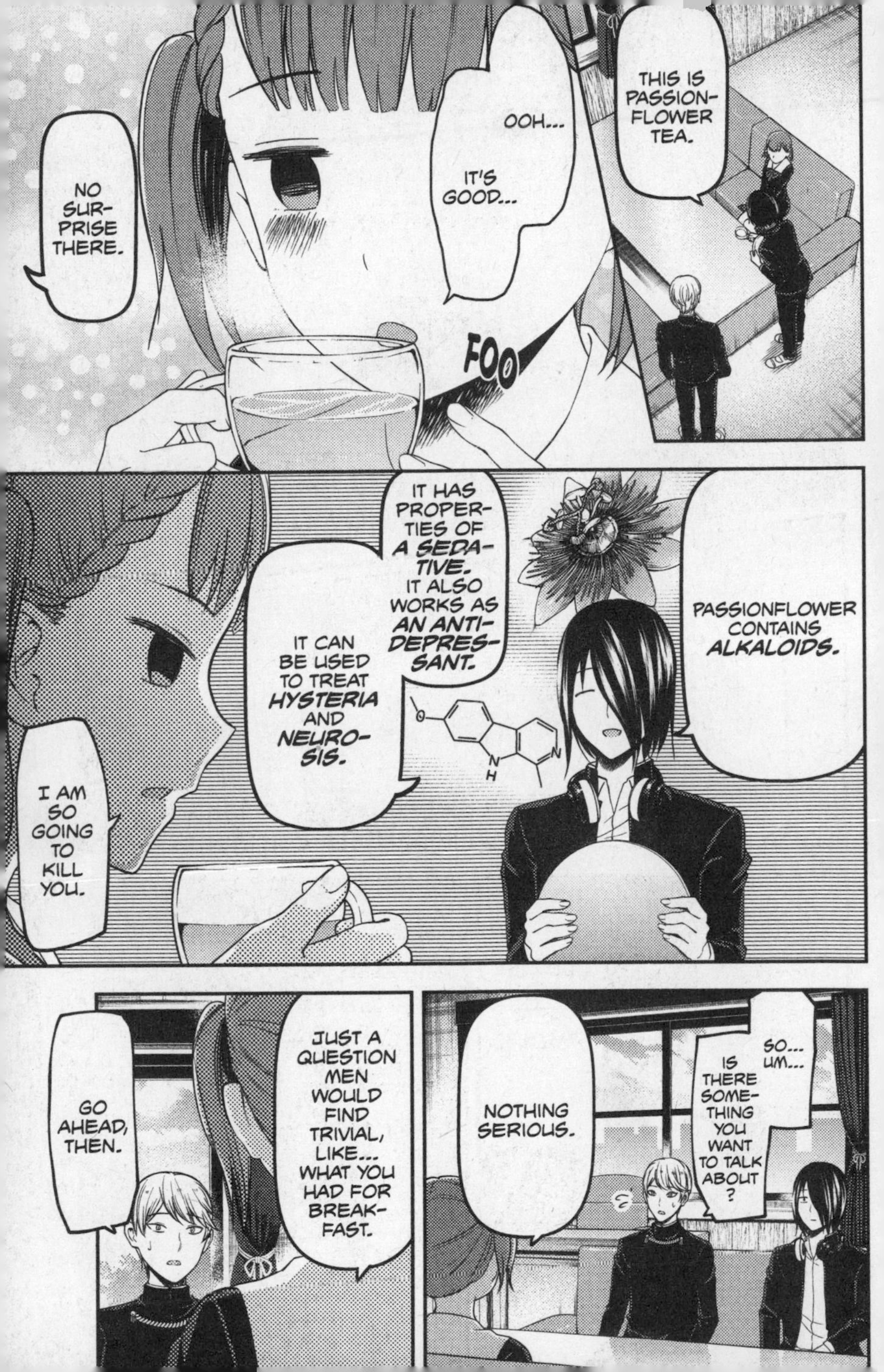
THIS IS PASSIONFLOWER TEA.
OOH...
IT'S GOOD...
FOO
NO SURPRISE THERE.
PASSIONFLOWER CONTAINS ALKALOIDS.
IT HAS PROPERTIES OF A SEDATIVE. IT ALSO WORKS AS AN ANTIDEPRESSANT.
IT CAN BE USED TO TREAT HYSTERIA AND NEUROSIS.
I AM SO GOING TO KILL YOU.
SO... UM...
IS THERE SOMETHING YOU WANT TO TALK ABOUT?
NOTHING SERIOUS.
JUST A QUESTION MEN WOULD FIND TRIVIAL, LIKE... WHAT YOU HAD FOR BREAKFAST.
GO AHEAD, THEN.

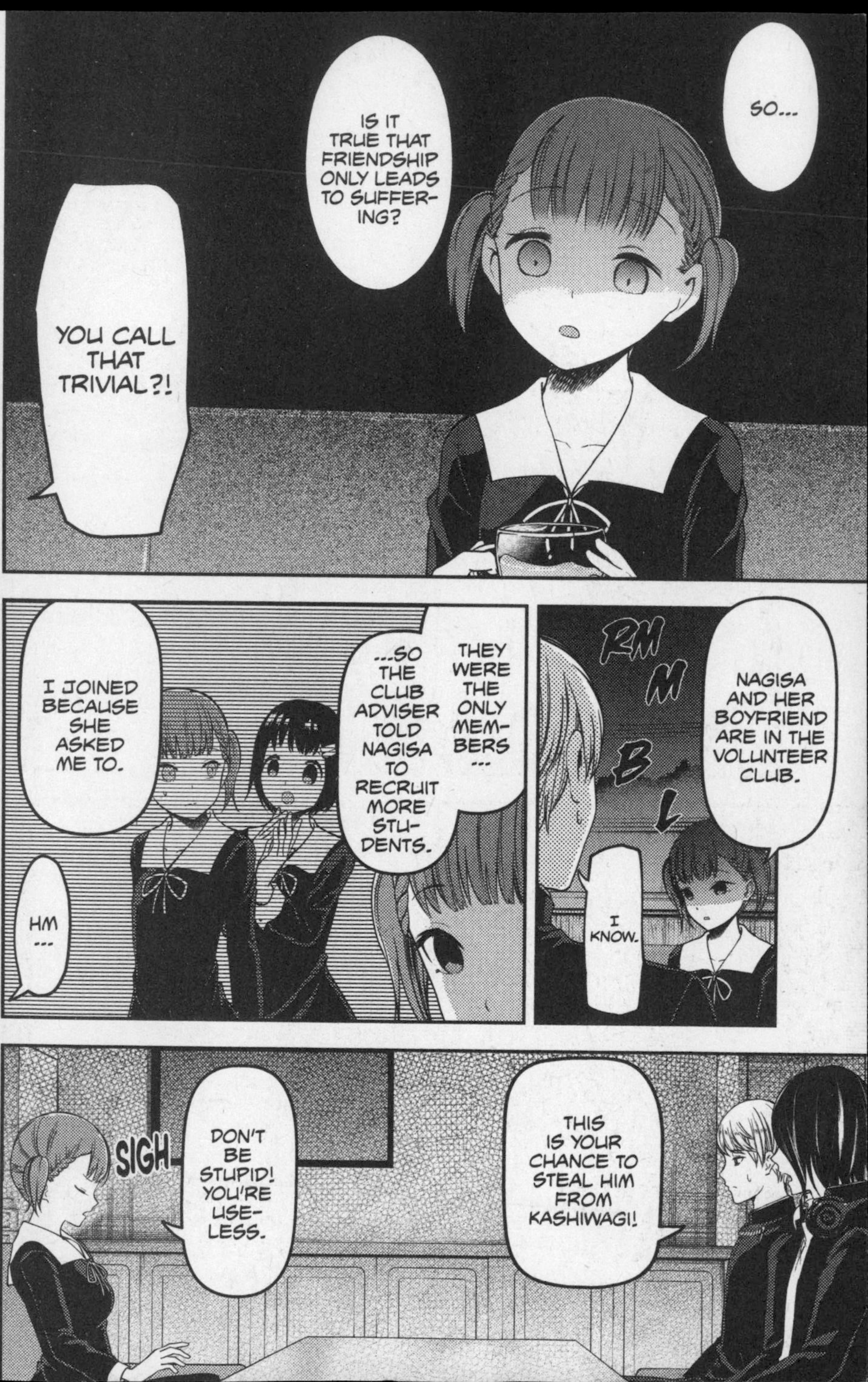
SO...
IS IT TRUE THAT FRIENDSHIP ONLY LEADS TO SUFFERING?
YOU CALL THAT TRIVIAL?!
NAGISA AND HER BOYFRIEND ARE IN THE VOLUNTEER CLUB.
RMMBL
I KNOW.
THEY WERE THE ONLY MEMBERS...
...SO THE CLUB ADVISER TOLD NAGISA TO RECRUIT MORE STUDENTS.
I JOINED BECAUSE SHE ASKED ME TO.
HM...
THIS IS YOUR CHANCE TO STEAL HIM FROM KASHIWAGI!
SIGH
DON'T BE STUPID! YOU'RE USELESS.

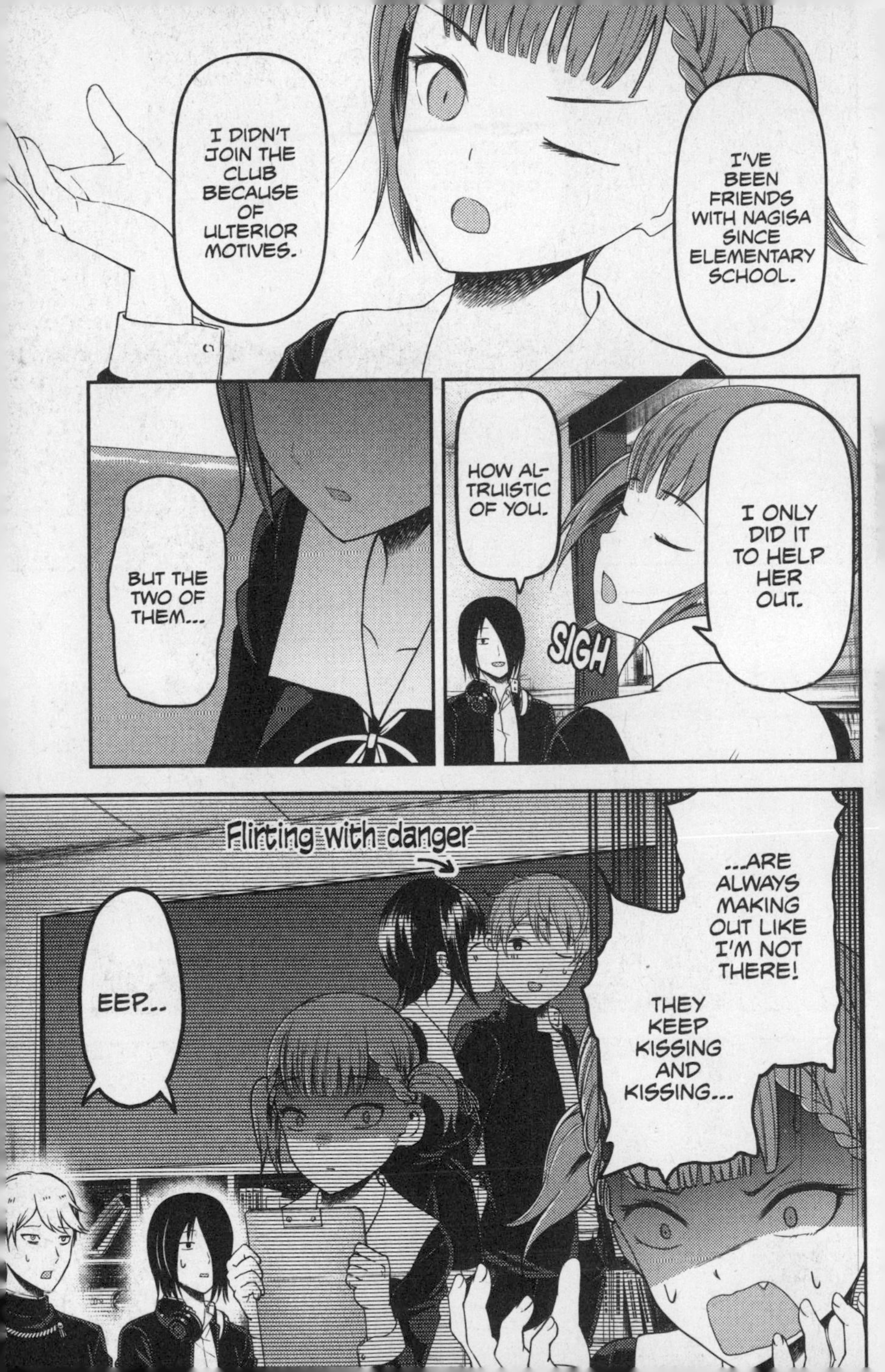
I'VE BEEN FRIENDS WITH NAGISA SINCE ELEMENTARY SCHOOL.
I DIDN'T JOIN THE CLUB BECAUSE OF ULTERIOR MOTIVES.
I ONLY DID IT TO HELP HER OUT.
SIGH
HOW AL-TRUISTIC OF YOU.
BUT THE TWO OF THEM...
...ARE ALWAYS MAKING OUT LIKE I'M NOT THERE!
THEY KEEP KISSING AND KISSING...
Flirting with danger
EEP...

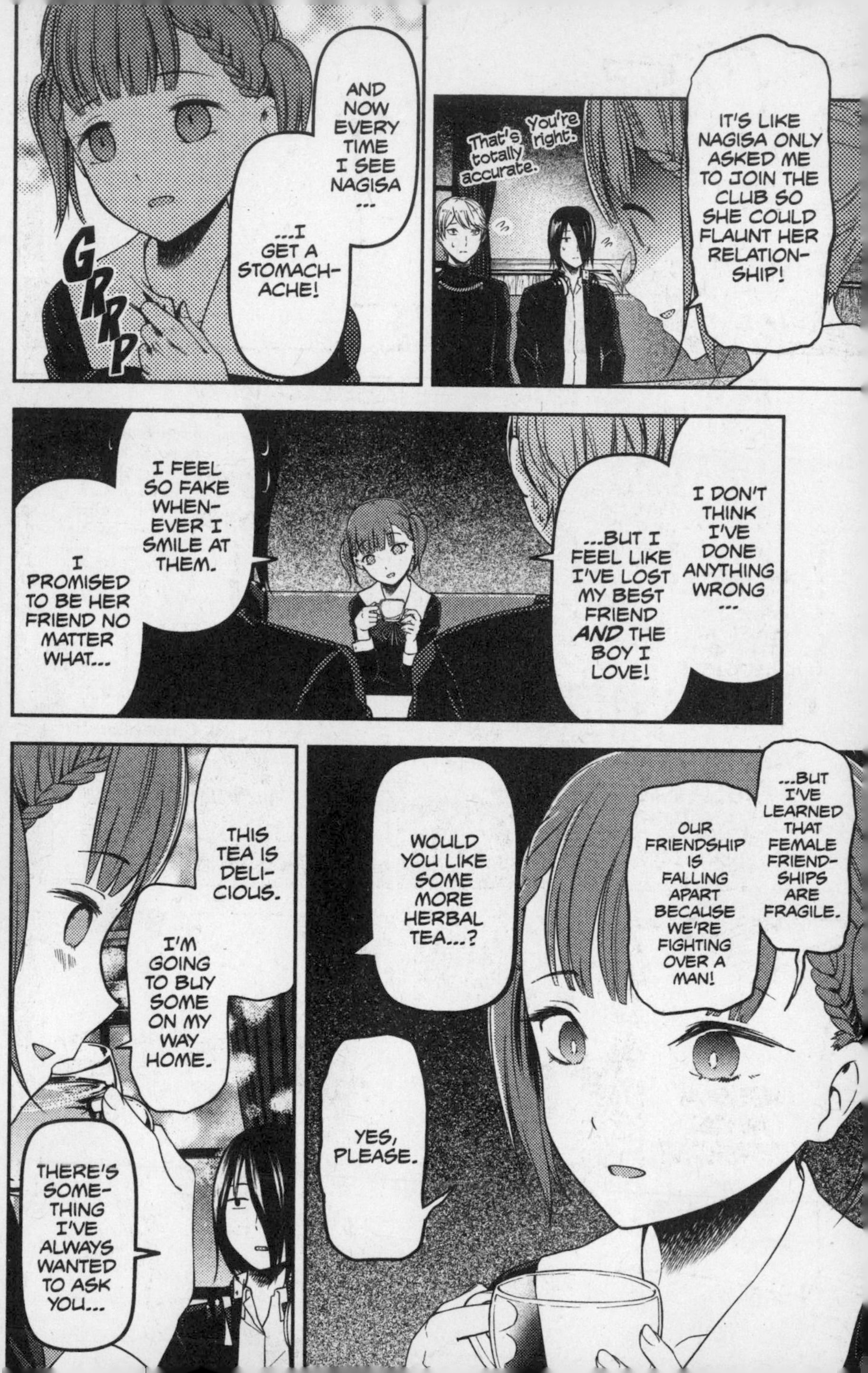

IT'S LIKE NAGISA ONLY ASKED ME TO JOIN THE CLUB SO SHE COULD FLAUNT HER RELATIONSHIP!
You're right.
That's totally accurate.
AND NOW EVERY TIME I SEE NAGISA...
...I GET A STOMACHACHE!
GRRP
I DON'T THINK I'VE DONE ANYTHING WRONG...
...BUT I FEEL LIKE I'VE LOST MY BEST FRIEND AND THE BOY I LOVE!
I FEEL SO FAKE WHENEVER I SMILE AT THEM.
I PROMISED TO BE HER FRIEND NO MATTER WHAT...
...BUT I'VE LEARNED THAT FEMALE FRIENDSHIPS ARE FRAGILE.
OUR FRIENDSHIP IS FALLING APART BECAUSE WE'RE FIGHTING OVER A MAN!
WOULD YOU LIKE SOME MORE HERBAL TEA...?
YES, PLEASE.
THIS TEA IS DELICIOUS.
I'M GOING TO BUY SOME ON MY WAY HOME.
THERE'S SOMETHING I'VE ALWAYS WANTED TO ASK YOU...

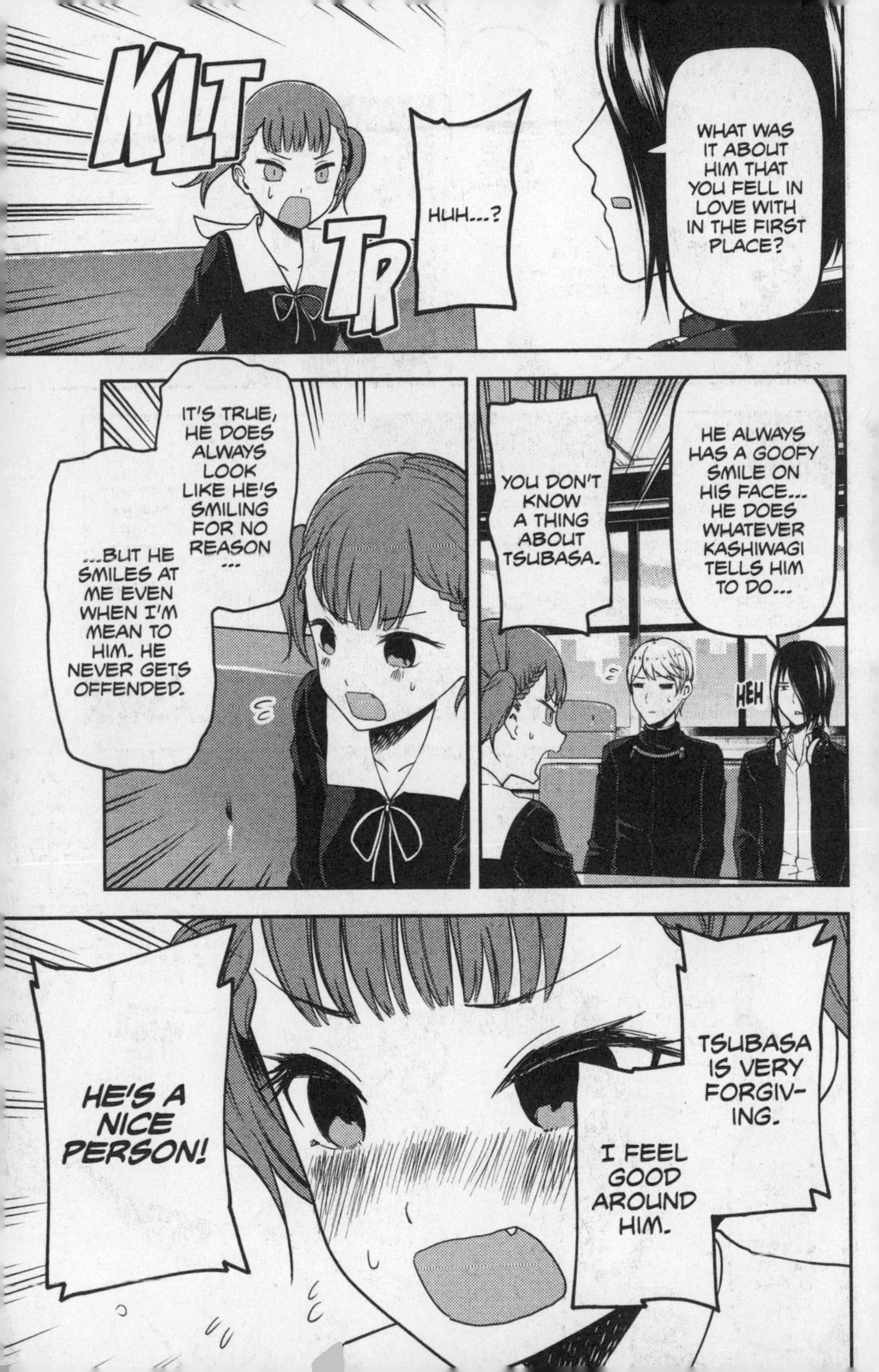
WHAT WAS IT ABOUT HIM THAT YOU FELL IN LOVE WITH IN THE FIRST PLACE?
HUH...?
TR
KLT
HE ALWAYS HAS A GOOFY SMILE ON HIS FACE... HE DOES WHATEVER KASHIWAGI TELLS HIM TO DO...
HEH
YOU DON'T KNOW A THING ABOUT TSUBASA.
IT'S TRUE, HE DOES ALWAYS LOOK LIKE HE'S SMILING FOR NO REASON...
...BUT HE SMILES AT ME EVEN WHEN I'M MEAN TO HIM. HE NEVER GETS OFFENDED.
TSUBASA IS VERY FORGIV-ING.
I FEEL GOOD AROUND HIM.
HE'S A NICE PERSON!

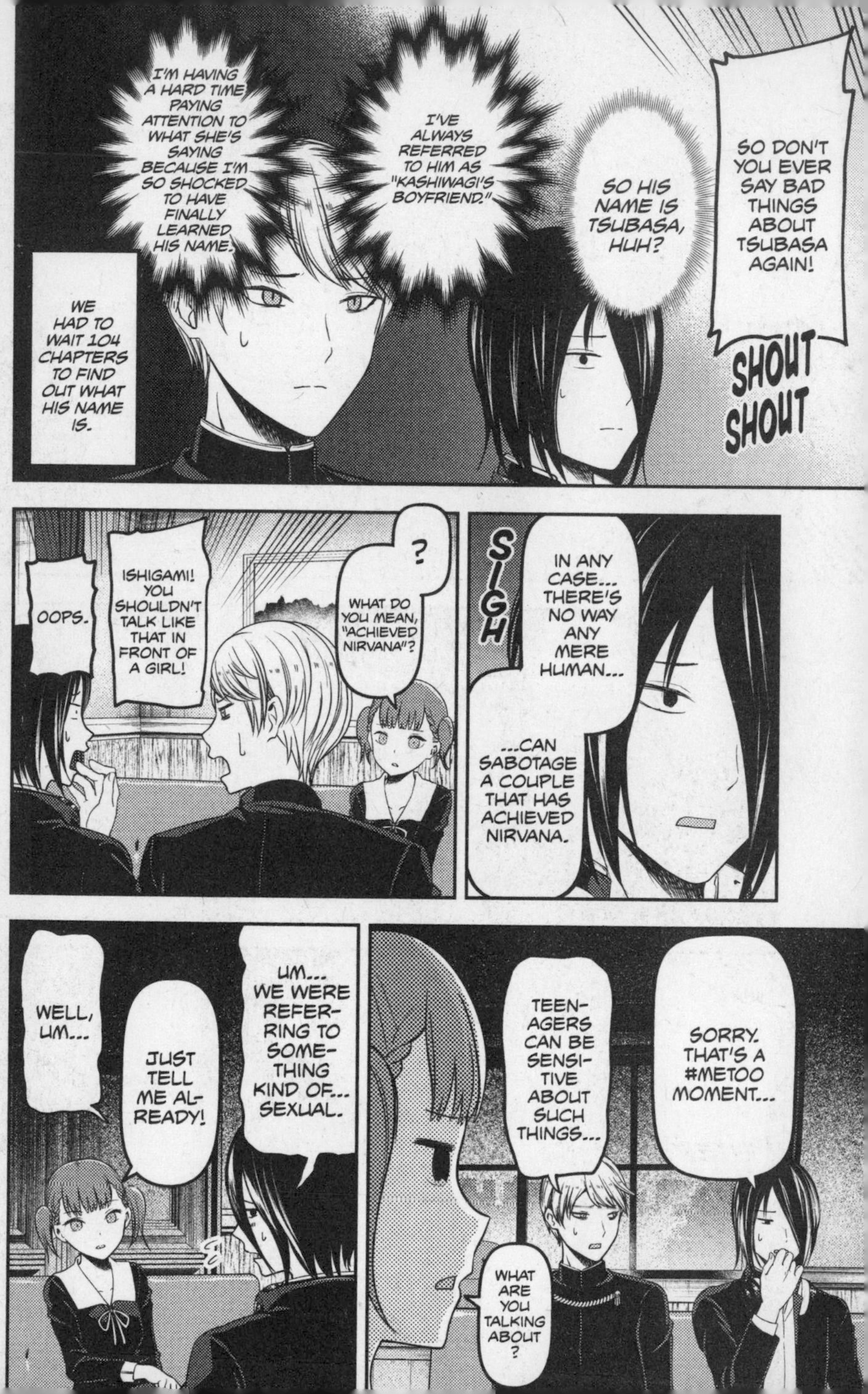
SO DON'T YOU EVER SAY BAD THINGS ABOUT TSUBASA AGAIN!
SHOUT SHOUT
SO HIS NAME IS TSUBASA, HUH?
I'VE ALWAYS REFERRED TO HIM AS "KASHIWAGI'S BOYFRIEND."
I'M HAVING A HARD TIME PAYING ATTENTION TO WHAT SHE'S SAYING BECAUSE I'M SO SHOCKED TO HAVE FINALLY LEARNED HIS NAME.
WE HAD TO WAIT 104 CHAPTERS TO FIND OUT WHAT HIS NAME IS.
SIGH
IN ANY CASE... THERE'S NO WAY ANY MERE HUMAN...
...CAN SABOTAGE A COUPLE THAT HAS ACHIEVED NIRVANA.
?
WHAT DO YOU MEAN, "ACHIEVED NIRVANA"?
ISHIGAMI! YOU SHOULDN'T TALK LIKE THAT IN FRONT OF A GIRL!
OOPS.
SORRY. THAT'S A #METOO MOMENT...
TEEN-AGERS CAN BE SENSI-TIVE ABOUT SUCH THINGS...
WHAT ARE YOU TALKING ABOUT?
UM... WE WERE REFER-RING TO SOME-THING KIND OF... SEXUAL.
JUST TELL ME AL-READY!
WELL, UM...

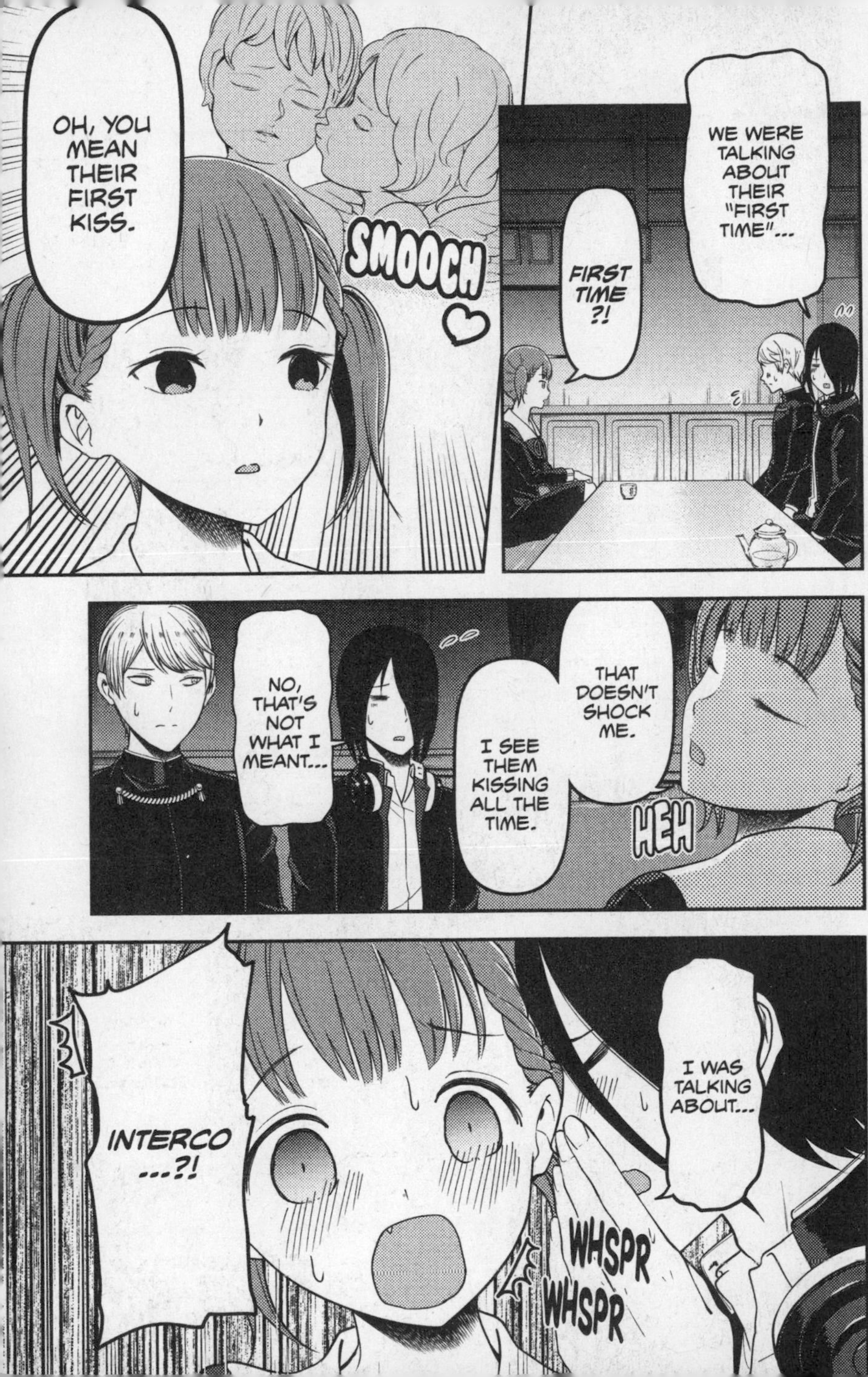
WE WERE TALKING ABOUT THEIR "FIRST TIME"...
FIRST TIME ?!
OH, YOU MEAN THEIR FIRST KISS.
SMOOCH
THAT DOESN'T SHOCK ME.
I SEE THEM KISSING ALL THE TIME.
HEH
NO, THAT'S NOT WHAT I MEANT...
I WAS TALKING ABOUT...
WHSPR
WHSPR
INTERCO ...?!

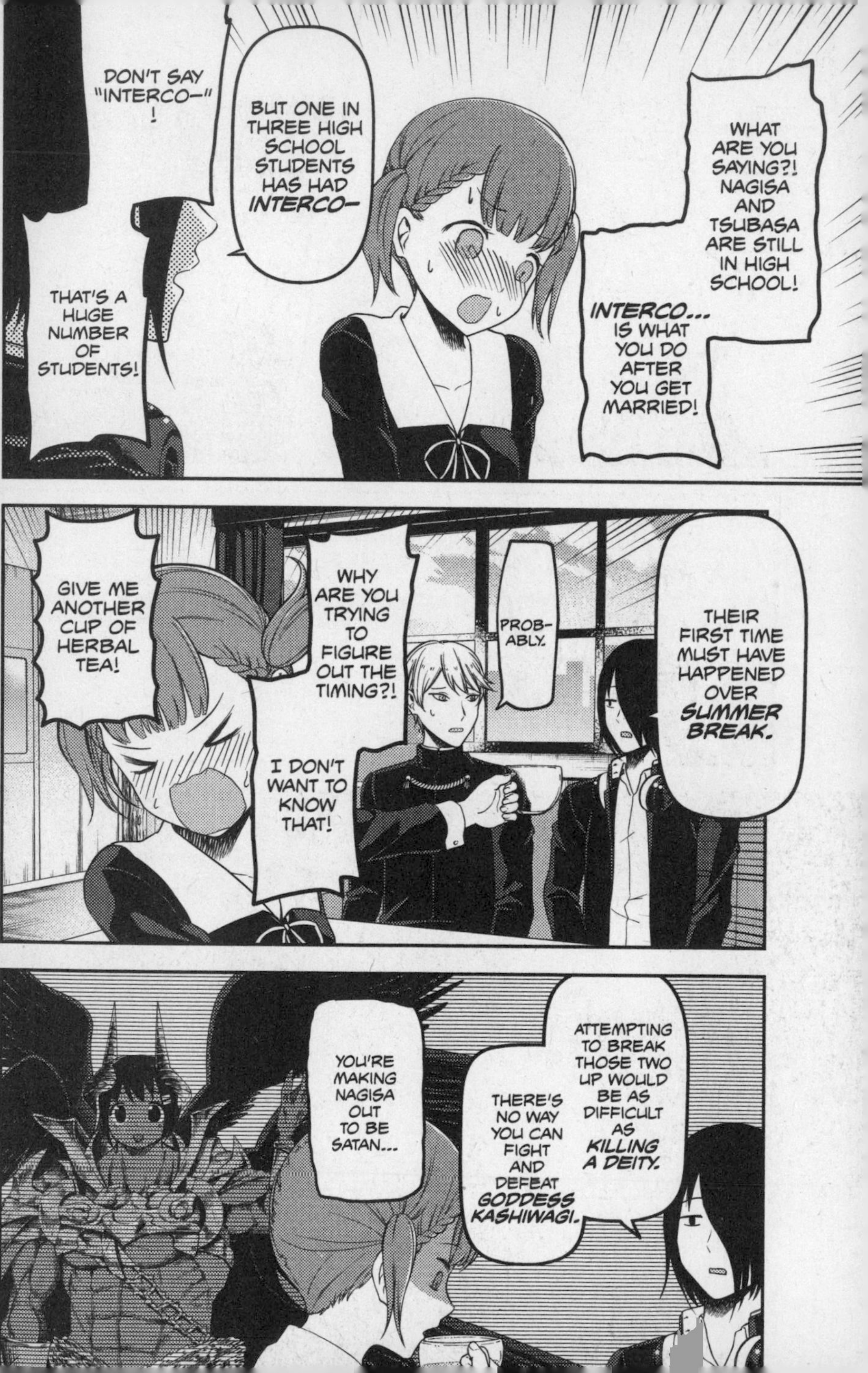
WHAT ARE YOU SAYING?! NAGISA AND TSUBASA ARE STILL IN HIGH SCHOOL!
INTERCO... IS WHAT YOU DO AFTER YOU GET MARRIED!
BUT ONE IN THREE HIGH SCHOOL STUDENTS HAS HAD INTERCO—
DON'T SAY "INTERCO—"!
THAT'S A HUGE NUMBER OF STUDENTS!
THEIR FIRST TIME MUST HAVE HAPPENED OVER SUMMER BREAK.
PROBABLY.
WHY ARE YOU TRYING TO FIGURE OUT THE TIMING?!
I DON'T WANT TO KNOW THAT!
GIVE ME ANOTHER CUP OF HERBAL TEA!
ATTEMPTING TO BREAK THOSE TWO UP WOULD BE AS DIFFICULT AS KILLING A DEITY.
THERE'S NO WAY YOU CAN FIGHT AND DEFEAT GODDESS KASHIWAGI.
YOU'RE MAKING NAGISA OUT TO BE SATAN...

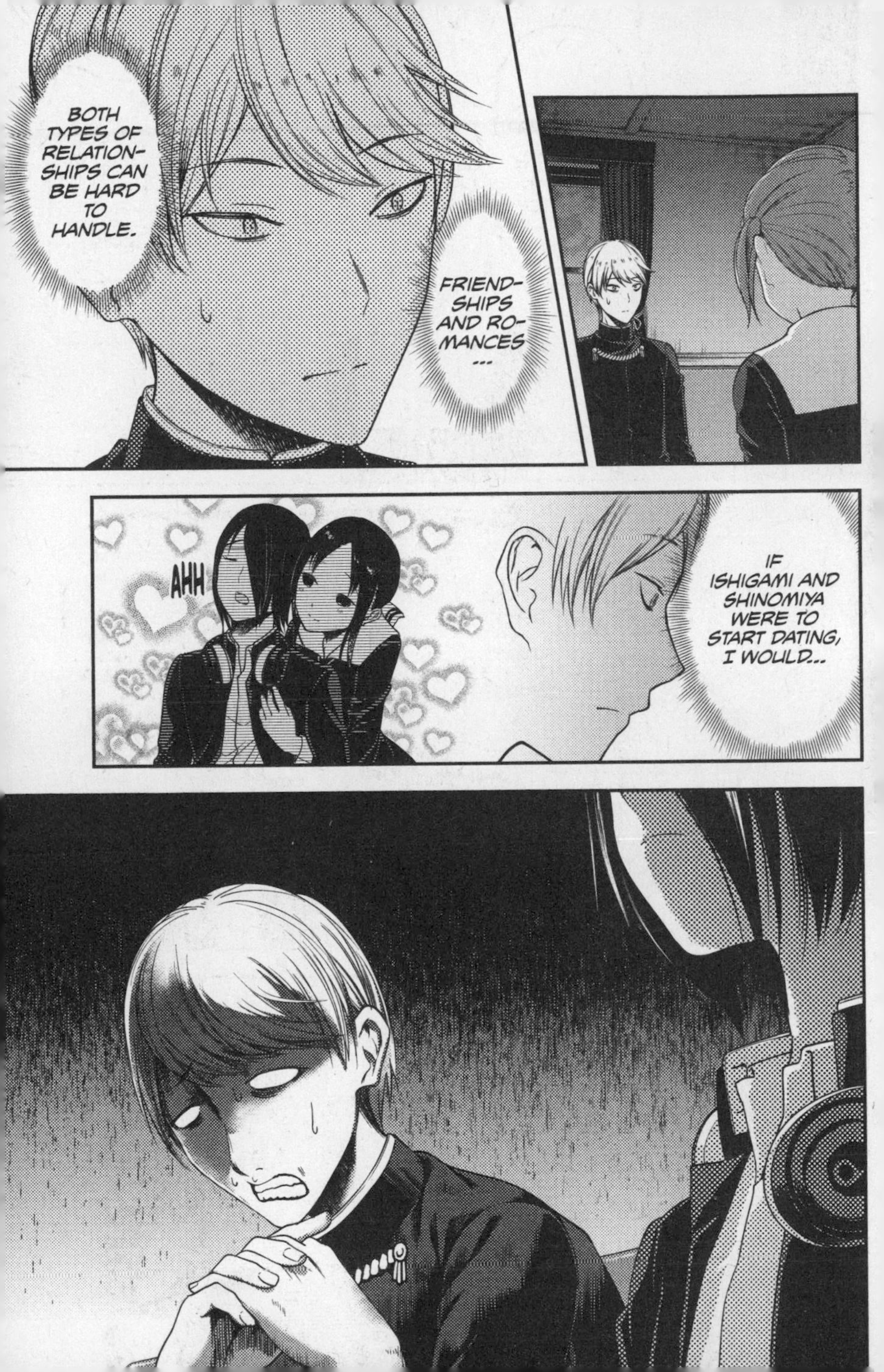
FRIEND-SHIPS AND RO-MANCES...
BOTH TYPES OF RELATION-SHIPS CAN BE HARD TO HANDLE.
IF ISHIGAMI AND SHINOMIYA WERE TO START DATING, I WOULD...
AHH

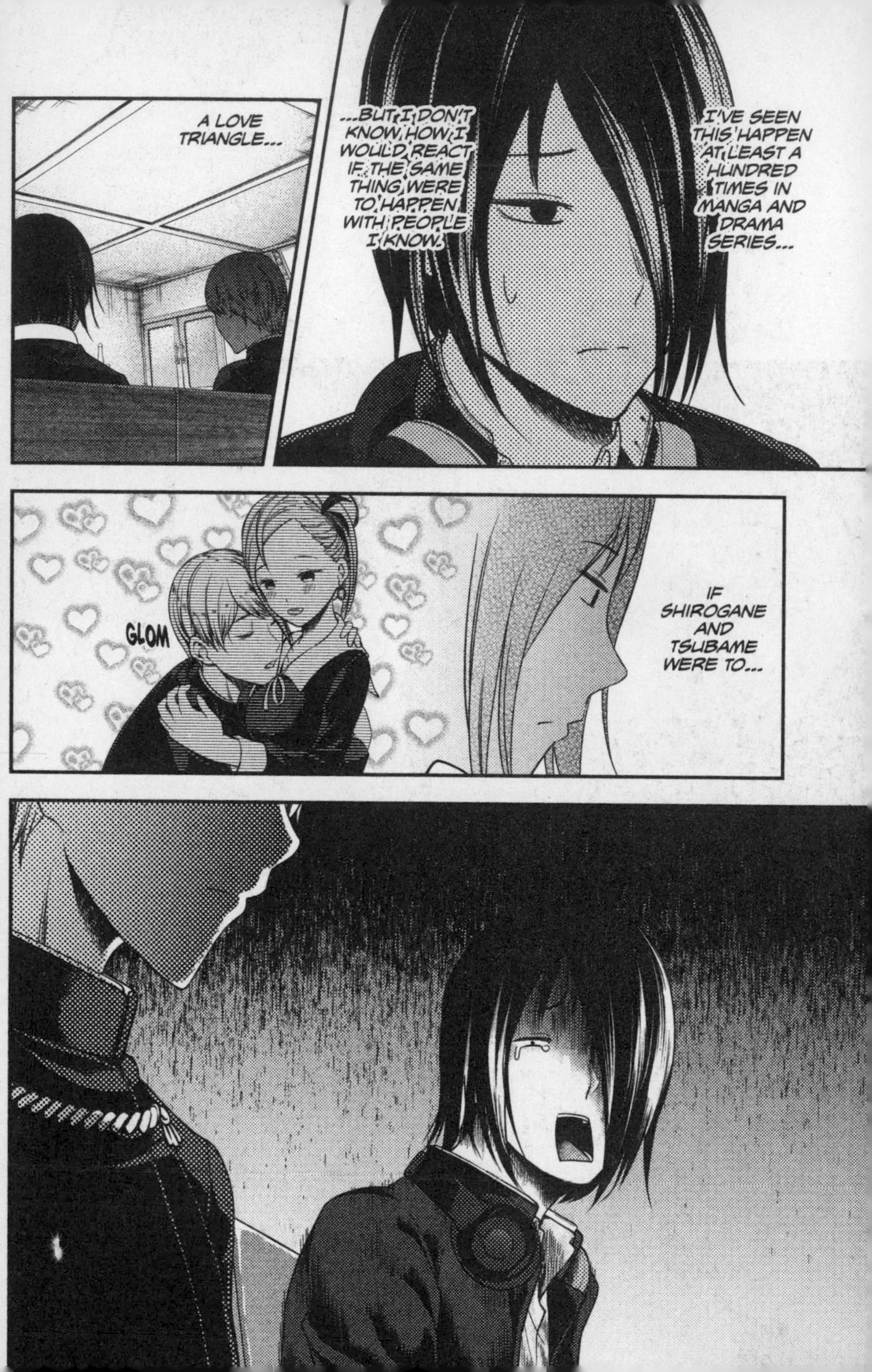
I'VE SEEN THIS HAPPEN AT LEAST A HUNDRED TIMES IN MANGA AND DRAMA SERIES...
...BUT I DON'T KNOW HOW I WOULD REACT IF THE SAME THING WERE TO HAPPEN WITH PEOPLE I KNOW.
A LOVE TRIANGLE...
IF SHIROGANE AND TSUBAME WERE TO...
GLOM

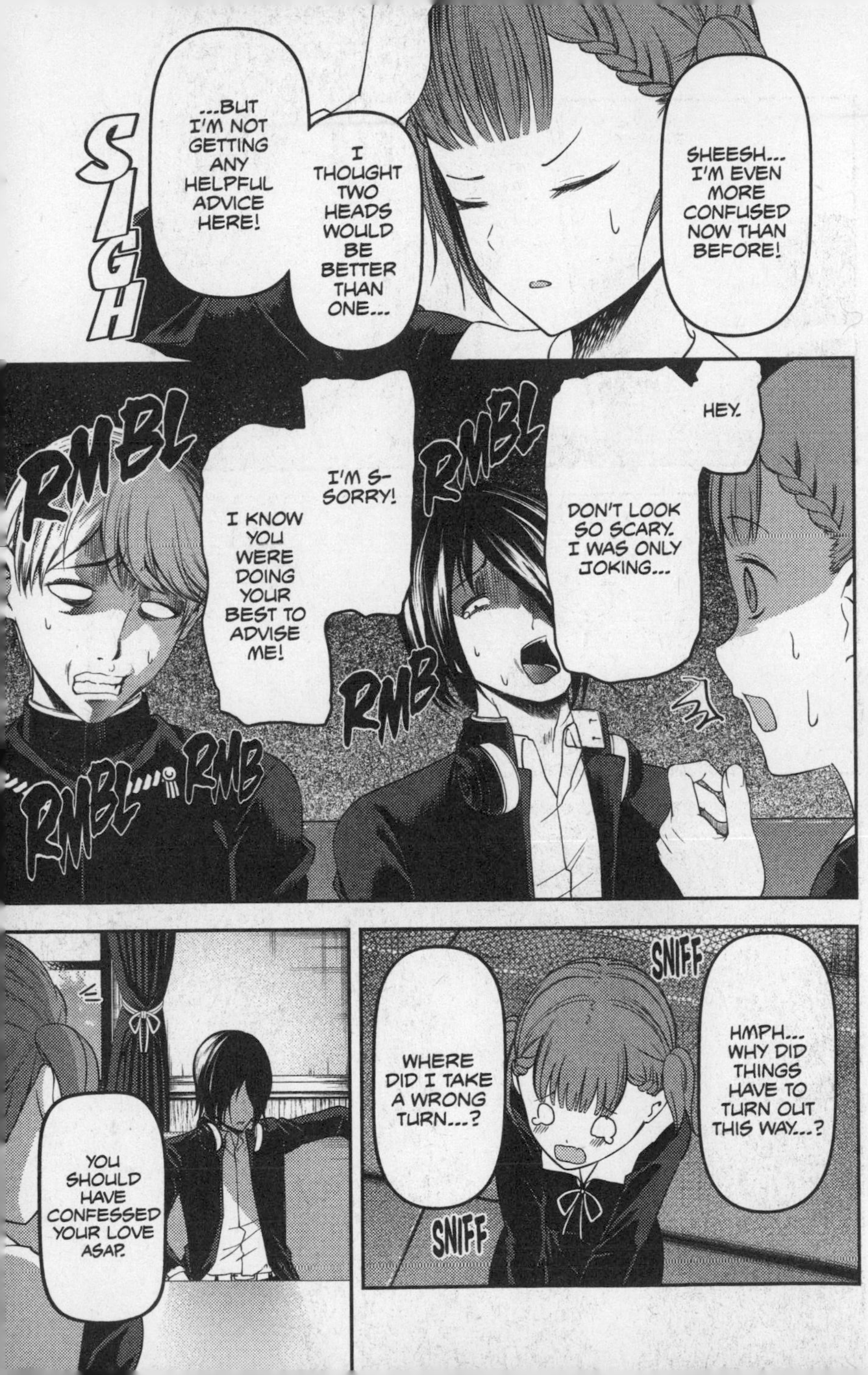
SHEESH... I'M EVEN MORE CONFUSED NOW THAN BEFORE!
I THOUGHT TWO HEADS WOULD BE BETTER THAN ONE...
...BUT I'M NOT GETTING ANY HELPFUL ADVICE HERE!
SIGH
HEY.
DON'T LOOK SO SCARY. I WAS ONLY JOKING...
RMBL
RMB
I'M S-SORRY!
I KNOW YOU WERE DOING YOUR BEST TO ADVISE ME!
RMBL
RMBL
RMB
SNIFF
HMPH... WHY DID THINGS HAVE TO TURN OUT THIS WAY...?
WHERE DID I TAKE A WRONG TURN...?
SNIFF
YOU SHOULD HAVE CONFESSED YOUR LOVE ASAP.

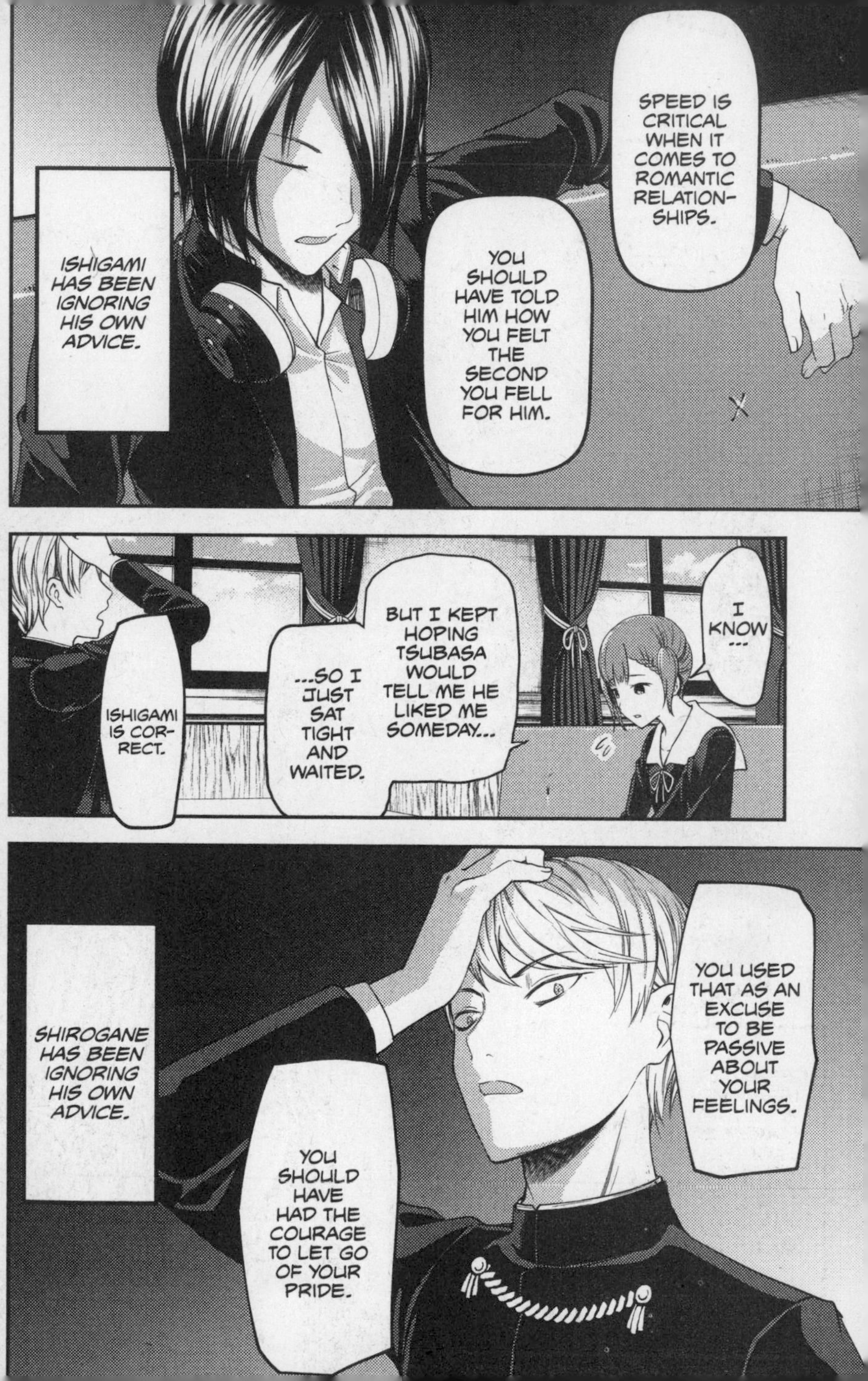
SPEED IS CRITICAL WHEN IT COMES TO ROMANTIC RELATIONSHIPS.
YOU SHOULD HAVE TOLD HIM HOW YOU FELT THE SECOND YOU FELL FOR HIM.
ISHIGAMI HAS BEEN IGNORING HIS OWN ADVICE.
I KNOW...
BUT I KEPT HOPING TSUBASA WOULD TELL ME HE LIKED ME SOMEDAY...
...SO I JUST SAT TIGHT AND WAITED.
ISHIGAMI IS CORRECT.
YOU USED THAT AS AN EXCUSE TO BE PASSIVE ABOUT YOUR FEELINGS.
YOU SHOULD HAVE HAD THE COURAGE TO LET GO OF YOUR PRIDE.
SHIROGANE HAS BEEN IGNORING HIS OWN ADVICE.

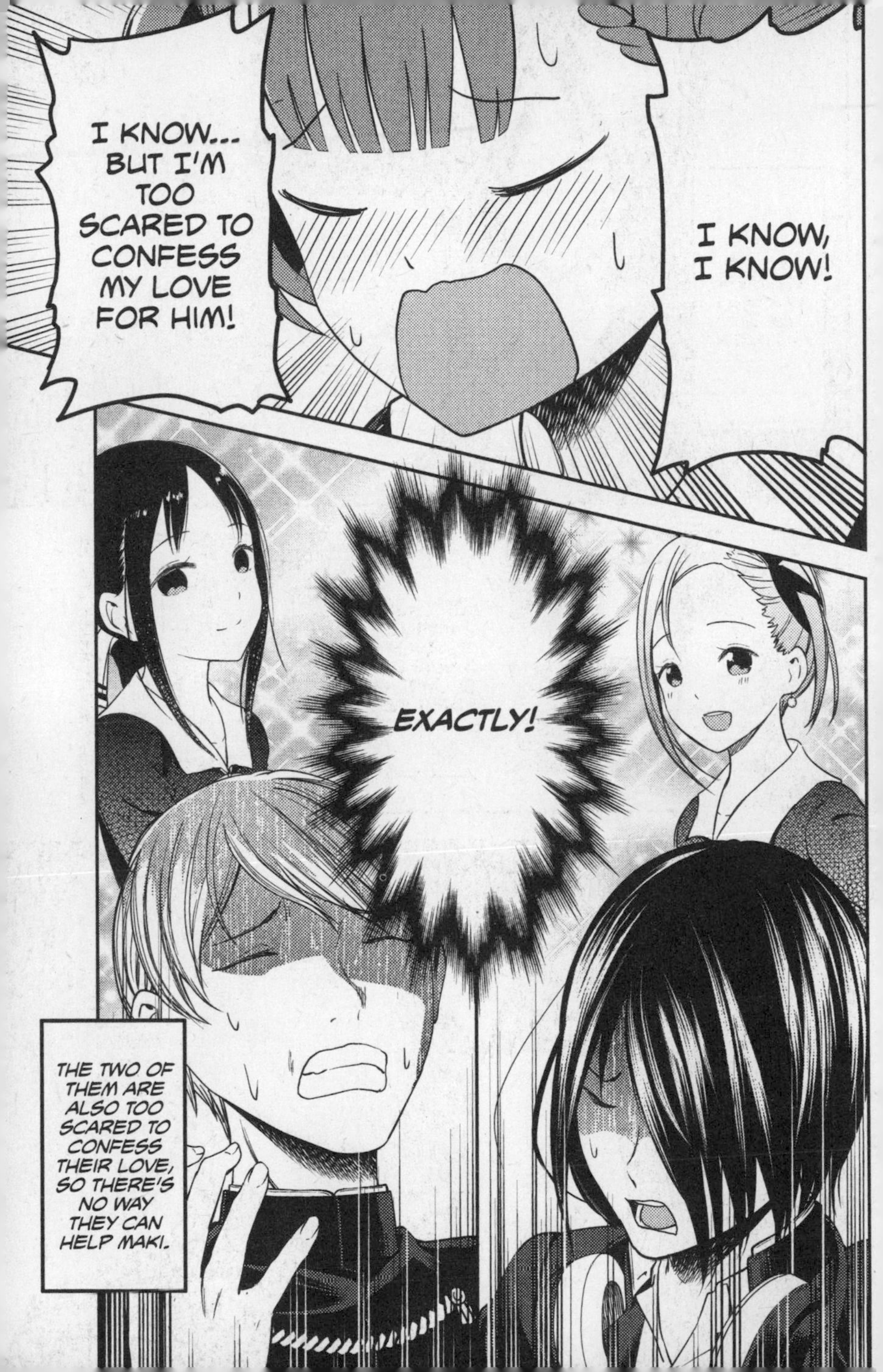
I KNOW, I KNOW!
I KNOW... BUT I'M TOO SCARED TO CONFESS MY LOVE FOR HIM!
EXACTLY!
THE TWO OF THEM ARE ALSO TOO SCARED TO CONFESS THEIR LOVE, SO THERE'S NO WAY THEY CAN HELP MAKI.

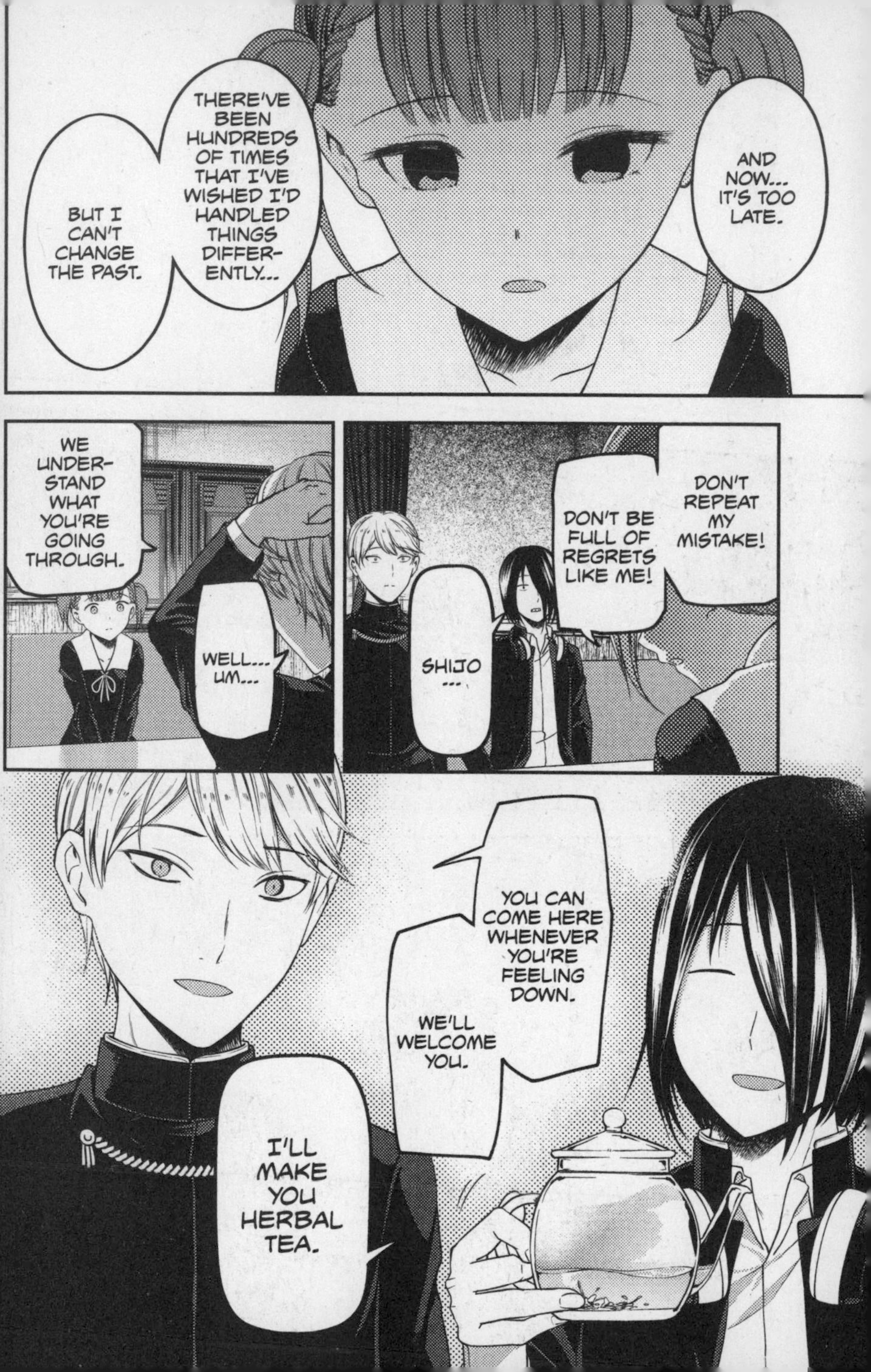
AND NOW... IT'S TOO LATE.
THERE'VE BEEN HUNDREDS OF TIMES THAT I'VE WISHED I'D HANDLED THINGS DIFFER-ENTLY...
BUT I CAN'T CHANGE THE PAST.
DON'T REPEAT MY MISTAKE!
DON'T BE FULL OF REGRETS LIKE ME!
SHIJO...
WE UNDER-STAND WHAT YOU'RE GOING THROUGH.
WELL... UM...
YOU CAN COME HERE WHENEVER YOU'RE FEELING DOWN.
WE'LL WELCOME YOU.
I'LL MAKE YOU HERBAL TEA.

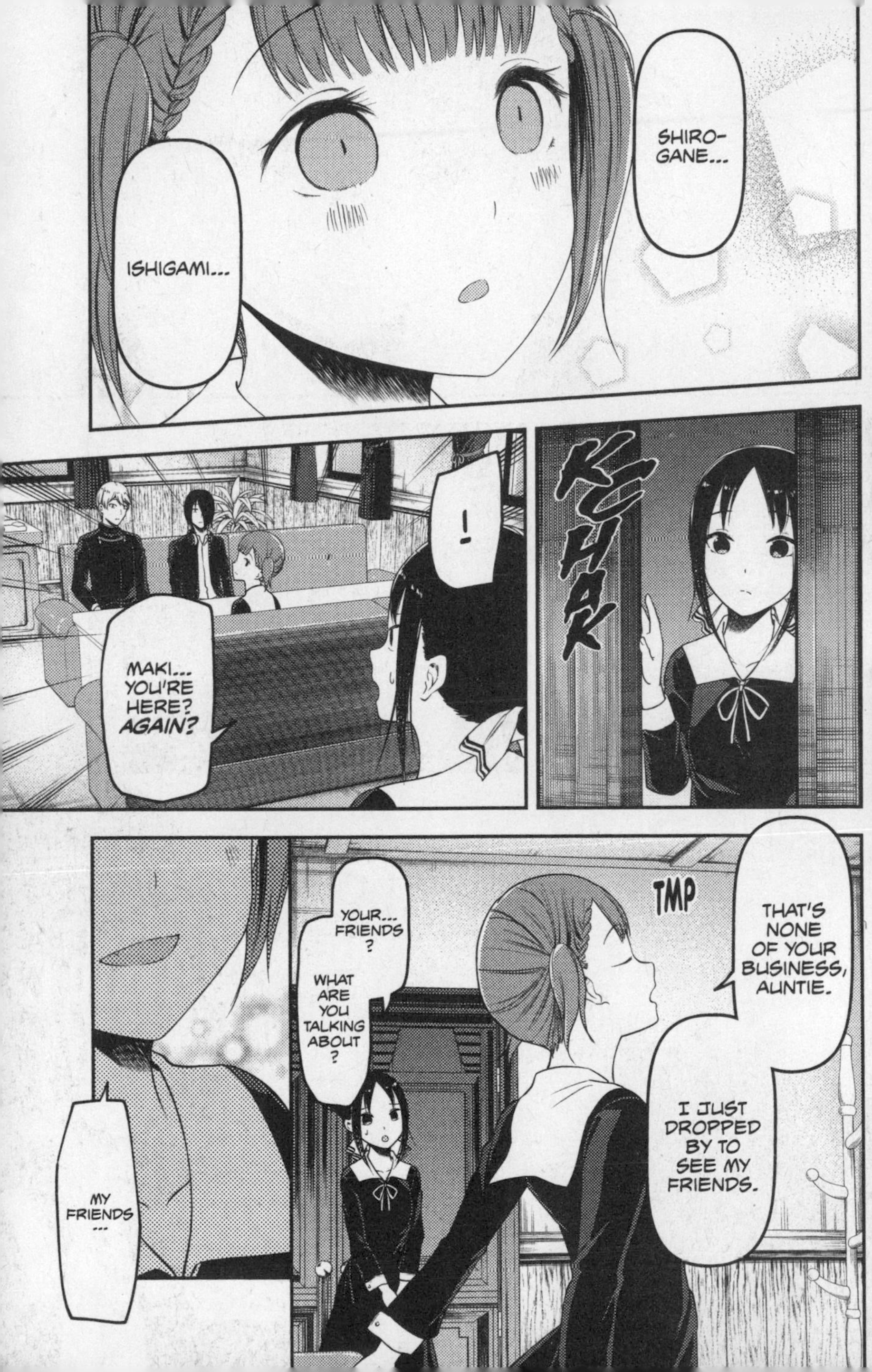
SHIRO-GANE...
ISHIGAMI...
KCHAK
!
MAKI... YOU'RE HERE? AGAIN?
TMP
THAT'S NONE OF YOUR BUSINESS, AUNTIE.
I JUST DROPPED BY TO SEE MY FRIENDS.
YOUR... FRIENDS?
WHAT ARE YOU TALKING ABOUT?
MY FRIENDS...

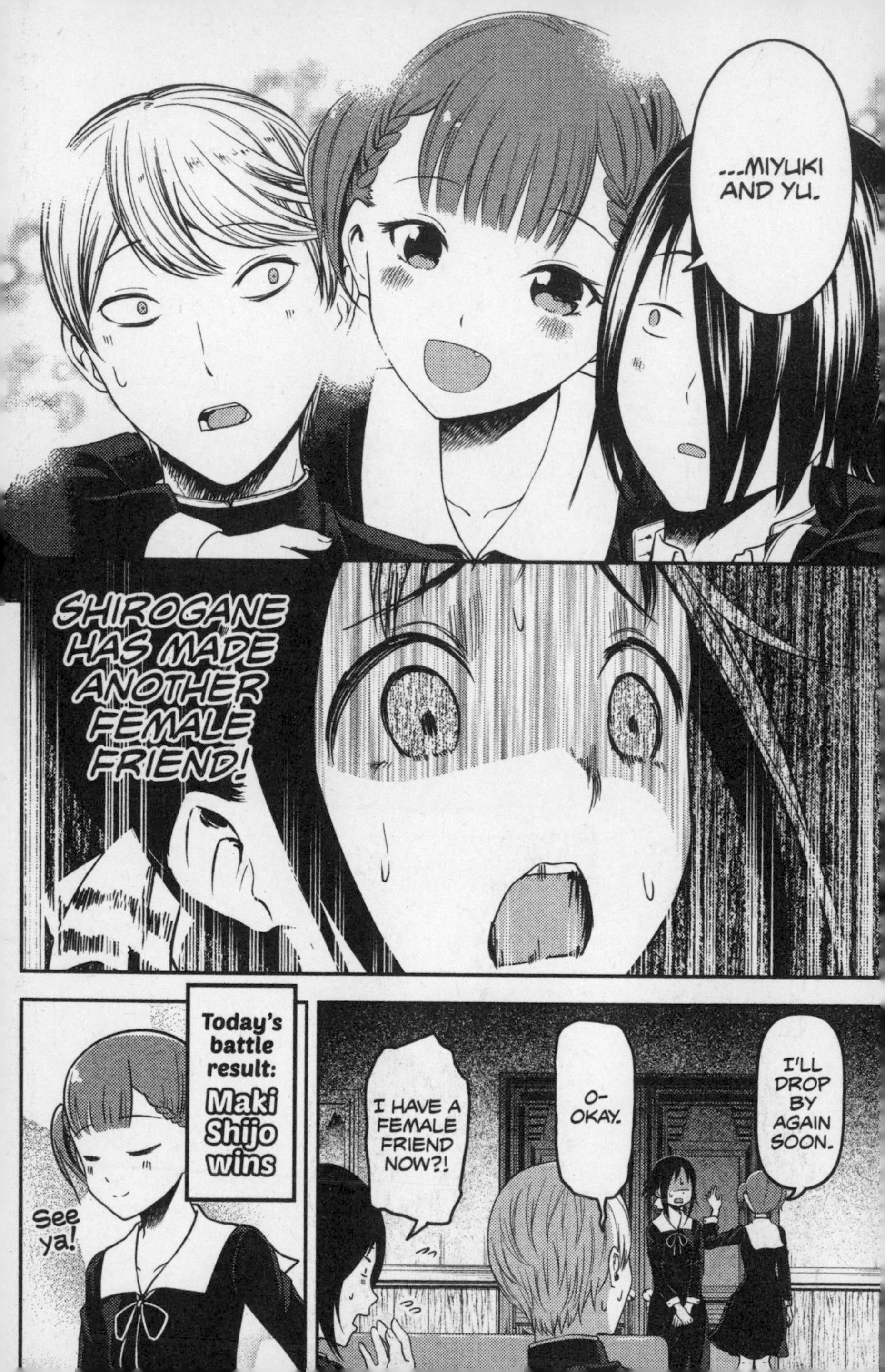
...MIYUKI AND YU.
SHIROGANE HAS MADE ANOTHER FEMALE FRIEND!
I'LL DROP BY AGAIN SOON.
O-OKAY.
I HAVE A FEMALE FRIEND NOW?!
Today's battle result: Maki Shijo wins
See ya!

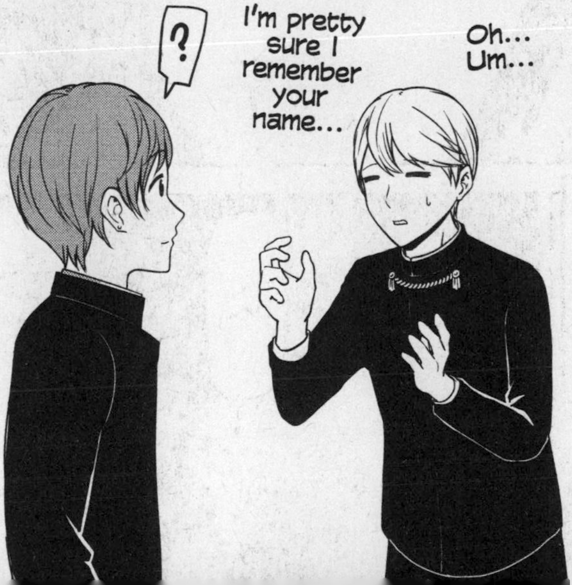
Oh... Um...
I'm pretty sure I remember your name...
?

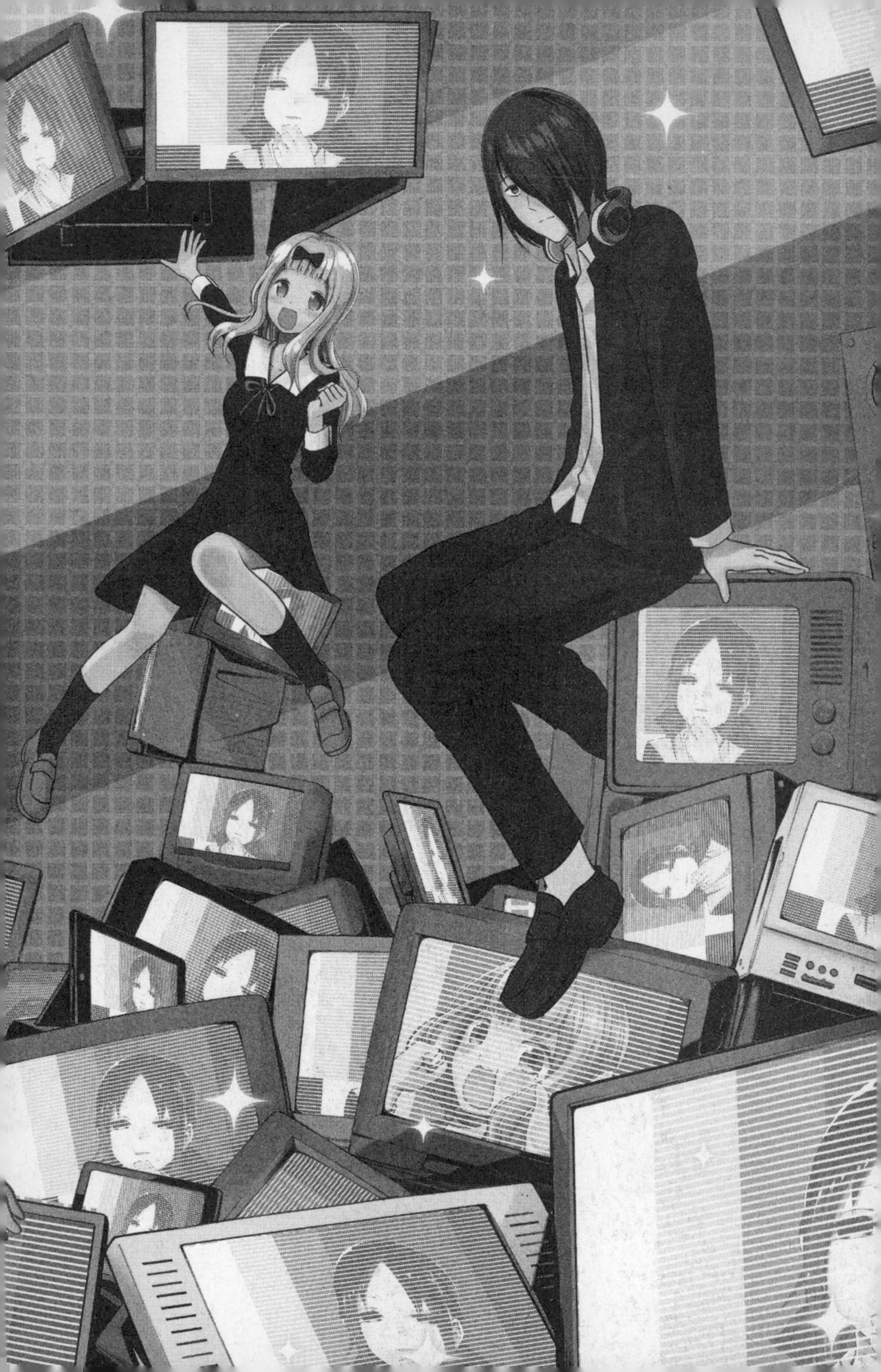

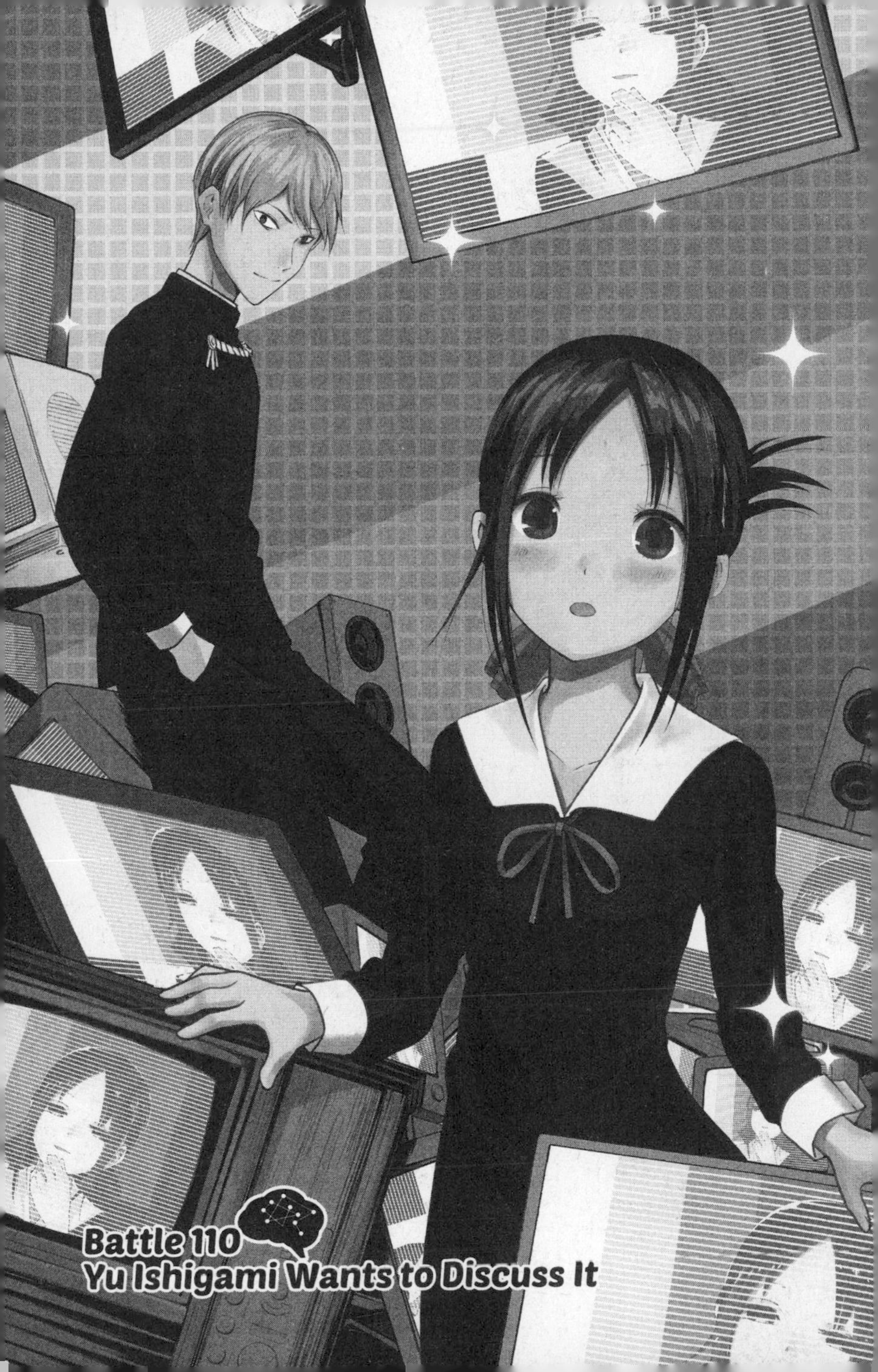
Battle 110
Yu Ishigami Wants to Discuss It

KAGUYA-SAMA

LOVE IS WAR

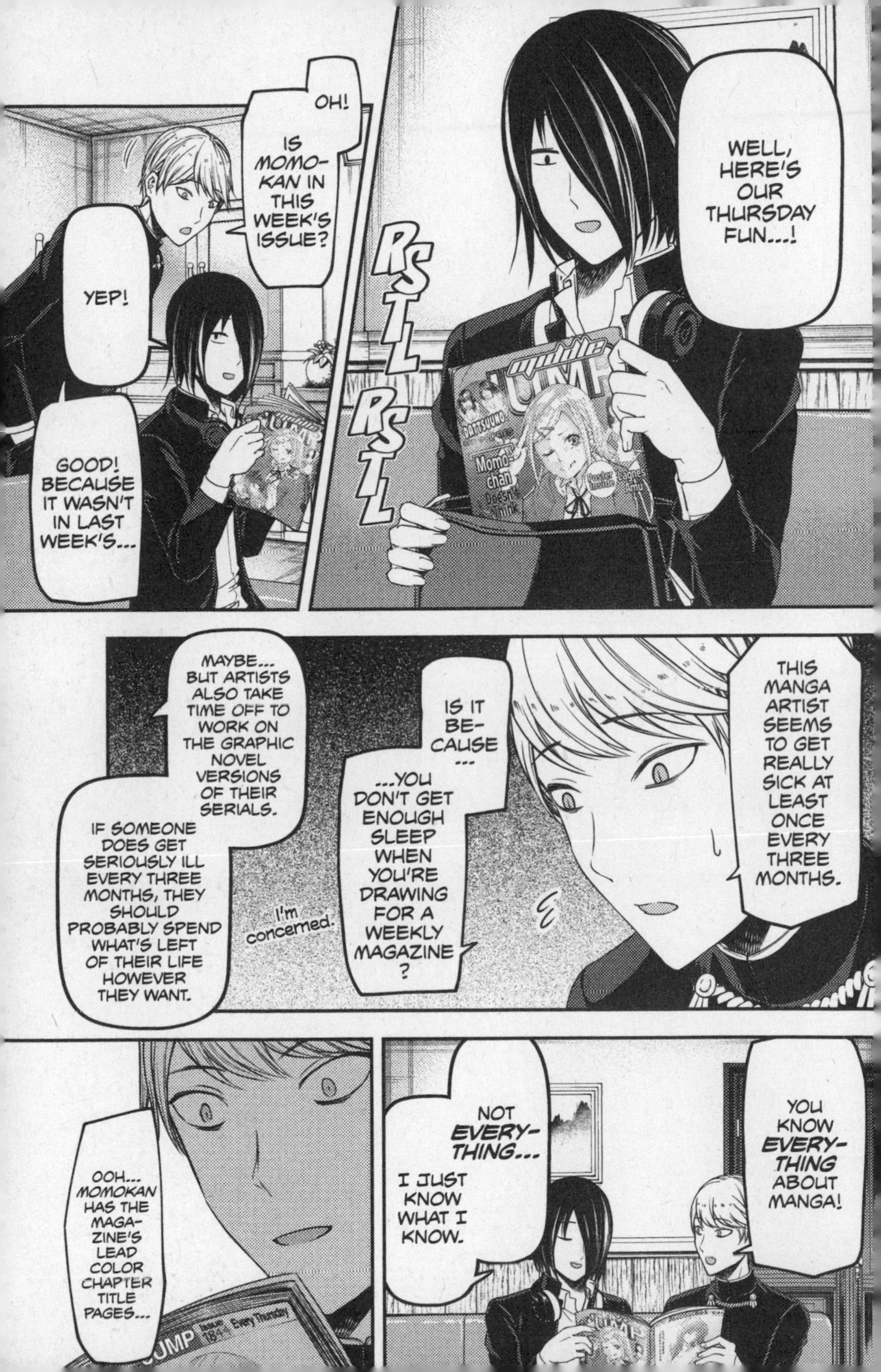
WELL, HERE'S OUR THURSDAY FUN...!
RSTL RSTL
OH! IS MOMO-KAN IN THIS WEEK'S ISSUE?
YEP!
GOOD! BECAUSE IT WASN'T IN LAST WEEK'S...
THIS MANGA ARTIST SEEMS TO GET REALLY SICK AT LEAST ONCE EVERY THREE MONTHS.
IS IT BE-CAUSE ...
...YOU DON'T GET ENOUGH SLEEP WHEN YOU'RE DRAWING FOR A WEEKLY MAGAZINE ?
I'm concerned.
MAYBE... BUT ARTISTS ALSO TAKE TIME OFF TO WORK ON THE GRAPHIC NOVEL VERSIONS OF THEIR SERIALS.
IF SOMEONE DOES GET SERIOUSLY ILL EVERY THREE MONTHS, THEY SHOULD PROBABLY SPEND WHAT'S LEFT OF THEIR LIFE HOWEVER THEY WANT.
YOU KNOW *EVERY-THING* ABOUT MANGA!
NOT *EVERY-THING...*
I JUST KNOW WHAT I KNOW.
OOH... *MOMOKAN* HAS THE MAGA-ZINE'S LEAD COLOR CHAPTER TITLE PAGES...

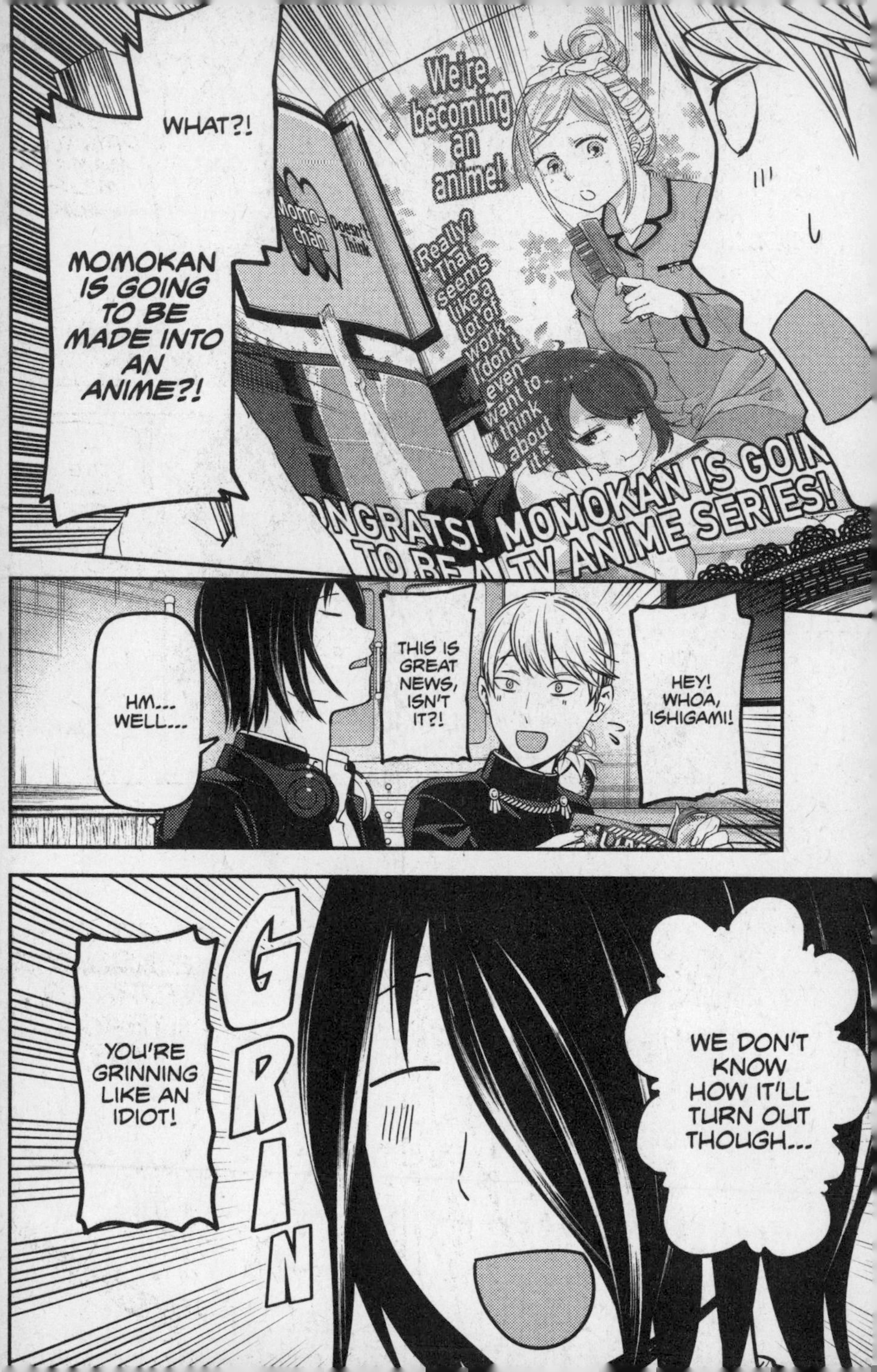

We're becoming an anime!
Really? That seems like a lot of work. I don't even want to think about it.
Momo-chan Doesn't Think
ONGRATS! MOMOKAN IS GOIN
TO BE A TV ANIME SERIES!
WHAT?!
MOMOKAN IS GOING TO BE MADE INTO AN ANIME?!
HEY! WHOA, ISHIGAMI!
THIS IS GREAT NEWS, ISN'T IT?!
HM... WELL...
WE DON'T KNOW HOW IT'LL TURN OUT THOUGH...
GRIN
YOU'RE GRINNING LIKE AN IDIOT!

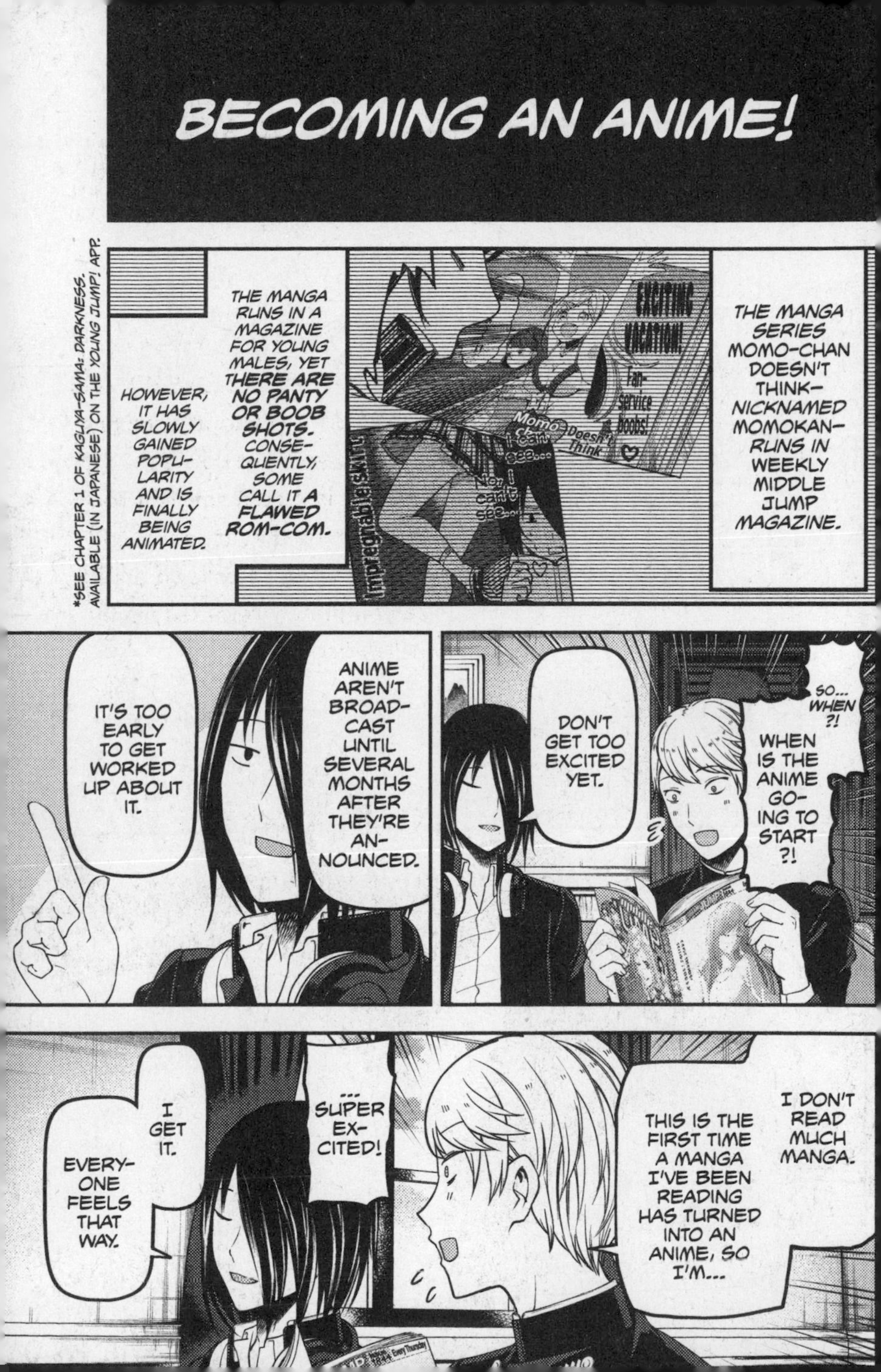
BECOMING AN ANIME!
THE MANGA SERIES MOMO-CHAN DOESN'T THINK—NICKNAMED MOMOKAN—RUNS IN WEEKLY MIDDLE JUMP MAGAZINE.
EXCITING VACATION!
Fan-service boobs! ♡
Momo-chan Doesn't Think
I can see...
No, I can't see...
Impregnable skirts
THE MANGA RUNS IN A MAGAZINE FOR YOUNG MALES, YET THERE ARE NO PANTY OR BOOB SHOTS. CONSEQUENTLY, SOME CALL IT A FLAWED ROM-COM.
HOWEVER, IT HAS SLOWLY GAINED POPULARITY AND IS FINALLY BEING ANIMATED.
*SEE CHAPTER 1 OF KAGUYA-SAMA: DARKNESS. AVAILABLE (IN JAPANESE) ON THE YOUNG JUMP! APP.
SO... WHEN?!
WHEN IS THE ANIME GOING TO START?!
DON'T GET TOO EXCITED YET.
ANIME AREN'T BROADCAST UNTIL SEVERAL MONTHS AFTER THEY'RE ANNOUNCED.
IT'S TOO EARLY TO GET WORKED UP ABOUT IT.
I DON'T READ MUCH MANGA.
THIS IS THE FIRST TIME A MANGA I'VE BEEN READING HAS TURNED INTO AN ANIME, SO I'M...
...SUPER EXCITED!
I GET IT.
EVERYONE FEELS THAT WAY.

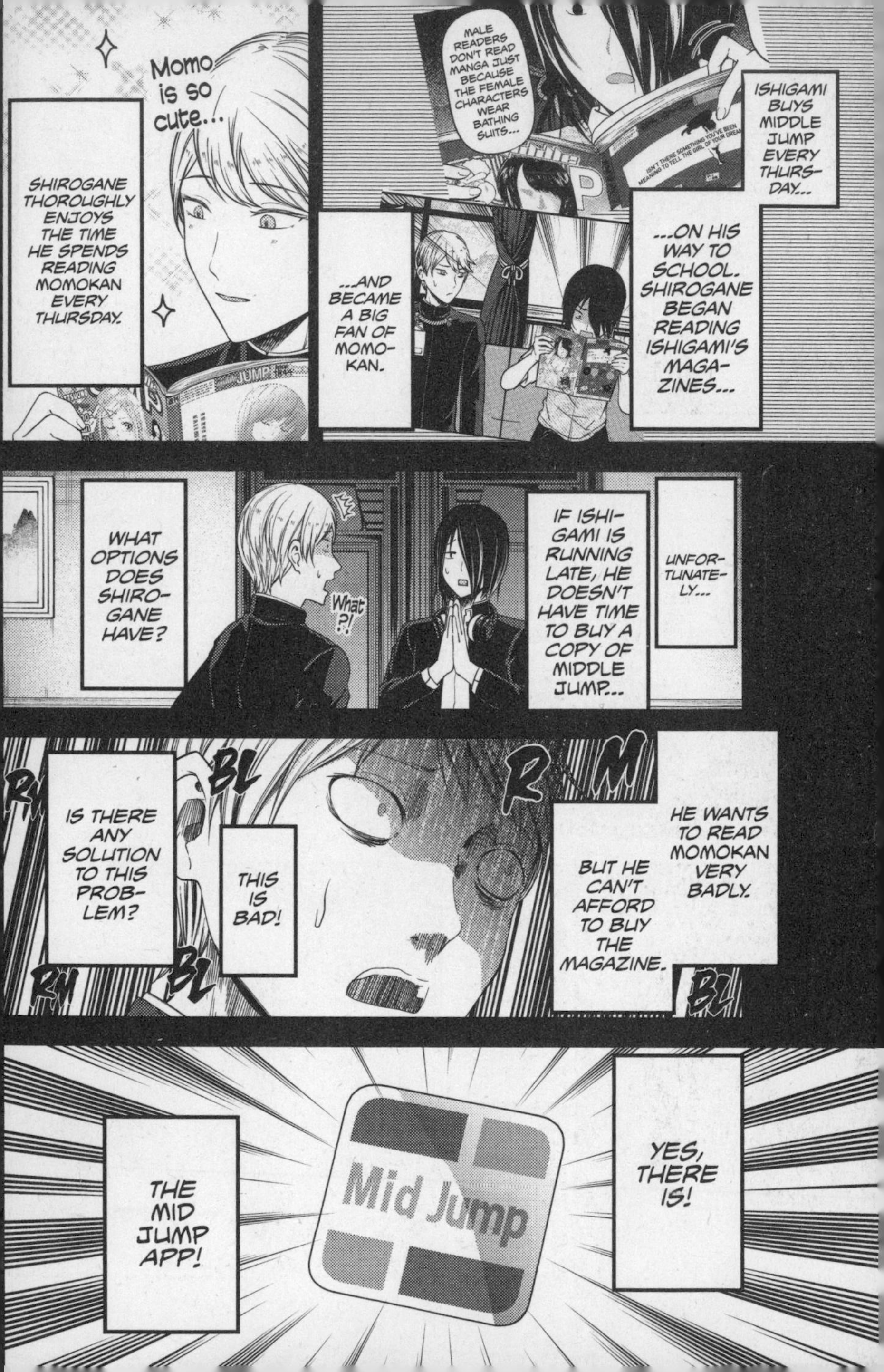
ISHIGAMI BUYS MIDDLE JUMP EVERY THURSDAY...
MALE READERS DON'T READ MANGA JUST BECAUSE THE FEMALE CHARACTERS WEAR BATHING SUITS...
...ON HIS WAY TO SCHOOL. SHIROGANE BEGAN READING ISHIGAMI'S MAGAZINES...
...AND BECAME A BIG FAN OF MOMOKAN.
Momo is so cute...
SHIROGANE THOROUGHLY ENJOYS THE TIME HE SPENDS READING MOMOKAN EVERY THURSDAY.
UNFORTUNATELY...
IF ISHIGAMI IS RUNNING LATE, HE DOESN'T HAVE TIME TO BUY A COPY OF MIDDLE JUMP...
What?!
WHAT OPTIONS DOES SHIROGANE HAVE?
HE WANTS TO READ MOMOKAN VERY BADLY.
RM
BUT HE CAN'T AFFORD TO BUY THE MAGAZINE.
BL
THIS IS BAD!
IS THERE ANY SOLUTION TO THIS PROBLEM?
YES, THERE IS!
Mid Jump
THE MID JUMP APP!

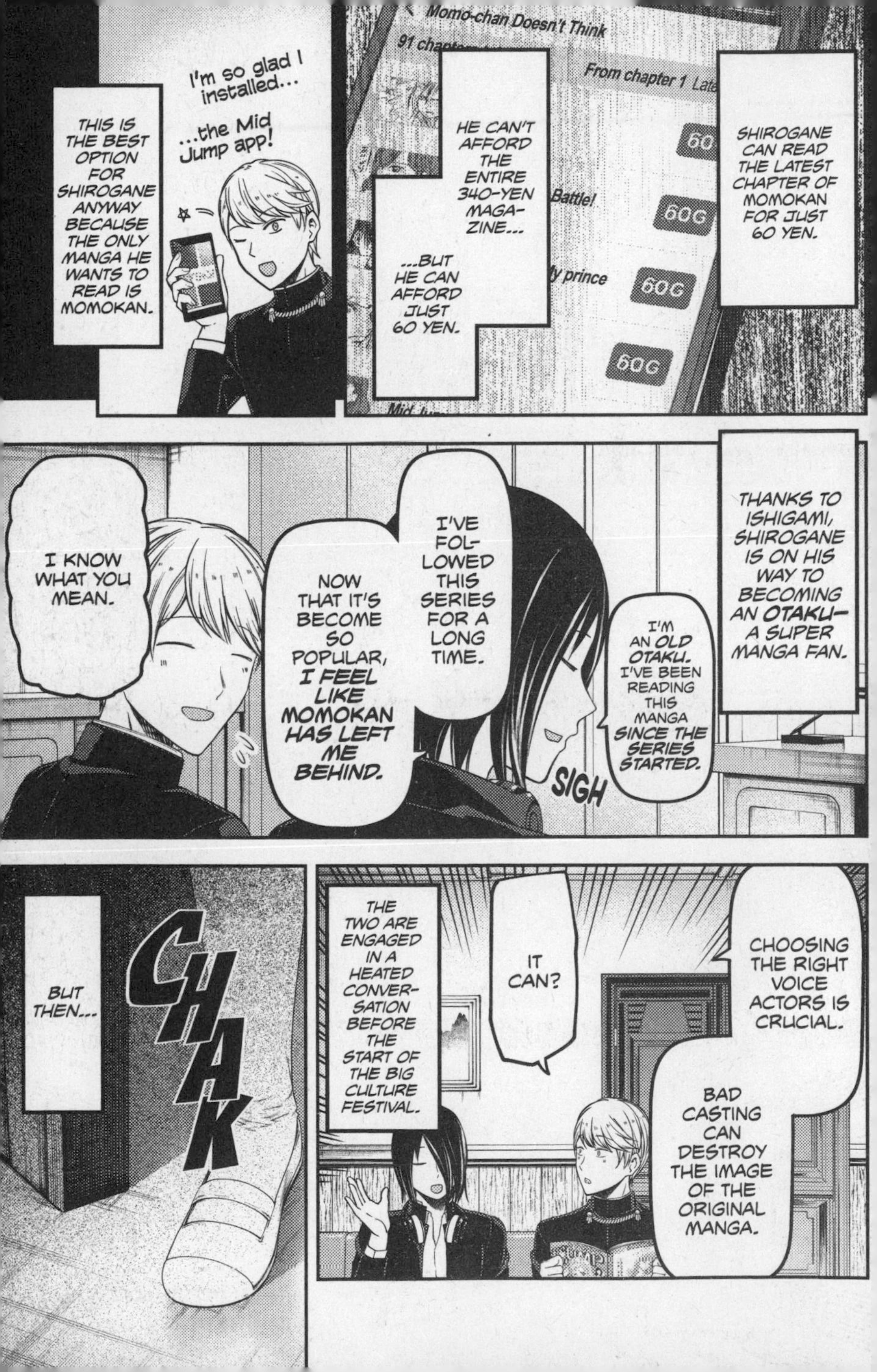
SHIROGANE CAN READ THE LATEST CHAPTER OF MOMOKAN FOR JUST 60 YEN.
Momo-chan Doesn't Think
From chapter 1
Battle!
60G
60G
60G
60G
HE CAN'T AFFORD THE ENTIRE 340-YEN MAGAZINE...
...BUT HE CAN AFFORD JUST 60 YEN.
I'm so glad I installed...
...the Mid Jump app!
THIS IS THE BEST OPTION FOR SHIROGANE ANYWAY BECAUSE THE ONLY MANGA HE WANTS TO READ IS MOMOKAN.
THANKS TO ISHIGAMI, SHIROGANE IS ON HIS WAY TO BECOMING AN **OTAKU**—A SUPER MANGA FAN.
I'M AN *OLD OTAKU*. I'VE BEEN READING THIS MANGA **SINCE THE SERIES STARTED.**
SIGH
I'VE FOLLOWED THIS SERIES FOR A LONG TIME.
NOW THAT IT'S BECOME SO POPULAR, **I FEEL LIKE MOMOKAN HAS LEFT ME BEHIND.**
I KNOW WHAT YOU MEAN.
CHOOSING THE RIGHT VOICE ACTORS IS CRUCIAL.
BAD CASTING CAN DESTROY THE IMAGE OF THE ORIGINAL MANGA.
IT CAN?
THE TWO ARE ENGAGED IN A HEATED CONVERSATION BEFORE THE START OF THE BIG CULTURE FESTIVAL.
CHAK
BUT THEN...

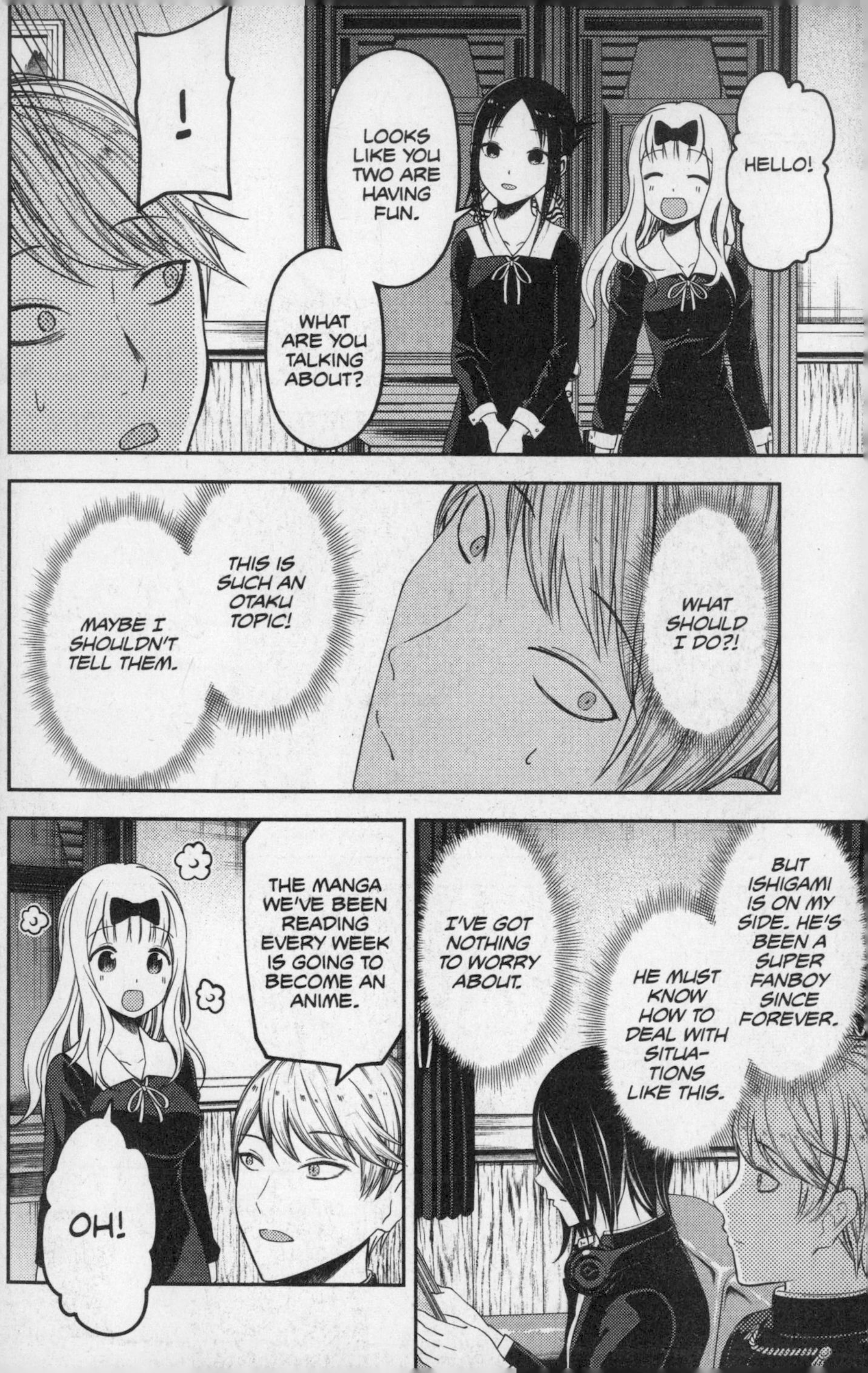
HELLO!
LOOKS LIKE YOU TWO ARE HAVING FUN.
WHAT ARE YOU TALKING ABOUT?
!
WHAT SHOULD I DO?!
THIS IS SUCH AN OTAKU TOPIC!
MAYBE I SHOULDN'T TELL THEM.
BUT ISHIGAMI IS ON MY SIDE. HE'S BEEN A SUPER FANBOY SINCE FOREVER.
HE MUST KNOW HOW TO DEAL WITH SITUA-TIONS LIKE THIS.
I'VE GOT NOTHING TO WORRY ABOUT.
THE MANGA WE'VE BEEN READING EVERY WEEK IS GOING TO BECOME AN ANIME.
OH!

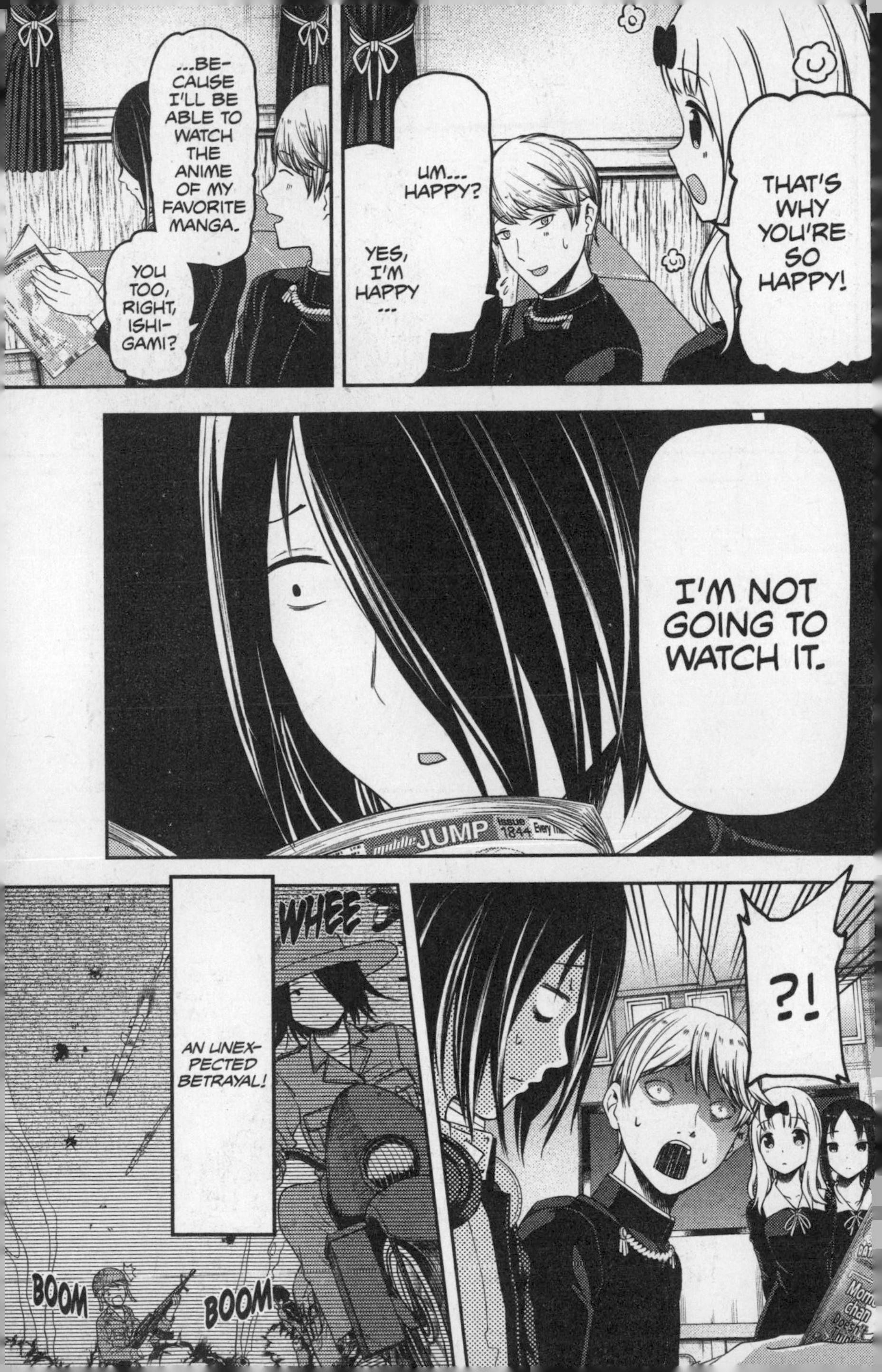
THAT'S WHY YOU'RE SO HAPPY!
UM... HAPPY?
YES, I'M HAPPY ...
...BE-CAUSE I'LL BE ABLE TO WATCH THE ANIME OF MY FAVORITE MANGA.
YOU TOO, RIGHT, ISHI-GAMI?
I'M NOT GOING TO WATCH IT.
JUMP
?!
WHEE
AN UNEX-PECTED BETRAYAL!
BOOM
BOOM

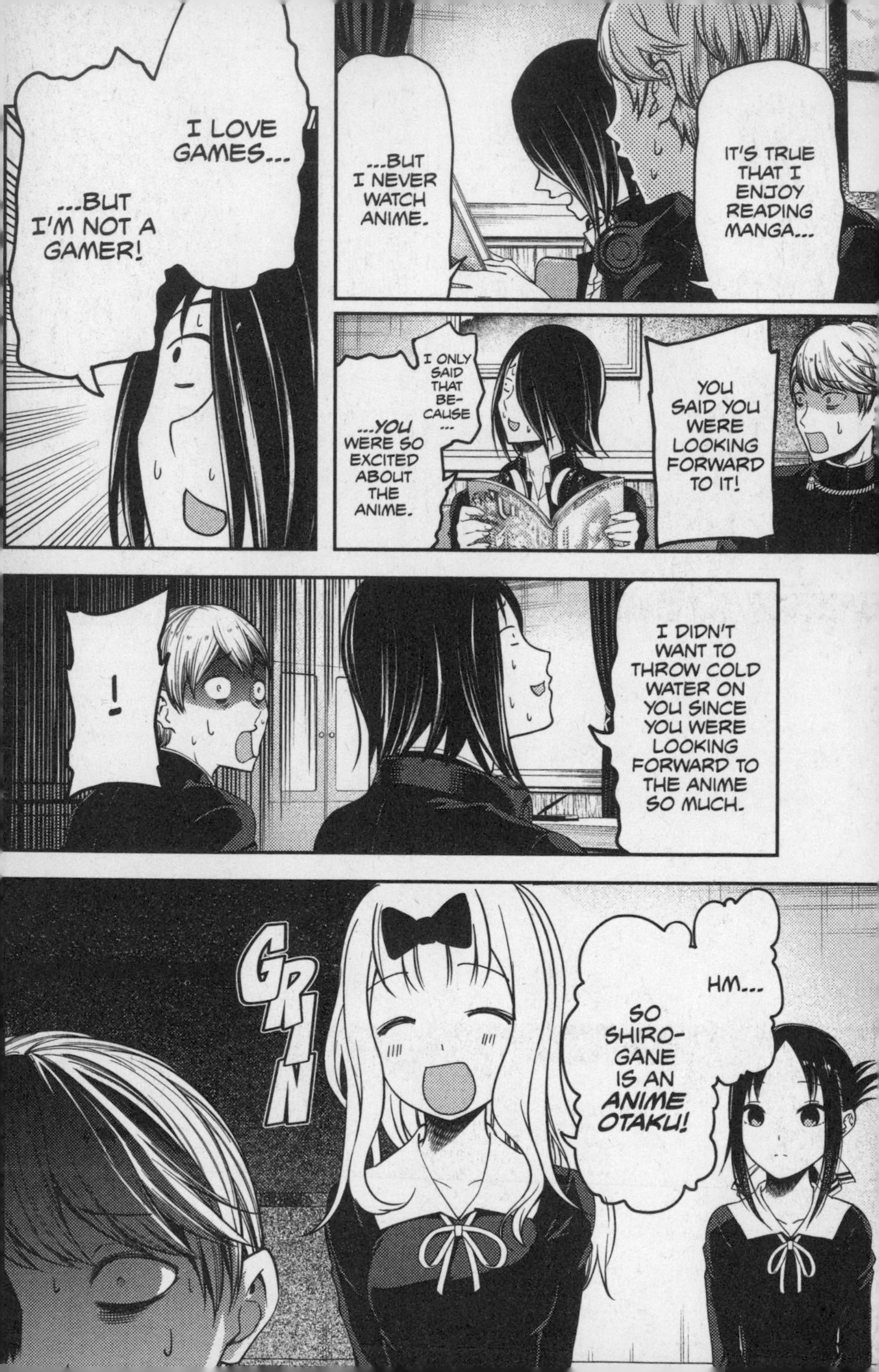
IT'S TRUE THAT I ENJOY READING MANGA...
...BUT I NEVER WATCH ANIME.
YOU SAID YOU WERE LOOKING FORWARD TO IT!
I ONLY SAID THAT BE-CAUSE...
...*YOU* WERE SO EXCITED ABOUT THE ANIME.
I LOVE GAMES...
...BUT I'M NOT A GAMER!
I DIDN'T WANT TO THROW COLD WATER ON YOU SINCE YOU WERE LOOKING FORWARD TO THE ANIME SO MUCH.
!
HM...
SO SHIRO-GANE IS AN *ANIME OTAKU*!
GRIN

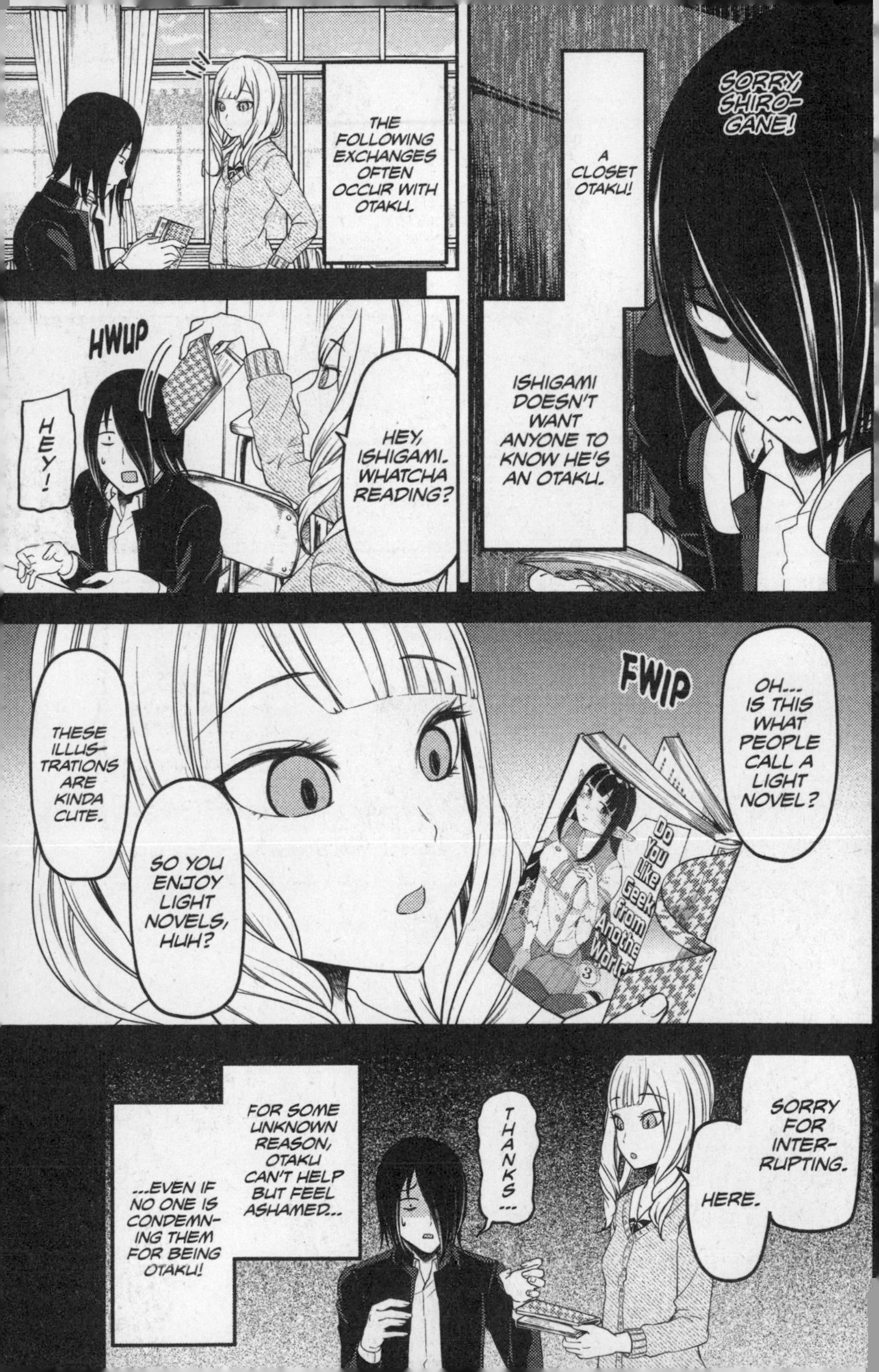
SORRY, SHIRO-GANE!
A CLOSET OTAKU!
ISHIGAMI DOESN'T WANT ANYONE TO KNOW HE'S AN OTAKU.
THE FOLLOWING EXCHANGES OFTEN OCCUR WITH OTAKU.
HEY, ISHIGAMI. WHATCHA READING?
HWUP
HEY!
OH... IS THIS WHAT PEOPLE CALL A LIGHT NOVEL?
FWIP
THESE ILLUS-TRATIONS ARE KINDA CUTE.
Do You Like Geek from Anothe World 3
SO YOU ENJOY LIGHT NOVELS, HUH?
SORRY FOR INTER-RUPTING.
HERE.
THANKS...
FOR SOME UNKNOWN REASON, OTAKU CAN'T HELP BUT FEEL ASHAMED...
...EVEN IF NO ONE IS CONDEMN-ING THEM FOR BEING OTAKU!

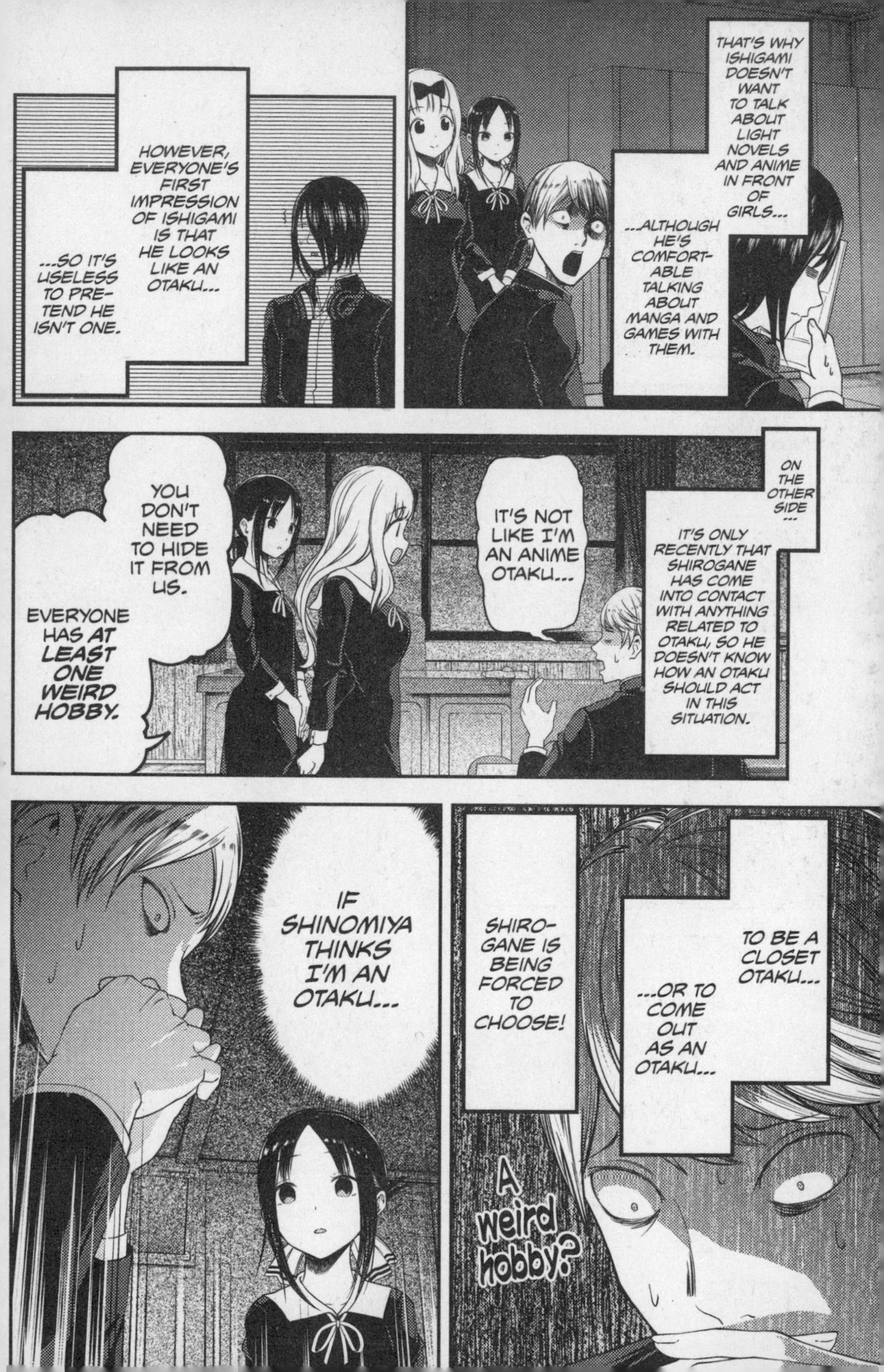
THAT'S WHY ISHIGAMI DOESN'T WANT TO TALK ABOUT LIGHT NOVELS AND ANIME IN FRONT OF GIRLS...
...ALTHOUGH HE'S COMFORTABLE TALKING ABOUT MANGA AND GAMES WITH THEM.
HOWEVER, EVERYONE'S FIRST IMPRESSION OF ISHIGAMI IS THAT HE LOOKS LIKE AN OTAKU...
...SO IT'S USELESS TO PRETEND HE ISN'T ONE.
ON THE OTHER SIDE...
IT'S ONLY RECENTLY THAT SHIROGANE HAS COME INTO CONTACT WITH ANYTHING RELATED TO OTAKU, SO HE DOESN'T KNOW HOW AN OTAKU SHOULD ACT IN THIS SITUATION.
IT'S NOT LIKE I'M AN ANIME OTAKU...
YOU DON'T NEED TO HIDE IT FROM US.
EVERYONE HAS AT LEAST ONE WEIRD HOBBY.
TO BE A CLOSET OTAKU...
...OR TO COME OUT AS AN OTAKU...
SHIROGANE IS BEING FORCED TO CHOOSE!
A weird hobby?
IF SHINOMIYA THINKS I'M AN OTAKU...

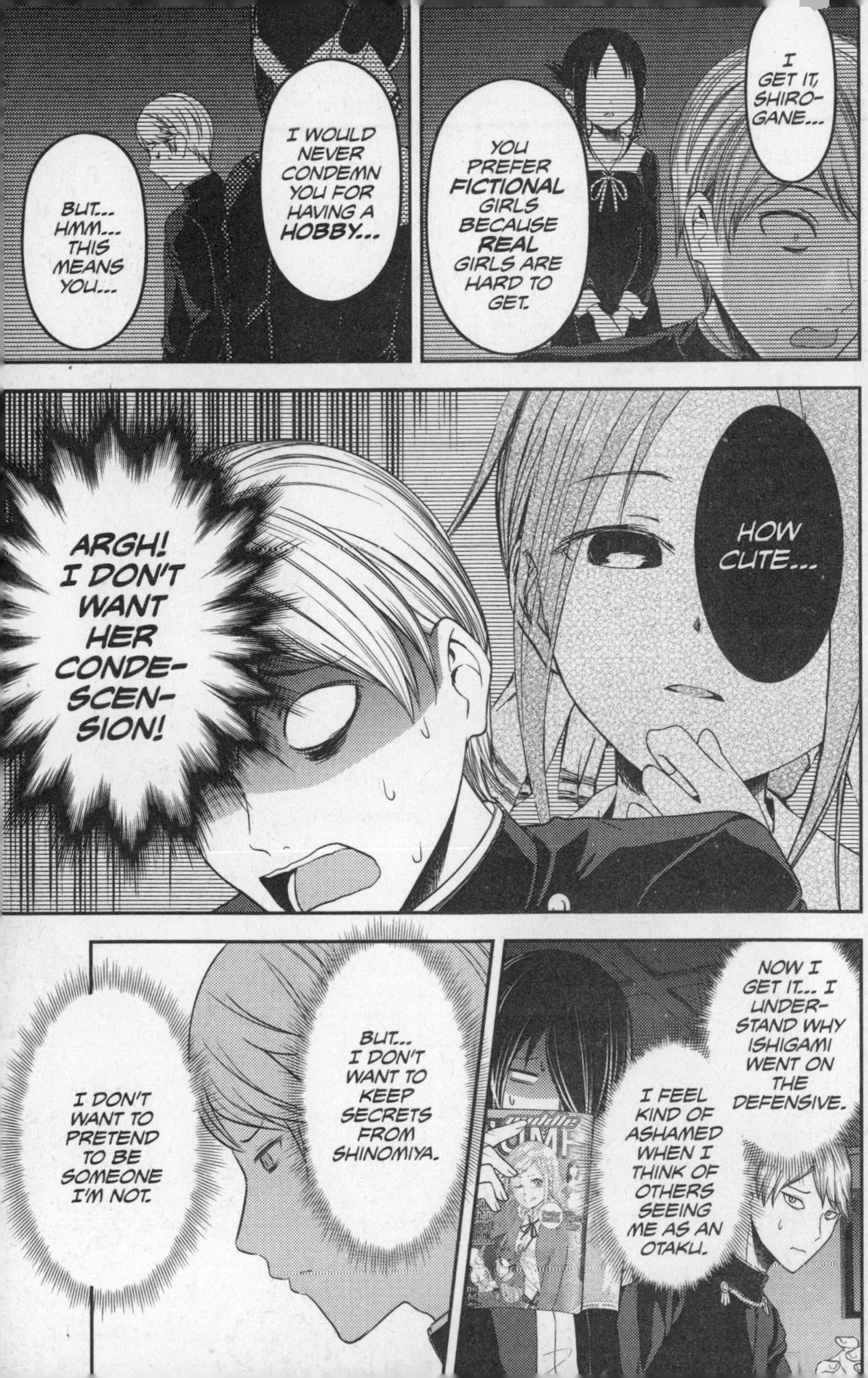
I GET IT, SHIROGANE...
YOU PREFER FICTIONAL GIRLS BECAUSE REAL GIRLS ARE HARD TO GET.
I WOULD NEVER CONDEMN YOU FOR HAVING A HOBBY...
BUT... HMM... THIS MEANS YOU...
HOW CUTE...
ARGH! I DON'T WANT HER CONDESCENSION!
NOW I GET IT... I UNDERSTAND WHY ISHIGAMI WENT ON THE DEFENSIVE.
I FEEL KIND OF ASHAMED WHEN I THINK OF OTHERS SEEING ME AS AN OTAKU.
BUT... I DON'T WANT TO KEEP SECRETS FROM SHINOMIYA.
I DON'T WANT TO PRETEND TO BE SOMEONE I'M NOT.

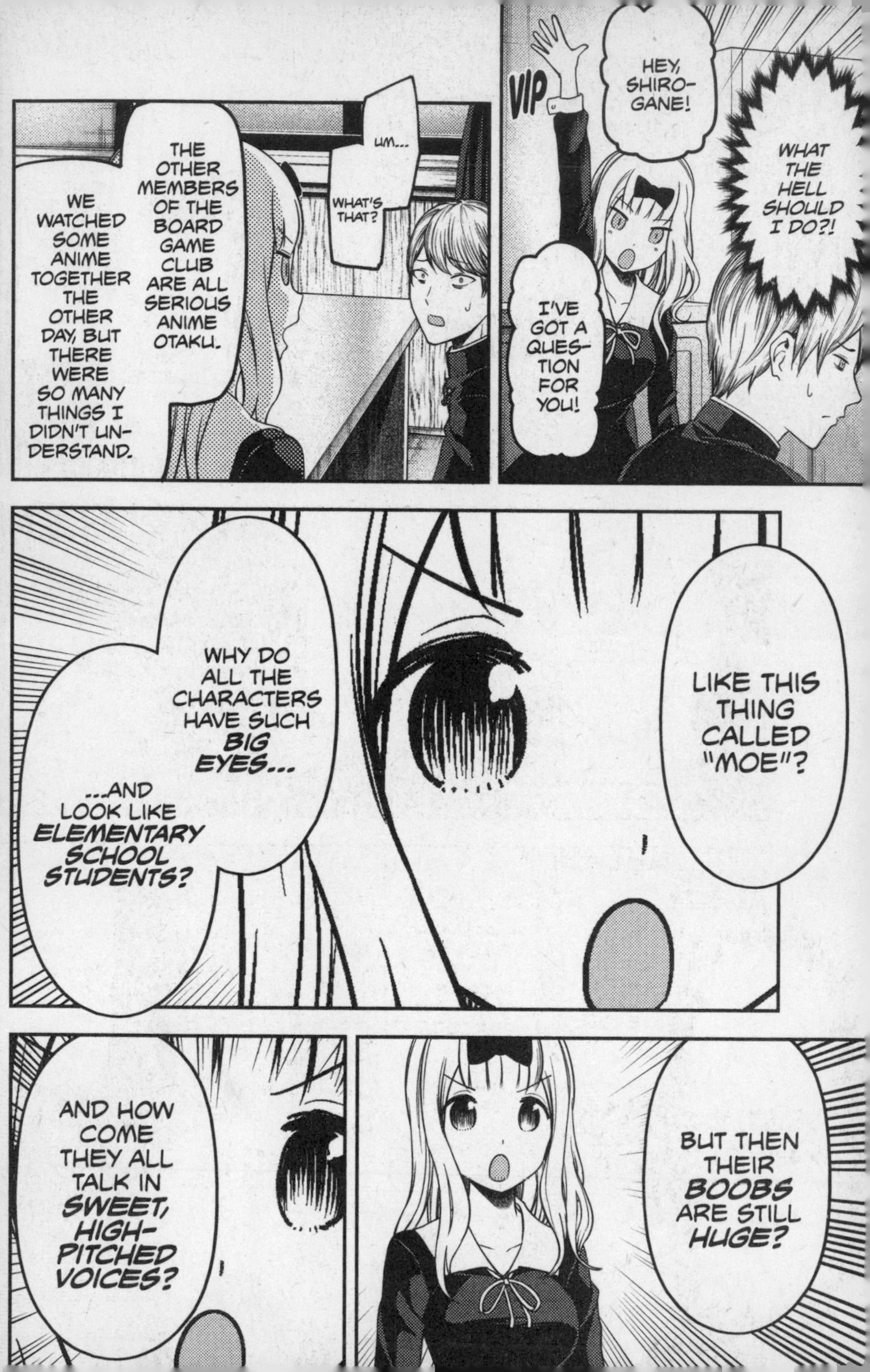

WHAT THE HELL SHOULD I DO?!
HEY, SHIRO-GANE!
VIP
I'VE GOT A QUESTION FOR YOU!
UM...
WHAT'S THAT?
THE OTHER MEMBERS OF THE BOARD GAME CLUB ARE ALL SERIOUS ANIME OTAKU.
WE WATCHED SOME ANIME TOGETHER THE OTHER DAY, BUT THERE WERE SO MANY THINGS I DIDN'T UN-DERSTAND.
LIKE THIS THING CALLED "MOE"?
WHY DO ALL THE CHARACTERS HAVE SUCH BIG EYES...
...AND LOOK LIKE ELEMENTARY SCHOOL STUDENTS?
BUT THEN THEIR BOOBS ARE STILL HUGE?
AND HOW COME THEY ALL TALK IN SWEET, HIGH-PITCHED VOICES?

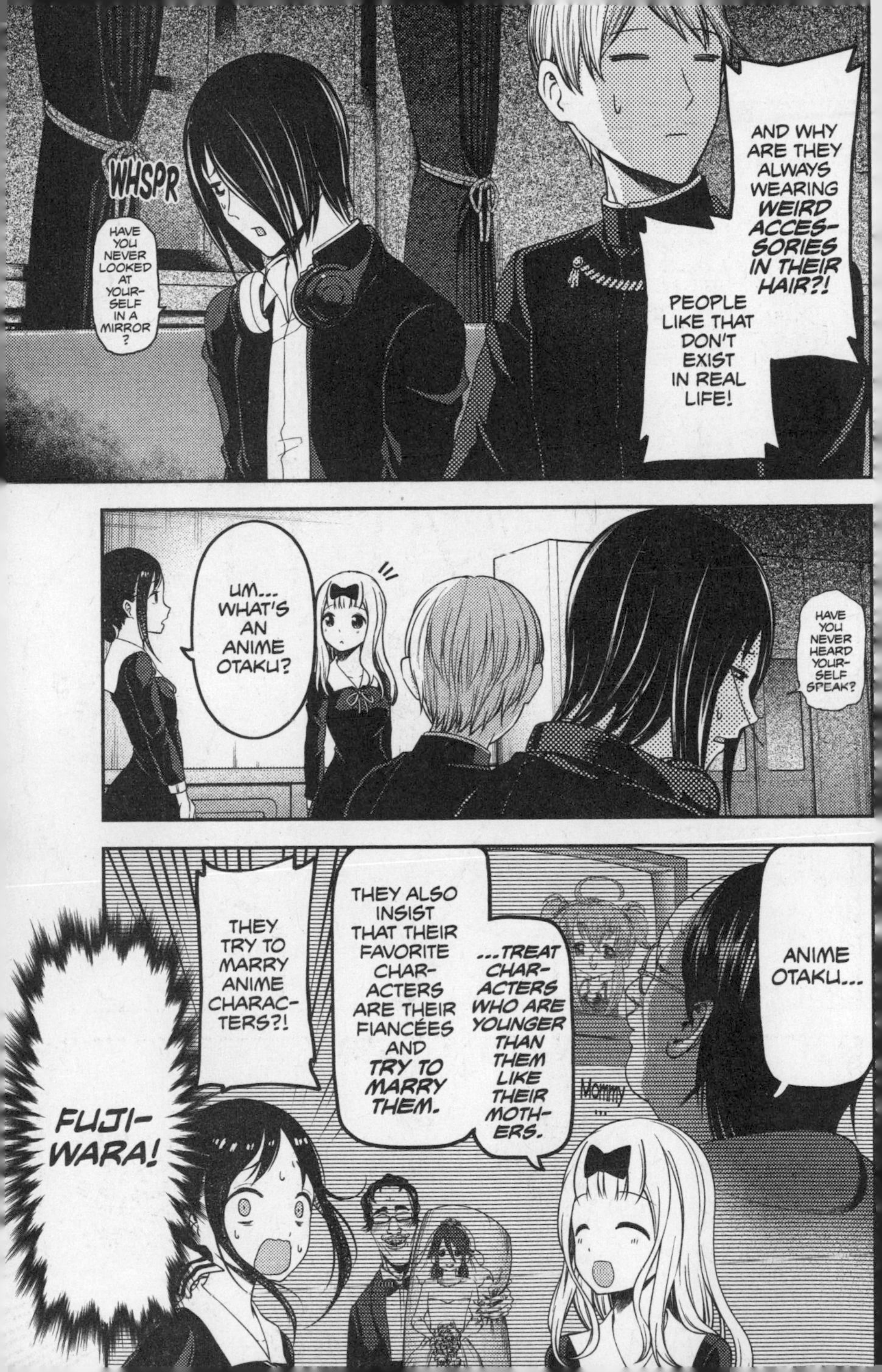
AND WHY ARE THEY ALWAYS WEARING *WEIRD ACCESSORIES IN THEIR HAIR?!*
PEOPLE LIKE THAT DON'T EXIST IN REAL LIFE!
WHSPR
HAVE YOU NEVER LOOKED AT YOURSELF IN A MIRROR?
HAVE YOU NEVER HEARD YOURSELF SPEAK?
UM... WHAT'S AN ANIME OTAKU?
ANIME OTAKU...
...TREAT CHARACTERS WHO ARE YOUNGER THAN THEM LIKE THEIR MOTHERS.
Mommy...
THEY ALSO INSIST THAT THEIR FAVORITE CHARACTERS ARE THEIR FIANCÉES AND *TRY TO MARRY THEM.*
THEY TRY TO MARRY ANIME CHARACTERS?!
FUJIWARA!

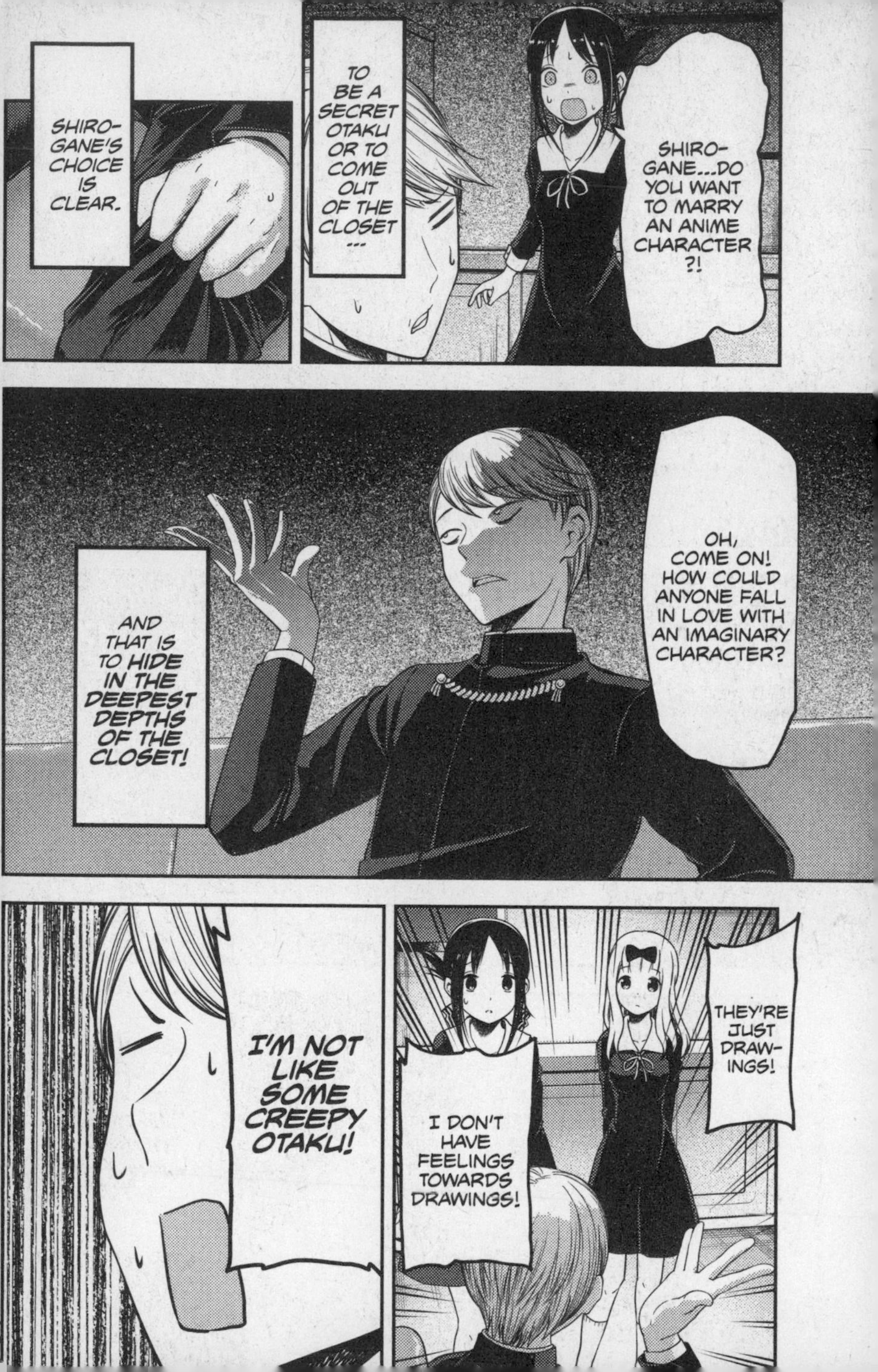
SHIRO-GANE...DO YOU WANT TO MARRY AN ANIME CHARACTER?!
TO BE A SECRET OTAKU OR TO COME OUT OF THE CLOSET...
SHIRO-GANE'S CHOICE IS CLEAR.
OH, COME ON! HOW COULD ANYONE FALL IN LOVE WITH AN IMAGINARY CHARACTER?
AND THAT IS TO HIDE IN THE DEEPEST DEPTHS OF THE CLOSET!
THEY'RE JUST DRAW-INGS!
I DON'T HAVE FEELINGS TOWARDS DRAWINGS!
I'M NOT LIKE SOME CREEPY OTAKU!

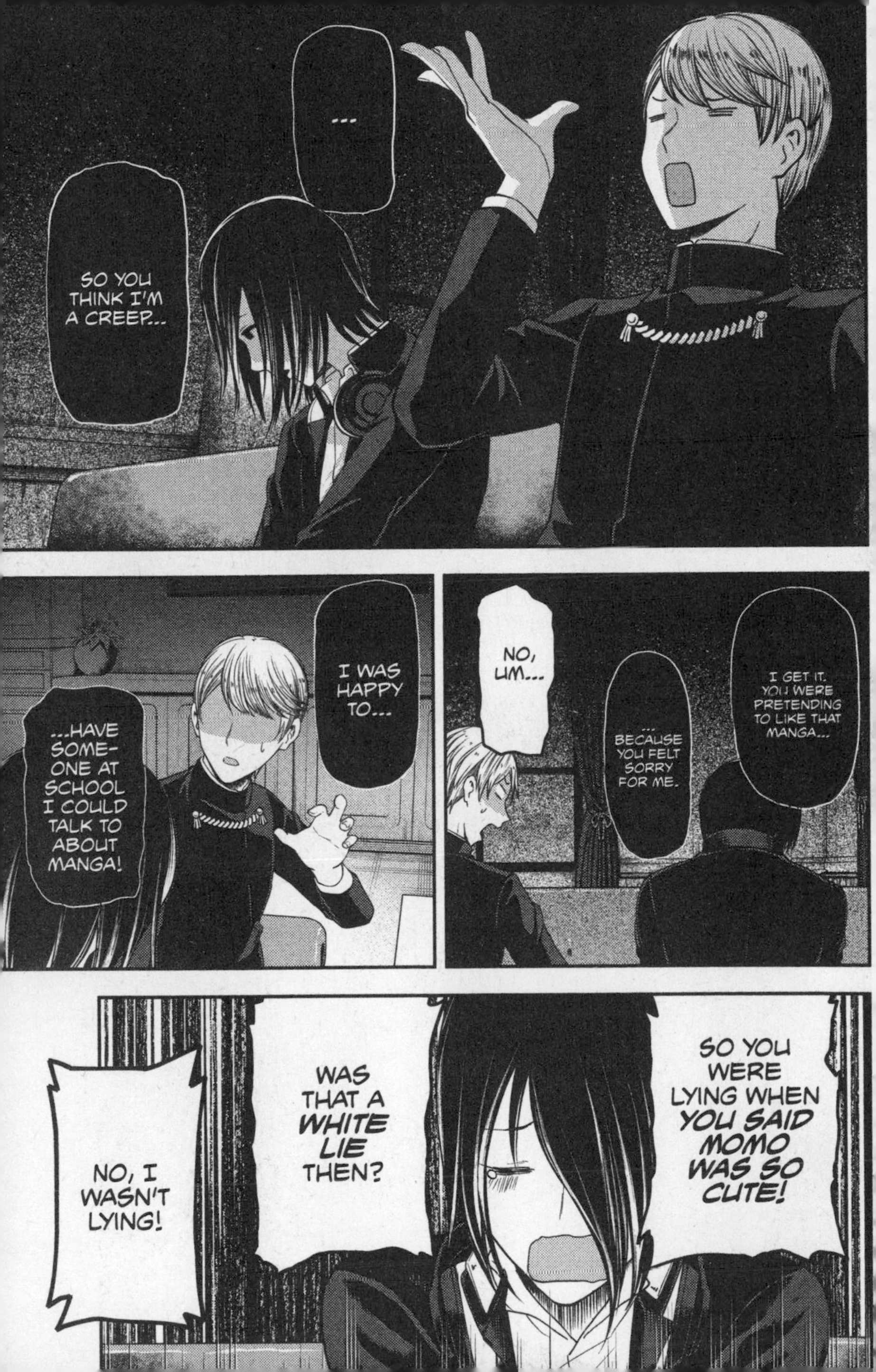
...
SO YOU THINK I'M A CREEP...
I GET IT. YOU WERE PRETENDING TO LIKE THAT MANGA...
...BECAUSE YOU FELT SORRY FOR ME.
NO, UM...
I WAS HAPPY TO...
...HAVE SOME-ONE AT SCHOOL I COULD TALK TO ABOUT MANGA!
SO YOU WERE LYING WHEN *YOU SAID MOMO WAS SO CUTE!*
WAS THAT A *WHITE LIE* THEN?
NO, I WASN'T LYING!

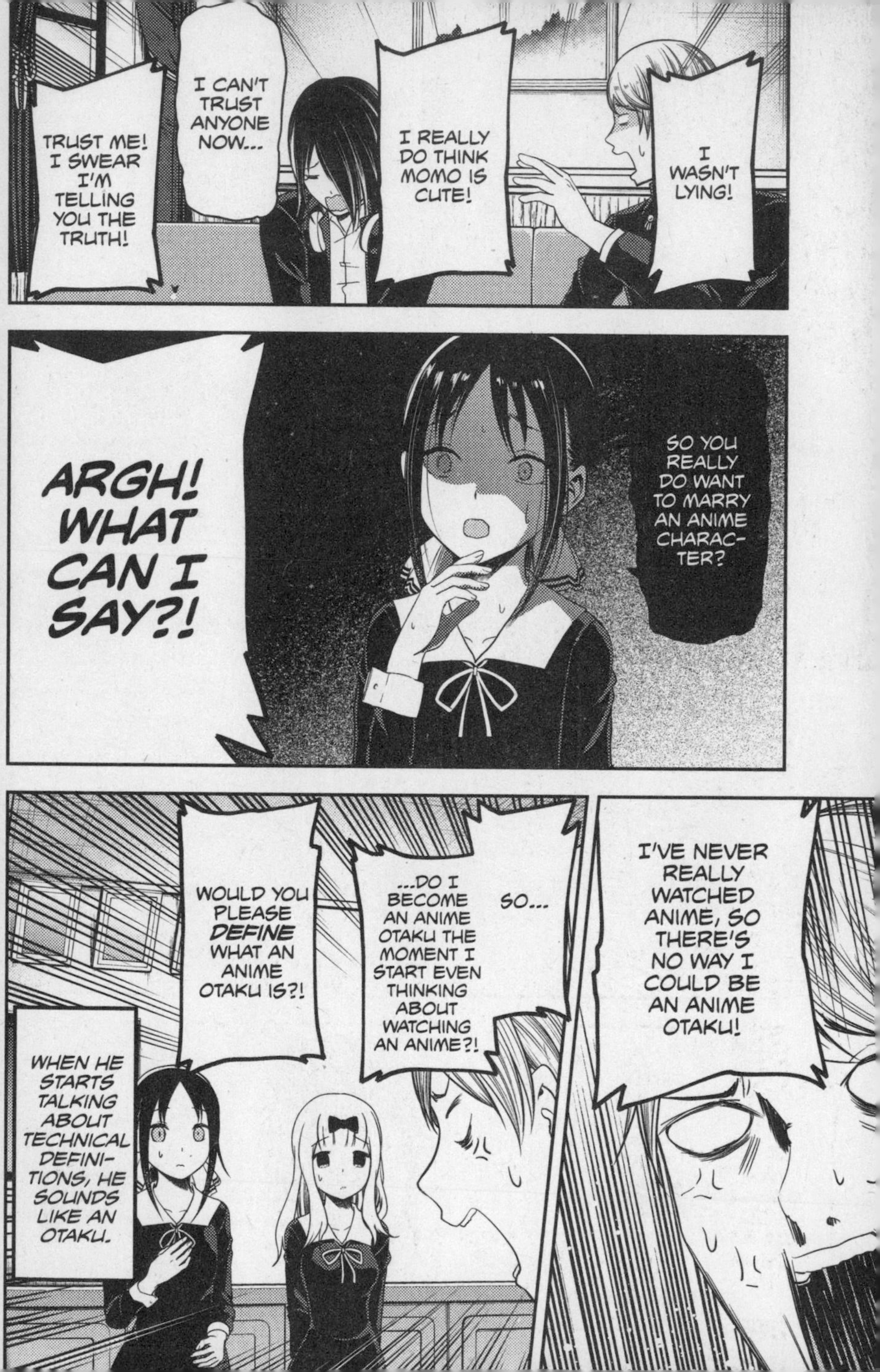
I WASN'T LYING!
I REALLY DO THINK MOMO IS CUTE!
I CAN'T TRUST ANYONE NOW...
TRUST ME! I SWEAR I'M TELLING YOU THE TRUTH!
SO YOU REALLY DO WANT TO MARRY AN ANIME CHARACTER?
ARGH! WHAT CAN I SAY?!
I'VE NEVER REALLY WATCHED ANIME, SO THERE'S NO WAY I COULD BE AN ANIME OTAKU!
SO...
...DO I BECOME AN ANIME OTAKU THE MOMENT I START EVEN THINKING ABOUT WATCHING AN ANIME?!
WOULD YOU PLEASE *DEFINE* WHAT AN ANIME OTAKU IS?!
WHEN HE STARTS TALKING ABOUT TECHNICAL DEFINITIONS, HE SOUNDS LIKE AN OTAKU.

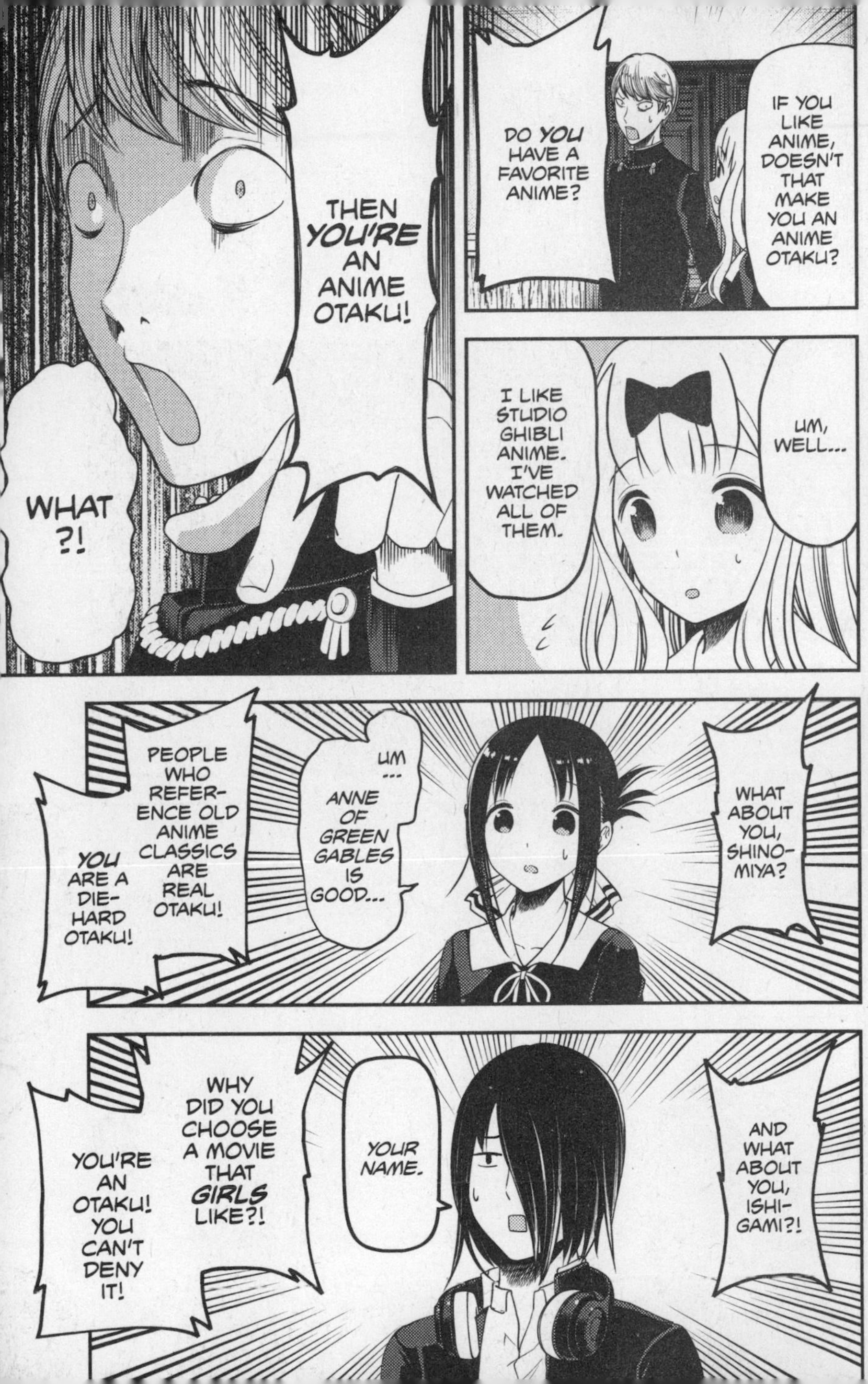
IF YOU LIKE ANIME, DOESN'T THAT MAKE YOU AN ANIME OTAKU?
DO YOU HAVE A FAVORITE ANIME?
UM, WELL...
I LIKE STUDIO GHIBLI ANIME. I'VE WATCHED ALL OF THEM.
THEN YOU'RE AN ANIME OTAKU!
WHAT?!
WHAT ABOUT YOU, SHINOMIYA?
UM... ANNE OF GREEN GABLES IS GOOD...
PEOPLE WHO REFERENCE OLD ANIME CLASSICS ARE REAL OTAKU!
YOU ARE A DIE-HARD OTAKU!
AND WHAT ABOUT YOU, ISHIGAMI?!
YOUR NAME.
WHY DID YOU CHOOSE A MOVIE THAT GIRLS LIKE?!
YOU'RE AN OTAKU! YOU CAN'T DENY IT!

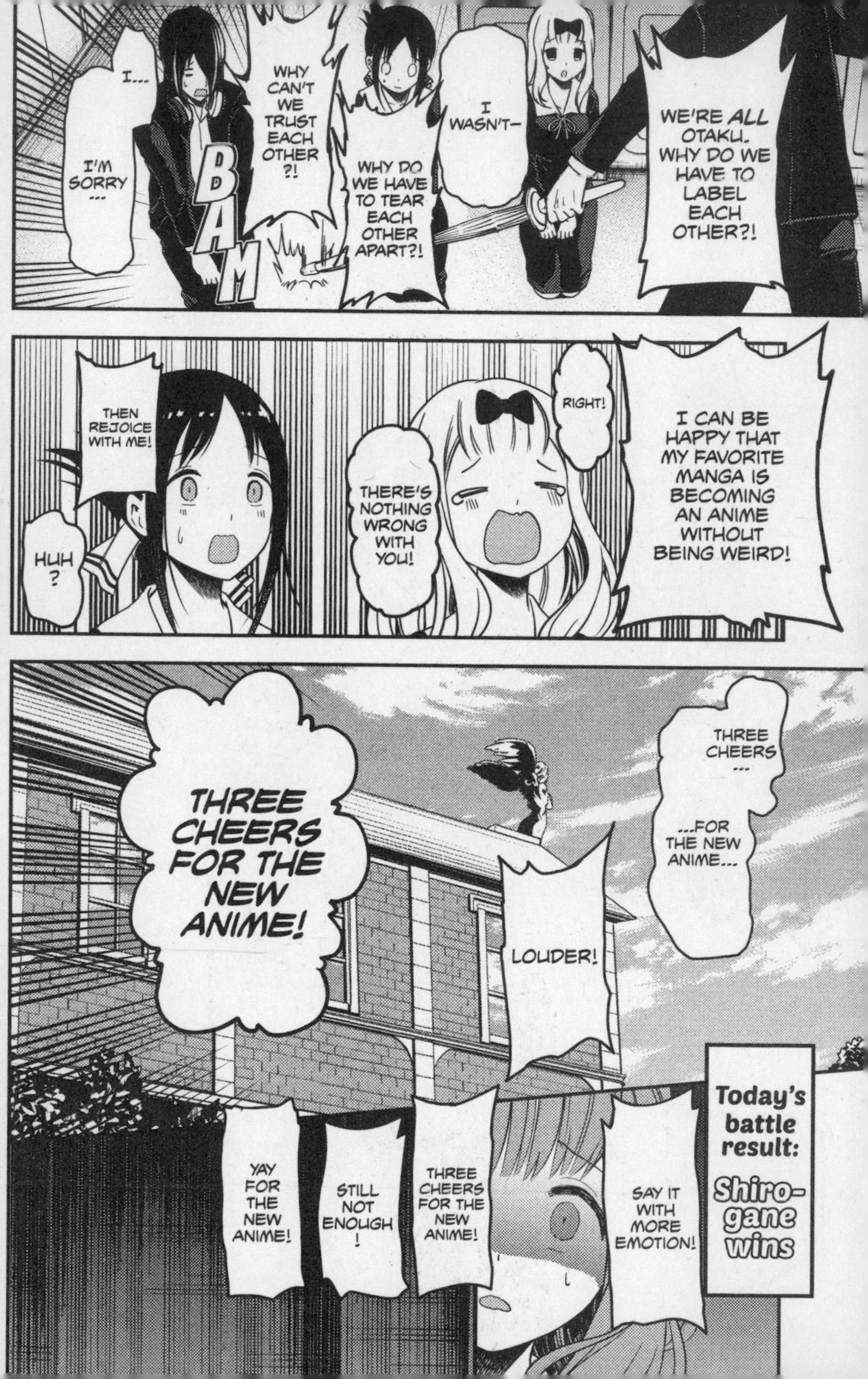
WE'RE ALL OTAKU. WHY DO WE HAVE TO LABEL EACH OTHER?!
I WASN'T—
WHY DO WE HAVE TO TEAR EACH OTHER APART?!
WHY CAN'T WE TRUST EACH OTHER?!
BAM
I...
I'M SORRY...
I CAN BE HAPPY THAT MY FAVORITE MANGA IS BECOMING AN ANIME WITHOUT BEING WEIRD!
RIGHT!
THERE'S NOTHING WRONG WITH YOU!
THEN REJOICE WITH ME!
HUH?
THREE CHEERS...
...FOR THE NEW ANIME...
LOUDER!
THREE CHEERS FOR THE NEW ANIME!
Today's battle result: Shirogane wins
SAY IT WITH MORE EMOTION!
THREE CHEERS FOR THE NEW ANIME!
STILL NOT ENOUGH!
YAY FOR THE NEW ANIME!

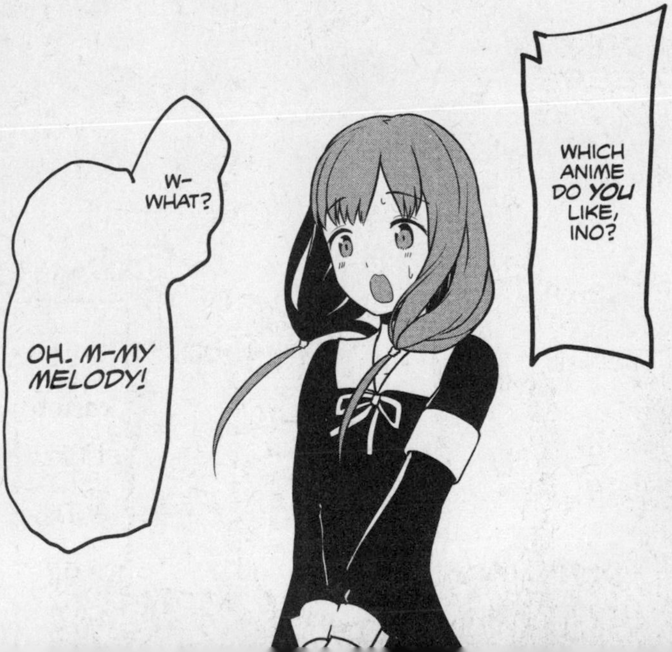
WHICH ANIME DO *YOU* LIKE, INO?
W- WHAT?
OH. M-MY MELODY!

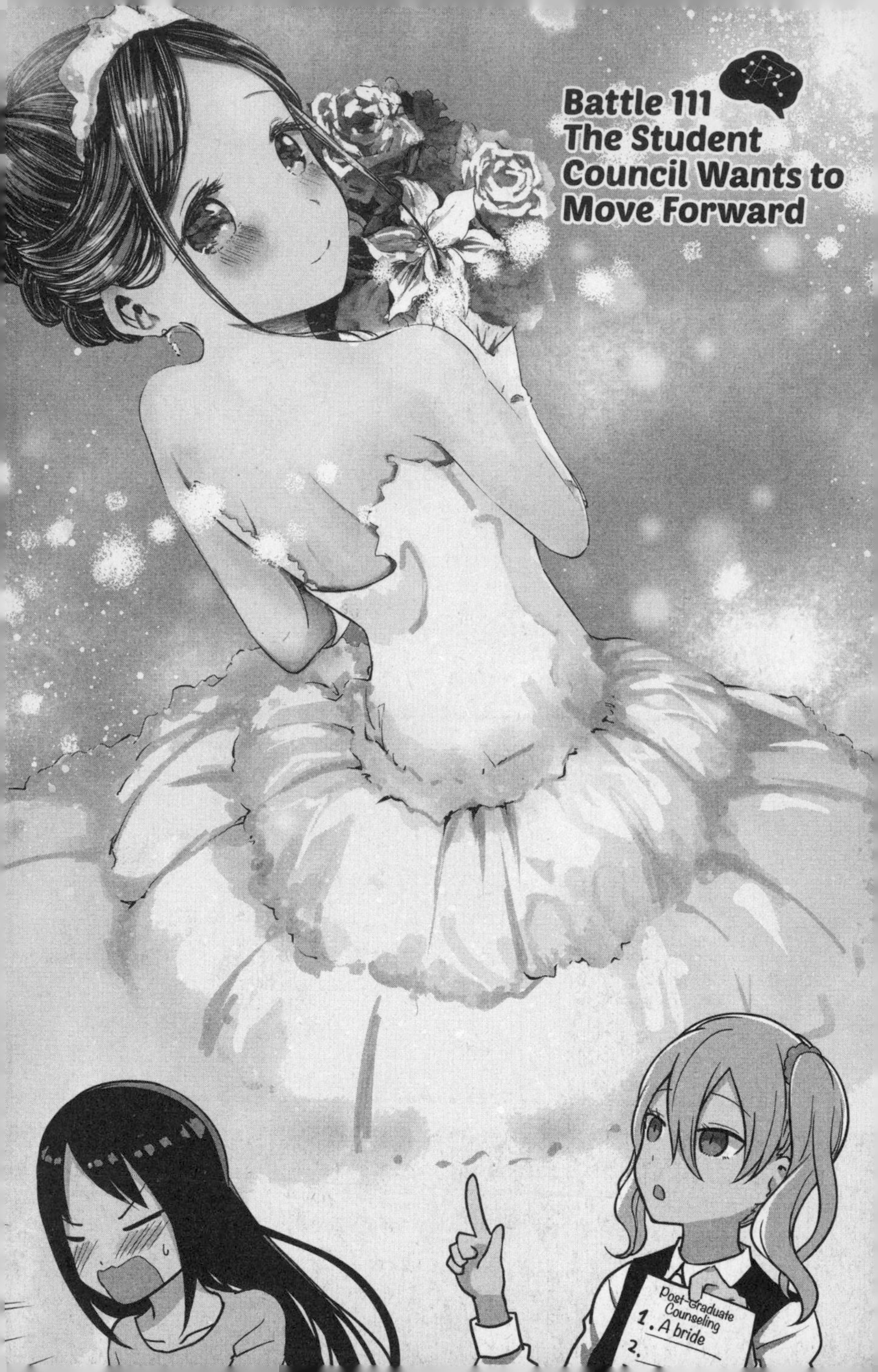
Battle 111
The Student Council Wants to Move Forward
Post-Graduate Counseling
1. A bride
2.

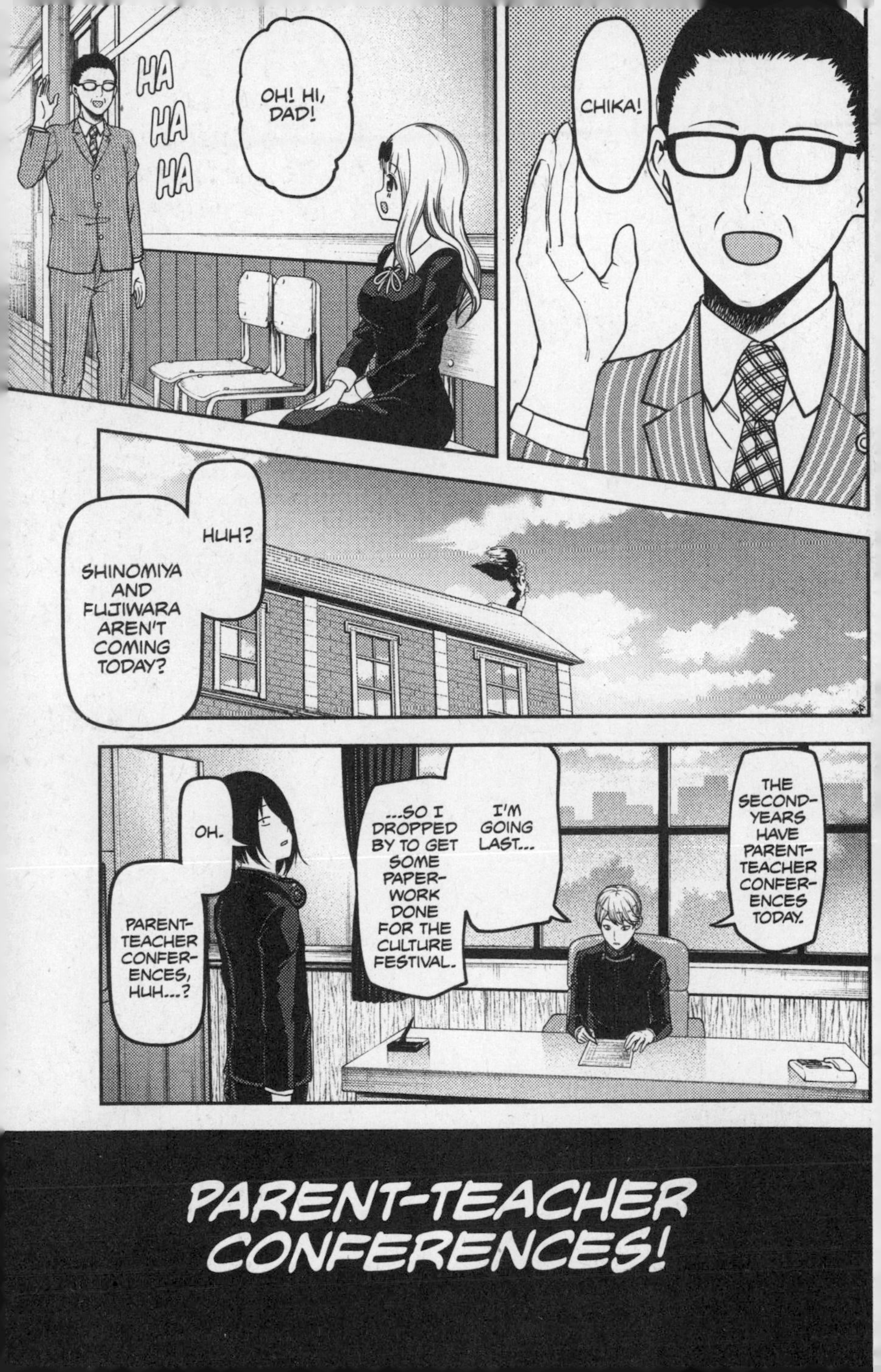
CHIKA!
OH! HI, DAD!
HA HA HA
HUH?
SHINOMIYA AND FUJIWARA AREN'T COMING TODAY?
THE SECOND-YEARS HAVE PARENT-TEACHER CONFERENCES TODAY.
I'M GOING LAST...
...SO I DROPPED BY TO GET SOME PAPERWORK DONE FOR THE CULTURE FESTIVAL.
OH.
PARENT-TEACHER CONFERENCES, HUH...?

PARENT-TEACHER CONFERENCES!

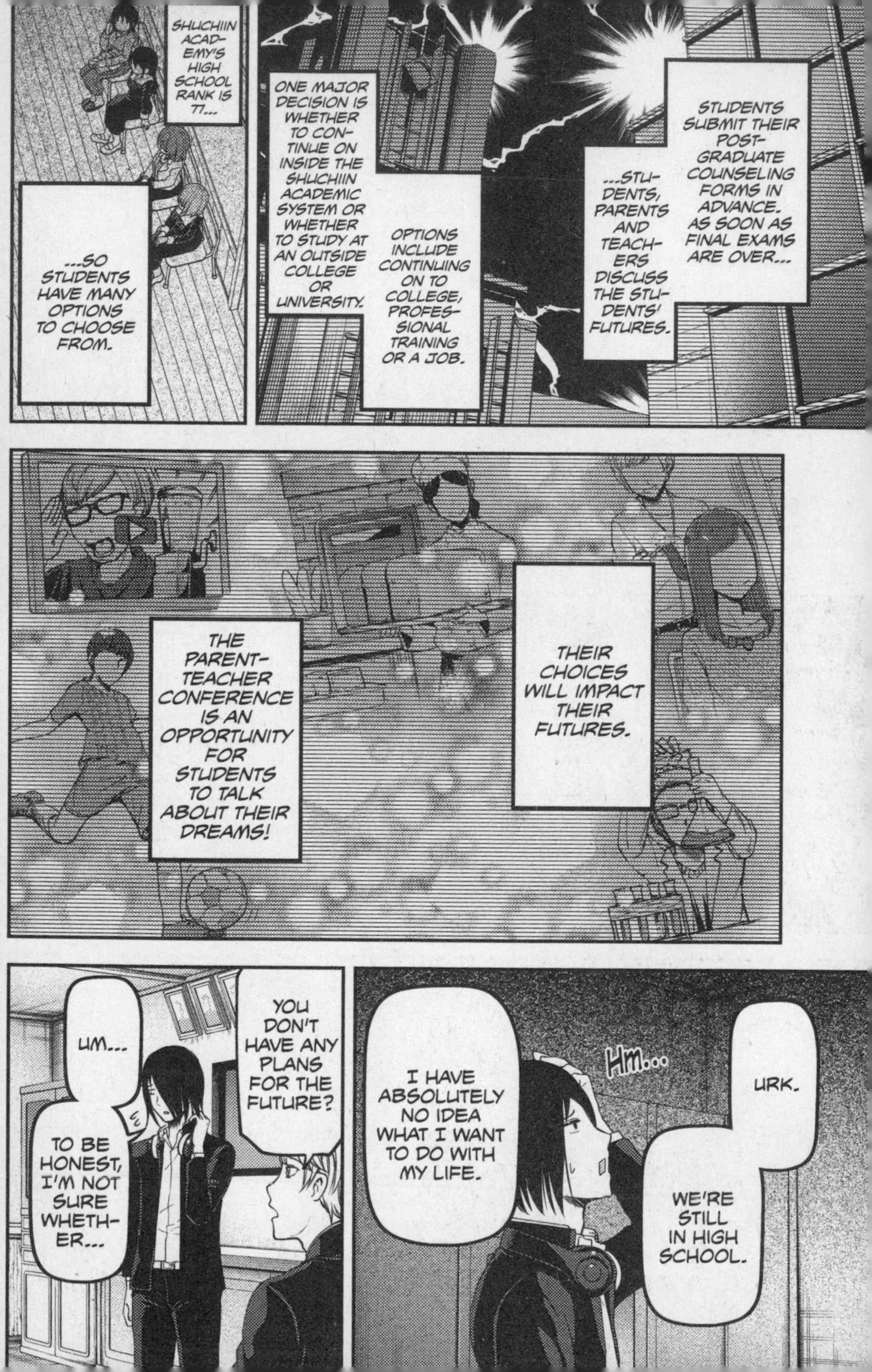
STUDENTS SUBMIT THEIR POST-GRADUATE COUNSELING FORMS IN ADVANCE. AS SOON AS FINAL EXAMS ARE OVER...
...STUDENTS, PARENTS AND TEACHERS DISCUSS THE STUDENTS' FUTURES.
OPTIONS INCLUDE CONTINUING ON TO COLLEGE, PROFESSIONAL TRAINING OR A JOB.
ONE MAJOR DECISION IS WHETHER TO CONTINUE ON INSIDE THE SHUCHIIN ACADEMIC SYSTEM OR WHETHER TO STUDY AT AN OUTSIDE COLLEGE OR UNIVERSITY.
SHUCHIIN ACADEMY'S HIGH SCHOOL RANK IS 77...
...SO STUDENTS HAVE MANY OPTIONS TO CHOOSE FROM.
THEIR CHOICES WILL IMPACT THEIR FUTURES.
THE PARENT-TEACHER CONFERENCE IS AN OPPORTUNITY FOR STUDENTS TO TALK ABOUT THEIR DREAMS!
URK.
Hm...
I HAVE ABSOLUTELY NO IDEA WHAT I WANT TO DO WITH MY LIFE.
WE'RE STILL IN HIGH SCHOOL.
YOU DON'T HAVE ANY PLANS FOR THE FUTURE?
UM...
TO BE HONEST, I'M NOT SURE WHETHER...

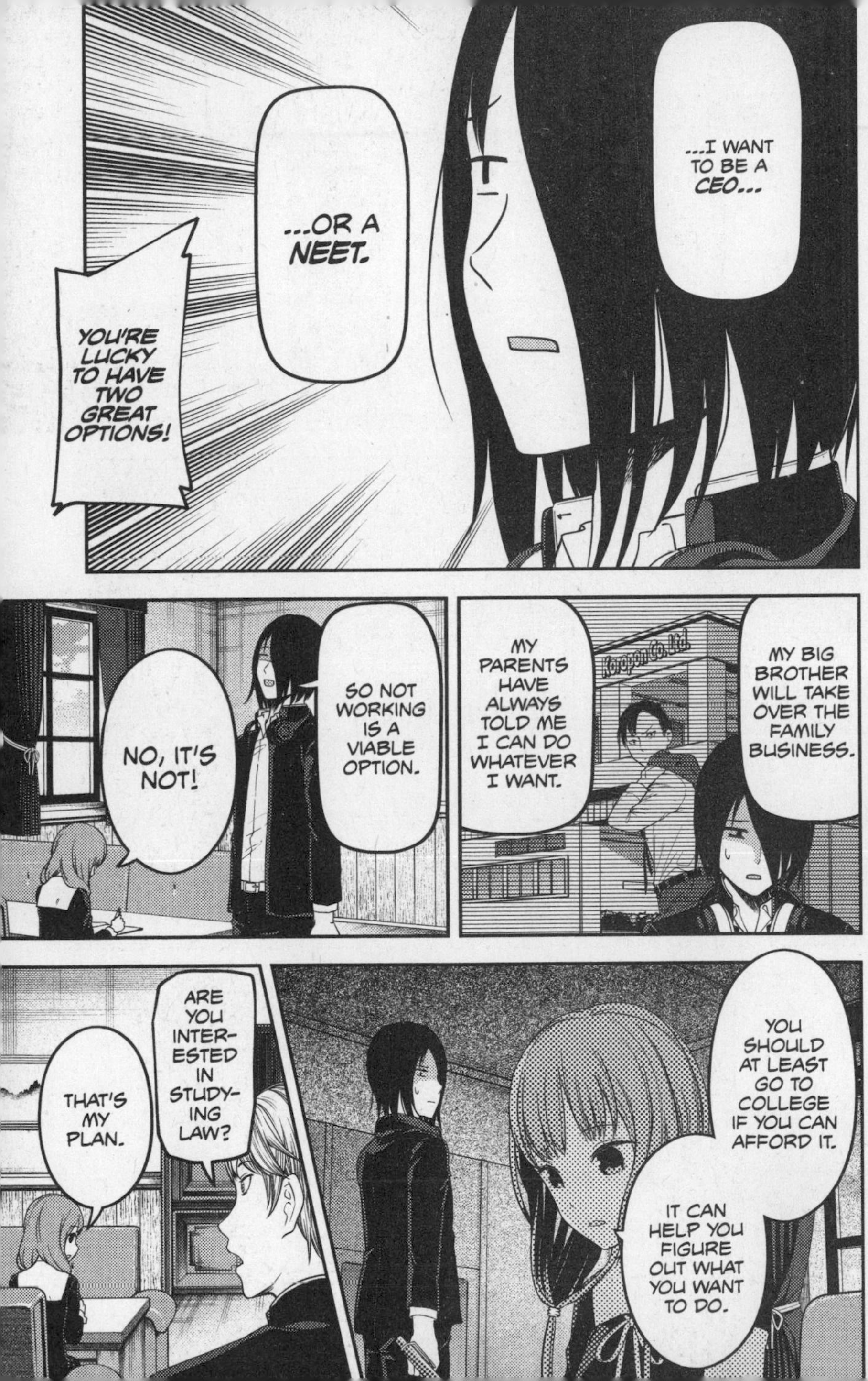
...I WANT TO BE A CEO...
...OR A NEET.
YOU'RE LUCKY TO HAVE TWO GREAT OPTIONS!
MY BIG BROTHER WILL TAKE OVER THE FAMILY BUSINESS.
MY PARENTS HAVE ALWAYS TOLD ME I CAN DO WHATEVER I WANT.
SO NOT WORKING IS A VIABLE OPTION.
NO, IT'S NOT!
YOU SHOULD AT LEAST GO TO COLLEGE IF YOU CAN AFFORD IT.
IT CAN HELP YOU FIGURE OUT WHAT YOU WANT TO DO.
ARE YOU INTERESTED IN STUDYING LAW?
THAT'S MY PLAN.

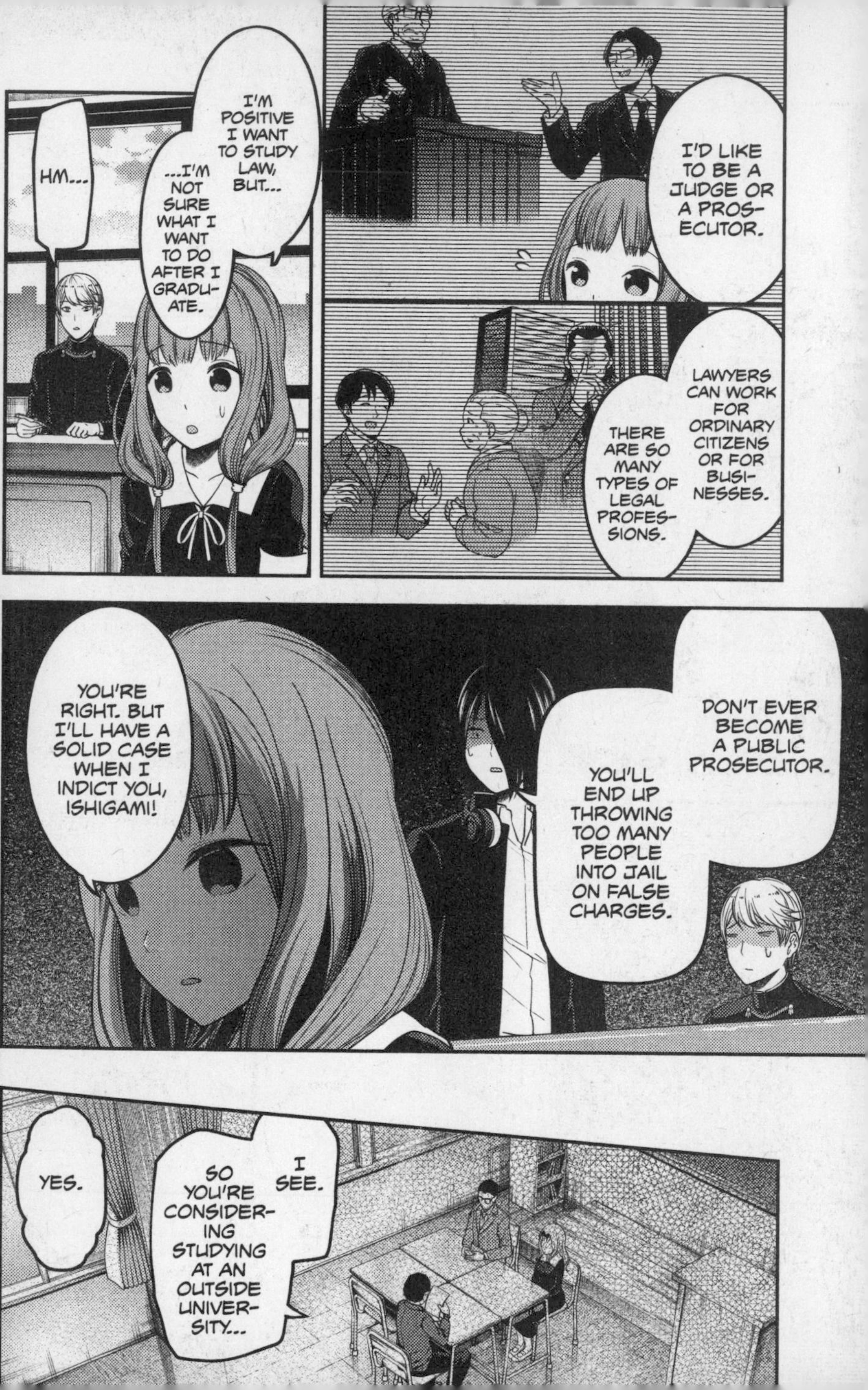
I'D LIKE TO BE A JUDGE OR A PROSECUTOR.
LAWYERS CAN WORK FOR ORDINARY CITIZENS OR FOR BUSINESSES.
THERE ARE SO MANY TYPES OF LEGAL PROFESSIONS.
I'M POSITIVE I WANT TO STUDY LAW, BUT...
...I'M NOT SURE WHAT I WANT TO DO AFTER I GRADUATE.
HM...
DON'T EVER BECOME A PUBLIC PROSECUTOR.
YOU'LL END UP THROWING TOO MANY PEOPLE INTO JAIL ON FALSE CHARGES.
YOU'RE RIGHT. BUT I'LL HAVE A SOLID CASE WHEN I INDICT YOU, ISHIGAMI!
I SEE.
SO YOU'RE CONSIDERING STUDYING AT AN OUTSIDE UNIVERSITY...
YES.

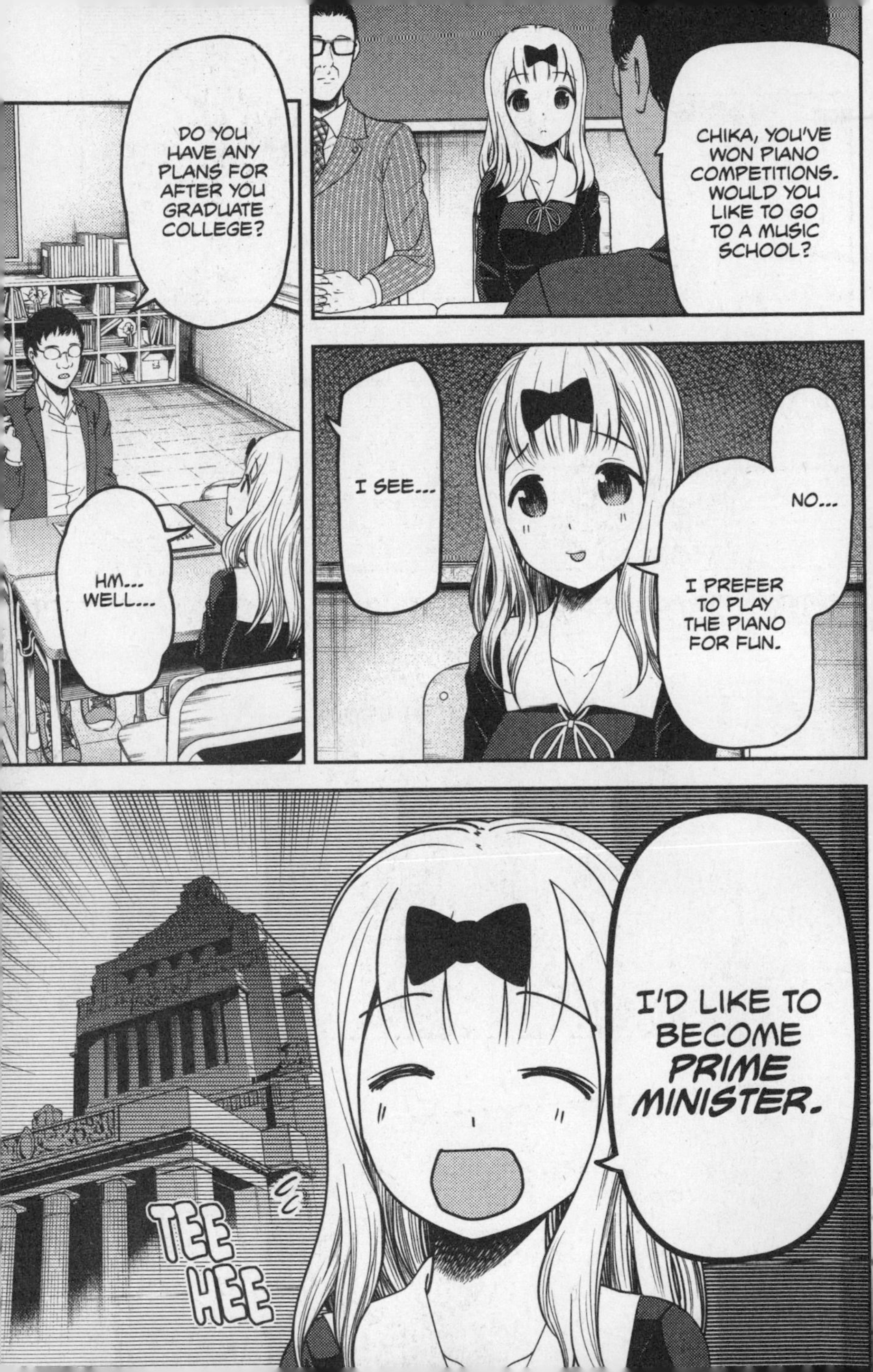

CHIKA, YOU'VE WON PIANO COMPETITIONS. WOULD YOU LIKE TO GO TO A MUSIC SCHOOL?
NO...
I PREFER TO PLAY THE PIANO FOR FUN.
I SEE...
DO YOU HAVE ANY PLANS FOR AFTER YOU GRADUATE COLLEGE?
HM... WELL...
I'D LIKE TO BECOME *PRIME MINISTER*.
TEE HEE

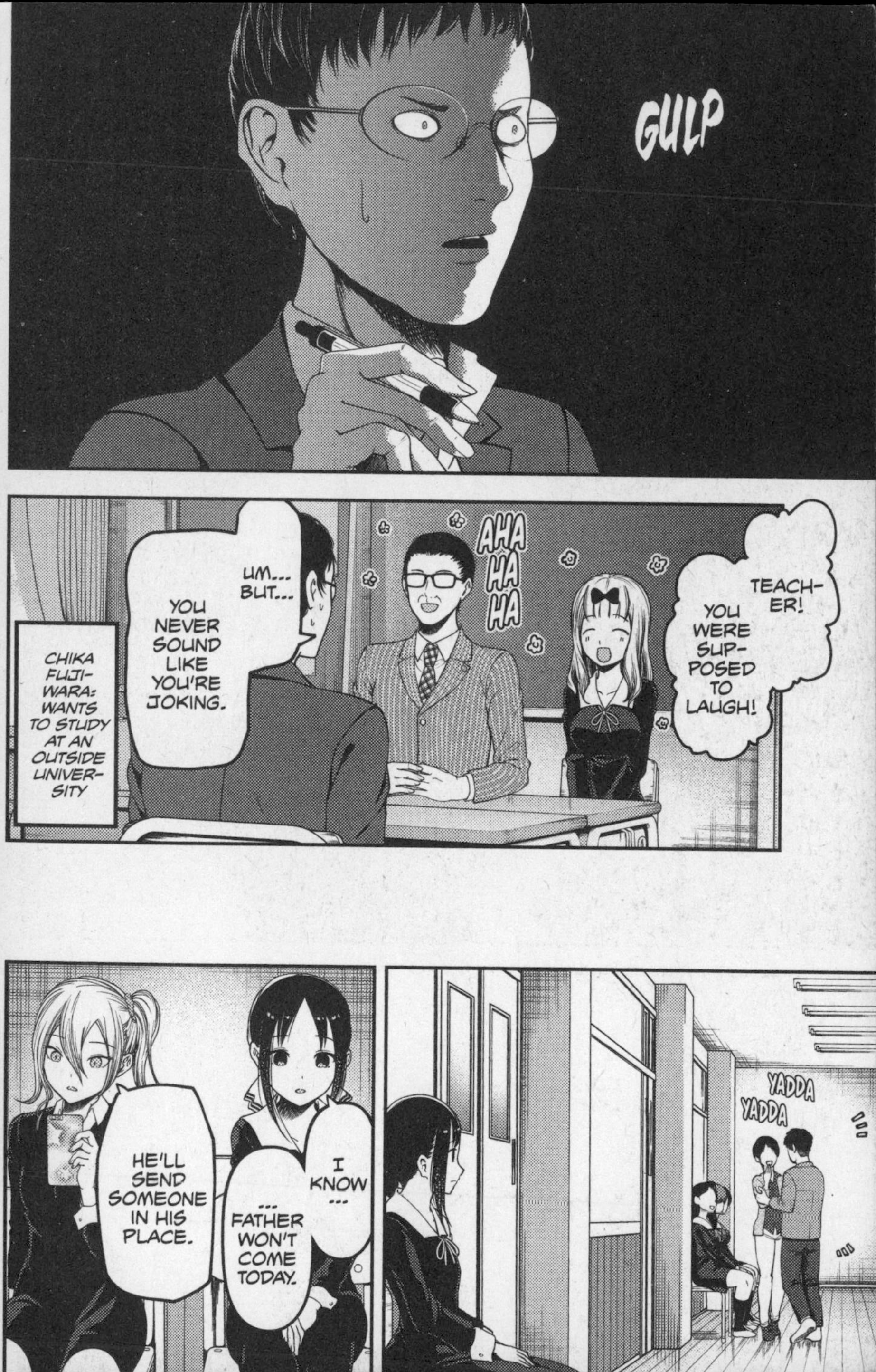
GULP
TEACHER! YOU WERE SUPPOSED TO LAUGH!
AHAHAHA
UM... BUT... YOU NEVER SOUND LIKE YOU'RE JOKING.
CHIKA FUJIWARA: WANTS TO STUDY AT AN OUTSIDE UNIVERSITY
YADDA YADDA
I KNOW...
...FATHER WON'T COME TODAY.
HE'LL SEND SOMEONE IN HIS PLACE.

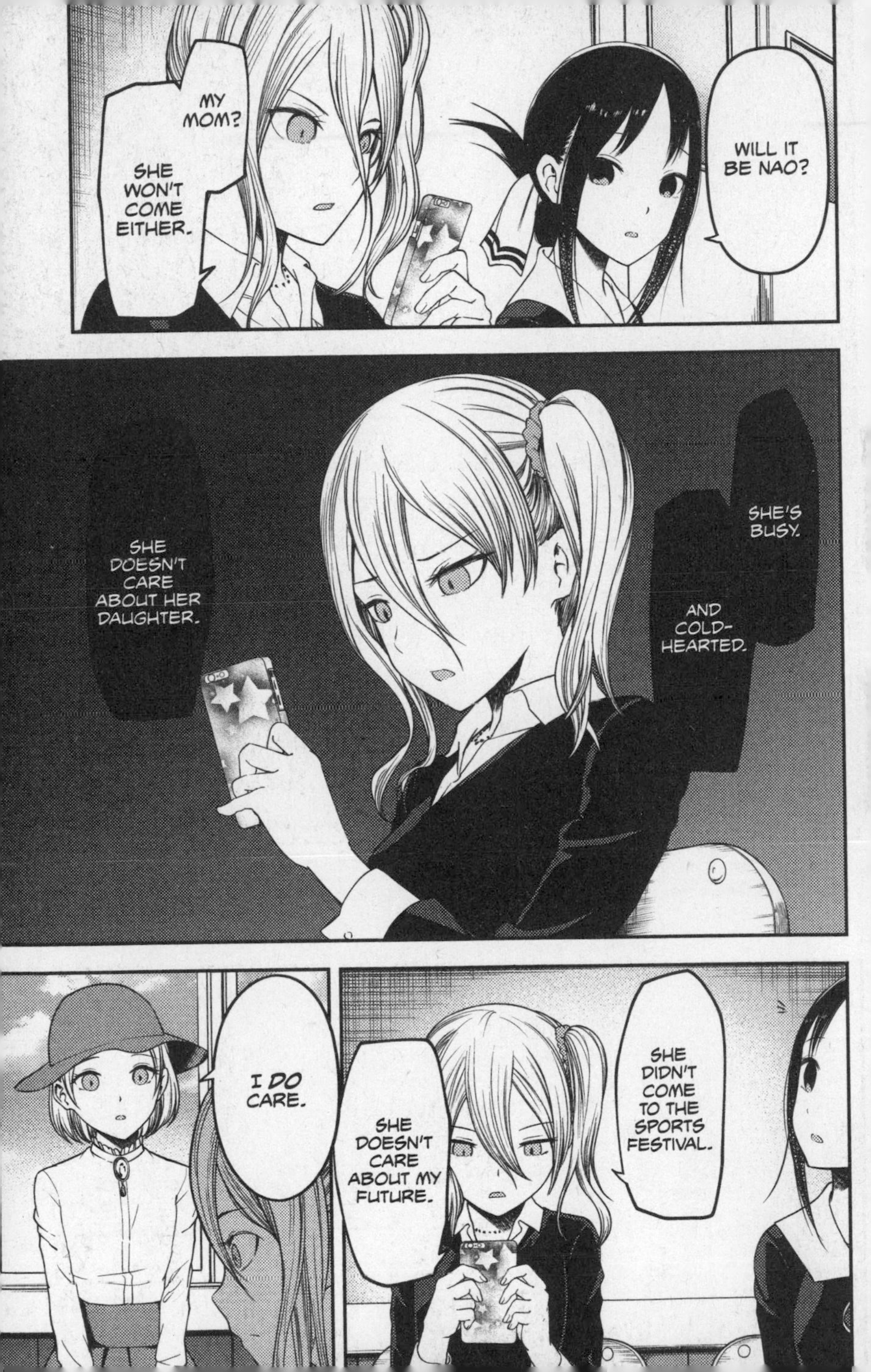
WILL IT BE NAO?
MY MOM?
SHE WON'T COME EITHER.
SHE'S BUSY.
AND COLD-HEARTED.
SHE DOESN'T CARE ABOUT HER DAUGHTER.
SHE DIDN'T COME TO THE SPORTS FESTIVAL.
SHE DOESN'T CARE ABOUT MY FUTURE.
I DO CARE.

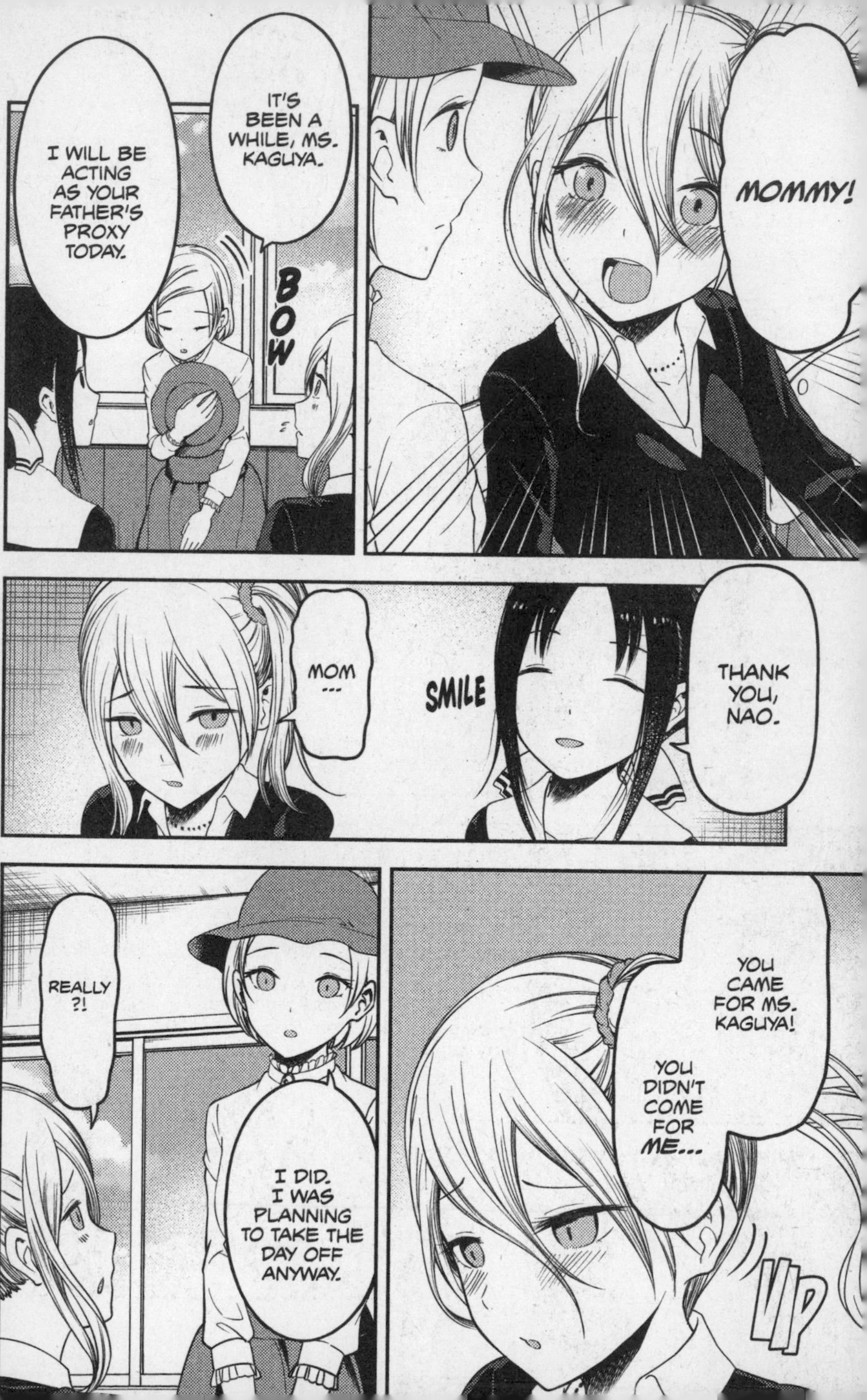
MOMMY!
IT'S BEEN A WHILE, MS. KAGUYA.
BOW
I WILL BE ACTING AS YOUR FATHER'S PROXY TODAY.
THANK YOU, NAO.
SMILE
MOM...
YOU CAME FOR MS. KAGUYA!
YOU DIDN'T COME FOR ME...
REALLY?!
I DID. I WAS PLANNING TO TAKE THE DAY OFF ANYWAY.

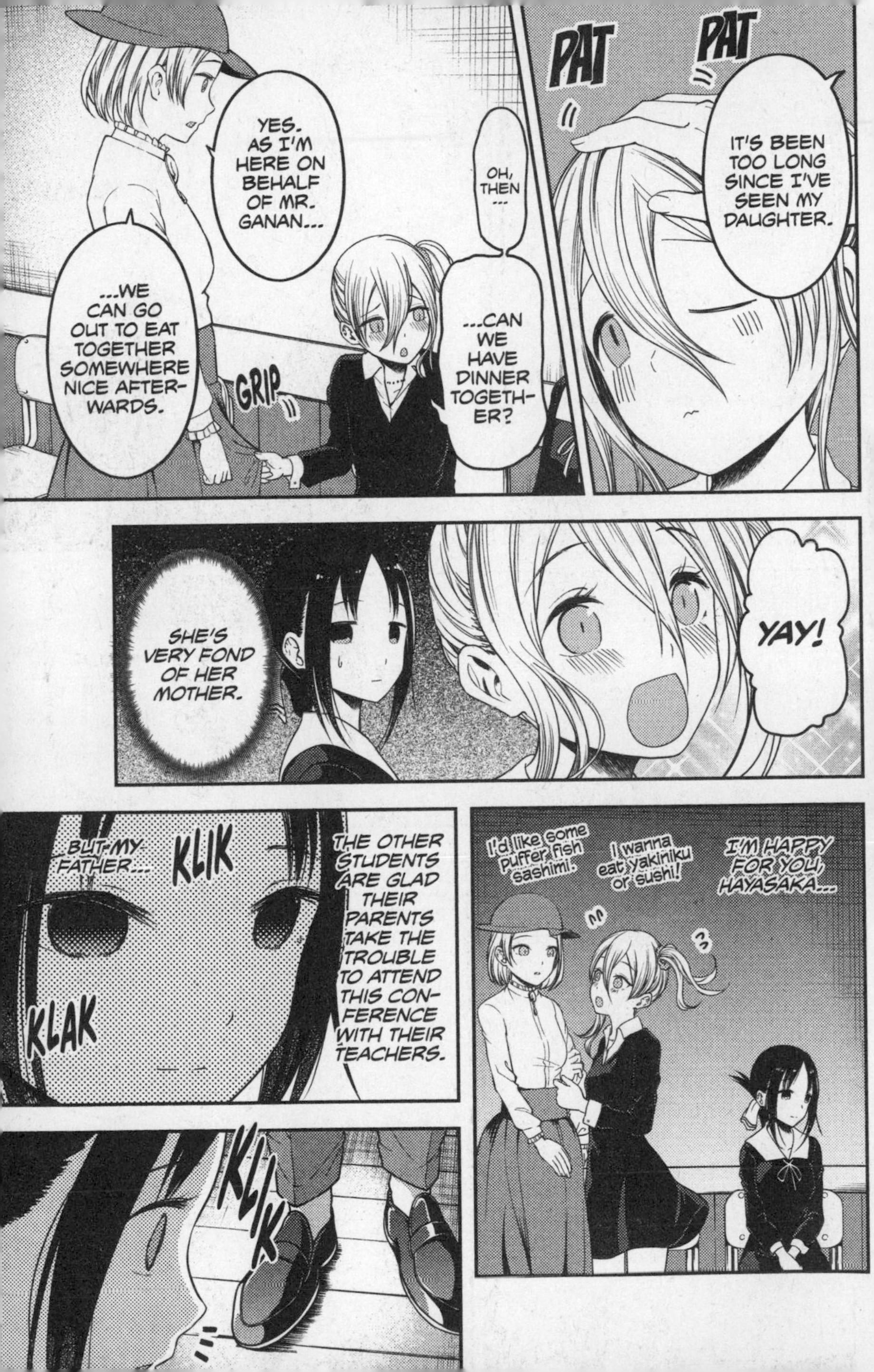
PAT
PAT
IT'S BEEN TOO LONG SINCE I'VE SEEN MY DAUGHTER.
OH, THEN...
...CAN WE HAVE DINNER TOGETHER?
YES. AS I'M HERE ON BEHALF OF MR. GANAN...
GRIP
...WE CAN GO OUT TO EAT TOGETHER SOMEWHERE NICE AFTER-WARDS.
YAY!
SHE'S VERY FOND OF HER MOTHER.
I'M HAPPY FOR YOU, HAYASAKA...
I wanna eat yakiniku or sushi!
I'd like some puffer fish sashimi.
THE OTHER STUDENTS ARE GLAD THEIR PARENTS TAKE THE TROUBLE TO ATTEND THIS CON-FERENCE WITH THEIR TEACHERS.
KLIK
BUT MY FATHER...
KLAK
KLIK

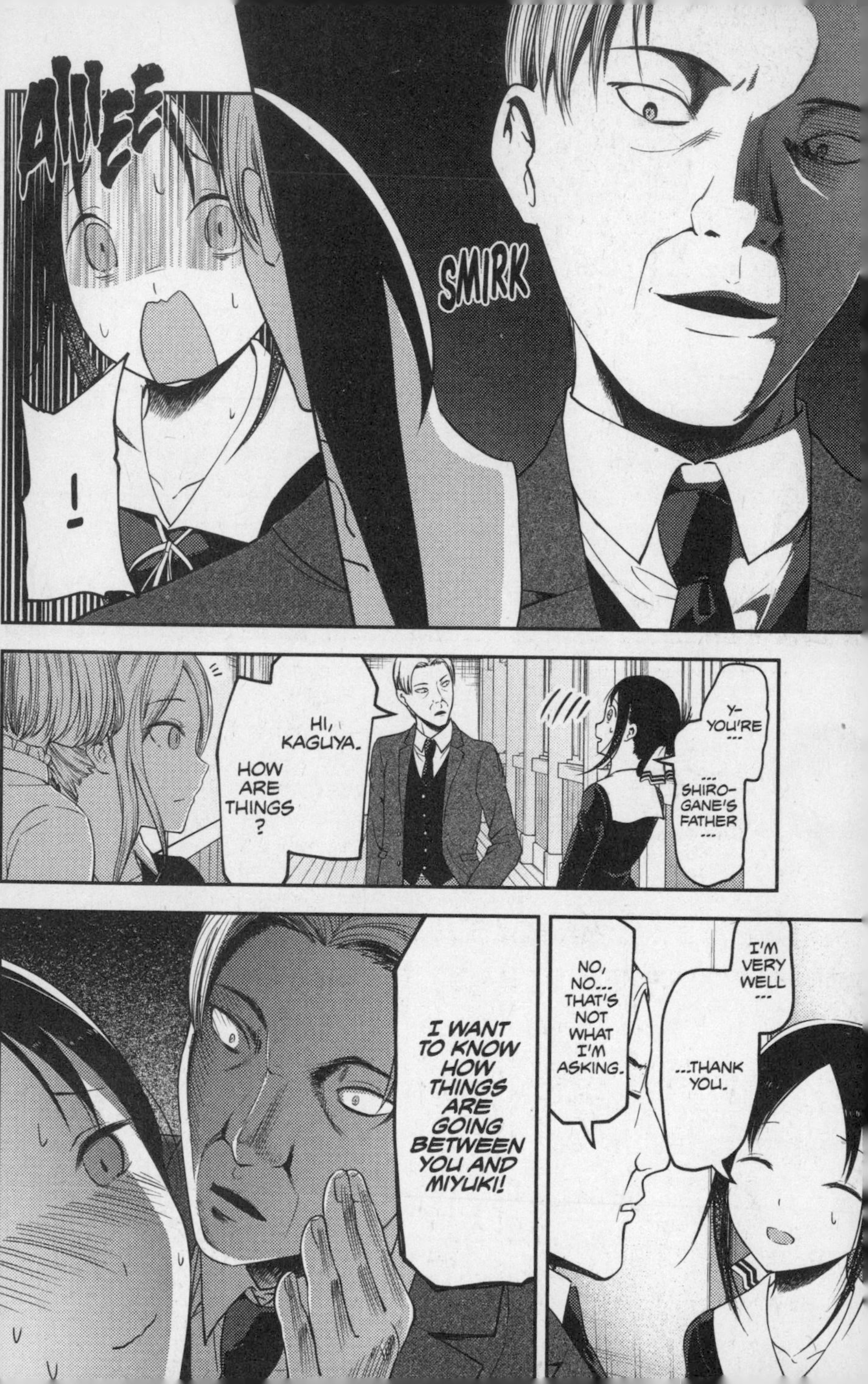
SMIRK
AWEE
!
Y-YOU'RE... ...SHIRO-GANE'S FATHER...
HI, KAGUYA. HOW ARE THINGS?
I'M VERY WELL... ...THANK YOU.
NO, NO... THAT'S NOT WHAT I'M ASKING.
I WANT TO KNOW HOW THINGS ARE GOING BETWEEN YOU AND MIYUKI!

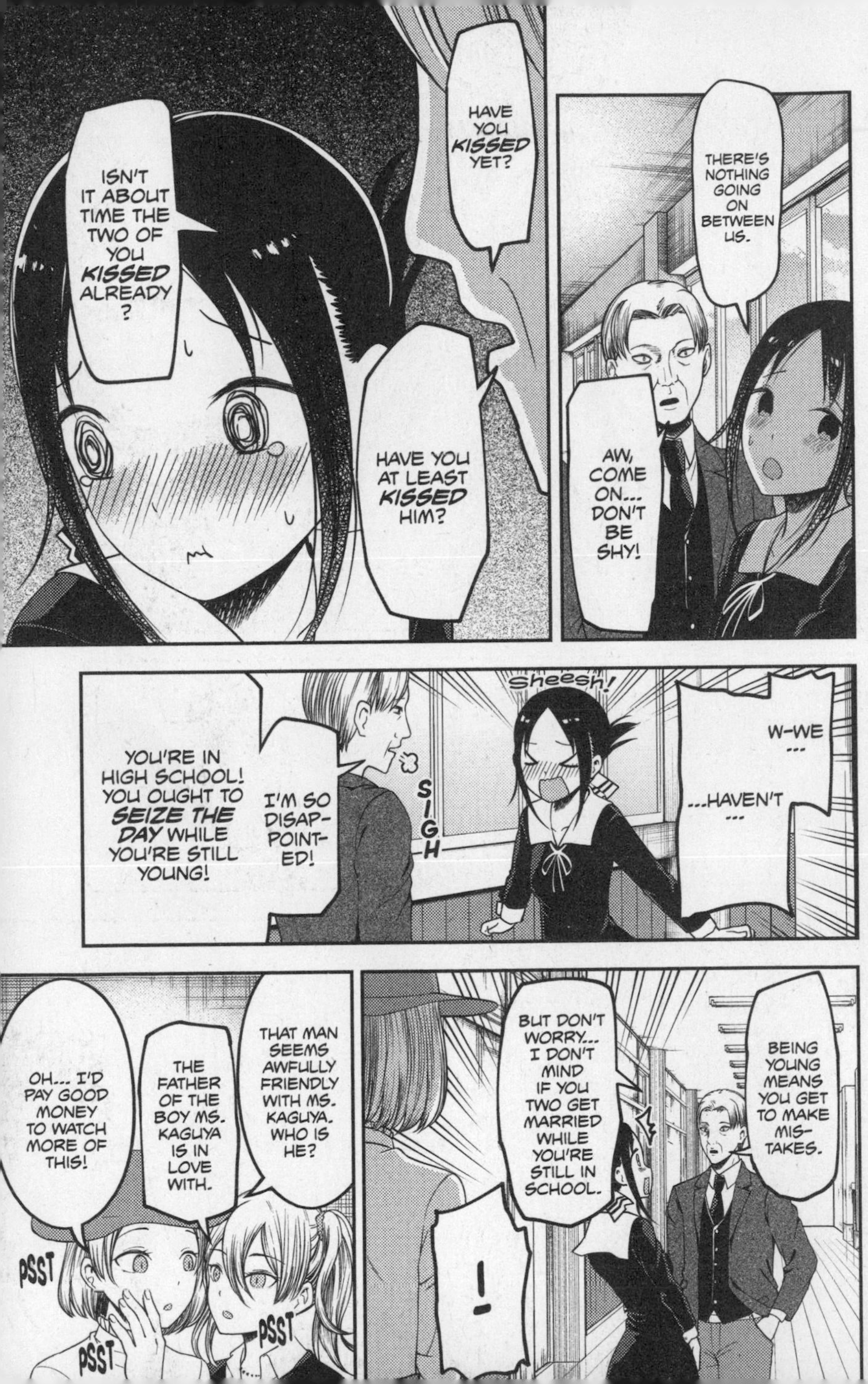
THERE'S NOTHING GOING ON BETWEEN US.
AW, COME ON... DON'T BE SHY!
HAVE YOU KISSED YET?
HAVE YOU AT LEAST KISSED HIM?
ISN'T IT ABOUT TIME THE TWO OF YOU KISSED ALREADY?
W-WE... ...HAVEN'T...
Sheesh!
SIGH
I'M SO DISAPPOINTED!
YOU'RE IN HIGH SCHOOL! YOU OUGHT TO SEIZE THE DAY WHILE YOU'RE STILL YOUNG!
BEING YOUNG MEANS YOU GET TO MAKE MISTAKES.
BUT DON'T WORRY... I DON'T MIND IF YOU TWO GET MARRIED WHILE YOU'RE STILL IN SCHOOL.
!
THAT MAN SEEMS AWFULLY FRIENDLY WITH MS. KAGUYA. WHO IS HE?
THE FATHER OF THE BOY MS. KAGUYA IS IN LOVE WITH.
OH... I'D PAY GOOD MONEY TO WATCH MORE OF THIS!
PSST
PSST
PSST

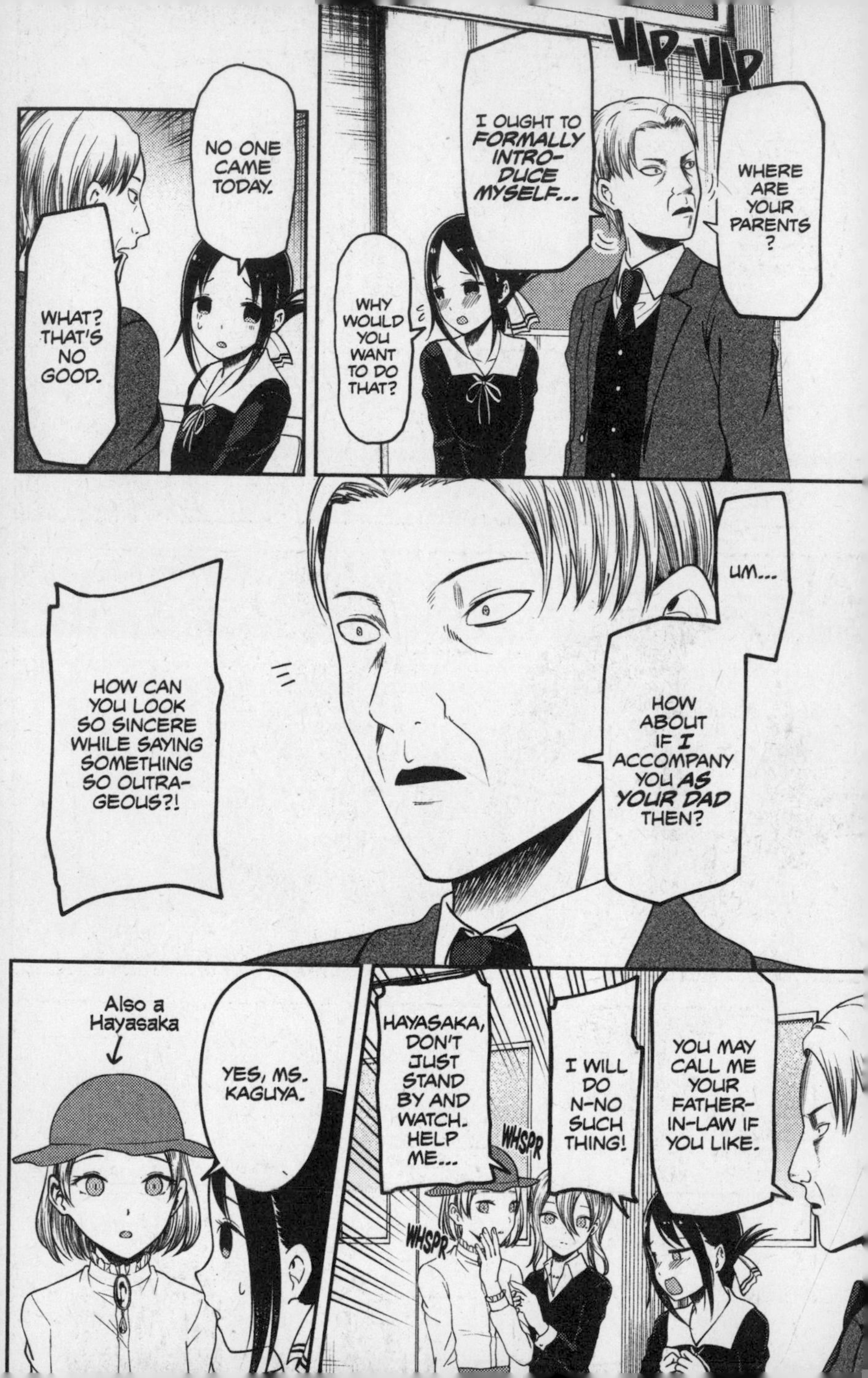
VIP VIP
WHERE ARE YOUR PARENTS?
I OUGHT TO FORMALLY INTRODUCE MYSELF...
WHY WOULD YOU WANT TO DO THAT?
NO ONE CAME TODAY.
WHAT? THAT'S NO GOOD.
UM...
HOW ABOUT IF I ACCOMPANY YOU AS YOUR DAD THEN?
HOW CAN YOU LOOK SO SINCERE WHILE SAYING SOMETHING SO OUTRAGEOUS?!
YOU MAY CALL ME YOUR FATHER-IN-LAW IF YOU LIKE.
I WILL DO N-NO SUCH THING!
WHSPR
HAYASAKA, DON'T JUST STAND BY AND WATCH. HELP ME...
WHSPR
YES, MS. KAGUYA.
Also a Hayasaka

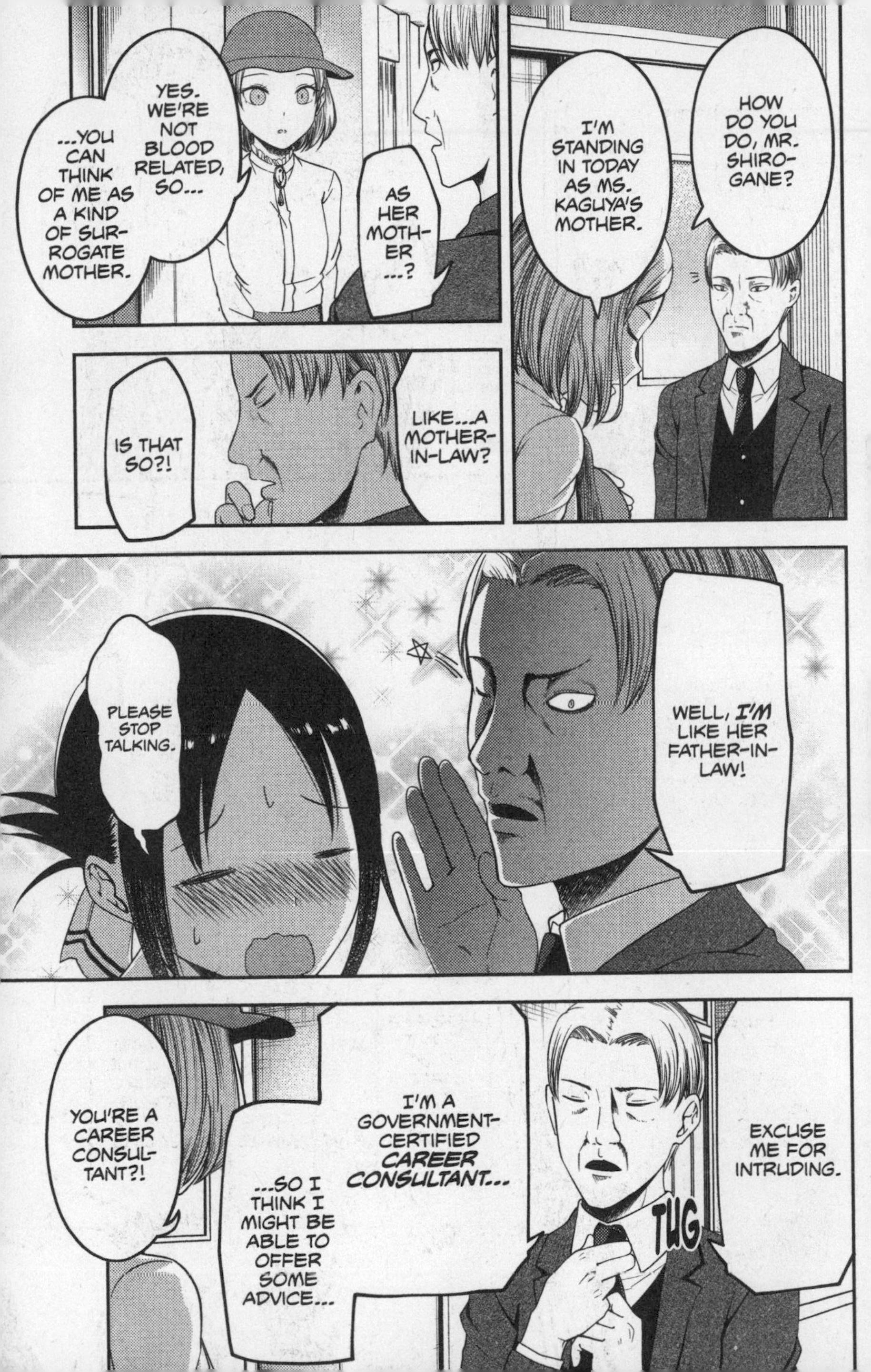
HOW DO YOU DO, MR. SHIROGANE?
I'M STANDING IN TODAY AS MS. KAGUYA'S MOTHER.
AS HER MOTHER...?
YES. WE'RE NOT BLOOD RELATED, SO...
...YOU CAN THINK OF ME AS A KIND OF SURROGATE MOTHER.
LIKE...A MOTHER-IN-LAW?
IS THAT SO?!
WELL, *I'M* LIKE HER FATHER-IN-LAW!
PLEASE STOP TALKING.
EXCUSE ME FOR INTRUDING.
TUG
I'M A GOVERNMENT-CERTIFIED *CAREER CONSULTANT...*
...SO I THINK I MIGHT BE ABLE TO OFFER SOME ADVICE...
YOU'RE A CAREER CONSULTANT?!

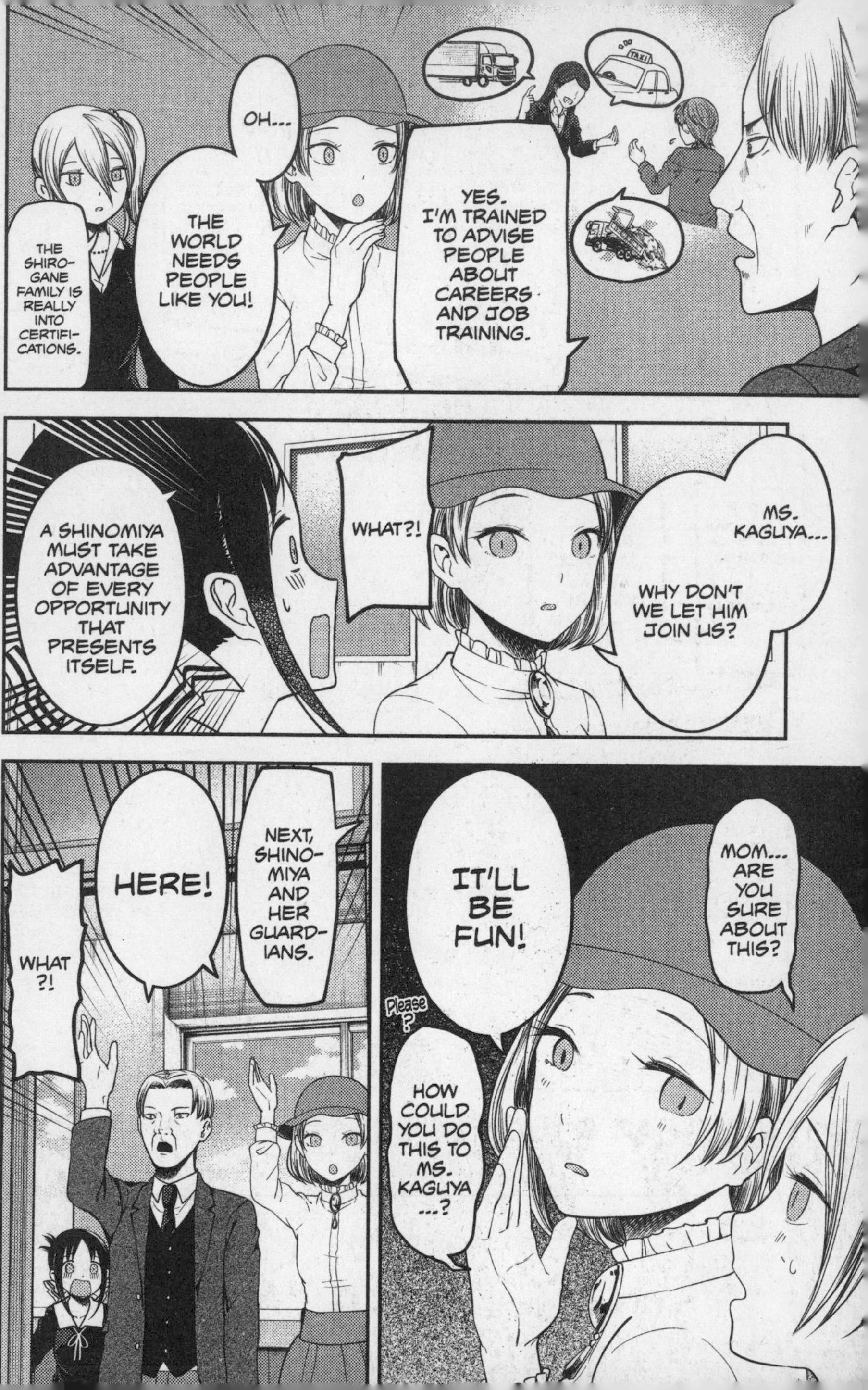
YES. I'M TRAINED TO ADVISE PEOPLE ABOUT CAREERS AND JOB TRAINING.
OH...
THE WORLD NEEDS PEOPLE LIKE YOU!
THE SHIROGANE FAMILY IS REALLY INTO CERTIFICATIONS.
MS. KAGUYA...
WHY DON'T WE LET HIM JOIN US?
WHAT?!
A SHINOMIYA MUST TAKE ADVANTAGE OF EVERY OPPORTUNITY THAT PRESENTS ITSELF.
MOM... ARE YOU SURE ABOUT THIS?
IT'LL BE FUN!
Please?
HOW COULD YOU DO THIS TO MS. KAGUYA...?
NEXT, SHINOMIYA AND HER GUARDIANS.
HERE!
WHAT?!

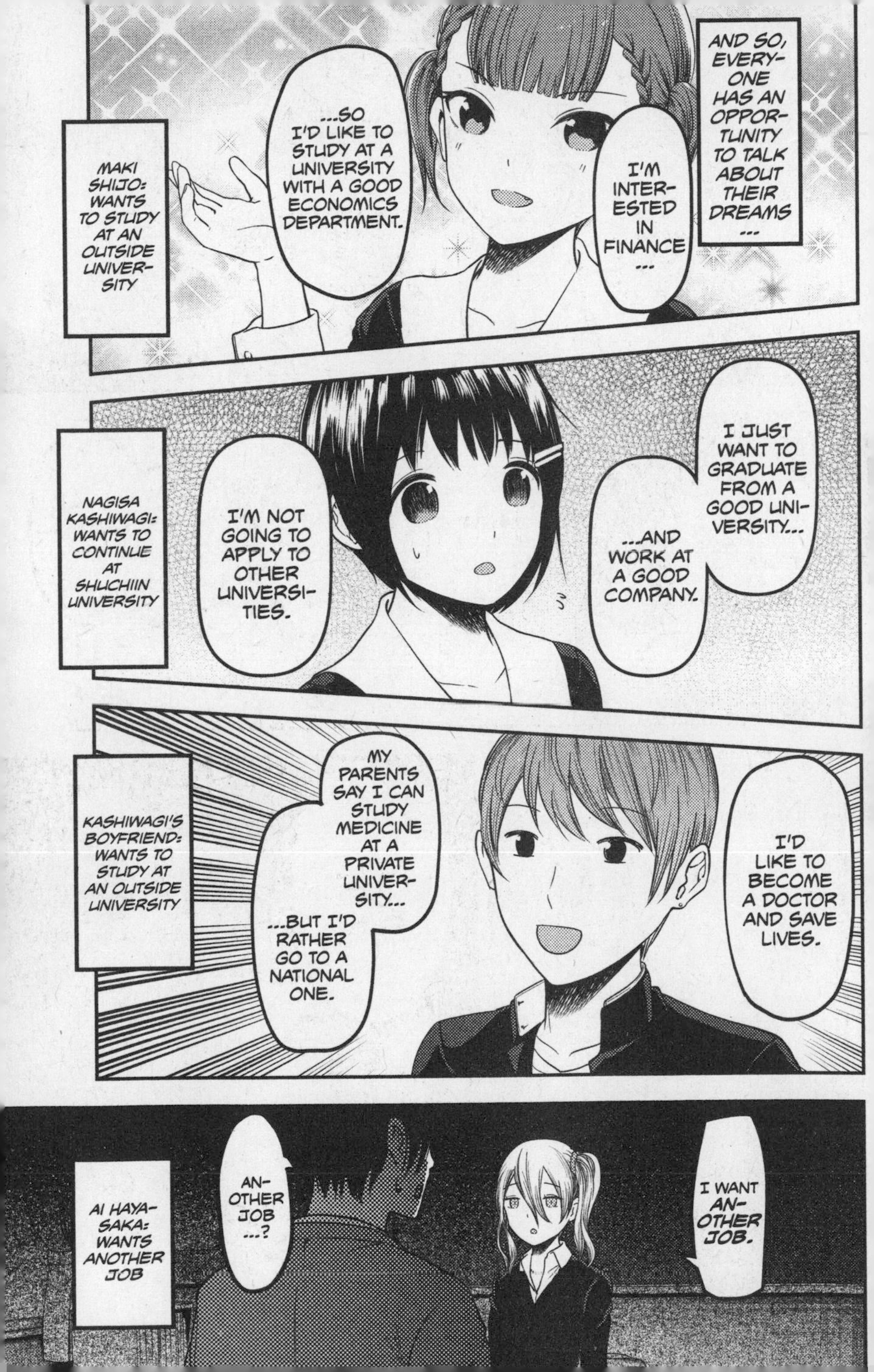
AND SO, EVERYONE HAS AN OPPORTUNITY TO TALK ABOUT THEIR DREAMS...
I'M INTERESTED IN FINANCE...
...SO I'D LIKE TO STUDY AT A UNIVERSITY WITH A GOOD ECONOMICS DEPARTMENT.
MAKI SHIJO: WANTS TO STUDY AT AN OUTSIDE UNIVERSITY
I JUST WANT TO GRADUATE FROM A GOOD UNIVERSITY...
...AND WORK AT A GOOD COMPANY.
I'M NOT GOING TO APPLY TO OTHER UNIVERSITIES.
NAGISA KASHIWAGI: WANTS TO CONTINUE AT SHUCHIIN UNIVERSITY
I'D LIKE TO BECOME A DOCTOR AND SAVE LIVES.
MY PARENTS SAY I CAN STUDY MEDICINE AT A PRIVATE UNIVERSITY...
...BUT I'D RATHER GO TO A NATIONAL ONE.
KASHIWAGI'S BOYFRIEND: WANTS TO STUDY AT AN OUTSIDE UNIVERSITY
I WANT ANOTHER JOB.
ANOTHER JOB...?
AI HAYASAKA: WANTS ANOTHER JOB

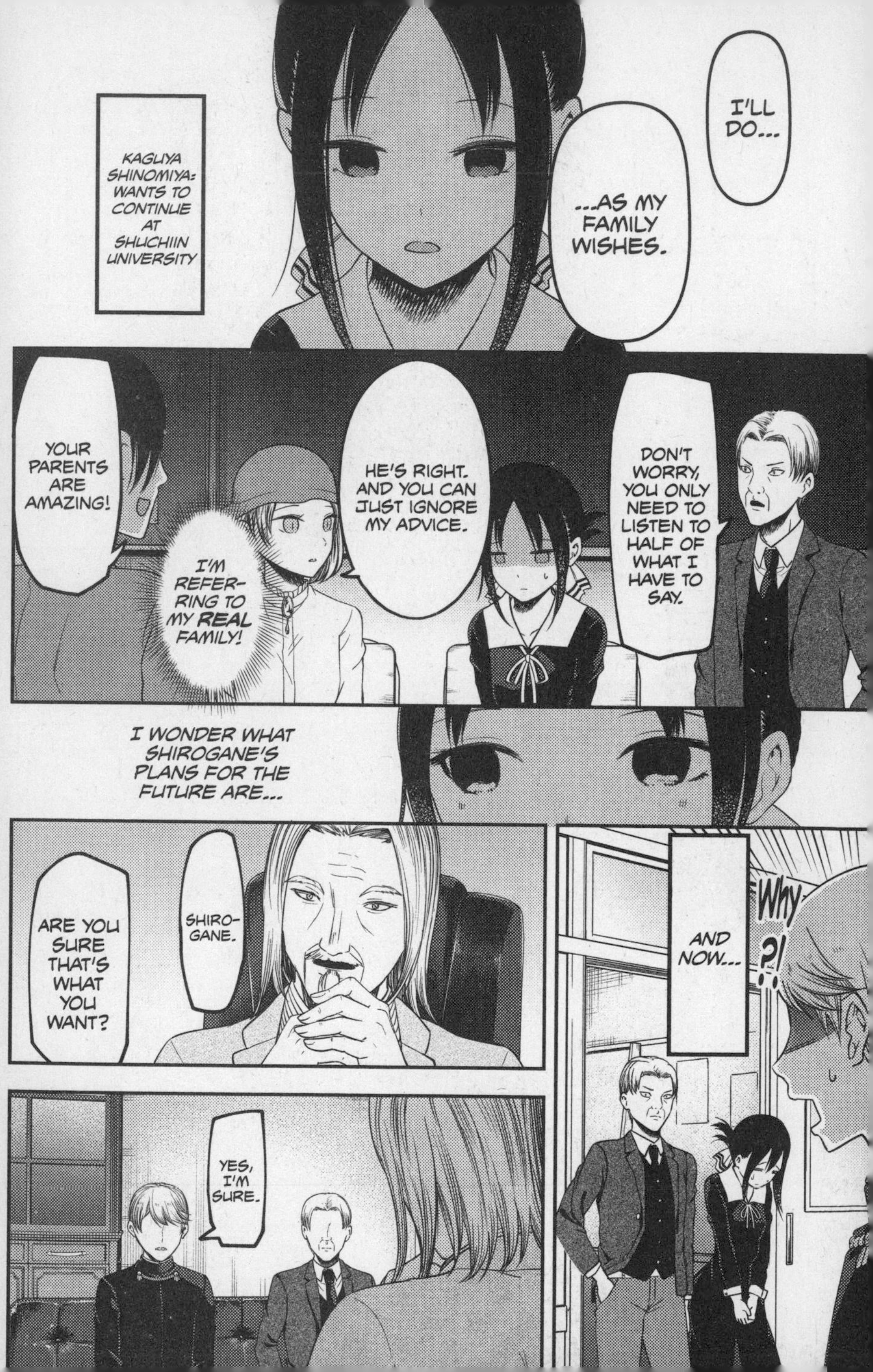
I'LL DO...
...AS MY FAMILY WISHES.
KAGUYA SHINOMIYA: WANTS TO CONTINUE AT SHUCHIIN UNIVERSITY
DON'T WORRY, YOU ONLY NEED TO LISTEN TO HALF OF WHAT I HAVE TO SAY.
HE'S RIGHT. AND YOU CAN JUST IGNORE MY ADVICE.
I'M REFERRING TO MY **REAL** FAMILY!
YOUR PARENTS ARE AMAZING!
I WONDER WHAT SHIROGANE'S PLANS FOR THE FUTURE ARE...
AND NOW...
Why?!
SHIROGANE.
ARE YOU SURE THAT'S WHAT YOU WANT?
YES, I'M SURE.

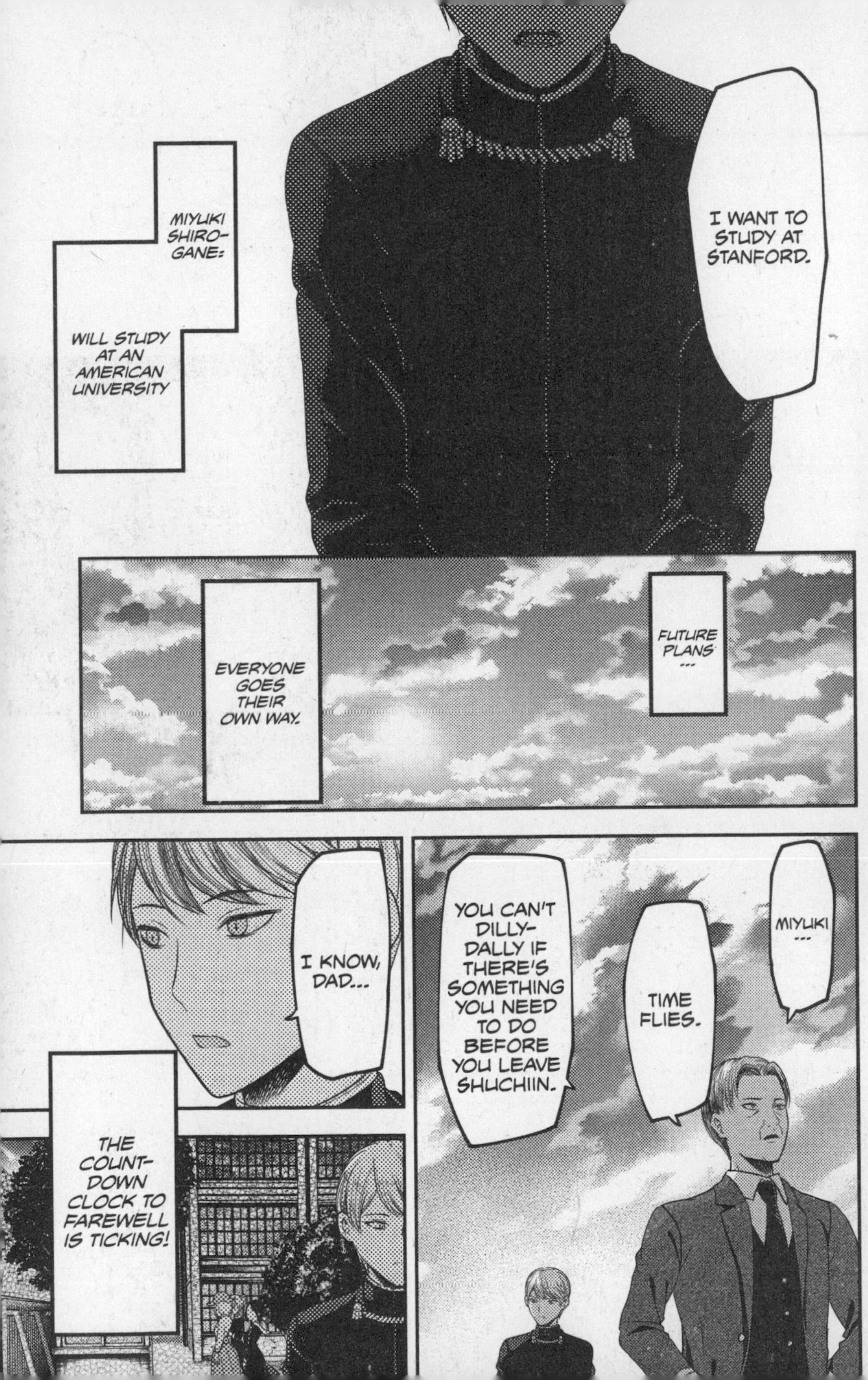
I WANT TO STUDY AT STANFORD.
MIYUKI SHIROGANE:
WILL STUDY AT AN AMERICAN UNIVERSITY
FUTURE PLANS...
EVERYONE GOES THEIR OWN WAY.
MIYUKI...
TIME FLIES.
YOU CAN'T DILLY-DALLY IF THERE'S SOMETHING YOU NEED TO DO BEFORE YOU LEAVE SHUCHIIN.
I KNOW, DAD...
THE COUNTDOWN CLOCK TO FAREWELL IS TICKING!

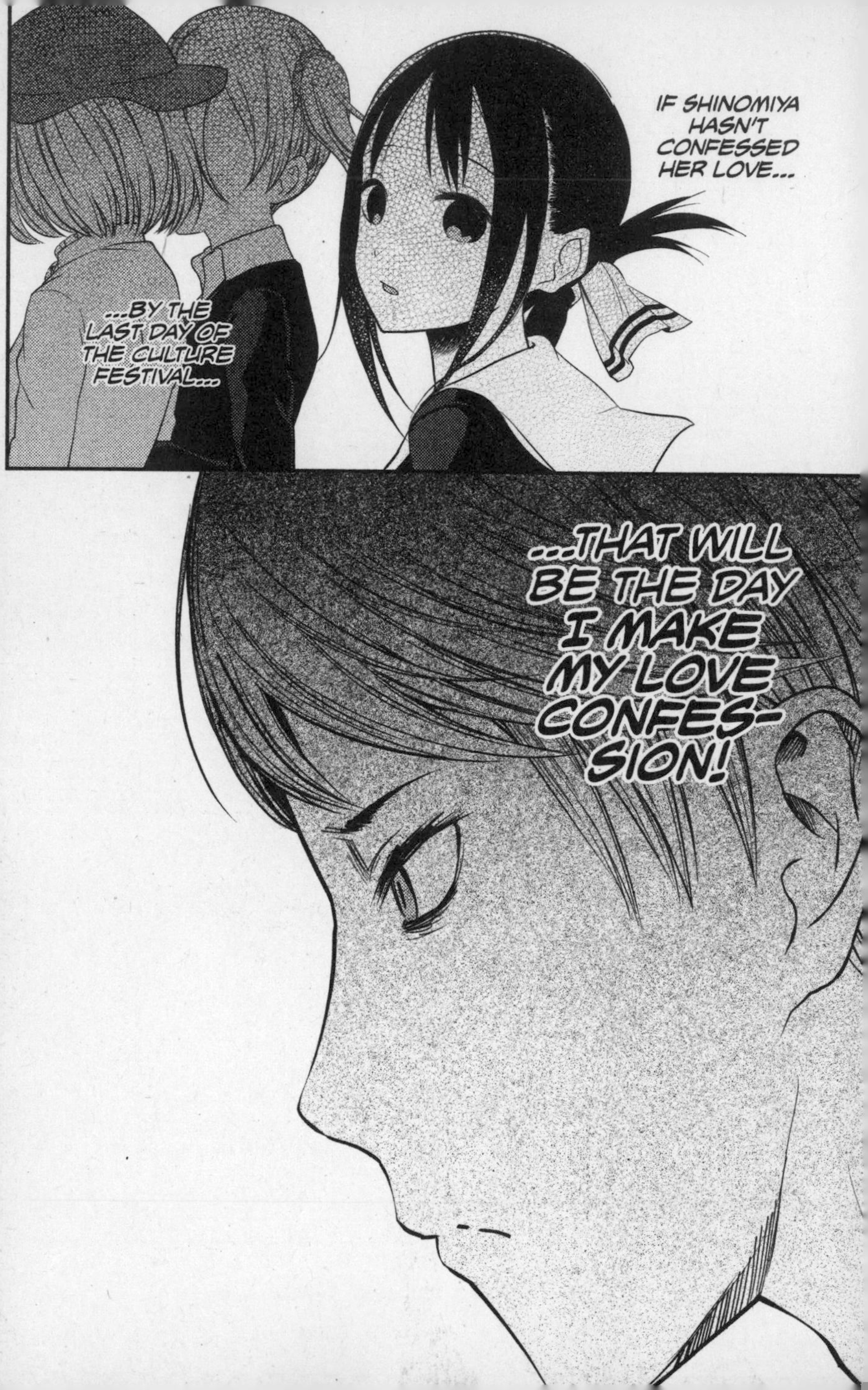
IF SHINOMIYA HASN'T CONFESSED HER LOVE...
...BY THE LAST DAY OF THE CULTURE FESTIVAL...
...THAT WILL BE THE DAY I MAKE MY LOVE CONFES-SION!

Continued in
volume 12!

THE PERSONAS THAT PEOPLE ADOPT CAN TRANSFORM THEIR TRUE NATURE, FOR BETTER OR WORSE.

AKA AKASAKA

Aka Akasaka got his start as an assistant to Jinsei Kataoka and Kazuma Kondou, the creators of *Deadman Wonderland*. His first serialized manga was an adaptation of the light novel series *Sayonara Piano Sonata*, published by Kadokawa in 2011. *Kaguya-sama: Love Is War* began serialization in *Miracle Jump* in 2015 but was later moved to *Weekly Young Jump* in 2016 due to its popularity.

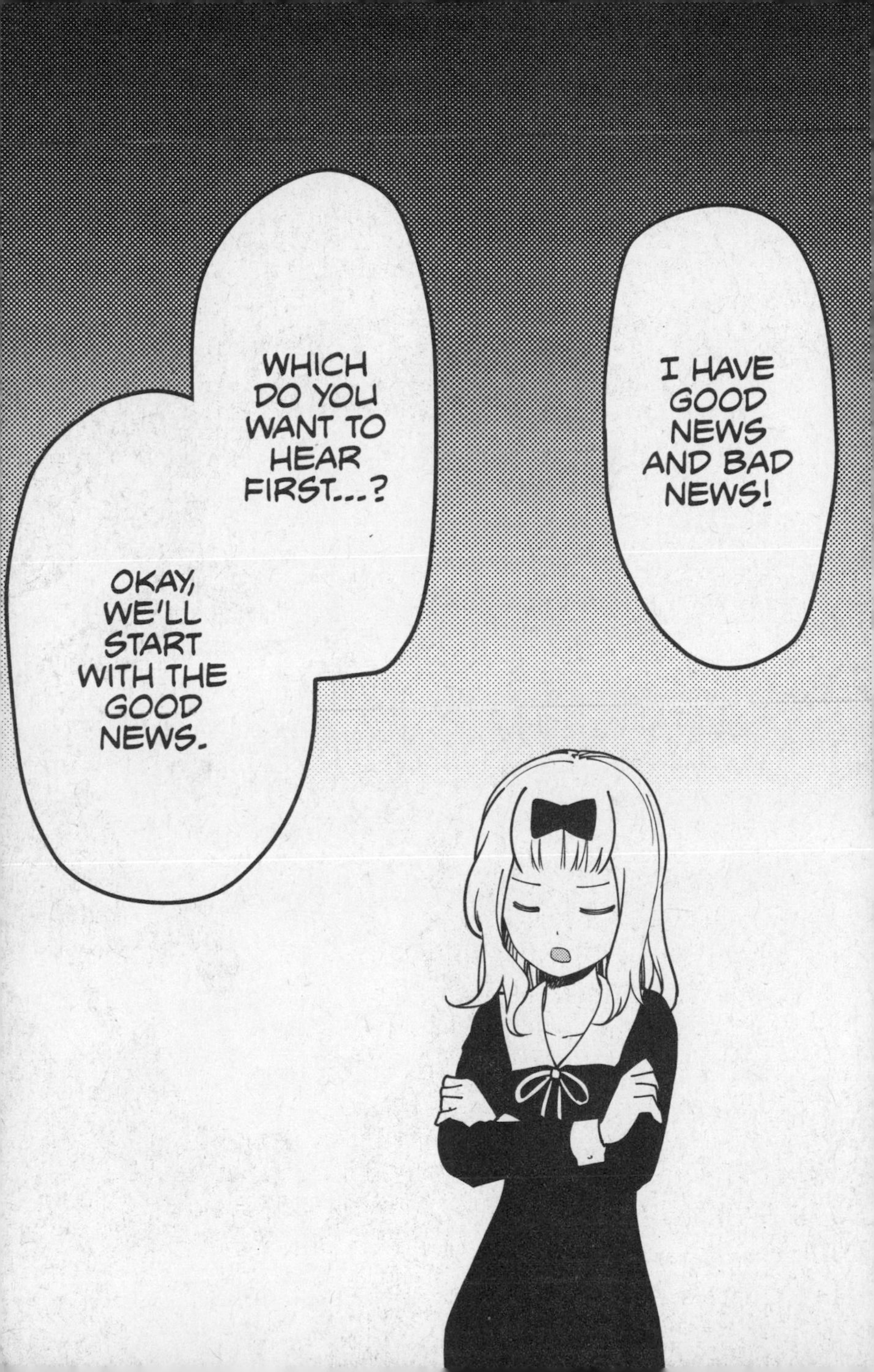
I HAVE GOOD NEWS AND BAD NEWS!
WHICH DO YOU WANT TO HEAR FIRST...?
OKAY, WE'LL START WITH THE GOOD NEWS.

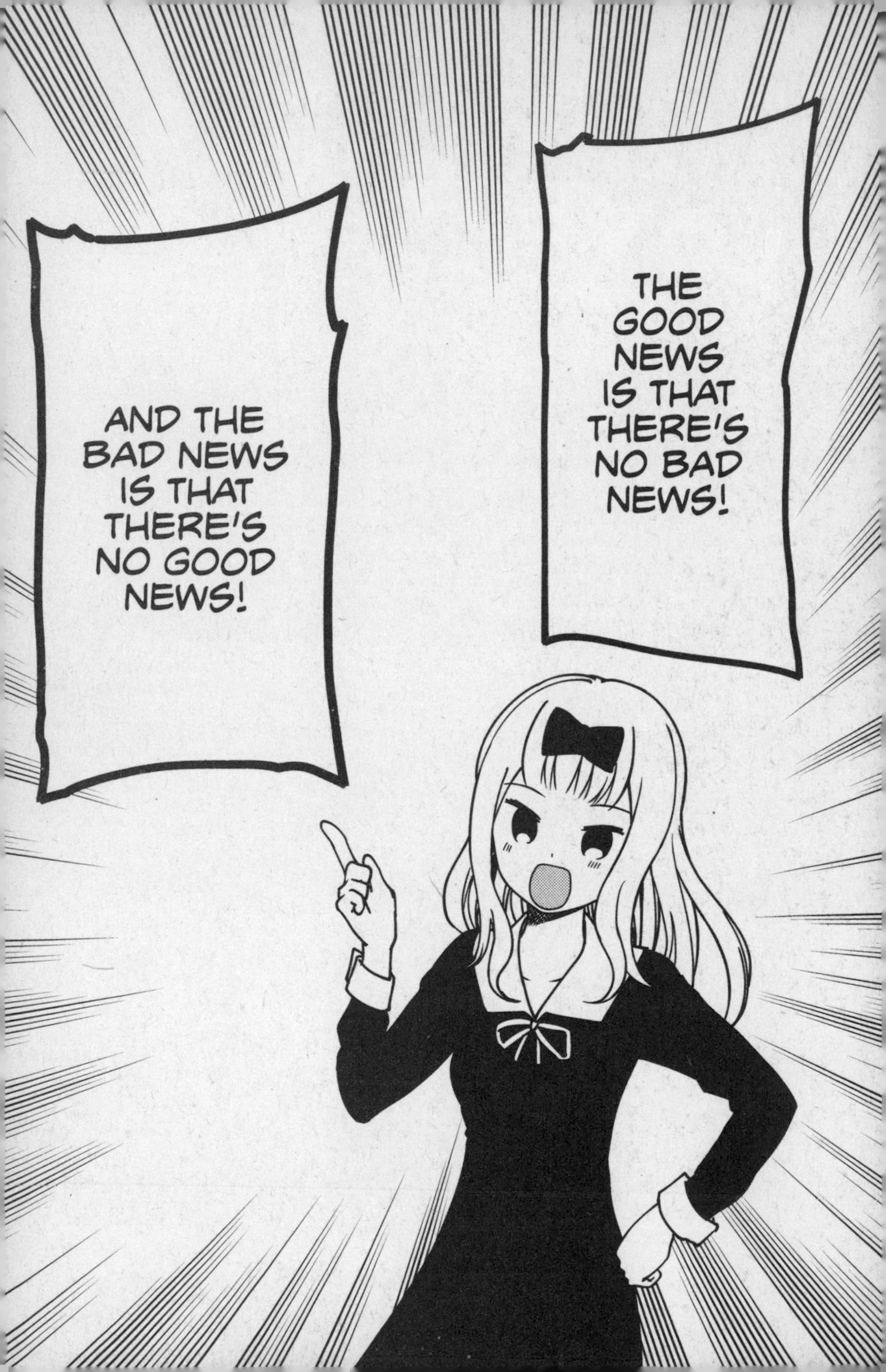
THE GOOD NEWS IS THAT THERE'S NO BAD NEWS!
AND THE BAD NEWS IS THAT THERE'S NO GOOD NEWS!

KAGUYA-SAMA
LOVE IS WAR

SHONEN JUMP MANGA EDITION

11

STORY AND ART BY
AKA AKASAKA

Translation/Tomoko Kimura
English Adaptation/Annette Roman
Touch-Up Art & Lettering/Stephen Dutro
Cover & Interior Design/Alice Lewis
Editor/Annette Roman

KAGUYA-SAMA WA KOKURASETAI~TENSAITACHI NO REN'AI ZUNO SEN~
© 2015 by Aka Akasaka
All rights reserved.
First published in Japan in 2015 by SHUEISHA Inc., Tokyo.
English translation rights arranged by SHUEISHA Inc.

Printed in Canada

Published by VIZ Media, LLC
P.O. Box 77010
San Francisco, CA 94107

10 9 8 7 6 5 4 3 2 1
First printing, November 2019

VIZ MEDIA
viz.com

SHONEN
JUMP
shonenjump.com

COMING NEXT VOLUME

KAGUYA-SAMA
LOVE IS WAR

12

STORY & ART BY
AKA AKASAKA

Will Shirogane ever admit to his insignificant but seemingly infinite lack of nonacademic talents? And what of the other student council members? Are any of them willing to view themselves objectively? Then, it's time for the school culture festival, which harkens back to a legend of ancient personal sacrifice that inspires the present-day students—symbolically, at least. Plus, a student council arm wrestling competition, balloon animals and a flashback episode about Shirogane's first awkward weeks as an outsider at Shuchiin High.

Cosplay makes the woman.

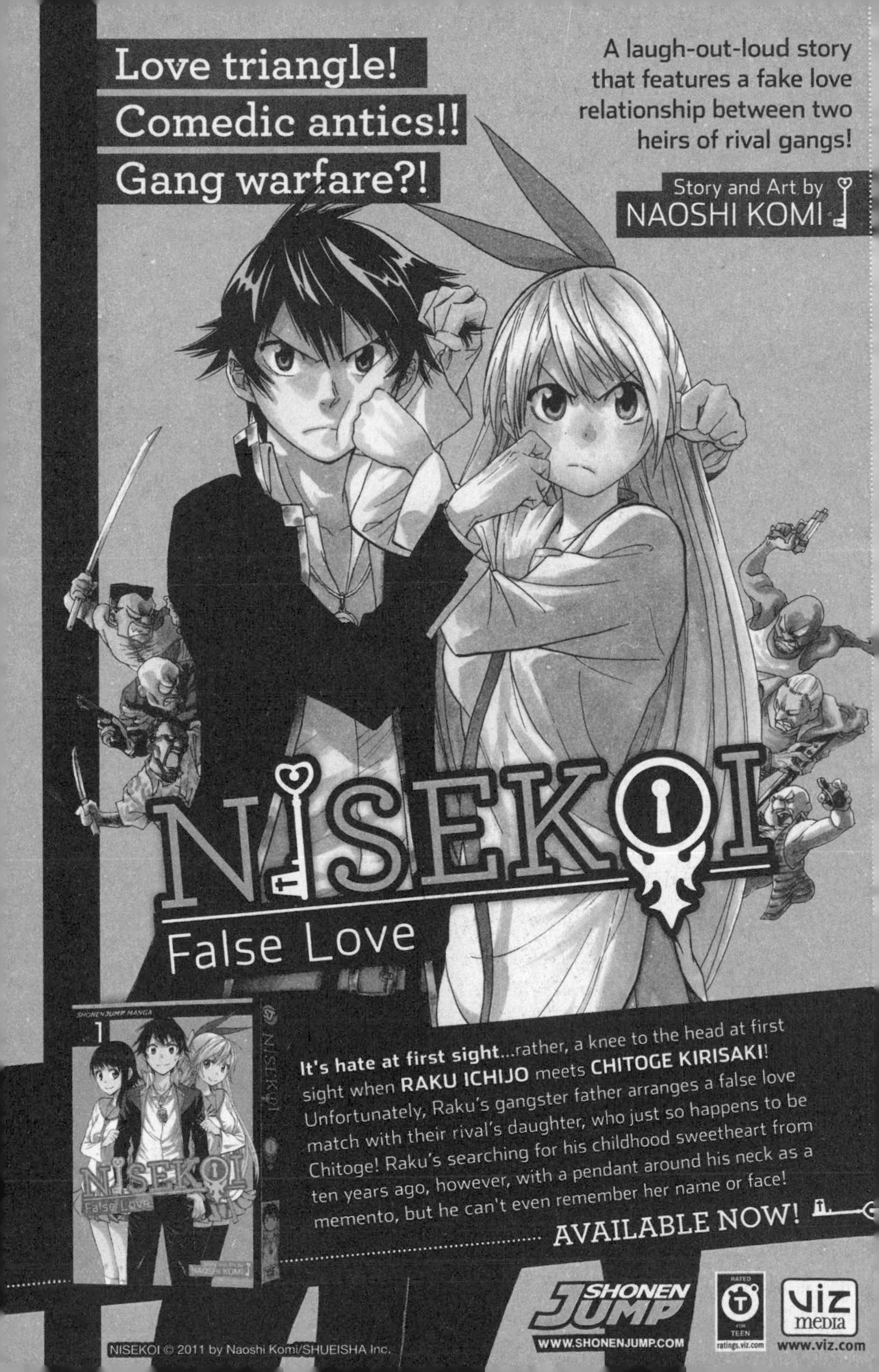
Love triangle!
Comedic antics!!
Gang warfare?!
A laugh-out-loud story that features a fake love relationship between two heirs of rival gangs!
Story and Art by
NAOSHI KOMI
NISEKOI
False Love
SHONEN JUMP MANGA
1
NISEKOI
False Love
NAOSHI KOMI
It's hate at first sight...rather, a knee to the head at first sight when RAKU ICHIJO meets CHITOGE KIRISAKI! Unfortunately, Raku's gangster father arranges a false love match with their rival's daughter, who just so happens to be Chitoge! Raku's searching for his childhood sweetheart from ten years ago, however, with a pendant around his neck as a memento, but he can't even remember her name or face!
AVAILABLE NOW!
SHONEN JUMP
WWW.SHONENJUMP.COM
RATED T FOR TEEN
ratings.viz.com
viz media
www.viz.com
NISEKOI © 2011 by Naoshi Komi/SHUEISHA Inc.

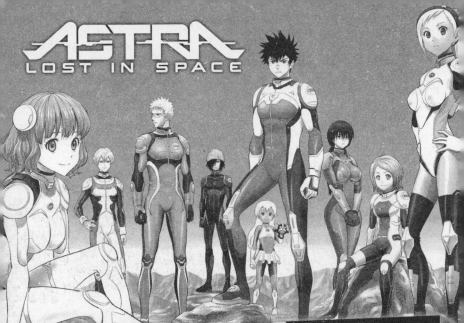

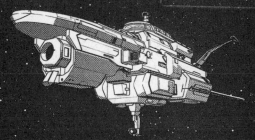 

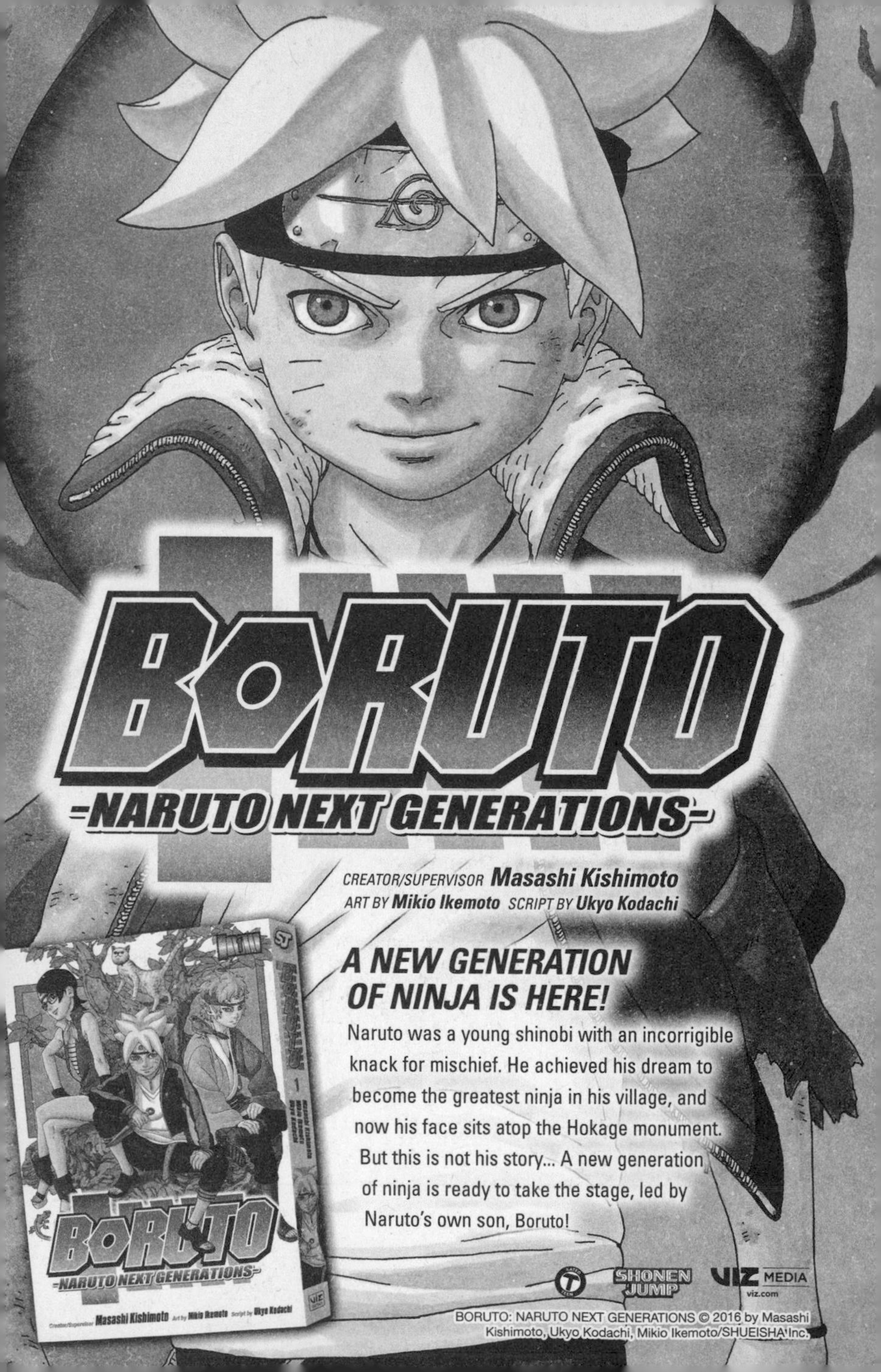
BORUTO
-NARUTO NEXT GENERATIONS-
CREATOR/SUPERVISOR Masashi Kishimoto
ART BY Mikio Ikemoto SCRIPT BY Ukyo Kodachi
A NEW GENERATION OF NINJA IS HERE!
Naruto was a young shinobi with an incorrigible knack for mischief. He achieved his dream to become the greatest ninja in his village, and now his face sits atop the Hokage monument. But this is not his story... A new generation of ninja is ready to take the stage, led by Naruto's own son, Boruto!
BORUTO
-NARUTO NEXT GENERATIONS-
SHONEN JUMP
VIZ MEDIA
viz.com
BORUTO: NARUTO NEXT GENERATIONS © 2016 by Masashi Kishimoto, Ukyo Kodachi, Mikio Ikemoto/SHUEISHA Inc.